BALTIC SEA

OCCUPIED
BY RUSSIA

●Koenigsberg

Danzig

EAST PRUSSIA

OCCUPIED
BY POLAND

OCCUPIED
BY
POLAND

Stettin

P
O
L
A
N
D

Vistula

⊠ WARSAW

Frankfurt-
on-Oder

Warta

S
I
L
E
S
I
A

Oder

●Breslau

PRAGUE

SLOVAKIA

AUSTRIA

Danube

VIENNA ⊠

GERMANY

🖤 Places with over 500,000 inhabitants

● Places with less than 500,000 inhabitants

▶■◀ German frontiers of 1937

----- Land boundaries of the Federal Republic

| 0 | 50 | 100 | 150 | 200 km |
| 0 | 50 | | 50 | 100 Eng. Mi. |

JE

RETURN TO POWER

RETURN
TO POWER

a report on the new Germany

BY ALISTAIR HORNE

Frederick A. Praeger, New York

Contents

1   "We Must Learn to Trust Each Other"   1
2   Rearming Two Germanys   23
3   Adenauer's Legacy   41
4   Herr Blank's Sea of Troubles   73
5   Krupp, the Special Case   102
6   Occupiers and Occupied   121
7   Saar Tug-of-War   131
8   Germany Ratifies   146
9   The Naumann Plot   160
10   Tightening the Screw   183
11   The Snapping of the Spring   198
12   West Germany Prepares for Elections   214
13   The Chancellor's Victory   230
14   Shaping the New Government   247
15   Hard Work and a Hard Currency   264
16   Atoms and Aircraft   310
17   The Phoney Peace Conference   333
18   Otto John Goes East   354
19   Adenauer's Defeat and Triumph   373
20   The Dangerous Way Ahead   388
     Index   407

To Renira

RETURN TO POWER

1

"We Must Learn

to Trust Each Other"

ON MAY 26, 1952, SEVERAL HUNDRED JOURNALISTS OF ALL NA-tions crowded into an austere room of what had once been a teachers' college on the bank of the river Rhine. The room was now the Upper Chamber of the West German parliament at Bonn — a few miles from the historic Remagen bridge where little more than seven years ago Allied forces had swept across the Rhine to bring the war against Germany to its conclusion. Outside the building the rain was coming down in a steady grey drizzle in keeping with the dreary character of the country's provisional capital. Inside, the journalists were witnessing an act which no other event in Bonn's history could rival in importance — except perhaps the birth of Beethoven. Seated at a table covered with a drab grey cloth, the Foreign Ministers of the United States, France, Great Britain and Western Germany were appending their signa-tures to one of the most unusual documents in all Europe's rav-aged history. It was formally known under the uninspiring alter-native titles of "The Contractual Agreements" and "The Bonn Conventions," by the West Germans as "The General Treaty," and by the Communists as the "General War Pact." On the same evening, the four ministers and their entourages left for Paris to sign the document's twin sister, the European Defense Commu-nity Treaty.

As he entered the signatory chamber in Bonn, M. Robert Schuman of France said with dramatic simplicity: "We must learn slowly to trust each other again." After the signing, the British Foreign Secretary, Mr. (now Sir) Anthony Eden, added: "It is now within the power of statesmanship and the wisdom of nations to close the chapter of wars which have tortured two generations."

Although neither of the two treaties signed in Bonn and Paris was to achieve enactment, they established a unique and historic principle, radically altering the alignment of world powers as it had existed over the past eighty cataclysmic years, and beyond. The Treaties marked the end of the wartime "Grand Alliance," the seeds of whose dissolution had already been sown at the Potsdam Conference of 1945, and the beginning of a new epoch of European co-operation. They marked Germany's return to power in world affairs. They were intended to mark the laying aside of the historic Franco-German enmity. *Revanchiste* sentiments which engendered Versailles were to have been finally exorcised at Bonn. In face of the common threat, German and Frenchman were to join a common army, less than a decade after the ending of the bitterest war in their histories. It was a monumental conception.

Since the story to be told in this book returns again and again to the EDC, its fate, and the alternatives to it, a rather detailed analysis of it is required. This may momentarily impede the flow of the narrative, but an understanding of the essential points will make much clearer what is recounted later on. This material is indispensable background. For many months the EDC was the focus of interest of all those, and notably Dr. Adenauer, who were concerned with the integration of Europe politically and defensively, to meet the encroachments on Europe of the Soviet Union.

Under the Bonn Conventions West Germany was restored her sovereignty with limitations; the EDC Treaty required that she provide a defense contingent of 500,000 men for a European Army. A unique feature of the Treaties was that they were indivisibly tied together, so that one could not enter into force without the other. Thus the price West Germany had to pay for her sovereignty was to pledge herself to irrevocable military alliance with the western world which she had so recently overrun, and which, in turn, had become her conqueror. But, for a nation which had been so utterly defeated after inflicting hideous carnage upon the world, the terms were remarkably generous. Few Germans doubted that the terms would have been a great deal harsher had the Allies retained their wartime cordiality.

The Bonn Conventions provided that the Occupation Statute, with its wide powers over German life and property, be repealed and the Allied High Commission abolished. The Federal Republic was to have almost full authority over both its internal and external affairs; thus it would no longer have to approach the Allies to negotiate a minor agreement with a foreign country on its behalf, or obtain their approval before changing its Constitution. There were, however, three important limitations to its full sovereignty, imposed in the form of "reserved rights." The first was the reservation of the previously held rights protecting the security of the Allied forces in Germany, which, under the EDC, were now to become "defense forces" as opposed to "occupation troops." Moreover, in the event of a "situation" arising which neither the Federal Government nor the EDC were able to control, the Allies would be empowered to proclaim a state of emergency — throughout the whole country if need be. (In addition to an attack from outside, the Conventions defined that a "situation" warranting Allied action would also be created by "subversion of the liberal-democratic basic order." Thus the Allies would be authorized to intervene in case of any attempt to seize power illegally in Western Germany — whether by neo-Nazis disguised as nationalists or by Communist agents.)

Secondly, the Allies retained their rights in Berlin, which still remained a quadripartite responsibility and outside the jurisdiction of the Federal Republic.

Thirdly, the reserved rights to carry on all negotiations aimed at German reunification or a four-power peace settlement. Thus the West Germans were precluded from entering into direct ne-

gotiation with the Soviets on this topic of paramount importance
to all Germans — or from "doing a deal" with the Russians, depending on one's point of view.

The Conventions contained a mass of complex detail covering
the liquidation of the heritage of war and occupation. Allied laws
were to remain in force until repealed by the Germans. The Federal Government pledged itself to execute the Allies' deconcentration program designed to split up the heavy industry and IG
Farben combines; it acknowledged its responsibility to resettle
and compensate the victims of Nazism, and to honor Germany's
pre-war external debts. In return the Allies agreed to waive
claims to more than two billion dollars for post-war aid. The
Germans would be allowed to fly civil airlines again. In a separate letter to the three Allied Governments, Dr. Adenauer declared that the German economy was not yet in a condition to
undertake the construction of its own aircraft, but when the occasion did arise, the Federal Republic would seek their approval.

The Conventions made it clear that they were essentially a provisional arrangement, and in no way a substitute for a Peace
Treaty for all Germany, to which the Russians would have to be
party. The Western Allies declared that such a German Peace
Treaty still remained their ultimate aim. As a result, the Conventions left all German frontier questions, especially the contested
Oder-Neisse line, to be settled at the peace conference. Pending
the peace settlement, the Conventions added, the western powers
and the Federal Republic would co-operate to achieve by peaceful means "a *unified Germany* enjoying a liberal-democratic constitution, like that of the Federal Republic and *integrated within
the European Community.*" It was this clause in particular which
caused the German critics of the Treaties — notably the Social
Democrats — to boggle at the Allied terms. They feared — not
without good reason — that the Russians would never agree to
any reunification of Germany which might place both halves
firmly within the western camp; thus the division of Germany
threatened to become a permanency. There was, however, an
escape clause providing that in the event of German reunification

the Conventions could be modified — but only with the agreement of all four signatories.

The EDC Treaty had had a past which was as long, and nearly as stormy, as its future was to be. In June, 1950, the North Koreans plunged into South Korea, and the German interzonal frontier at once assumed the potential menace of a 38th Parallel. A dangerous vacuum existed in West Germany. In face of the new aggressive mood of Communism, the NATO Council launched the idea of rearming Germany at its meeting in New York in September, 1950. On October 24th the EDC was born in France, in the form of the "Pleven Plan," which envisaged integration of German forces on the "combat team" or brigade level under non-German command, thus putting the German contingent almost on the basis of a mercenary foreign legion. In this form it was not likely to be acceptable to the Germans, who were already insisting on full equality of rights as terms for their participation. In Great Britain, Mr. Ernest Bevin accepted for the Labor Government the principle of German rearmanent on November 29th, 1950, with the words: "If unhappily aggression were to take place in Europe, we are satisfied that its defense would have to take place as far east as possible, and that means that Western Germany must be involved; and if Western Germany is to be defended, it seems to us only fair and reasonable that the people of Western Germany should help in their own defense." In February, 1951, the Paris Conference began work on the basis of the Pleven Plan. On February 5th, 1952, Mr. Eden, Foreign Secretary of the newly elected Conservative Government, defined Great Britain's future relationship with the EDC: "British forces on the Continent will operate as closely as possible with the European Defense Forces and be linked with them in matters of training, administration and supplies." The view of the Conservative Government was that it would not join the EDC because it was the acknowledged precursor of European Federation, to which Britain did not wish to be committed. Britain's refusal to participate was the first of the blows which were to kill the EDC two and a half years later.

The EDC Treaty in its final draft consisted of 132 articles, and a mass of supplementary annexes, parallel treaties with the USA and Great Britain, and cross-links to the Bonn Conventions.

It was an even more complicated document than the Conventions and, had it been enforced, would undoubtedly have provided a great many lawyers with ample work during the fifty years of its life. Although the Germans learned from the constant reiterations of their leaders roughly what the EDC stood for, public-opinion polls subsequently conducted showed that only a fractional percentage of the population really understood the implications and responsibilities entailed by the European Army. Judging from reports from France in the last two years, even fewer Frenchmen were aware of the sacrifices of national sovereignty which the EDC demanded, or that they might one day find themselves in a Corps d'Armeé commanded by a "Boche" general. Nevertheless, in spite of all its flaws, it is doubtful that any scheme could have been devised to provide for German rearmament with greater safeguards once the principle of *full equality* for any German military contingent had been established.

First and foremost among these safeguards, there would be no new Wehrmacht and no German General Staff. The basic national unit of the European Army would be a *groupement,* or light division, and no army corps could contain more than two divisions of the same nationality. Thus would the German contingent of twelve divisions (a total fixed by NATO) be spread out and assimilated among the other thirty provided by France, Italy and the Benelux countries. All would wear the same European uniform with only their national flag as a shoulder-flash to identify them. German staff officers would be tightly integrated within the various EDC commands, all coming under the control of the EDC Board of Commissioners, consisting of nine members — two each from Germany, France and Italy, one from each of the Benelux countries — appointed for six years.

This body would be endowed with the most far-reaching authority. The extent of the supra-national powers of these nine men over the internal affairs of the six member countries would have been staggering. If one could imagine it on a European scale, their competence would embrace many of the functions fulfilled in Great Britain or the United States by Ministries or Departments of Defense, Army, Navy, Air Force, Treasury, Commerce, and the Chiefs of Staff. Apart from issuing orders on the mobilization and disposition of the forty-two EDC divisions and the two-million-odd men under its command, the Board would be responsible for the common defense budget and the collection of financial contributions; the placing of arms contracts; the control of arms manufacture (as well as the powers of supervising and inspecting member countries' munitions factories); the export and import of weapons; and the co-ordination of recruiting and conditions of service and training. The Board in turn was responsible to an *EDC Assembly* (based on the structures of the Schuman Plan Assembly). There was further to be a *Council* whose task it was to "harmonize" the activities of the Board of Commissioners with the policies of the various member governments, and a High Court to settle disputes. Composed of the Defense Ministers of the six countries, the Council was the only high EDC organ to retain national characteristics. Its members were initially to be endowed with voting rights in the ratio of three votes each for Germany, France and Italy, two each for Belgium and the Netherlands, and one for Luxemburg. Eventually, however, these would depend on the size of each nation's defense contribution.

As her financial contribution to European Defense, the Treaties stipulated that Western Germany should begin by paying 850 million marks a month (approximately 210 million dollars per month) from the date of their enforcement until June 30th, 1953, after which time contributions would be fixed on the NATO scale. Of this monthly payment, 551 million marks would go to meet Allied defense costs in Germany (i.e., what were formerly occupation costs) during the first six months; dwindling to 319 million for the next three months and steadily diminishing as the expanding German contingent demanded more money.

Depending on the strategic requirements of NATO, the strength of the German EDC contingent was tentatively fixed at 500,000 men. 400,000 of these would be recruited for the twelve divisions of her ground forces; 80,000 for her air forces, consisting of 1,500 planes (mostly fighter-bombers); and the remaining 20,000 for her naval forces (to be limited to light coastal units). Beyond these the Germans would be permitted no forces outside the jurisdiction of the EDC, with the exception of a small detachment of troops allocated for the President's ceremonial guard. The same stipulations applied for all the other EDC members, although special concessions were made to recognize France's position as a country with overseas territories to be policed and defended. The Treaty thus granted her the right to maintain separate national forces in these territories but it ruled that they should "not be so large as to jeopardize" France's contribution to the EDC. In the event of a major crisis in one of her overseas possessions, France could withdraw troops from the EDC, but such a move could obviously be made *only* with the sanction of the NATO Supreme Commander. As will be seen later, these were stipulations that were to cause the gravest dissatisfaction in France long after the Treaty had been signed.

The EDC offered the following safeguards against a revival of German aggressive militarism once the nation had been rearmed:

1. The whole structure and aim of the EDC was keyed to defense rather than attack.
2. There would be no German General Staff.
3. There would be no German forces able to act independently of the EDC.
4. All training would be co-ordinated within the EDC.
5. The German defense budget, arms production and arms allocation, and weapon research would be closely controlled and supervised by the EDC Board of Commissioners. In addition to this, Western Germany, as a "strategically exposed area," was barred from producing atomic, chemical or biological

weapons, long-range guided missiles or "V" bombs (with the
exception of anti-aircraft rockets of specified size and limited
range), heavy naval vessels or military aircraft.

6. The present Allied forces were to remain in West Germany,
   and would presumably be reinforced by foreign EDC contingents. This, combined with the wide powers of inspection possessed by the Board of Commissioners, would make any secret
   arms manufacture or the training of a *Black Reichswehr* like
   that of the 1920's virtually impossible.

In spite of all these safeguards against a renewal of German
aggression, France wanted more. At the very last moment before
its signature, the Treaty very nearly collapsed because of French
misgivings. They feared that the Treaty had insufficient powers
to bind Germany for the fifty years of its life, and that a revital-
ized and rearmed Germany might one day break away from it,
leaving France and the other four with their armies inextricably
integrated within the EDC.

Late on the night of May 23rd, after M. Schuman had already
left for Bonn, the French Cabinet held a five-hour meeting, concluding that it would not ask Parliament to ratify the EDC without obtaining greater safeguards against a German withdrawal.
This was a form of French statecraft which was to repeat itself
in the ensuing months. There were some hasty and heated negotiations between M. Schuman and the British and American
deputations in Bonn, and much agitated telephoning between
Bonn and the Quai d'Orsay during the weekend. By Sunday
morning Dr. Adenauer, Mr. Acheson and Mr. Eden had agreed
upon the final text of the Treaties to be signed on the Monday
and Tuesday, but M. Schuman was still awaiting his Government's assent.

Finally, after another Cabinet meeting on Sunday night, the
French announced that they would sign the Treaties. It was clear
in Bonn that their eleventh-hour diplomacy had triumphed. On
Tuesday in Paris an additional joint declaration was attached to
the EDC in which the British and United States Governments
pledged in strong terms: "If any action from whatever quarter

threatens the integrity or unity of the Community the two Governments will regard this as a threat to their own security." Further, Britain and the USA resolved to maintain in Europe such troops as were "necessary" for the defense of the NATO area and relevant to the "integrity of the EDC." There was little doubt that a German secession was the "threat" to the EDC's "integrity" against which the two powers' guarantee was directed.

To the observer abroad, the way would now have seemed clear for ratification in the French Parliament. The prospects then seemed less clear in the Bundestag where 165 Socialists and Communists were already dedicated to opposing the Treaties. But, alas, it was to be two years, three months and a few days before the Treaties were even presented before the National Assembly for their final and humiliating dismissal. As the *Daily Telegraph* commented in a leader on May 26th, 1952: "The French doubts would seem to be the reflection of the still lingering and widespread misgivings about any form of German rearmament rather than matters calling for fresh decisions of policy on the part of Britain and the United States." To dispel these misgivings, the Germans could themselves offer no better "guarantees" than their own behavior over a period of time. The next two years, with the Germans becoming more and more their own masters (although still tantalizedly awaiting restoration of their sovereignty), were to provide an important test.

Meanwhile, during all this diplomatic activity of the West, the Russians and their vassals had not been inactive. Since Russian intransigence made the division of Germany a fact shortly after the ending of the war, a vast game of poker has been going on between East and West, with each trying to raise the other's bid. On March 18th, 1948, the Soviet zone created a "People's Council," elected from a single list after the usual custom of Communist countries, and two days later Marshal Sokolovsky, the Soviet Military Governor, walked out of the quadripartite Control Council. Two weeks later the Russians began the blockade of Berlin. In June of the same year, the Western Allies adopted a new currency, based on the Deutsche Mark, for their three zones, but the Russians refused to follow suit. Thus the schism between the economies of East and West Germany became firmly established. In May, 1949, the Constitution of the Federal Republic was drawn up in the West and the Russians lifted the blockade after the attempt to grab Berlin by a 13½ month siege was frustrated by the brilliant Allied airlift. On August 14th of the same year, a West German Parliament was freely elected by the populations of the three Allied zones. In October the East replied, creating the "German Democratic Republic" (DDR). By no stretch of the imagination could the DDR's government be called a freely elected one, formed as it was of representatives of the Soviet Zone "People's Councils" by a formal decree. In 1950, the West launched the Schuman Plan, forwarding the integration of the West German economy within a European Community. In reply, the Russians consolidated the bonds of their satellites by making the new East German Government agree with the Poles to accept the Oder-Neisse line as a finality.

Outwardly, the Allies generally appeared to be one move ahead of the Russians — although in fact they were loosening their grip on Western Germany (with the object of gaining German goodwill in exchange for occupation control) while the Russians were all the time tightening their stranglehold on Eastern Germany. Then, in 1950, the Allies took up cudgels in the cause of German reunification — the desire dearest to most Germans' hearts, once the immediate post-war problems of hunger and material insecurity had been met. On May 26th the Allied High Commissioners transmitted to the Soviet Supreme Commander a plan for conducting free All-German elections, based on resolutions of the Federal Government. Without even mentioning the Allied proposals, Herr Grotewohl, the East German Prime Minister, followed up in November with a letter to Dr. Adenauer recommending the setting up of an All-German Constituent Council, composed of equal representations from East and West Germany, to draft a peace treaty.

Since the battle for German reunification had begun, disagreement between the East and the West was centered around the sequence in which reunification should be effected. The Western program, endorsed by the Federal Republic, prescribed the following sequence: (1) Free All-German elections, leading to (2) formation of an All-German Government with whom the four Occupying Powers could sign (3) a freely negotiated peace treaty.

The Russian reunification formula was: (1) Formation of a provisional government from East and West Germany. (On the basis of the Grotewohl letter, which laid down the axiom "Germans around one table," Eastern Germany with its eighteen million inhabitants would gain bargaining equality with the Federal Republic with a population of forty-eight million and an area nearly three times as big. It would also annul the present quadripartite ratio of 3:1 against the Russians.) The provisional government would then (2) draw up with the Four Powers a peace treaty requiring the withdrawal of all occupation troops. (3) "Free elections" for a permanent All-German government would take place in a Germany hermetically sealed off from the West. Recalling the technique of the Communist seizure of power in Czechoslovakia, and the sobering fact that the only armed forces left in Germany to "supervise" these elections would be the East German "People's Police," the Soviet design behind the proposals was as plain as a pikestaff.

In September, 1951, the West German Bundestag unanimously approved a procedure for All-German elections, involving the setting up of a neutral supervisory commission to be provided by the United Nations. The proposal was passed on to the Allies, who in turn put it before the UN. Meanwhile, with discussion on EDC by now in full swing, Herr Wilhelm Pieck, the East German President, resumed the Soviet attack in a threatening letter to his West German opposite number, Professor Heuss. With prospects of the Federal Republic's incorporation within the "aggressive Atlantic Pact," warned Herr Pieck, "the danger is growing of an indescribably dreadful war of which the whole German people will be the victim."

By the end of 1951, the UN had appointed a supervisory electoral commission consisting of representatives from Iceland, Holland, Pakistan, Poland and Brazil. On the Kremlin's orders, however, Poland withdrew, and on January 9th, 1952, Herr Grotewohl followed up by refusing to recognize the UN decision. It was, he said, an "intervention in the domestic affairs of the German people."

Then, on March 10th, 1952, with signature of the EDC Treaty imminent, the Russians opened up their big guns in a note to each of the Governments of the three western powers. It proposed that the conclusion of a German peace treaty be "accelerated," because of the "danger of a revival of German militarism." Germany was to be reunited as a single State allowed "national land, sea and air forces essential for the defense of the country." All foreign troops were to be withdrawn within one year of the peace treaty coming into force. Ex-Nazis were to be restored full equality of rights. Included was a clause of rather sinister implications, "the existence of organizations hostile to democracy and the cause of maintaining peace must not be allowed on the territory of Germany." There was little doubt that, in Soviet eyes, most of the West German political parties would come within this definition, and suffer the fate of their kin in the Soviet satellites.

But the most important provision was that Germany was to pledge herself "not to enter into any coalitions or military alliances whatsoever directed against any power which has taken part with armed forces in the war against Germany." The proposal was a direct attack on the EDC and aimed at nothing more nor less than the complete neutralization and isolation of Germany. Nevertheless it offered distinct attractions to the West German opponents of EDC, the "unity-firsters," the "third forceists," and many ex-Nazis disaffected by their treatment under Allied denazification legislation. The bait was readily seized by the Social Democrats in Western Germany and, among others, the Bevanites of Great Britain, who urged the Allies to go slow on EDC and give most serious consideration to the Soviet proposals.

There can be little doubt that the Russian proposals of March 10th were an attempt to throw a wrench into the works of EDC. The Russians knew the terms would be unacceptable to the Allies, especially at this moment when they had become diplomatically so deeply embroiled in pushing signature of the Treaties. At best, opposition to the Treaties provoked in the West by the Russian proposals might have forced the Allies to accept an endless conference *à la* Panmunjom. In view of the lengths to which the Russians have gone, both before and after March, 1952, to consolidate their hold on Eastern Germany, only a Candide could believe that they would ever permit reunification of Germany except on terms offering clear prospects of bringing all 66 million Germans under the hammer and sickle.

The exchange of notes between the four Governments, each knowing in advance what the other's answer would be, continued until September, 1952, when the Russians disengaged. On May 24th, the day the three foreign ministers arrived in Bonn to sign the Conventions, a third excellently timed Russian note arrived. With its eye on the German populace, it shifted the blame for prolonging the division of Germany upon the Allies by rejecting the Russian peace treaty proposals. Signature of the Treaties with the West, it added, created for Western Germany "new difficulties in the path of unification with the Eastern part of Germany." The West Germans were thus offered the hideous dilemma of electing either isolation from the West and a chance of reunification on Russian terms, or integration with the West and the possibility of perpetuating the division of Germany.

The propaganda value of the Soviet notes was backed up with every sort of threat by the East German puppet leaders. Herr Ulbricht, the loathed boss of the Socialist Unity Party (SED), threatened at a press conference in East Berlin that any West German politician who voted for the Treaties would be "punished by the German people." The Treaties had military objectives, he declared, but they would end in Ostend, not the Urals. On the day the Treaties were signed, Herr Ulbricht warned ominously that their results would be "very clearly felt" in Berlin.

A fortnight before the signing of the Treaties, the Communists attempted a trial of strength in Essen. Some 30,000 Communists, brought from distant parts of the Federal Republic and stiffened with "specialists" from the Soviet Zone, marched on the police under banners inscribed "Make May 11th a day of battle for youth against Western war treaties and for the Soviet Peace Treaty." The police opened fire with their pistols, wounding several Communists and killing 21-year-old Philip Müller, who received immediate canonization as a party martyr. The West German Communists have to date never again been able to muster such forces.

In Paris, on the day after the signature of the EDC Treaty, there were even bloodier Communist-sponsored riots.

But the brunt of the East's offensive against the Treaties was to be taken by Berlin, as threatened by Herr Ulbricht, and along the interzonal frontier. Immediately after the EDC signing on May 28th, the Soviet Zone Government announced the new retaliatory measures: a "death strip" was established along the whole 500-mile length of the interzonal frontier, totally cutting off traffic between East and West. The "death strip" was a belt ten yards deep in which all trees were chopped down, houses levelled, and shrubbery and all other obstacles removed. It stretched from the Baltic to Czechoslovakia, and within it anyone was to be fired upon at sight. Wooden control towers equipped with searchlights and machine-gun posts were set up at frequent intervals by the East German People's Police. Behind the ten-yard "death strip" there was a "forbidden zone" 500 yards wide and a further "security belt" three miles deep within the Soviet Zone.

Inside the 500-yard belt, all theaters, inns, restaurants and hotels were closed, and a strict curfew established forbidding any sort of work out of doors during the hours of darkness. Inhabitants were screened for "political trustworthiness" by visiting authorities. Those who failed the test were given twenty-four hours to pack up their belongings and move eastwards to an unknown destination, probably the uranium mines of Saxony. Exit from and entry into the three-mile *cordon sanitaire* required special passes from the People's Police, and then movement was only allowed via specified roads. Security precautions in the South of England in the weeks before the Normandy landings were hardly as stringent. Thus did the Russians intend to bring home to the Western Germans, brutally and dramatically, the full significance of the division of their land, which their Government's endorsement of the Treaties would perpetuate.

The immediate sequel to the sealing-off of the frontier was a westward trek of farmers and other inhabitants of the security belt, fleeing before the People's Police could make the frontier totally uncrossable. Hundreds got over, but many died in the attempt — either shot in the "death strip" or drowned while trying to ford the fast-flowing Werra on ramshackle rafts made from oil drums. There were many such tragedies as that of the farmer's 18-year-old daughter who fainted from fright and exhaustion within sight of the Western boundary posts while her family, helpless in safety, watched as People's Police dragged her back.

The Soviets opened their attack on Berlin with a reconnaissance probe against the Allies, by barring Western military patrols along the interzonal autobahn. Simultaneously with the sealing of the frontier, all telephone cables from West Berlin to the Federal Republic and the Soviet Zone were severed without warning, and the frontier between West Berlin and the Soviet Zone closed. More than half of the 255 streets connecting East and West Berlin were blocked, and some three hundred railwaymen who lived in West Berlin, but worked in the Eastern sector, were told not to come back to their work after the signature of the Treaties. As an extra Communist pinprick, West Berlin owners of weekend houses within the Soviet Zone were driven out of them in the middle of the Whitsun holiday, and their property occupied by the "Vopos" (People's Police).

During the preceding months, feverish work had been observed on rail and canal links in the Soviet Zone designed to by-pass the West Berlin communications system, and senior Allied officials seriously wondered whether the Russians were not intending to reinstate the Berlin blockade — but this time on a more effective and permanent basis. With American air strength heavily committed in Korea, it would certainly have proved much more difficult to put the costly air lift back into operation. But the Russians did not resume the blockade: one felt they were reserving this ultimate card against Berlin until the final ratification of the Treaties. Perhaps they were also deterred by the Allied declaration at the signing of the Treaties that they would regard any attack upon Berlin as an attack upon themselves.

As further proof of Allied determination, both Mr. Eden and Mr. Acheson made separate prestige visits to the encircled city after the signing of the Treaties. Speaking at the Berlin Assembly Hall, Mr. Eden repeated the Allied guarantees. "We shall not be influenced by threats," he said; "these are strong and, I hope, reassuring words. They establish beyond doubt our abiding interest in Berlin." On the day of his visit, May 29th, the Soviets organized an incursion into the Western sectors of some 6,000 Communist youth agitators. There was a short, sharp battle with the West Berlin police, in which 280 Communists were arrested, a great many more injured, and the rest driven back over the sector boundaries.

The pinpricks continued. The Soviets presented the British and Americans with telephone bills — probably the largest in history — totalling about $19,000,000, for the use since 1945 of cables running through the Soviet Zone! One day Russian troops suddenly "occupied" three small enclaves belonging to the Allied sectors, on the periphery of the city — Steinstücken (American), Eiskeller and West Staaken (British). For some time, Allied countermeasures were limited to notes of protest, but suddenly the British took action and played one of the few cards in the Allied hand in Berlin. This was to seal off the Soviet Zone radio headquarters, which for some extraordinary reason was still housed in a building in the British sector of Berlin.

The blockade of the Radio House, which lasted for about a week, was my introduction to Berlin. I found a most anomalous situation. There, in the middle of the Soviet Zone, lay beleaguered Berlin — an island of the free West in a Communist sea.

In the middle of West Berlin, only a few hundred yards from British Army HQ, was yet a smaller island — the Soviet Radio House, incessantly pouring out vilification against the British and the West at large. For years the Allies had been under pressure from the Berliners to liquidate this last remnant of quadripartite days. During the blockade a courageous French general had dynamited its aerial mast in the French sector, but that had been all. Now, on the orders of Major-General Coleman, the British city commandant, nobody was to be allowed to enter the Radio House. Its staff could leave but not re-enter. During the night, a company of the Royal Scots had surrounded the building with barbed-wire barricades and sat down to await developments. In the morning the day staff, numbering about a thousand, tried to gain entrance but were turned away. A large crowd of Berliners assembled to hurl taunts at the night staff, who refused to leave the premises.

At first the Berliners were delighted that at last, after putting up with so much from the Russians, the Allies were getting tough with them. But after a few days their elation was replaced by acute disappointment when they realized the British were going to do no more than besiege the building. On one of my frequent trips down to the Radio House, a young West Berlin policeman asked me why the British did not force an entry, drive out its occupants, and make an end to it once and for all.

"You British always do things by half-measures," he complained. "If you would give us proper weapons, we would soon send them scurrying."

A flat-nosed Russian guard was scowling at us through the iron gate of the Radio House, and I remarked to the Berliner that we were surrounded by some three hundred thousand Russian troops, only a mile or two distant, and that the suggestion he had made was just the sort of thing some of the Allies feared the Germans would do as soon as they got arms.

"Never mind," he replied, "once we get arms, they will be so much more respectful, and will not dare treat Berlin as they do now."

It was, I think, the only time I ever heard a German private citizen speak so enthusiastically about rearmament — but he was a Berliner.

As a display of defiance, the twenty-one members of the night staff still in the building refused to leave throughout the blockade, and continued their broadcasts with much melodrama. During the day they played jazz records and Communist marching songs at full volume over loud-speakers, interspersed with propaganda harangues in English aimed at the bored Scottish soldiers. Obviously the British action had been anticipated for some time, for the building was as well stocked with provisions as Noah's Ark. Periodically my chief, R. H. C. Steed, would telephone Herr von Schnitzler, the head Communist radio commentator, to enquire how the supplies were holding out. Herr von Schnitzler would reply defiantly: "We shall stay here half an hour longer than your troops will stay when our comrades from the East come to liberate us." Eventually, apparently on higher orders, he would no longer answer our calls.

On one occasion I got into conversation with a man carrying a 'cello case outside the Radio House. He was very disgruntled. Every morning he came down to take up his place in the radio orchestra, and every morning a kilted soldier barred the way. He was not interested in politics.

"I am a German and an artist, and I think you and the Russians are being equally childish," he said as he stalked away.

Nevertheless, half-hearted though it seemed, the British action proved its point, and after a week of siege the Russians withdrew from the Western enclaves they had occupied.

Before they did this, I paid a visit to one of the enclaves, West Staaken, on the fringe of the British sector, where the Russians had cut off the 3,000 inhabitants from the rest of Berlin. The new demarcation line arbitrarily imposed by the Russians ran down the center of the main road. It was strictly one way; on one side you were in the free West, but if you wanted to turn round and drive back you came under the dictatorship of the proletariat. Remembering that my insurance policy did not cover accidents behind the Iron Curtain, I discreetly left my car in a side street. Near the Soviet control point there was a newspaper and candy stand. I went over and asked its inhabitant for information. Spitting angrily out of his booth, he pointed to a worried-looking old woman he had been talking to before I came up.

"Her nephew is dying in West Staaken and they will not let her in. They will not let people visit the graveyards of their relatives over there, nor would they let us go to the Protestant Church at Whitsun. Mongol swine!"

At this moment two young Russian soldiers came by on the far side of the road, tommy-guns slung over their shoulders. The embittered boothkeeper provocatively held out a hand full of caramels, as if enticing a dog. The Russians stopped and smiled uncertainly. The boothkeeper shouted what sounded like an oath in Russian at them. They made an angry gesture and moved on. The booth rocked with derisive laughter.

"The poor swine, even though their army stretches from here to China, they've never in their lives seen a caramel. But they wouldn't dare accept one from me. Ha ha ha!"

I looked around nervously for cover before the shooting began.

That boothkeeper, as well as the policeman at the Radio House, was a typical Berliner, I discovered. How easily the Reds could double over that half-street and carry off both him and his diminutive booth into the Communist void! There might be an Allied protest, but it would avail him little. Yet he was defiant to the point of folly. I found myself frequently comparing the unafraid Berliners, with their whimsical humor at their city's impossible position, to the tough Serbs I had met in Belgrade shortly after the break with Russia. Of all the Germans, the Berliners were the most resolutely anti-Bolshevik. As Brigadier Claude Dewhurst, the talented former head of the British liaison mission to the Russians in Berlin, notes in his book *Close Contact* the "Reddest" district in Berlin, Wedding, voted 50 per cent Communist and 20 per cent Socialist in pre-war days. But after the Russian capture of the city, not one Communist member was elected to Wedding's council in the first free elections, in spite of a 93 per cent poll. "The nearer you get to Communism, the less you like it."

A rally in honor of a visiting delegation from North Korea gave me my first glimpse of the Communist half of Berlin. Much has been written about the uniqueness of Berlin as a window through the Iron Curtain, and on the fantastic contrasts between East and West, but what always struck me most forcibly were the contrasts in people themselves. In West Berlin the people are not smartly but adequately well dressed. They go about with a bustle and a certain vivacity. You cross through the shanty no-man's-land into the Potsdamer Platz, with its massive placards and pictures of Ulbricht and Pieck, and suddenly you notice the people: shabby in the extreme, walking about with no apparent aim or enthusiasm, hungry yellow faces with expressionless features. The abrupt contrast shocks you.

On the way to the meeting, I passed several columns of Free German Youth and men and women of the People's Police in their blue uniforms and blouses, carrying their rifles slung Russian style. Their faces showed no emotion of either depression or elation — just machine-like fixity. Were they just unwilling victims of the most monstrous press-gang on earth, or were they revelling in the return of the old *Kameradschaft* they had not experienced since the Nazis? It was impossible to tell.

Inside the meeting, I found, to my concern, that I was seated in the midst of a large detachment of young Vopos. As far as I could see, I was the only Western correspondent there. On the arrival of the North Koreans, who were accompanied by Herr Grotewohl, and at appropriate intervals during the speeches, the section leader of the Vopos shouted "*Auf!*" and all leaped to their feet to applaud with slow rhythmic clapping — the sort that a first night flop gets at home. I did not see why I should clap too, so I remained seated, in face of much muttering and scowling. Mass emotion is a terrifying thing if you run counter to the current, and after about the tenth "*auf*" I began to wonder if my nerves would hold out to the end. Fortunately they did.

The North Korean spokesman told a harrowing tale of the

suffering which the war (launched by the reactionary Syngman Rhee) had brought to his country, embroidered with imaginative descriptions of the various pests dropped on North Korea by the villainous Americans. Then Grotewohl rose and the point of the North Korean visit became all too obvious. Dr. Adenauer was another Syngman Rhee; the United States had just signed "General War Treaties" with him, aimed at launching an invasion of the *German Democratic Republic*. If the East German people were not prepared, they too, like their North Korean brothers, would suffer the ghastly fate of biological warfare. Therefore they must be ready and equipped. I could sense the young Vopos being deeply impressed by Grotewohl's words. There was no doubting it. The tenseness grew as I still remained seated, and a tremendous burst of applause greeted the words "we must be prepared." It was all very frightening and I was glad to get back to West Berlin that night.

A few days later Herr Grotewohl formally announced the creation of an East German army. The country had been, he said, "compelled in the interests of peace" to take this step.

2

Rearming Two Germanys

THE ANNOUNCEMENT OF THE FORMATION OF THE EAST GERMAN army was in fact just another Soviet hoax designed to frighten West Germans and the world at large away from the EDC. While intensifying the hypnotic beat on their monotonous peace tom-tom, the Soviets endeavored to show themselves as a poor defenseless nation, threatened by the aggressive designs of Western Germany's twelve EDC divisions, and thus forced — most unwillingly — to rearm the East Germans.

But in truth rearming of the East Germans had been going on slowly for years, and long before the EDC was even thought of. The first step in the establishment of the East German Army actually took place in July, 1948, when about 6,000 ex-Wehrmacht soldiers were recruited and allotted to groups, 250 strong, described as "Training Units of the Frontier Police Alert Detachments." They were then equipped with German World War II arms. A year later the force was reorganized into thirty-nine "Alert Detachments" under the People's Police. In 1950 the Alert Detachments came under the command of a Moscow-trained East German, Wilhelm Zaisser, who led the International Brigade in Spain under the name of "General Gomez." He later became head of the East German State Security Service, to suffer (in consequence of the 1953 uprisings) the fate common to most

Communist secret police chiefs. The next commander was General Heinz Hoffmann, also a Spanish Civil War leader, who had adopted Russian nationality during World War II. Under his control the units received most rigorous ideological indoctrination and a quantity of heavy Russian equipment, including T34 tanks. Training was on completely Russian lines, emphasizing tactics of fanatical attack on the basis of overwhelming numerical superiority. By the beginning of 1951, the force numbered 65,-000 and that summer it held its first maneuvers, under the guise of "summer camps." Even before Korean War, General Hoffmann is on record as having boasted, "We are not policemen, we are soldiers. When we fight we shall fight side by side with the Red Army." Yet on August 11th of the same year, Herr Grotewohl stated blandly at a press conference in East Berlin, "The People's Police has no military character." On December 21st some 6,500 officers graduated from military schools, and on January 1st, 1952 the "Alert Detachments" were transformed into divisional cadres with a nominal strength of between 2,500 and 3,500 men, intended for expansion into Soviet-type motorized divisions of 8,000 men. By June of 1952, while the Soviets were pouring vitriol on the West for forming a West German army under "Hitlerite Generals," in East Germany they were extending invitations to all former Nazi officers to join the "new" National Army — or *Barracked* People's Police" (KVP) as it became known after the Grotewohl announcement. (In 1955, when all West Germany was reading *Discipline Is All* by Kurt Halbritter, a book of brilliant anti-militarist satires, the same book was being confiscated in the Soviet Zone by the State Security Service.) In October 1952, the KVP formally appeared for the first time at a parade in honor of the founding of the East German Republic, wearing loose-cut olive-green uniforms almost indistinguishable from those of the Russian Army. Meanwhile arms production in East German industry had already been a fact for several years.

Some idea of the planned size of the East German army may be gained from the fact that by the end of 1951 about a quarter of the force's total strength were officers. On this basis, Western military observers in 1952 estimated the East German army would consist of over twenty divisions — or be nearly twice the size of the West German EDC contingent, based on a supporting population little more than a third as numerous and less than a tenth as industrialized. At the end of 1952, before one single West German soldier had been recruited, the figures published by the Foreign Office showed that more than 100,000 East Germans were already under arms. A fully trained three-division strong Army Corps had already been established at Pasewalk in the north, equipped with 350 tanks and 200 guns, including self-propelled units. An embryo navy of four flotillas of minesweepers, and a nucleus air force of 5,000 had also been set up. This was not bad going for an army only "created" six months earlier, and it was conservatively estimated that West German rearmament would then have taken at least eighteen months to catch up.

Nor did militarization of the Soviet Zone end with the "Barracked People's Police." In May, 1952, a youth training organization called "Sport and Technics" was formed for boys and girls between 13 and 18, whose para-military scope far exceeded that of the Hitler Youth. Under its edicts all schools were to provide children with an hour's "military education" — including shooting lessons for all boys and girls over 12, and jumping from parachute towers for the older children. By the following May Day, the organization could provide a detachment of a thousand pathetic little creatures in outsize uniforms to march with sub-calibre rifles in the procession, from a total of 800,000 members already enrolled. The brown shirt of the Hitler Youth had been simply exchanged for the blue shirt of the "Free German Youth."

None of this long-term rearmament program made the Russian reunification proposals of 1952 ring very true, and the trends bore an alarming resemblance to developments in North Korea prior to 1950. This time, fortunately, the West had the bitter experience of Korea to forewarn them, and the peephole of Berlin to inform them of what was afoot in the Soviet Zone. With the memory of Korea still very fresh in 1952, the Soviet's progressive rearmament of Eastern Germany (which is, after all, the womb of Prussian militarism) would have seemed adequate cause for the West to organize the West Germans in their own defense. But over and beyond this, the relative East-West strengths in this part of the world were frighteningly disproportionate, and it may be well to mention here some statistics which made the West's need for West German defense participation so compelling.

In 1952, the Russians themselves had over three million men, in 175 divisions, mobilized in their land forces alone most of which were on an active war footing. (These figures have remained more or less constant to date, but the striking power of the Russian divisions had been increased by modernization.) Twenty-two divisions, most of them armored or motorized infantry, were stationed in Germany, backed up by a further sixty divisions facing west in Russia herself. The East European satellite armies then disposed of an additional sixty to seventy divisions, inclusive of the East German forces. As against this the US, French and British forces in West Germany totalled little more than ten divisions, and many of these were (and, indeed, are still) severely under strength. The remainder of the NATO forces in Western Europe, which had already fallen well behind schedule, totaled about twenty standing divisions. Even with NATO's projected expansion, the Western line of defense between the North Cape and the Mediterranean would still be dangerously thin. Moreover, it was only with considerable strain to their economies that France and Britain could maintain their present commitments, which in 1952 included Korea, Indo-China, Malaya, Egypt, North Africa and Austria — as well as Germany. When the Mau Mau menace emerged in Kenya later, Britain had to scrape the very bottom of the barrel of her home reserves for reinforcements. Had the situation in Malaya greatly deteriorated, or a new emergency sprung up elsewhere, she would undoubtedly have been forced to move troops away from Germany and leave agape the tempting gateway over the North German plains to the Ruhr and Calais.

What was even more alarming was the fact that little more

help could be expected from the United States in terms of manpower. Even her seemingly inexhaustible reserves had reached their peacetime limit, if one can accept the depressing statistics given by General Mark Clark in his book *From the Danube to the Yalu.* "In 1953," the former UN commander in Korea writes, "American military commitments required the deployment of a million men abroad, not counting those in Korea. Just to meet present peacetime standards would require the draft of one million new soldiers every year for the next decade." But, according to General Clark's figures, the current draft could only raise a little more than 800,000 youths a year between the ages of 18 and 26 without having to re-draft older men. Not until 1959 would the American demands of a million a year be satisfied.

This critical manpower shortage, at a time when America finds herself at loggerheads with the most numerous race on earth, General Clark explains as being rooted in the "seven lean years" of the great US depression, when nobody wanted to have the children who should now be coming of military age. General Clark expresses the fear that in the event of war "the Communists would outman us numerically everywhere we fought." This has for a long time been a more or less accepted fact.

The reverse of the picture is the West's technical and atomic superiority. But some very disquieting thoughts were raised recently by the first full-scale NATO maneuvers to use atomic cannon and other atomic weapons — exercise "Battle Royal" in September, 1954. There, in the very area of Germany where a possible Russian attack in Europe would have to be countered, a side with numerical superiority but minimum atomic support launched an "offensive" against a numerically inferior side possessing superiority in tactical atomic weapons. The lesson of the exercise seemed to point to a fairly clear victory by the numerically superior attacking side. If one can accept General Ridgway's reasoning in the New York *Times* of July 15, 1955, nuclear superiority — even if the West still possesses it — may never obviate the need for large standing armies, especially in "localized" wars *à la* Korea, or Indo-China.

Apart from the critical manpower shortages of the West vis-à-vis the 750 million men at the disposal of the Communists, there were compelling economic reasons why the West Germans should take over the burden of their own defense. As Mr. Eden put it in the House of Commons on July 7th, 1952: "If the Germans take no part in rearmament it would mean that they alone of the free nations would be able to continue to devote their full industrial capacity to civil needs and export trade." The British High Commissioner, Sir Ivone Kirkpatrick, put it even more concisely in my first interview with him on August 12th, 1952: "If we do not support a German arms contribution, we shall be encouraging competition in the field of foreign trade which may eventually ruin us. Ask Coventry what they think!" To another correspondent, Sir Ivone, a diplomat with a long experience of both pre- and post-war Germany, and considerable reservations about the German national character, said: "I fear German tractors more than German tanks." It always seemed astonishing that the hard-headed British trade-unionists who bellowed most loudly against "arming the Hun" during the next two years, should also complain equally loudly about "unfair" German trade competition, without apparently noticing the interdependence of the two. The figures were revealing: in the fiscal year 1952–53, Britain's defense expenditures were budgeted at $4,847,000,000, or 12.8 per cent of her gross national product (America: 17.6 per cent). Germany was then paying only $1,680,000,000 (i.e. about 6.7 per cent of the national product) a year on occupation costs, and it was fairly obvious that, once the principle of ending the Occupation had been established, she could hardly be expected to maintain payment much longer in the absence of EDC or a similar defense arrangement. Thus if Britain, together with France and America, considered it necessary to keep troops stationed in Germany, an additional $560 million would devolve on the British taxpayer.

From the point of view of economic resources, it would be ludicrous to think of any West European defense system on present boundaries from which Germany was excluded by neutralization. Whether for arms or civil production the coal mines and steel industries of the Ruhr are vital to the rest of Europe. In 1952, the whole of Western Europe (including Great Britain and Western Germany) produced 547 million tons of coal and 55 million tons of finished steel; compared with a total production by the USSR and her European satellites of 460 millions tons of coal and 38.5 million tons of steel. In the event of Germany being neutralized, the balance between Western Europe and the Eastern bloc would become just about even. In the event of Germany becoming completely detached from the West and assimilated into the Eastern bloc, the remainder of Western Europe would be completely outmatched in the basic products — to say nothing of the vast chemical, machine, aluminum and other highly developed industries of Western Germany. Once again the lesser European countries dependent on Ruhr coal would find themselves in a dire position similar to that of the 1930s when they had to pay homage to Hitler to insure fulfilment of their needs. The whole economic life of Europe would be subservient to the whim of the Kremlin.

Thus, only seven years after the war, the full partnership of Western Germany had become militarily, strategically and economically essential to the survival of the western world. Through no deeds of her own she found herself in the immensely favorable position of being the balance between East and West.

Yet, for Europeans who had suffered fearful injuries at the hands of the Germans, the realization that these same Germans were perforce to become once more a major armed power was extremely unpalatable. Coming so soon after the unconditional surrender and the Allies' stringent "re-education" program, the new status of Germany had a bewildering, and in many ways unfortunate, psychological effect on the Germans themselves. In many of the war generation it created the dangerous illusion that, at least where Russia was concerned, the Allies had been wrong and Hitler had — at least to a certain extent — been right. There were also Germans who, although by no means unrepentant Nazis, were still sufficiently nationalistic and impregnated with the Hegelian sense of German destiny to see Germany's enlistment on the side of the West as an opportunity for gaining peacefully the leadership in Europe which she had been denied in two wars. Some of these even found their way into the front ranks of the diversified parties which constituted Dr. Adenauer's Bonn Coalition. The knowledge that these and comparable ideas were finding expression in Western Germany could not but raise misgivings abroad that an old spirit was reviving.

Against all this stood the towering figure of the Federal Chancellor, Dr. Adenauer, and the genuine spirit of European co-operation he had instilled into his Christian Democrat followers, and thence into a wide cross-section of the German people. The great, visionary aim of all Dr. Adenauer's foreign policy is contained in one simple sentence of a radio interview of December 17th, 1952: "My policy is, and remains, directed towards the United States of Europe."

As the New York *Times* rightly noted in April, 1952: "So far as Germany is concerned, the success of the whole defense program depends upon one man — Chancellor Adenauer." Dr. Adenauer's own views on European defense and Germany's role were outlined in a speech in Berlin of October 1951:

> A United Europe can never be an aggressor. The plurality of the members of which it would consist would never permit aggression or an aggressive policy. A United Europe will not attack, but it will be able to defend itself against an attack. No power which wishes for peace can object to this. In this integrated Europe, Germany will be a very strong factor for peace. Germany experienced the last war with all its horrors on her own soil and at very close quarters. She knows well that another war would be still more terrible, still more cruel, and she knows too that she lies geographically nearest the danger zone. Germany therefore — and I repeat and emphasize this — will be a particularly strong element of peace in a United Europe.

Even after the disillusioning collapse of the EDC in 1954, Dr. Adenauer astounded members of his own Party by persisting in his simple conviction that a European political union would yet come to pass. But his greatest ambition of all has been to take his place in history as the German statesman who effected a reconciliation with France, an ambition that goes back to the chaotic period after the first world war when he sympathized with plans to set up a separatist pro-French Rhineland, removed from the shadow of Prussia. Needless to say, his part in this separatist movement, indistinct though it appears to have been, has been much used by his more nationalistically inclined opponents.

As the man whom Sir Winston Churchill once deemed the "wisest German statesman since Bismarck," Dr. Adenauer, until he reached the end of his biblically allotted span, had led a remarkably sequestered life by comparison with most other world leaders. He did not make his debut in national politics until he was in his seventies, and had never been outside Germany until he was 75 — the age at which Bismarck was making his final retirement to Friedrichsruh. In fact, any comparison between Adenauer and Bismarck begins and ends with their stature as German statesmen. Whereas Bismarck had no scruples about constantly playing one nation against another to achieve his supreme aim of German unity, Adenauer has never allowed even the paramount call of reunification to swerve him from his determination to align Germany with the West. Most of his active life he had spent in the city administration of Cologne, his birthplace, of which he became *Oberbürgermeister* (Lord Mayor) in 1917. From then until 1933 he filled this post efficiently, but without gaining exceptional distinction outside of the city. In 1933 he refused to fly the Nazi swastika from the Cologne City Hall, and was deposed shortly thereafter. The next year Dr. Adenauer, who is a devout Catholic, spent in semi-refuge at the Benedictine monastery of Maria Laach, near Koblenz. In 1934 he was arrested after the Roehm *putsch,* but released again. He was arrested a second time after the abortive anti-Hitler bomb plot in July 1944, and consigned to a concentration camp for several months.

During the twelve years of Hitler's reign, Dr. Adenauer retired to complete seclusion and political inactivity in the small village of Rhöndorf on the Rhine south of Bonn, which is still his home. These were the years of Toynbeean "withdrawal" equivalent to St. John in the wilderness, Lenin in Siberia, or (one hesitates to draw the comparison) Hitler in Landsberg, during which time Dr. Adenauer read and reflected and developed his ideas on European integration and Franco-German coexistence.

When the end of the war came, he was reinstated as Oberbürgermeister of Cologne by the Allies but shortly afterwards let go by the British for "incompetence" — a fact which Germans now never let one forget! However, his star was from then onwards in the ascendant; he was elected Chairman of the Christian Democrat Party (CDU) — first in the British Zone, later as leader of the whole West German party. On September 15th, 1949, the Bundestag voted him with a majority of only one to be first Chancellor of the Federal Republic. He was then 73.

Apart from their very different lives Dr. Adenauer and Sir Winston Churchill have certain things in common. Like Sir Winston, Dr. Adenauer thrives on a minimum of sleep, to the distress of his younger assistants. His working day begins at 6 a.m., and members of his staff have frequently been roused at 7 a.m. to continue discussion on some point left over from the previous night's work. Dr. Adenauer works until past 10 o'clock in the evening. He often works a seven-day week. After the lightning State tour of Greece and Turkey in 1954, an exceptionally robust 45-year-old member of the Chancellor's entourage told me that he was so exhausted that he slept for twenty-four hours. Dr. Adenauer was at his desk the morning after his return.

In his private life, Dr. Adenauer leads the somewhat solitary existence of a man who has outlived two wives, although he had as constant companion, until she married in 1954, his youngest daughter, Lotte. His seven children are all grown up, and have provided him with thirteen grandchildren. As relaxation from the cares of statesmanship, in place of Sir Winston's painting and bricklaying, Dr. Adenauer has the cultivation of prize-winning roses, a voracious appetite for detective stories, and a lust for being driven at hair-raising speeds. He differs from Sir Winston in being a non-smoker, and only an occasional imbiber of Rhine wine; in all, the epitome of Dr. Johnson's temperate man.

It may well be the hours spent in his garden which give Dr. Adenauer his remarkably slim and erect bearing, and a handshake firm enough to make many a younger man wince. But undoubtedly the secret of his undiminished vigor also lies largely in his complete imperturbability — which probably has a value comparable to Sir Winston's alleged ability to find complete repose in a ten-minute nap. Dr. Adenauer's almost Amerindian features (he suffered severe facial injuries in a car accident in 1917) are rarely seen to drop their impassive composure, or register any emotion. Typical of Adenauer was his reaction when, one evening in June, 1955, his state secretary telephoned him at home the news that the Russians had invited him to participate in talks on Germany in Moscow. The invitation probably represented the peak of Dr. Adenauer's career, the crowning glory of his policy, but after hearing the news, Adenauer replied calmly, "That seems like a very significant piece of news; but I'm in the midst of listening to a concert — we'll talk about it tomorrow morning." That was almost Drake with his bowls at Plymouth Hoe before sailing to meet the Spanish Armada! During my time in Germany I never once saw Adenauer show excitement in a speech, or let the tenseness of the moment disturb the inflexible calmness of his delivery. Whereas his great opponent, Schumacher, would work his voice up into a high-pitched hysteria to win a point in a debate, Dr. Adenauer dispatches his enemies with an icy cold logic, often tinged with an inimitable quality of Rhenish irony. It is the cold Adenauer rebuff that his own close collaborators and leaders of the coalition fear most. He rarely comes off second best; I recall one occasion, when an unknown Austrian had the last laugh, in a correspondence to *Der Spiegel* in 1955. Shortly after the signing of the Austrian Treaty, relations between Austria and the Federal Republic became strained over the question of former German property held in Austria as war reparations. Dr. Adenauer remarked caustically that "if the Austrians should demand further reparations from us, then we will send them the bones of Adolf Hitler." The Austrian correspondent to the *Spiegel* replied, "That sounds like a threat, but in fact it isn't — for what an invasion of tourists there would be (especially from the Federal Republic) if we had these precious remains in our country!"

In his speeches, Adenauer never resorts to pathos or dialectics. His most effective rhetoric weapon is his simplicity — especially since it is a gift almost unknown to German orators. His words are simple, and his sentences short and easily translatable into any language (a fact which enhances his popularity with the foreign press!). The theme of all his speeches is simple, and invariable — thus by constant repetition the majority of the German people have come to gain a crystal-clear impression of his policies, as opposed to the aura of indefinition which usually surrounds the utterances of the Social Democrat Opposition.

This simplicity and composure, added to a great natural dignity, also provide him with his greatest strength in Party and Cabinet dealings. In contrast to Sir Winston, he has no mind for detail or for engaging in technical matters within the specific realm of his various ministers. As one of his personal assistants told me, at Cabinet meetings he refuses to become involved in discussions on such technical subjects as finance or economics, or let himself get immersed in detail. Having listened attentively to the discussion he will intervene to give a clear-cut decision, showing a complete understanding of the factors at issue, while being able to see the wood a good deal more clearly than his tree-bound colleagues.

Like Sir Winston, Dr. Adenauer is open to constant attack for the patriarchal, authoritarian manner with which he tends to rule Party, Cabinet and Government alike. Being Germans, the Christian Democrats complain less than the Tory back bench; although in 1954 a CDU deputy, Herr Schmidt-Wittmack, alleged he was driven East by the autocratic behavior of his chief. The very first of the many apocryphal Adenauer anecdotes I heard on coming to Bonn told of a very senior Cabinet Minister who dared to raise his hand three times to be heard while the Chancellor was laying down the law at a Cabinet meeting. Twice he was ignored, but on the third attempt Dr. Adenauer remarked coldly, "You should know by now, Herr —, that you are entitled to leave the room if you need without requesting my permission."

Indeed, as Dr. Adenauer magically restored order to an unruly Bundestag with an admonitory forefinger, he often recalled a stern schoolmaster disciplining his boys. His autocratic manner is frequently rankling to German political leaders. He has a habit of delegating little authority to his collaborators; when he goes away from Bonn, officials relax and journalists snatch a few days' holiday in the certainty that no decisions will be taken in his absence.

At the end of the first Bundestag in 1953, a leading member of one of the coalition parties commented to me: "He may be autocratic, but it was better that he *led* the Bundestag than that we had a new government every three months, like the French." Any German exercising authority tends, in the light of the past, to awaken fears abroad, but a calm authoritative personality like the Chancellor's was just what the Germans needed to restore to sanity a country filled with the neurotic and the shell-shocked. If any German can bring about a Franco-German conciliation, Dr. Adenauer, with his great patience and vision is ideally suited to the task.

In complete contrast to Dr. Adenauer stood a man nearly twenty years younger — the late Kurt Schumacher, the embittered, tragic leader of the Social Democrats. Somebody once aptly remarked that Adenauer symbolized the restoration of the good old days of Germany, while Schumacher represented the ruins of its more recent past. At the beginning of World War I, Schumacher lost his right arm. Becoming an intense pacifist after the war, he joined the Social Democrats and gained a seat in the Reichstag in 1930. On Hitler's seizure of power, he was flung into a concentration camp, where he remained almost uninterruptedly for twelve years until liberated by the Allies. When he emerged his health was shattered and his mind deeply engrained by his experiences under the Nazis. In October, 1945, he was elected

Chairman of the Social Democratic Party in preference to two other candidates, Herr Erich Ollenhauer and Herr Otto Grotewohl. Schumacher's heroic record under the Nazis gave him precedence over Ollenhauer who had led the Party from exile in Czechoslovakia, France, and then England; fortunately for Germany, the surviving remnants of the SPD would not elect Grotewohl because of his desire to merge with the Communist Party. Under Schumacher's dedicated and fanatical guidance, the Social Democrat Party was given a discipline and a drive that it had never had in pre-war days. It also became the most rabidly nationalistic of the big German political parties in the early postwar days. In the 1949 election, the Social Democrats all but tied with the Christian Democrats, but steadfastly refused to form a coalition.

While being an uncompromising foe of Communism, Schumacher held the most bitter and fundamental hostility for Dr. Adenauer, at whom he once growled: "You are the Chancellor of the Allies!" Under him the Social Democrats adopted an attitude of unyielding opposition to the Treaties and Adenauer's whole policy of integration with the West. To the Social Democrats, German reunification had a special significance; with the traditionally Socialist areas of Prussia and Middle Germany back in the fold, the SPD could reckon to become the supreme power in the land. At one moment he went so far in his fight against the Treaties as to threaten that anybody who voted for them would cease to be a German. It sounded curiously like an utterance of the Nazis. In his demand for German unity without attachments, he was as single-minded as Dr. Adenauer in his policy of Western integration. Even the SPD building in Bonn was constructed on his orders in sections, so that it could be dismantled and transported to Berlin as soon as it became once more the capital. No longer a pacifist, his terms for rearmament were a German national army under German command, arming behind a "shield of Western force," with the thinly veiled ultimate objective of regaining Eastern Germany.

Had Schumacher lived, the development of Western Germany

over the past two years might well have been different; there is little doubt that he would have used organized labor to fight against the Treaties with mass strike actions, and with his personality still at the helm the Christian Democrats would have been hard put to it to win the 1953 election.

But Schumacher was a stricken man. At a conference in London in 1948 he was suddenly taken ill with a terrible pain in his left leg. He was at once flown back to Germany, where doctors diagnosed a chronic circulation ailment, stemming from the neglect of the concentration camps. The leg was amputated, and for the remaining few years of his life, a hopeless cripple, he used to be half carried to his seat in the Bundestag by his loyal followers, whence he hurled searing invective at the Government. On the night of August 20th, 1952, he died, thus depriving Germany of one of her two great public figures. The grief within the SPD — who, even down to the girl secretaries, regarded Schumacher as a demigod — surpassed all belief. Like a dead king, for two days his body lay in state in the Party headquarters in Bonn, with leaders of the Party keeping watch.

His successor was Herr Ollenhauer, the man who had spent five years in London and had indeed acquired something of the aroma of Transport House — down to the pipe-smoking and baggy trousers. Standing roughly on the right — or at least, moderate — wing of the SPD, he was by temperament a German Herbert Morrison to Schumacher's Bevan; unimposing, amorphous, tubby and owl-like — and an incredibly dull speaker. Even the West German weekly, *Der Spiegel,* which tends to be sympathetic towards the Social Democrats, commented: "The career of the politician Ollenhauer appears so deadly boring even to his comrades . . ." As a counterfoil to Schumacher's brilliant, irrational mind, Ollenhauer's steady, reflective personality provided the qualities of the ideal lieutenant. With Schumacher gone, the Social Democrats were without a leader.

In German politics, Herr Ollenhauer had already gained the reputation of a man open to compromise. Hopes were raised in the coalition that the Social Democrats' opposition to the Treaties would gradually lessen. But they were disappointed. At the first post-Schumacher SPD congress in October 1952, Herr Ollenhauer, speaking under a larger-than-life portrait of Schumacher, declared that the Party would continue in the steps of the dead leader. They would not support the Treaties because they considered that their enforcement would remove all prospects of German reunification. "If the Government accepts the Contractual Agreements and the EDC Treaty against the wishes of the Social Democrat Party, we shall fight from the first day onwards for their radical revision by new negotiations on a new basis," Herr Ollenhauer threatened. The statement clearly had one eye on the French Assembly, which would obviously think twice about ratifying the EDC, thus binding France to the Treaty until the end of the century, if it was to be repudiated by the German Socialists as soon as they should come to power.

Here one must go back briefly to review the turbulent course towards ratification along which the Treaties had been launched after their signature in May 1952. It was more or less decided in principle among the six signatories of the EDC that the others should wait until Germany had ratified. In his earliest timetable, Dr. Adenauer hoped to have ratification completed by the parliamentary recess in July. Then the first of many snags occurred when — under Socialist pressure — the Bundesrat (Upper House) decided that the Treaties could on no account be ratified without their approval. And they insisted that the Treaties be granted the most careful study by the various Bundestag committees. The Chancellor was placed in an awkward position since he was by no means sure of a majority in the Bundesrat, but he managed to push the first of the three readings on the Treaties through the Bundestag (Lower House) at the beginning of July. In his opening address he warned the House that if the Treaties were rejected "the confidence we have won among the Western Powers and in the whole world would be lost. Russia would in all probability succeed in her plans for the neutralization of Germany, and the integration of Europe would become impossible without Germany."

During the debate the most brutal kidnapping took place in West Berlin of Dr. Linse, a leading member of an organization called the "League of Free Jurists." The "Free Jurists" were a body of lawyers, with their headquarters in West Berlin, who collected information on specific cases of injustice and inhumanity in the Soviet Zone with a view to eventual prosecution of those responsible. They were reputed to have an extremely effective intelligence network in the Zone, which appears to have been largely broken up as a result of information extorted from Linse. His movements betrayed by his secretary (who was later discovered to have been a Communist agent), he was spirited off by a group of young East German criminals who had been offered amnesty if they carried out this abduction. In spite of repeated pleas by his distraught wife, and notes of protest by the US High Commissioner, the Russians persistently denied all knowledge of Linse. His fate is still unknown. The Bundestag was deeply shocked when it heard of this latest Russian monstrosity, and as the leader of the West German Communist Party, Herr Max Reimann, rose to speak, all but his thirteen fellow Communists trooped out of the Chamber.

The Treaties were then handed over to seven different parliamentary committees for examination, prior to their being submitted to the vote in the second and third readings in the Bundestag. These were tentatively fixed, before the House went into recess, to take place on September 3rd and 5th. But when September arrived it was discovered that the committees — impeded by the delaying tactics of their Social Democrat members — were still far from completing their work on the Treaties. September ran into October and October into November, and still, to Dr. Adenauer's intense concern, the Treaties were not ready for the second reading. Meanwhile, hovering over the parliamentary scene was a menacing cloud puffed up by the Socialists, who had filed a plaint to the Federal Constitutional Court designed to block the Treaties on the ground that they required an amendment to the Constitution. In the event that the Court concurred with the Socialists, the Coalition Government would have to drum up a two-thirds majority in both Houses to alter the Constitution, which it could never do under the existing balance of power.

Then, before the hectic summer was over, the Russians backed up their barrage of notes on German reunification by sending to Bonn a five-man delegation from the East German "People's Chamber" with a message to the Bundestag. It was purely a propaganda stunt and one which few West Germans fell for. With much misgiving the Bundestag President, Dr. Ehlers, decided to receive the deputation — but no more. As the East German deputies rolled across the Rhine Bridge into Bonn in their Russian "Zim" cars, some 200 angry Bonners tried to drag them out of their cars, shouting, "Give us back Dr. Linse!" The visit ended the following day in a hail of rotten eggs at a luncheon to which the Foreign Press Association had amiably invited the delegates. As is, alas, so often the case, it was the journalists who took the brunt.

While Dr. Adenauer and his followers were exerting every sinew to get the Federal Parliament to accept the Treaties ending the Occupation and rearming Western Germany, some disquieting reports from Germany were beginning to reach the western world. Both Americans and Europeans who, in the bitter light of past experience, had never accepted German rearmament as anything other than a necessary evil, now became extremely alarmed by the news of increasing activity among the neo-Nazis. At the same time, an emotional campaign to free the war criminals still in Allied prisons was reaching its climax in Western Germany, arousing the fear abroad that the German attitude towards the crimes of Nazism might be undergoing an unpleasant distortion.

3

Adenauer's Legacy

IT IS NOT COMFORTABLE TO BECOME LEGAL SUCCESSOR TO A regime responsible for the most lethal war and the most monstrous crimes in history. This was the Federal Government's inheritance in 1949. Leaving no doubts as to his own personal repugnance for the deeds committed by Germans under the swastika, Dr. Adenauer realized on coming to power that Germany could never be accepted as an equal among the free nations till the world at large was convinced that a decent Germany had risen from the ashes of the old. The Federal Government had to show that the Nazis could never return to power in any form in Western Germany, and that it would do all that lay in its power to redress the wrongs committed in the twelve-year rule of Nazism. To the press of the outside world, watching to detect any signs of waywardness in the new Germany, the criteria applied were: what are the Germans doing to prevent a resurgence of Nazism? — what are they doing to recompense decimated European Jewry, and to stifle the rebirth of any fresh anti-Semitism? — and how do they now regard German crimes of the past?

With the switch of Allied policy toward Russia, the regrowth of German national pride following on the Western Zones' postwar recovery, and the lifting of Allied controls on political activity, the stage was set for surviving incorrigibles of Nazidom to raise their heads again. In 1949, a neo-Nazi Party was formed in Lower Saxony called the Socialist Reich Party (SRP). Essentially a party of the lunatic fringe, it carried not the slightest weight in the Federal Republic as a whole, and at its peak never boasted more than 40,000 subscribing members. But on its first appearance the SRP evoked concern abroad as a potential recrudescence of Nazism, heightened when it gained 11 per cent of the total votes in the Lower Saxon *Land* elections of 1951. The question was raised, why did the Federal Government not prove its good faith by prohibiting the SRP? The answer was, initially, that its advisers were against setting a precedent which would inevitably lead to the outlawing also of the Communist Party. Such a step, the West Germans feared, could create a secret Communist underground difficult to control, and also complicate reunification with East Germany. But in 1952, embarrassed by the wild rantings of the SRP leaders, the Federal Government took action, and applied to the Supreme Court at Karlsruhe to prohibit both Parties on the grounds that their constitutions were "not in accordance with democratic principles."

The Socialist Reich Party was generally linked in Germany with the name of its founder and nominal leader, ex-Major-General Otto Ernst Remer, for in Remer's past was to be found the reason for the SRP's existence. Remer was one of those nonentities brought to fame by the accident of having been in the right place at the right time when history was being made. On July 20th, 1944, when Colonel Count Stauffenberg set off his bomb at the "Wolf's Lair" in East Prussia, Remer was a major in command of a home defense battalion outside Berlin. But it was Remer who, acting on Goebbels' orders, rounded up the unsuccessful conspirators in Berlin.

For his services, he was made a Major-General and awarded the Knight's Cross with Diamonds, one of the highest German decorations. His only active command in this exalted rank was of a division in the Ardennes offensive, in which he hardly distinguished himself. At the time of the bomb plot, Remer was not even an outstandingly staunch Nazi supporter, but from then on he became the loyalest of the loyal and after Hitler's death he looked upon himself as the St. Paul of the movement. When Remer was sentenced to three months' imprisonment in March 1952 for slandering the memory of the 20th of Julyists, whom he had called "traitors," the judge noted that "the accused evidently still lives in the conceptions of 1944, and cannot free himself from these conceptions even seven years after the end of the war." (After the trial ended, Remer's defending counsel, Dr. Wehage, received a number of hostile letters from Germans who had followed the trial; one of them, from a young German who had grown up under Hitler, commented: "After what I have heard in the courtroom, and what you defended there, I am thankful that we did not win the war, although I myself fought stubbornly for the cause, and my father died for it.")

Thus the SRP had a completely backward-looking platform aimed at reincarnating the "best" of Nazism, but it had none of the revolutionary zeal of the Nazis in their early days (partly because Remer was no Führer) and soon lost way after its first successes in 1951. It was chiefly a party for those with a grudge — particularly against the Western occupiers. (Lower Saxony had the greatest concentration of occupation troops — all British — and was the scene of most of the big-scale maneuvers.) Others were those who described themselves as "victims of denazification." Denazification, which placed the ex-Nazis in one of four categories according to their past importance, could entail (instead of, or in addition to, a prison sentence) confiscation of wealth, blocking of property and accounts, loss of civil rights over a period up to ten years, disenfranchisement, exclusion from any government post, disqualification from the teaching, legal, journalistic and medical professions, and other highly restrictive penalties. In January, 1948, the British authorities terminated their denazification activities, but they were later carried on — with considerable zeal — by the local German authorities. Already by 1948, in the British Zone alone, 347,667 ex-Nazis had been removed from private or public positions, and a total of 572,195 placed under the restrictions of the two lesser categories.

The SRP also played upon the misery of the thousands of refugees from the East, crowded into primitive camps and often unable to find employment, and upon the disillusion of a number of professional ex-soldiers who had been disgusted by the Socialists' violent anti-Wehrmacht campaign of the earliest post-war days, which went so far as the declaration that any soldier who had fought for Hitler was a criminal.

In July, 1952, the Supreme Court issued a temporary injunction against the SRP forbidding it to organize meetings or distribute printed matter. A few days later the Party disintegrated from internal stresses, even before the Court in October pronounced a final verdict prohibiting it as "a successor organization to the National Socialist Party." All the SRP's Parliamentary seats were declared forfeit, including the sixteen in the Lower Saxon *Land* Diet. The leaders of the Party fell out of the limelight, and little was heard of them again. In March of the following year, Remer fled the country for Egypt to escape serving his suspended three months' prison sentence, but his own countrymen on General Naguib's staff prevailed upon the Egyptians to refuse him entry. After a year and a half of wanderings he returned to Germany in 1954 in search of a pardon under the new Amnesty Act. It is unlikely that he will find a place in any existing political party.

If the SRP movement had little effect on the West German political scene, it demonstrated that the alliance between Nazism and Communism was not just a freak phenomenon that lived and died with the Molotov-Ribbentrop pact. The Party had from the beginning shown itself open to collusion with the Soviets. Its one member in the Bundestag, Dr. Dorls, frequently stated that he considered the 1939 pact with Russia one of Hitler's greatest triumphs, and its collapse the greatest tragedy of the Nazi era. Dorls felt that a National Socialist Germany would eventually be able to assert its superiority in an alliance with the Soviets. In July, 1952, Dr. Lehr, the Federal Minister of the Interior, revealed to the foreign press that his Ministry had concrete evidence that the SRP was receiving funds from the Soviet authorities in East Germany. Later, Herr Stern, chairman of the SRP's Berlin branch, swore under oath that Count Westarp had received substantial funds from the *West Kommission* (the organization entrusted with infiltration and "agit-prop" functions within West Germany) of the Socialist Unity Party in East Berlin. After the outlawing of the Party, it was reported that the West German Communist Party had offered SRP functionaries posts in their own Party, provided they would take a training course in Russia. Some apparently went, and have not yet reappeared. Dorls himself was observed in conference with Herr Renner, one of the leaders of the Communist Party, and was reported by the German press to have asked for asylum in East Germany. The Communists hastened to cover their tracks, and issued a statement declaring that Renner had ordered Dorls "never to set foot in his office" and condemning Dorls' action as a "maneuver to discredit the Party with the people."

Links with the East were common to nearly all the lesser neo-Nazi splinter organizations. A group called the *Brüderschaft* (Brotherhood) had been riven by internal disputes and collapsed in 1951 in a manner similar to the SRP; its founder, Alfred Franke-Grieksch, an ex-SS Colonel, disappeared to the Soviet Zone and has not been seen since. The president of the *Brüderschaft* was Karl Kaufman, one of the seven men to be arrested with Dr. Naumann in January 1953. Such is the eternal intimacy between Bolshevism and Nazism.

An attraction of the Communist system of East Germany to the ex-Nazis was the absence of the severe Western "denazification" program. Being a totalitarian power, the Russians had more effective ways of stamping out Nazism in their zone than the West, and — perhaps wisely — ceased discrimination against past Nazi Party members shortly after the East German Republic was set up. Wherever they could use him, the Communists would not hesitate to give an ex-Nazi a government or military appointment. To the practical-minded Russians, the neo-Nazis in West Germany, with their hatred of the moderate Adenauer regime and bitter hostility to its policy of co-operation with the West, were invaluable allies, supplementing the wobbly Communist Party and its assorted fellow-travelling neutralists. With utmost cynicism they vituperated the Federal Government for employing reformed Nazis in its service, while they themselves were financing the most unrepentant Nazis in the West for the most undemocratic services.

The employment of ex-Nazis in West German Government offices has constituted one of Bonn's recurrent headaches. In 1952 a Parliamentary committee was set up to examine charges by the Social Democrats that ex-Nazis in the Foreign Office had used their influence to bring in men with dubious records under Hitler. In July that year it delivered its report, finding the charges proved in four specific cases, one of which was the German Ambassador to Greece, Dr. Werner von Grundherr. All four were forced to resign from the Foreign Office, and the committee advised that a further three diplomats should not be employed in the personnel department, and three more should not be given foreign posts. The report supplied figures showing that of the 542 persons employed, 184 were former Party members, 153 had belonged to Ribbentrop's Foreign Office and 88 had been victims of Nazi persecution.

The Social Democrats were not satisfied with the report or the action taken, and public opinion abroad was disturbed to learn that two-thirds of the men responsible for contemporary German foreign policy had served under the Nazis. In 1953 the attack switched to a closer assault on Dr. Adenauer personally for appointing four Cabinet Ministers in his new Government who had Nazi backgrounds, and for retaining the services of Dr. Globke as his personal State Secretary in the Chancellery. Globke's copybook was blotted by the fact that his acute legal brain had been enlisted by the Nazis to write a commentary on the infamous Nuremberg Race Laws. To his credit it is said that his commentary did in fact mitigate the severity of the Law in the earliest days of the Third Reich's persecution of the Jews. Moreover — as Dr. Adenauer replied to his detractors — Dr. Globke was an extremely competent State Secretary.

The whole problem was a constant embarrassment to Dr. Adenauer — especially because of the adverse, and often unintelligent, comment it provoked abroad. There can be no doubt that if Dr. Adenauer had his way, in an ideal situation, there would be no ex-Nazis in the Foreign Office. But under the practical exigencies of the moment this was impossible in a country where over six million Nazi Party members — an eighth of the total population — had survived the war. Many of the pre-war diplomats and civil servants had become Party members under compulsion, to hold their jobs. A great number of those who now claimed they had been refused jobs under the Nazis — apart from the comparatively few who had been genuine victims of Nazism — would have found it equally hard to get jobs under any democratic regime. To have barred every member of the Nazi Foreign Service from employment in the Federal Foreign Office would have been comparable to the Labor Party in 1945 firing every foreign service employee who had held office under the previous Tory Governments. The training of diplomats is a slow business, and the suggestion that the Federal Government should have "trained" an entirely new corps from scratch was totally unrealistic.

In October, 1952, 5,000 former *Waffen SS* toughs held a reunion in the picturesque Hansel and Gretel town of Verden in Lower Saxony. The meeting was convened principally to exchange information about missing comrades and would have been a harmless affair but for the remarks of a guest speaker, ex-General Ramcke. Speaking extemporaneously, Ramcke — a much decorated paratroop commander — tempestuously demanded an amnesty for all German ex-soldiers still in Allied prisons, claiming that the Allies had been just as guilty of war crimes. "Who are the war criminals?" he asked. "They are those who made the Versailles Treaty; they are those who shattered German cities like Dresden for no tactical reasons; they are those who dropped atom bombs on Nagasaki and Hiroshima, and who are producing new atom bombs. But they are *not* the German front-line soldier." General Gille, who later repudiated Ramcke's remarks, passed him repeated notes while he was speaking, but the speaker only grew more and more excited. Ramcke, who had himself been released on parole from a five-year war crimes sentence in France the previous year, continued with the prophecy that the Allied black lists would "become lists of honor."

Ramcke's speech was hotly attacked in the West German press, and deplored by spokesmen of all political parties, as well as most of the veterans' organizations — including the SS. Dr. Adenauer wrote a special letter to Sir Ivone Kirkpatrick, expressing his Government's emphatic disapproval of the speech, and some weeks later an association of the holders of the Knight's Cross deliberately excluded Ramcke from invitation to their reunion. But some of his words appealed to many Germans of the war generation. There are few subjects on which all Germans, regardless of party or past, are more in agreement than war crimes.

Most Germans divide war crimes into two classes. First, those committed by members of the armed forces and either directly or indirectly connected with the conduct of the war, or committed in the heat of the moment (e.g. the lynching of shot-down Allied airmen during an air raid). Second, the crimes committed in cold blood by civilians — principally in the concentration camps and in connection with the mass exterminations and deportations in Eastern Europe and Russia.

If the Germans are unanimous in condemning the second group, the vast majority consider that their countrymen imprisoned for offenses in the first group are being wrongfully detained by the Allies. With monotonous regularity, they are referred to in the West German papers as the "*so-called* war criminals." The individual cases tend to be excused by reference to the belief that all war must "be terrible to be short," which seems to be a part of the German mystique as old as Hermann the Warrior. Once a war has been embarked upon it has to be won by every possible means.

The German case *for* the first category of war criminals is essentially one of *tu quoque*. In the past years the West German press have been quick to seize on any discreditable act by Allied troops in Korea, Malaya, Kenya, Indo-China or wherever fighting — and especially guerrilla fighting — has been in progress. They have also followed with the greatest interest the retrospective writings of Allied leaders.

In the First World War, the Kaiser wrote a letter to Emperor Franz Josef which was the first proclamation in this century of the creed of "total war":

> My soul is torn asunder, but everything must be put to fire and blood. The throats of men and women, children and the aged must be cut and not a tree nor a house left standing.
>
> With such methods of terror, which alone can strike so degenerate a people as the French, the war will finish before two months, while if I use humanitarian methods, it may prolong for years. Despite all my repugnance, I have had to choose the first system.

Germans now set against the Kaiser's famous letter the following extract from Sir Winston Churchill's war memoirs referring to the decision to use the atomic bomb against Japan; which, he declares, presented "the vision — fair and bright indeed it seemed — of the end of the whole war in one or two violent shocks." And later:

> There was never a moment's discussion as to whether the atomic bomb should be used or not. To avert a vast indefinite butchery, to bring the war to an end, to give peace to the world, to lay healing hands upon its tortured peoples by a manifestation of overwhelming power at the cost of a few explosions, seemed, after all our toils and perils, a miracle of deliverance.[1]

In January, 1954, *Der Heimkehrer,* a periodical for returning German prisoners-of-war, headlined the details of the first trial in Kenya of Captain Griffiths,[2] noting that he had been "acquit-

---

[1] *The Second World War* (Vol. VI, pp. 552–3).

[2] Griffiths was arraigned on charges of machine-gunning in the back two African wood-cutters arrested on an anti-Mau Mau patrol, and, some time later, administering a *coup de grâce* to one of the men. He was acquitted of murder on a technicality because the prosecution could not prove which of the Africans he had shot with his pistol. Griffiths later received a five-year sentence on other charges of cruelty to Africans.

ted for a deed for which British Military Courts have hanged German soldiers upon the gallows." Another case picked up by the German press was that of an American lieutenant in Korea charged in 1952 with administering a beating to a civilian which resulted in death. *Der Mittag* registered its approval of the conduct of the trial, but noted that three soldiers arrested with him had been released from trial "because they had been acting under his orders." *Der Mittag* commented that this was a defense which had been rejected by the Allied War Crimes Courts which had sentenced many "simple soldiers and officers" for carrying out the orders of a superior. The whole question of "superior orders" raised in the War Crimes Trials was one which struck most deeply at the fundamentals of German military thinking, as will be seen in a later chapter.

The category of war crimes about which the mass of West Germans feel most strongly is that which includes the actions taken to repress partisan warfare — principally in Russia and Eastern Europe, and chiefly by means of mass execution of hostages. There were charges which had brought sentences against a large number of senior — and popular — German commanders, such as Field Marshals Kesselring, List and Manstein, and Generals Rendulic and Mackensen. The defense at these trials, subsequently re-echoed by German public opinion, was that the Western Allies had no conception what partisan warfare meant — particularly on the scale waged by the Communists — and that massive counter-terror had been the only effective means of repressing it. The shooting of Jewish terrorist hostages in Palestine in 1946-48, and the reprisals against guerrillas in South Korea and against bandits in Malaya have provided the *tu quoque* apologists with ammunition. But in their confused thinking they fail to see that none of these actions ever exacted reprisals on the monstrous ratio of the Nazis, such as the execution in 1944 of 335 Italian hostages for deaths of thirty-two German policemen — a deed for which Field Marshal Kesselring was held responsible. The defense also tends to belie the other German excuse for brutality as a means to a speedy victory, because — as many

German military thinkers now themselves admit — German excesses against occupied populations (especially in the Ukraine and Yugoslavia) generally had the effect of stiffening anti-German resistance.

A glance at the war crimes dossiers of the generals and lesser military personnel shows that only a small percentage were sentenced for actions against partisans or hostages. It was difficult to see how the Germans who shouted for the release of all "front-soldiers" from Allied prisons could embrace in their appeal those senior doctors of the armed forces who were responsible for the carrying out of the most monstrous and cold-blooded experiments on human guinea-pigs far behind the lines. Yet *Die Zeit,* a leading German weekly, published on March 10th, 1954 a long article entitled "About Injustice in Landsberg" (the US war crimes prison), demanding the release of Lt.-General Oskar Schröder, "whose guilt," it claimed, "was in being medical chief of the Luftwaffe." It overlooked the fact that under General Schröder's supervision inmates of concentration camps were involuntarily subjected — among other horrors — to high-altitude decompression tests, which usually resulted in the victim literally exploding, like a deep-sea fish suddenly brought to the surface.

Die Zeit did not, however, overlook the *tu quoque* aspect, and adduced evidence of convicts of Sing-Sing who, in recent years, had been inoculated with malaria — which evidently resulted in the death of four. With such confused thinking perpetually emanating from their papers and politicians, it is hardly surprising that the West German populace were roused in 1952 by an emotional campaign to "free the soldiers" as a pre-requisite to joining in Western defense plans.

At the spearhead of the campaign was Dr. Erich Mende, 36-year-old Bundestag deputy of the Free Democrats — a sincere, straightforward and likeable ex-Major of the infantry, decorated with the Knight's Cross and several other awards for gallantry. Mende claimed to have a following of at least 20-25 coalition deputies who would refuse to vote for the Treaties if the Allies did not first release the bulk of the military prisoners. The issue

was picked up by sections of all parties — including, in a remarkable *volte face,* the Social Democrats, who only a few years
ago had been declaring all ex-soldiers of the Wehrmacht to be
criminals, but were now loth to miss an opportunity to chastise
the Chancellor and the Treaties.

Under the threat of losing his majority for the Treaties, Dr.
Adenauer urgently transmitted an appeal to the Allied High
Commissioners; although, as he confessed to Sir Ivone Kirkpatrick, he did so reluctantly, as he considered that most of the
prisoners still held by the Allies would be an embarrassment to
any government, and many of them were "unsocial elements."

Any mass amnesty for German war criminals — apart from
moral considerations — might well have proved political dynamite in all of the three occupying countries. Instead, as a sop to
the Germans, Britain and America (who between them held almost all the top-ranking German officers) decided — amid considerable official secrecy — to set about the gradual release of
the most senior officers, many of whom were elderly and in poor
health.

The two British-held Field Marshals, Kesselring and Manstein,[3] were allowed to leave Werl during the summer of 1952 to
undergo medical treatment in private clinics. In October Kesselring, who was 67, and supposedly dying of cancer of the throat,
was freed completely as an act of clemency. He made a remarkable recovery on gaining freedom, and was almost immediately
elected President of the *Stahlhelm* veterans' organization, for
which his mortal affliction has not prevented him from making
frequent and outspoken speeches. Manstein was sent home the
following May. He promptly produced a 700-page war memoir.

About the same time the Americans released Col.-General
Reinhardt — then serving a term of fifteen years' imprisonment.

---

[3] Kesselring had been sentenced to death, commuted to life imprisonment,
later reduced to twenty-one years, for responsibility in the shooting of the
335 Italian hostages. Manstein was sentenced to eighteen years' imprisonment (reduced to twelve years) on nine charges, including partial responsibility for the death of 10,840 Russian prisoners of war.

Within a few days of his release, he was appointed President of the *Kyffhäuser Bund,* another ex-soldiers' organization.

In July 1953, the British discharged the last senior officer in their custody — Col.-General von Falkenhorst, the commander of the German army in Norway. His twenty-year sentence was remitted on the grounds that he was suffering from angina.

Between 1952 and 1953 no less than eight of the eleven Field Marshals and full Generals held by the Allies were released with a minimum of publicity. In the autumn of 1953, when ratification of the Treaties was still being stalled by apparently endless French delays, the Allies agreed to the setting up of Mixed Consultative Boards in each of the three zones as a substitute for the Clemency Boards provided for under the Bonn Conventions. The stop-gap boards, consisting of both German and Allied representatives in each zone, reviewed each case and made recommendations for clemency to the appropriate High Commission. The result was a considerable acceleration in the rate of release of war criminals of all categories. In May, 1952, the total still held by the West was just under 1,000; by the end of 1954 it had fallen to little more than 300. At the same time, while the three Allied Governments made it clear they did not intend a mass amnesty of the war criminals, correspondents were no longer allowed access to the various case histories and the whole emphasis was laid on playing down this explosive topic. It was a curious swing of policy; as an American press official remarked to me wryly, "Time was when the order was to give all publicity to these b——s."

Although the German campaign for the freeing of the war criminals died down in 1953 after the bulk of the senior officers had been released, the widespread belief in their innocence tended to become even more firmly implanted as a result of the Allied concessions, which appeared to many a German mind as a confession of error. In August, 1952, two war criminals, Hans Kuhn and Wilhelm Kappe, escaped from a work party from Werl prison in the British Zone. A car was waiting for them, and the whole episode had the appearance of have been carefully planned from outside. Kappe was later arrested by the German police at his home town of Aurich, in Friesland. A massive press campaign was launched against the Aurich police, unpleasant slogans were painted on the local Mayor's house, and shortly before the British authorities arrived to escort Kappe back to Werl, he "escaped" again through an open window in the police station. Soon thereafter the Federal Minister of the Interior, Dr. Lehr, responding to political pressure, informed the British that he regretted that the German police could not be expected to continue the search for the escaped men. Kappe, who was serving twenty-one years for the ill treatment of captured British prisoners of war, has not been recaptured to date. Kuhn was later apprehended by British security personnel, but not before his life story had been serialized in a German illustrated magazine.

At Christmas in the same year, a group of seven war criminals escaped from the Dutch prison at Breda and made their way to the German frontier, where they claimed asylum as "political refugees." A local magistrate released them on payment of a fine for "illegally crossing the frontier." One of the escaped criminals was later received quite openly by Dr. Mende in his office in the Bundeshaus.

On another occasion, a concentration camp wardress released from Werl prison was promptly granted restitution money by the local German authorities under the "Late Homecomers" law. As the Jewish *Allgemeine* noted, this seemed a cynical use of public funds when many victims of the concentration camps were still awaiting compensation.

The campaign on behalf of the war criminals reached a ridiculous climax at the end of 1952, when a group of Germans wrote to the *Frankfurter Abendpost* offering to suffer imprisonment in Werl prison over Christmas in surety for an equal number of war criminals, so that these could go home to their relatives over the holidays. Sir Ivone Kirkpatrick promptly entered the lists with a timely and sharp letter to the *Abendpost* in which he described the volunteers as "victims of ignorance and confusion. Almost all the prisoners have been convicted of having been concerned in either the murder of defenseless prisoners of war or the murder and maltreatment of Allied nationals in slave labor camps or concentration camps. Unfortunately, I have to read the details of these cases and am sickened with the evidence."

Almost at the same time, the Germans received even more sobering treatment in the form of a remarkably forthright and courageous speech by their own President Heuss at the dedication of the Belsen Memorial.

> Germans must never be allowed to forget what members of their nation did. We knew what was going on. The deepest depravity of the age, and our own shame, is that such things could take place within the confines of a people from whose past sprang Lessing and Kant, Goethe and Schiller.

The President's speech wound up to a stinging blast against the *tu quoque* mentality: "To cite the injustice and brutality of others in order to establish a precedent for one's own is the technique of the amoral . . ."

Around 1948, the Western Allies in general [4] drew a line on war crimes prosecutions. From then on, cases that were pending — or subsequently came to light — were handed over for trial by the Germans themselves. Although penalties incurred under German law do tend as a whole to be more lenient than under the British or US systems (i.e. rape under American law can be punishable by death, whereas the standard sentence in West Germany is four years), the heads of the legal branches of the three Allied High Commissions each told me on separate occasions that they considered the results extremely unsatisfactory. The French representative commented that most of the sentences had been derisory.

One of the more notorious cases tried by the Germans in recent years was that of Emanuel Schäfer, the Nazi SD chief in Yugoslavia who telegraphed Hitler in 1942, *"Serbien ist Juden-*

---

[4] The French were the exception; by some tortuous process of Gallic justice, wretches are still being tried who have been in gaol awaiting trial for over ten years.

frei!" ("Serbia is free of Jews.") A German court found that he had transmitted an order from Hitler which resulted in the killing of between 5,000 and 6,000 Jewish women and children in Serbia. The judge, however, declared him to be a "basically clean and decent man" who had been too weak to resist recognizable wrong. For his flaw of judgment he was convicted of one charge of accessory to murder, and two of manslaughter, for which he was sentenced to six and a half years' imprisonment. As was the case in the defense of almost all German war crimes, the *actual* murderer was the dead Führer.

A similar case, adjudicated in May 1954, was that of Friedrich Noell and Emil Zimber. Noell was commanding an infantry company near Smolensk in 1941 when he received orders to shoot all the Jews in a neighboring village. Another company of the battalion had refused just such an order, but Noell passed on the instructions to his Sergeant-Major, Zimber, who reported back when the liquidations had been carried out. Noell was sentenced to four years' imprisonment, Zimber to three years. In its summing up the court, resorting to a remarkable piece of Teutonic legalism, found that what was particularly bad about Noell's case was not the actual shooting of the Jews, but the fact that he had attempted to pass the responsibility to his subordinate instead of carrying out the shootings himself.

Rather different sentences, however, were passed in two cases where Germans themselves had been the victims. One was the trial of Paul Schnurpfeil, which ended a few days after the Noell-Zimber case. Schnurpfeil, an ex-Communist, was found guilty of having handed three Nazis over to the Poles in the Neisse area in 1945. The Germans died as a result of subsequent maltreatment. The judge claimed that although Schnurpfeil had not actually murdered his compatriots, he was still responsible for their deaths. He was condemned to life imprisonment, the severest sentence under German law. Then there was the case of Albert Buchholz, who was sentenced in July, 1954, to eight years' hard labor for denouncing three German camp doctors in a Soviet prison camp. Two of the doctors had their terms prolonged as a result. All these trials took place many years after the war, when German public opinion — feeling that the Allied courts had had their innings — was sick of the protracted war crimes proceedings; nevertheless, the four cases make a curious comparison.

When in May, 1954, I tried to obtain some facts and figures on the German-conducted trials, I met almost universally with a blank wall. The Federal Ministry of Justice in Bonn informed me coldly that they "did not recognize" war crimes as such, and that no separate statistics had been kept on offenses that might fall within this category. In desperation I sent a questionnaire to the Ministries of Justice of each of the ten *Länder*. All the answers were more or less disappointing, and three-quarters of the *Länder* informed me that no specific statistics had been kept. This struck me as curious in a country with such a reverence for statistics.

However, after much trouble, I managed to find at least part of the figures I wanted in the Federal Statistics Office, which proved that someone somewhere *had* been making a separate tally of these cases. For the two years 1950–51, the records showed that courts in the Federal Republic and Berlin had tried 2,058 cases of war crimes. Of these only 730 had received sentences; the rest were acquitted. Of the 730, only ninety-six were sentenced to more than two years' imprisonment while 372 received purely nominal sentences of up to one year. In view of the massive political and emotional pressure to which the German judges found themselves subject, it is perhaps remarkable that so much justice had been done.

The German war crimes trials cannot but recall what happened at the Leipzig Trial after World War I. Under a provision of the Versailles Treaty, the Allies in 1919 handed the German Government a list of 896 Germans for extradition as war criminals, including such national heroes as Hindenberg, Ludendorff and Tirpitz. The demand caused such an outcry of indignation in Germany that it was abandoned in exchange for a German offer to try forty-five of the principal offenders. As a result three were sentenced to terms of less than a year, two were condemned to four years' imprisonment, while the remaining forty were simply acquitted. The two who received the relatively heavy sentences of four years were the famous U-boat officers, Lieutenants Dithmar and Boldt, who were found guilty of torpedoing — against orders — the British hospital ship *Llandovery Castle,* and later shelling the lifeboats in an attempt to conceal the crime, with the resulting death of 234. After the trial, German newspapers carried such headlines as "Four Years Imprisonment for U-boat Heroes." Like Kappe and Kuhn, both men "escaped" after a brief imprisonment.

In 1954, a remarkably interesting book was published in Germany, entitled *Bilanz des Zweiten Weltkrieges* ("The Balance Sheet of the Second World War"). It consists of a series of essays on every aspect of the conduct of the war, written by leading experts on each — such as Field Marshal Kesselring on the *Luftwaffe,* Col.-General Guderian on the Russian campaign, and Count Schwerin von Krosigk on the financing of the war. The book is a profound analysis of why Germany lost the war, bearing with it (as I intend to show in the next chapter) the dangerous seeds of a new "Stab-in-the-Back" legend. But in addition it contains some illuminating insights into that fatal flaw of the German character, which, I believe, is greatly responsible not only for the present blurred thinking on war crimes, but also for the fact that crimes *could* ever have taken place on the scale they did, unresisted by the mass of the population. This flaw is the total inability of the average German, in spite of his tremendous regard for the Law (with a capital "L"), to distinguish between what is constitutionally *legal* and what is morally *legitimate.* Hand in hand with this goes the belief, with a sort of Hobbesian resignation, that the powers-that-be, the *Obrigkeiten,* are infallible and that therefore those whom they persecute *must* stand outside the Law, and that the ultimate fates of these "outlaws" must be of no concern to "law-abiding" citizens.

A prime example is provided in *Bilanz des Zweiten Weltkrieges* in the chapter entitled "Food and Agriculture in the War," by ex-State Secretary Hans Joachim Riecke. Riecke gives an elaborate statistical table on the calorie values of the "normal consumer's" ration at various stages of the war, commenting that the *Existenzminimum* was 1,800 calories. Then, almost *en passant,* he notes that "political rations" for concentration camp inmates were, by State decree, 20 per cent less than that of the "normal consumer." On the basis of Herr Riecke's table, this provided an admission that from 1941 onwards the concentration camps were being fed substantially below the *Existenzminimum* of 1,800 calories. Without pausing to consider the monstrous consequences of this piece of State legislation, Herr Riecke goes on to remark that the principle of "political rations" must be "rejected"; but adds — *tu quoque* — that it was frequently proved during the Nuremberg Trials that these "political rations" had been in fact considerably higher than what the German "normal consumer" was receiving at the time of the Trials.

Again, Professor Pfeffer, writing in the same book on racial problems, comments that the Nazi treatment of the Jews was "mistaken" but never discusses whether the morality of the extermination policy might not have been somewhat faulty. As to the German people's reaction to war-time atrocities, he explains: "The population took notice of these things without especial interest, because they were so over-exerted by fighting, work and the air war, that they had hardly any interest in suffering which seemed to them to be no worse than that which they themselves experienced."

The prevalent German attitude to the whole ghastly problem of war crimes, strikes Western observers as one of the most disheartening features of the modern German scene, but it would be unfair to the Germans not to try briefly to look at it from their point of view. For the German confusion, at least a share of the fault must devolve upon the Allies; firstly, for not avoiding the stigma of "conquerors' justice" in the first place by making the war crimes' trials truly "International Tribunals" through the inclusion of representatives of neutral nations. Secondly, one of the greatest — and most harmful — mistakes ever committed by the Allies was the promulgation in the early post-war days of the "collective guilt" decree. Thus all Germans, good and bad, were placed on a level with thugs of Belsen, and it was perhaps not surprising that many, knowing their own personal innocence of war crimes, began in their mental processes to discount the monstrosities with which the Allies were charging the real criminals. Several Germans, including front-line soldiers, have told me that they were so stunned by the Allied revelations that even now they find it almost impossible to believe that Germans could really have committed such barbarities. I personally believe that the war crimes have made a much deeper impression on the average German's innermost conscience than any outsider would imagine from reading the frequent (and much publicized) demands inside Germany to release the war criminals.

A rather embittered young student from Bonn University told me that he and his friends had applauded Salomon's *Fragebogen* (which, with a sale of over a quarter of a million copies, has been the most widely read book in Germany since the war), although they disapproved of his rootless cynicism, because its details of brutality in American internment camps "revealed to us for the first time since the war that we Germans were not the only devils on earth." It is perhaps understandable — at least according to the principles of Freud — that a people with such a massive burden of guilt on their collective conscience should try to repress it, or seek an escape in the invariable *tu quoque*. But the fact that they do not talk about it does not mean that all Germans are now oblivious to what happened in the concentration camps.

No sane or decent German would agree with the ravings of Ramcke that one day the Allied Black Lists would become lists of honor, but there is another aspect which weighs strongly with all Germans. The war criminals, even the worst of the concentration camp thugs, are mostly Germans condemned by foreign powers. When President Heuss — who has himself campaigned incessantly to bring about a healthier attitude to war crimes in Germany — wrote to the 81-year-old von Neurath congratulating him on his release from the "martyrdom" of Spandau in November 1954, it was undoubtedly as one old Württemberger to another — and nothing more. Such is the respect of Germans for age and position that a great many consider it morally wrong that an elder statesman like von Neurath should have been imprisoned at all. We smugly assure ourselves that the concentration camps simply "couldn't happen" in England or America, and therefore it is extremely difficult for us to examine our souls objectively and imagine what our attitude would be in the event of large numbers of Englishmen or Americans being tried, and imprisoned or executed by foreign powers. One can only recall how Frenchmen reacted to Napoleon's exile to Elba; or, indeed more recently, the violent indignation generated in Alsace when a French Court in 1953 executed fourteen Alsatians for taking part in the Oradour massacre — although the Alsatians appear to have behaved with no less brutality than the German SS on that occasion.

In August 1954, shortly before the EDC Treaty was brought before the French Assembly for ratification, the former British Assistant Judge Advocate General of the Forces, Lord Russell of Liverpool, published a book entitled *The Scourge of the Swastika,* which he described as "A short history of Nazi war crimes." It was in fact a lurid anthology of horrors — and a remarkably unscholarly work for so distinguished a lawyer with all the facts at his finger tips. The book received maximum publicity from the Daily Express, which serialized it, and was clearly designed — appearing as it did so long after the events — to stir up emotions against German rearmament. Lord Russell was called upon by the Lord Chancellor either to suppress the book, on the grounds that it would influence contemporary controversial politics, or to resign his post. Lord Russell chose to publish and resign. In Germany, the book had the most mischievous results. Viewed as the work of a man with a personal grudge desiring to combat German rearmament with any weapon, its sole effect was to harden the prevalent attitude to war crimes — the precise opposite to Lord Russell's professed aim in publishing the book.

One cannot continue indefinitely to maintain the thesis of the "collective guilt" of fifty million people, especially since they are now bound, whether we like it or not, to our Western destiny. Such a book only serves to rake up the miseries of the past, whose perpetrators the Allies have had ample opportunity to bring to justice. Mr. Anthony Eden's words in March, 1954, when taxed in the House with the reburials of the German war criminals in Hamelin jail, are perhaps more appropriate: "I am not prepared to pursue hatred beyond the grave."

On August 14th, 1952, after a trial which had lasted seventeen months and in which 137 witnesses were heard, the former head of the Bavarian State Restitution Office, Philipp Auerbach, was found guilty by a Munich court on various charges of dishonesty while in office. He was sentenced to two and a half years' imprisonment. Two days later, Auerbach committed suicide. Under normal circumstances the case would not have raised a ripple of interest outside Germany, but Auerbach's attracted minutest attention throughout the world. The reason was that Auerbach was a Jew, and his case was the first important trial of a Jew to take place in post-war Germany.

Auerbach's story belongs to the legacy of misery and broken lives left behind by Hitler's concentration camps. Shortly after liberation from Buchenwald in 1945, Auerbach found himself appointed as chief of the Restitution Office in Bavaria. Bavaria had become the central gathering-point in Germany of all displaced persons and Auerbach was responsible for the rehabilitation and redisposal of all of them. Vast sums of money passed through his hands, both from US and German sources. In the post-war chaos that prevailed in the Bavarian Government these funds were not administered properly and petty embezzlement was rife throughout Bavarian Government Departments; the temptation for one who had suffered as much as Auerbach must have been enormous.

Right up to the end of his trial Auerbach pleaded his innocence, declaring dramatically in his last statement to the Court: "I have taken not a thread, not a shoe-string." The following night he took an overdose of sleeping tablets, leaving a letter to be published in which he declared, "My blood lies on the heads of my perjurers." At his funeral members of Munich's Jewish community paraded with banners inscribed "Down with the Nazi Dreyfus Trial."

In the course of the trial, Auerbach's counsel, Klibansky (later himself imprisoned by a Frankfurt Court for another offense) made every effort to whip up anti-semitic issues; the French press at once acclaimed the trial to be Germany's modern *Affaire Dreyfus,* and described Auerbach as "one more Nazi victim." In New York a "Committee for Fair Play for Auerbach" was founded during the trial, demanding that the Allied High Commission take responsibility for Auerbach's trial away from the Germans.

It was unfortunate that, despite Jewish protests, the trial started during Passover. It was even more unfortunate that, of the five judges trying Auerbach, three, including the President, were ex-Nazis. There was, however, little doubt in the minds of Allied observers that — in the strictly legal sense — the trial had been fair and the sentence a just one.

The world has now long forgotten the tragic Auerbach case, but the question it posed — What of anti-semitism in Germany now? — still remains one of the biggest questions about post-war Germany, and it will obviously continue as such for a good many years to come. As far as the present Federal Government is concerned, its policy towards the Jews both at home and externally has constituted one of the finer parts of its record since 1949. Under the guidance of Dr. Adenauer, a life-long opponent of anti-semitism, the Federal Government has from its earliest days declared a two-fold aim: to make material reparations for the persecutions of its predecessor, and to persuade the German people to a healthier attitude towards the Jews. The material reparations assumed three forms: first, individual claims for return of property of German Jews seized by the Nazis; secondly, restitution funds in compensation for the deprivation and torment that the surviving Jews had suffered under Hitler, designed to rehabilitate them in the new German society; and thirdly, "collective" reparations made to Israel for the great mass of European Jewry murdered under the Third Reich for whom there were no individual claimants.

The Israel Reparation Scheme, which might well be described as Western Germany's most "unsordid" act, received its first impetus in a now famous speech made to the Bundestag by Dr. Adenauer on September 27th, 1951, on the occasion of a greeting for the Jewish New Year. Dr. Adenauer proposed negotiations with Israel to come to a reparations agreement as "a spiritual purging of the unheard-of suffering perpetrated in the name of the German people" under the Nazis. The reparations would be designed to alleviate the economic straits in which Israel found herself through having to assimilate the floods of Jewish refugees caused by Hitler's persecution. At the same time the Federal Government pledged itself to prosecute "unrelentingly" any resurgent Jew-baiters in Western Germany. The reparation proposal was passed with a unanimous vote of acclaim, and at the end of the session the Bundestag rose and stood in silence for one minute as a gesture of abhorrence for the Nazi pogroms.

The German offer of conciliation, however, met from the beginning with most virulent opposition in Israel, where a very strong minority preferred to forgo the German reparations rather than have contact with the nation they held responsible for the massacre of European Jewry. Eventually, in September, 1952, Dr. Adenauer signed an agreement with the Israelis to give Israel goods to the value of $714,000,000 in instalments over a period of twelve years — a considerable burden to a country with ten million refugees of its own to assimilate. The signing ceremony was especially planned, in compliance with Jewish wishes, so that the Jews did not have to shake hands with the German delegates.

Almost immediately, the Arab nations threatened to boycott all German goods if the Federal Republic carried out the agreement. At that time the Arab countries constituted one of West Germany's major export markets, and implementation of the boycott might have had a crippling effect on the slowly recovering German economy. Nevertheless, the agreements were ratified by the Bundestag with the overwhelming majority of 238 to 34, with 86 abstentions, and to date have been scrupulously fulfilled by the Germans. (Fortunately for the West Germans the Arab threat never materialized.)

Jewish claims for restoration of pre-war property in Germany — totalling approximately $600,000,000 — had been almost completely satisfied by 1954. The second category of claims, the compensation of German Jews for sufferings almost impossible to assess in terms of marks and pfennigs, has not been liquidated quite so satisfactorily and has brought the German authorities constant criticism for the slowness with which the claims have been handled. But on investigation the delays turn out, with few exceptions, to be due to the elephantine workings of the German legislative system, and to the general shortage of all public funds, rather than to any deliberate discrimination against Jewish claimants. Indeed, the German refugees from Eastern Germany have themselves experienced similar interminable delays before receiving restitution funds redistributed under the "equalization-of-the-burden tax."

On its pledge to stamp out any resurgent anti-semitism in Germany and to "re-educate" the German people, the Federal Government has not lagged. Responsible German leaders have bent over backwards in their efforts to be conciliatory towards the Jews. President Heuss himself made a point of attending a special celebration in Germany, in July, 1954, in honor of the 750th anniversary of Maimonides. Frequent interviews on relations with the Jews have been given to leading German newspapers and over the German radio by Dr. Adenauer and in 1954 the Bureau for Home Service (A non-party organization set up by the Federal Government to undo the psychological effects left by the Nazis, and to publicize the workings of democracy in Western Germany) devoted a whole issue of its weekly publication *Das Parlament* to the problems of Israel — in addition to its frequent bulletins to factories and schools on the same theme.

Under present circumstances for a politician to express any sentiment that could be taken as derogatory to the Jews would be political suicide. It is difficult to banish the impression that political expediency rather than moral considerations is often the background of some pious utterances. But by and large the conciliatory aims of the leaders of the present Government should be considered as profoundly sincere.

Typical of the desire for atonement were some of the press comments on the death of Einstein in 1955. The *Frankfurter Allgemeine* wrote; "Einstein was a German, but had to leave Germany because he was a Jew. That we drove out one of the greatest scientists of our times will appear to coming generations not only as a folly but as a disgrace. Thus, the honor of providing one of the earth's great sons with research facilities has had to be ceded to another nation." The *Sueddeutsche Zeitung;* — "Let us not forget that he came from among us — and that we have been shamed by his emigration."

How far the Federal Government's drive against anti-semitism has succeeded among the German population is something most difficult for an outsider to gauge. For obvious reasons, Germans who were adults under the Nazis tend to be reserved in talking about anti-semitism to a foreigner, and their comments are more usually conditioned than spontaneous. One has to rely largely upon the experiences of Jews themselves. A recent survey carried out by the Jewish weekly newspaper *Allgemeine* concluded that between 50 and 60 per cent of the German population had adopted a tolerant and mainly friendly attitude towards the Jews. The remainder divided more or less equally into groups which are neutral or show distinct anti-semitic tendencies. The survey ended on the hopeful note that the younger generation who have grown up in post-Hitler Germany belong, with few exceptions, to the friendly 50 to 60 per cent, and are, as the *Manchester Guardian* put it, "growing up to regard Jews as ordinary human beings and not the agents of some obscure plot against 'Germanism.'" Herr Jakob Altmaier, one of the three Jewish deputies in the present Bundestag, commented in 1954: "I can say that during the last four years no anti-semitic utterance either open or veiled has ever been made known to me." On a visit to Munich in the summer of 1954, I discussed the attitude of the German population with two of the heads of the American Joint Distribution Committee, which had its headquarters there. They considered that, while there was much latent anti-semitism inevitably left ingrained by the twelve years of Nazi indoctrination, they never met with any overt manifestation of calculated anti-semitism. Returning German Jews often encountered difficulty attempting to settle down again in Germany, but they attributed that more to the average German's resistance to "foreigners" than to any articulate anti-semitism.

During the two and a half years that I spent in Germany, most of the reports of anti-semitism which appeared from time to time in British newspapers, generally proved to be gross exaggerations of trivial incidents occurring in the heat of the moment, and I can recall no case where there was any evidence of deliberate or studied anti-semitism.

A case in point was that of Herr Norbert Brandt, a Jewish pharmacist in Berlin, whose sad story was given great prominence by the *Daily Express* in August, 1954, as proof that anti-semitism was rife again in Germany. Brandt had been lessee of a Berlin pharmacy until 1936, when the Nazis forced him to give up his concession in favor of an "Aryan" pharmacist. Robbed of his livelihood, Brandt was subsequently removed to a Nazi concentration camp, where no less than nine members of his immediate family died, but he survived. At the end of the war he was given a job as pharmacist in the Jewish hospital in Berlin. By 1950 he had once again acquired the lease of a pharmacy, this time as lessee of the "Utrecht Apotheke" in the French sector of Berlin. In 1953 the owner of the "Utrecht" practice died and, by German law, with her death Brandt's lease came to an end. Brandt then applied to the Berlin Health Office to buy the practice of the "Utrecht Apotheke," believing that under the Restitution Laws he should be given preference as a victim of Nazism.

Without any reason being given, however, Brandt's application was rejected and the unfortunate man was apparently so dumb-founded that he forgot to renew his lease of the pharmacy, with the result that he lost that as well as the ownership of the practice which he had sought. To add a seeming insult to injury, the man who did acquire the practice of the "Utrecht Apotheke" — a Herr Forster — was an ex-Nazi who in 1937 had become lessee of another pharmacy through the forced removal of a Jewish apothecary in circumstances identical to Brandt's own case.

When he demanded a reason for the decision Brandt was told by the Berlin Health Office that the Restitution Laws only en-titled him to a position comparable to that which he had held before being removed by the Nazis; he could claim State assist-ance to be reinstated as lessee of a pharmacy but not as owner of a practice, and Herr Forster had a greater claim because of ten years' longer pharmaceutical experience.

It was a typical and tragic example of that confusion of "legal-ity" and "legitimacy" in the German official mind which I have referred to before, but even the head of the Jewish Restitution Office in Berlin, Dr. Löwenberg, admitted at the time that the Health Office had acted within the letter of the law and that there was no evidence that deliberate anti-semitism was involved. In its wider significance, though, the Brandt affair did have its bright side; this was the indication that non-Jewish Germans might not so supinely accept anti-semitism as in the days of Hit-ler's Jew-baiting. A flood of highly critical articles appeared in the Berlin press, deploring the Brandt affair and demanding a reversal of the Health Office's decision. A short time after the case was aired in the press, a petition signed by 1,200 private Berliners on behalf of Brandt was presented to the Berlin Senate.

The case was taken up in the Senate and the Minister for Health, Dr. Conrad of the Free Democrats, was repeatedly called upon to reverse his Department's decision on Brandt, or resign. He refused to do either but at the end of October, 1954, was forced to resign by a vote of no confidence in the Berlin House of Depu-ties, on the grounds of "displaying an attitude regarding a com-pensation for Nazi injustice which cannot be approved by anyone in this Parliament." The House promptly decided that the very first pharmacy practice should be allotted to Brandt.

If the present German attitude towards the Jews is healthier than at any time since 1918, much of it is undoubtedly due to the tragic truth that Jew-baiters cannot thrive where there are no Jews. Instead of the 600,000 Jews who lived in Germany before Hitler came to power, the Jewish community now numbers only 25,000. And unless there is a return of Jews to Germany on a much larger scale than in the post-war years, Hitler's "solution of the Jewish problem" in Germany threatens to become a fact within the next generation or two by the dying-out of the remainder of the German Jewish community. Over one-third of the 25,000 are over 65 years old, and the average age of the whole community is close to 55. Of the 251 surviving members of Hanover's Jewish community only 26 are under 30. Mixed marriages have become increasingly common because of the dearth of eligible mates of Jewish faith.

Of all the potential danger-spots of anti-semitism in post-war Germany, Munich has possessed the most explosive ingredients. When Munich was made the Jewish rehabilitation center in Germany shortly after the end of the war, the American Joint Distribution Committee set up its headquarters there to register the survivors of Hitler's concentration camps, and arrange their resettlement, or emigration to foreign countries. Moehlstrasse, the street outside the AJDC Office, became the center where all the pathetic remnants of European Jewry gathered to seek news of other members of their families who might have survived the holocaust. In the long wait for resettlement, small trading shanties sprang up, and with them — in the first chaotic post-war years — a thriving black market. This inevitably led to frequent brushes with the Munich police, and each time the police intervened there were cries of "anti-semitism" abroad.

Only a small number of the Jewish DP's actually settled down in the Moehlstrasse; the remainder lived in the DP camp at Foehrenwald, some twenty miles outside Munich, which itself became a major storm center. Foehrenwald soon earned a reputation in Germany of housing the most desperate and anti-social Jewish DP's. To Foehrenwald were channeled those whose re-habilitation presented almost insurmountable problems, and whom no country wanted as immigrants. At the time of writing Foehrenwald is the last DP camp in Germany and one of the last in Europe. The sad truth was that Foehrenwald contained not only the anti-social elements; it also included a vast number of psychologically shattered human beings who had lost all hope as a result of the years of horrors in the concentration camps, and had no wish to start another life outside Foehrenwald. It included, too, the incurably sick: out of some 1,400 inmates of Foehren-wald when I visited it in June, 1954, 350 were tubercular, 250 had some other chronic illness and another thirty were totally bedridden. There they lived in squalid barracks, divided by roads nostalgically named "Illinois," "Pennsylvania," "Kentucky" — after the promised land which would not accept them.

In May, 1952, an unpleasant and frightening episode took place at Foehrenwald. Because of the spate of black-market of-fenses in the Moehlstrasse, and reports of currency-smuggling into Switzerland, the Munich police decided to carry out a raid on the DP camp. They overplayed their hand and acted with excessive zeal. No less than 300 fully armed police descended on the camp; the sight of the black-clad figures pouring out of their lorries, barking guttural commands, revived a horrible terror in the hearts of the inmates; they barricaded themselves and fought a pitched battle. There were some ugly incidents; members of the police in the heat of battle were alleged to have cried such slogans as "We'll finish off what the gas chamber started," and they chalked up swastikas on the walls.

To avoid any further incident, the AJDC, in 1954, decided to liquidate Foehrenwald as soon as possible and to move their own headquarters to Frankfurt. But the problem of what to do with those inmates of Foehrenwald seems insuperable, although re-sponsibility for their care will eventually be turned over to the Germans. To add to the AJDC's worries, during 1953 and 1954 the numbers in the camp actually *increased* by the return of some

420 former DP's who had immigrated to Israel. It was a sadly ironical twist of fate. These were men and women who, in the first post-war years, had swarmed across the Mediterranean in leaky boats and under appalling conditions, eventually to enter Zion (then under British Mandate) as "illegal immigrants." In the ensuing years many of them had either found the work in Israel too exacting or the strained Israeli economy too limited to assimilate them, and had returned to Europe — to the land of their tormentors — again as "illegal immigrants." As Mr. Kohane of the AJDC told me: "Most of them are in fact not Germans, but have chosen Germany because they feel that the country owes them a living, and will be obliged to look after them." The "illegals" also presented a serious dilemma to the German authorities. Legally they could order their deportation, but — once again — for fear of comment abroad, they dared not take such a step.

So far, the AJDC leaders commented to me, the turbulent events of the past years at Foehrenwald, in the Moehlstrasse, and the Auerbach case, have not generated any new widespread feelings of anti-Jewish hatred in Munich. Curiously enough, the only rabidly anti-semitic literature to be circulated in Munich since the war has been the work of non-Germans: a lunatic rabble comprising the survivors of such East European fascist organizations as the Rumanian "Iron Guard," the Hungarian "Arrow Cross," and a white Russian organization called "RONDD," and others. As yet another instance of the West German authorities' determination to stamp out this sort of thing, the Bavarians in March, 1954, arrested two of the leaders of RONDD for trial on charges of "disturbing the population by utterances and actions of race hatred thereby endangering public order and security" — the first time that this post-war Bavarian law has been invoked.

One cannot leave this chapter on the sad legacy that Hitler's "solution of the Jewish problem" has left in Western Germany without noting what has happened in East Germany. There the Communist authorities have made no offer to Israel, nor to any organ of world Jewry, to make material compensation for the monstrosities of the Nazis, although the Government of the "People's Republic" is just as much a "successor organization" to the National Socialists as the Federal Government of West Germany (and indeed in many ways it has shown itself to be a very much closer successor). There has been no organized scheme of restitution and compensation for Jewish concentration camp survivors in Eastern Germany; and far from returning property seized by the Nazis, most private property which formerly belonged to Jews has been confiscated by the Communist State. Although, during the Brandt case, East German papers were ready to castigate the West Berlin Government as "Fascists," during the wave of Soviet-sponsored anti-semitism which succeeded the Slansky arrests in Czechoslovakia nearly half the small Jewish community of the Soviet Zone found sufficient cause to leave their homes and flee to the "Fascist" Federal Republic.

But of all the manifestations from the past that comprised Dr. Adenauer's legacy, undoubtedly the most disturbing was the reappearance of Dr. Goebbel's right-hand man, Dr. Werner Naumann. Dr. Naumann's activities, which make Otto Remer look like a rank amateur, were important enough to be discussed fully in a subsequent chapter.

4

Herr Blank's Sea

of Troubles

SOON AFTER THE SIGNATURE OF THE TREATIES IN MAY, 1952, public interest — both in Germany and abroad — not unnaturally began to focus on the organ set up to give birth to Western Germany's new armed forces. At the head of it was 45-year-old Herr Theodor Blank, appointed by Dr. Adenauer in November, 1950, with the imposingly vague title of "The Federal Chancellor's Commissioner for Questions relating to the Augmentation of Allied Troops." He was not invested with ministerial rank and nominally took his orders from the State Secretary in Dr. Adenauer's office.

Herr Blank (whose organization was commonly called the *Dienststelle Blank* — "Blank Office") was an ideal choice for the job in a country where the repute of the military was at a low ebb, and in a world where the mere thought of Germans in uniform evoked horrid images of jackboots and sabre-slashed cheeks. He was not a Prussian, nor a professional soldier, nor of the "Junker" caste. He was born of working-class parents in the industrial town of Elz-on-Lahn in the *Land* of Hesse — home of the traditional mercenary soldier of fortune. By trade he was a woodworker (he has a habit of rebuking would-be flatterers who call him Dr. Blank, with the proud rebuff, "Don't Herr Doktor me — I'm a carpenter!"), becoming secretary of the Christian

Factory and Transport Workers' Union at the age of 25, from which he was dismissed as soon as the Nazis came into power. He spent the six war years in the Wehrmacht, in which the highest rank he attained was Senior Lieutenant in an anti-tank unit. Shortly after the end of the war, he became one of the co-founders of the German Federation of Trade Unions (DGB), and was later appointed joint-Chairman of the coal miners' union. In 1949 he was elected Christian Democrat deputy for an industrial constituency in the Ruhr.

As a personality, Herr Blank is a tough and vigorous little man, courageous and extremely frank, with a great deal of working-class common sense. He likes his schnapps, and likes to call a spade a spade. In contrast to Wellington's famous remark — and unlike German civilian defense ministers of the Reichswehr period — he is not frightened of his generals, and appears to be held in considerable reverence by his staff, including the professional soldiers and members of the aristocracy serving under him.

To prepare the groundwork for the new forces, Herr Blank gathered around him a remarkable collection of high-minded idealists, professional ex-officers, lawyers and administrators. In their ranks were, by 1952, no less than twenty-four holders of the *Ritterkreuz* and a very large number of officers and civilians who had played a role in the 20th of July conspiracy against Hitler. As his military right and left hand, Herr Blank had selected ex-Generals Speidel and Heusinger. Lt.-Gen. Hans Speidel was Field Marshal Rommel's Chief of Staff in France in 1944, played an active role in the Western end of the anti-Hitler conspiracy, and only survived his chief by a slim margin of fortune. Lt.-Gen. Adolf Heusinger had been Army Chief of Operations in the Wehrmacht, and was in fact in the midst of reading out a report about the collapsing Eastern front at the Führer HQ when the Stauffenberg bomb exploded. He escaped with slight injuries. In spite of his ignorance of the conspiracy, he was arrested by the Gestapo on account of his attitude towards the regime. Required for employment in the Blank Office was a politically unimpeachable past, and Herr Blank was undoubtedly more rigid in this than other West German Government heads.

The problems facing Herr Blank and his team in 1952 were mountainous. There were not even the remnants of a defeated army on which he could build. The West German economy had been completely demilitarized and it would require monumental efforts to divert a proportion of it to the support of the new army. Herr Blank not only had to build his new army from scratch, but he also had to create an army which would avoid all the obnoxious features of past German armies. Even the choice of a name for the new forces was difficult. At a Foreign Press luncheon in October, 1954, Herr Blank remarked that the former names "Wehrmacht" and "Reichswehr" had had to be discarded because of their associations. (The tentative title chosen to embrace all three services was *Streitkräfte* — "Armed Forces.")

Early in June, 1952, Herr Blank gave some of the details of his plans. On the assumption that the EDC would be ratified by all signatories by late autumn, he said he hoped to make a start with training by January. Applications from volunteers were already coming in, but until enactment of the Treaties the Blank Office could do no more than acknowledge receipt. It was not until eighteen months later that the first questionnaires were sent out to would-be volunteers. To make up the total of 500,000 men required for all three services (of which 150,000 would be regulars), Herr Blank foresaw the necessity of a conscription law to ensure a steady flow of 18-year-olds. He hoped that the full complement would be reached by June, 1953. Large-scale training of the twelve army divisions would begin in January, 1954, and by the end of that year the German EDC contingent would be fully operational.

Alas for Herr Blank's calculations; because of the unexpected obstacles ahead in the path of EDC, even by the fall of 1955 there would still be not one single German soldier in uniform. Herr Blank rapidly expanded his office so that by autumn 1953 it was over 700 strong, with a deputation of more than 200 members serving on the EDC Interim Committee in Paris. Several of his officers told me then that they had long since completed their portion of the planning groundwork — as far as they could before ratification of the Treaties — and were now extremely concerned as to their future in the Blank Office. They apparently resorted to the time-honored War Office device of circulating immaterial minutes among themselves.

A large and important section of the Blank Office was engaged in studying how to overcome the considerable economic problems caused by the raising of a new army. In 1952, unemployment in Western Germany was still short of the two-million mark, and it seemed that this reserve of manpower would easily allow the recruiting of half a million men to take place. However, the additional $980,000,000 laid down as the first German defense contribution would undoubtedly represent a considerable strain on the heavily burdened German taxpayer. (By 1955 unemployment was down to the half-million mark, of which a sizeable proportion were in fact engaged in part-time work.) The needs of Herr Blank threatened to make serious inroads amongst technicians which the high degree of mechanization planned by Herr Blank would make indispensable. On the other hand, the parsimonious Finance Minister, Herr Schäffer, had hoarded away a large financial reserve from the defense costs, for which he had budgeted but which — because of the non-ratification of EDC — had never been drawn upon. Thus Herr Blank was able to express confidence to the Foreign Press in October, 1954, that the Government would not have to raise money for defense by floating a loan, or by increasing taxation. Herr Schäffer's accumulated reserves should be sufficient to foot the whole of the *Streitkräfte's* first bill — with the exception of its heavy arms, which the bountiful United States were expected to provide. When asked in the Bundestag in February, 1955, what he would do if rearmament costs exceeded the planned defense budget, Professor Erhard replied, "We shall let the Americans pay."

One of the major problems facing Herr Blank was the conversion to arms production of an economy which had been systematically stripped of its war potential. Although heavy industry in any country is rarely loath to accept arms contracts, initially Herr Blank met with considerable resistance from the Ruhr barons who had suffered the crippling effects of the Allied dismantlement program for an earlier participation in German armament — and who were now being kept very comfortably employed meeting expanding civilian consumer demands. At his press lunch in October, 1954, Herr Blank estimated that it would take five years before German industry could produce heavy weapons (i.e. tanks, medium and heavy artillery, and aircraft) in noteworthy numbers, but that the conversion to production of light arms and the thousand-and-one pieces of equipment required by a modern army could begin almost at once — without any serious disruption of industry. Herr Blank cited as an example that the West German shoe industry produces currently nine to nine and a half million pairs a month. Thus, even if the *Streitkräfte's* 500,-000 members were provided with four pairs of footwear each, this would still amount to less than a week's production. Similarly optimistic statistics were given for the textile industry's ability to clothe, and the building industry to house, the new forces.

Undoubtedly much of Herr Blank's optimism was intended for internal consumption — for the political opponents of German rearmament, the trade unions and the industrialists. However, if time justifies his optimism, it will tend to indicate that the original NATO estimate as to how great a defense effort the Germans could afford was very low. A hint as to how quickly German industry *could* rearm was given in the autumn of 1953, at the Blank Office's first display of equipment "with civilian applications," to show members of the NATO staff what German industry could produce. It was a most remarkable exhibition of German technical ability, and included every conceivable type of non-lethal military equipment — from Geiger counters to six-wheeled 15-ton ammunition carriers. Each of the vehicle prototypes on display (all realistically painted olive drab and many with cupolas already cut in the cabin roofs for fitting an AA machine gun) was put over a seemingly impossible obstacle

course, consisting of pits up to three feet deep. Every vehicle
cleared the various obstacles — each with an almost identical
clearance to spare — which showed that the individual manufacturers had all been building to close specifications, and suggested to what extent the Blank Office had already succeeded in
co-ordinating industry to its requirements.

Of all the troubles facing Herr Blank, by far the most serious
were certain deep-seated psychological issues. There is an enormously strong and widespread anti-militarist feeling in Western
Germany. The shattering defeat of 1945, the legacy of aerial
destruction, the disappearance into the eternity of Siberia of hundreds of thousands of German POW's, the Socialist defamation-
of-the-military campaign, the squalid pensions paid to war widows, and the Allied re-education program have all left their mark
on German youth — intensified by the fearful proximity of the
Russian colossus and the awareness that Germany will certainly
be a battlefield of the next World War. The *Ohne Mich* (count
me out) attitude is strong among the war generation but even
stronger among the 18- and 20-year-olds who have to face future
call-up. At every ex-servicemen's rally there are noisy counter-
demonstrations, not always organized by Communists or Socialists. In December, 1954, Herr Blank himself was struck in the
face by a beer mug thrown by an anti-militarist youth after a
political meeting at Augsburg. Of the many university students
I have talked to, and teen-aged hikers I have picked up on the
autobahn, I cannot recall a single one showing enthusiasm for
rearmament. At best one would get the luke-warm reply, "I sup-
pose it's necessary, but I hope it won't take me"; but much more
often their attitude was one of downright opposition and neutralism. One student at Bonn University explained to me:

"You can hardly expect us to be enthusiastic when only the
other day the Allies — and our own leaders — were hammering
into our heads *'Nie wieder Soldat, nie wieder Soldat!'*"

A prominent West German educationalist struck another, more
fundamental chord:

"It's not only anti-militarism; the trouble with our truncated, democratic Federal Republic is that it is so colorless; its virtues are as yet essentially negative ones and there is little enough about it that can inspire a young man's imagination; let alone an ideal strong enough for him to fight for."

In May, 1952, EMNID, the West German public-opinion poll, asked a cross-section of 2,000 people if they considered it "right" that their menfolk should become soldiers again. Only 21 per cent answered in the affirmative, 63 per cent said definitely "No," and 16 per cent were undetermined. More recent polls have shown only a slight increase in favor of remilitarization. By autumn 1954, after more than two years of heavily publicized existence, the Blank Office had still received only some 120,000 applications from volunteers, many of whom were refugees or unemployed. Moreover, a surprisingly high percentage had applied for non-combatant service, with a particular predilection for the Army Pay Corps! The Blank Office feared that, after rigorous selection, the applications to date would provide only a fraction of the manpower needed for the "regular army." The induction of officers also promises to be difficult — if for no other reason than the extremely high standards which will be required of them. The establishment calls for 22,000 regular officers, including forty generals. There are some 1,400 surviving generals from World War II living in Western Germany, but, as Herr Blank has remarked, most of them are either over age, or politically "not right."

There is one factor which has been, and is, playing a most significant part in the German attitude towards remilitarization. That is the very healthy revulsion throughout the nation — and especially among the veterans — towards the return of the *Kommissgeist* — or everything that a foreigner understands by "Prussian discipline." Next to *Fragebogen* the book with biggest circulation in post-war Germany has been a novel called *0815,* an extremely entertaining mockery of all the heel-clicking and bullying that has characterized every previous German army. But amid the barrack-room humor there is a very serious moral contained in the revolt against the system by a number of independently-minded young soldiers, who — though under highly fictional circumstances — actually gain the reform they seek by achieving the downfall of their swinish sergeant-major. The film of *0815* had equal success.

Symptomatic of the feelings that memories of past militarism generated in Western Germany was the wave of intense anger caused by the return home in January, 1955, of Hitler's youngest Field Marshal, Ferdinand Schoerner. Schoerner commanded the senseless, fanatical last ditch defense of Prague in May, 1945, when Germany was already in the throes of defeat; a defense he was only able to maintain by resort to most brutal disciplinary measures. After the war, the Russians sentenced Schoerner to 25 years imprisonment for war crimes; then, some nine years later — without any prior warning — Schoerner was sent home. To the average West German, Schoerner was the epitome of the *Kommissgeist* and of all that was beastly and brutal about the *Wehrmacht;* the mere mention of his name made a shudder of horror run down the spines of old soldiers. West German newspapers greeted his homecoming with such epithets as "the butcher of Riga" and "bloody Ferdinand." So violent was public opinion that a Federal Cabinet minister, Herr Strauss, gave voice to the belief that the Soviets had deliberately released him at this critical time with the sole purpose of "frightening our young people from joining up."

In a sincere attempt to make the *Streitkräfte* more palatable to young Germans, Herr Blank (who himself suffered much as a soldier under the spirit of Prussianism) has repeatedly stated that *Kommiss* would have no place in the new forces. The old steel-tipped jackboots would disappear and the rigid, tight-fitting Prussian type tunics be replaced by something very similar to the loose-cut American style. Saluting will be required only for the soldier's immediately superior officers and very senior officers. The obsequious third person plural when addressing a superior will no longer be used. Parade ground drill will be dropped almost entirely. The *Schleifer* — the bullying type of NCO who dominated all previous German barrack-rooms and made the simple soldier's life a senseless horror — will be banned.

The motto of the reform scheme was "Citizens in Uniform." Instead of the soldier being a slave of the barrack-room, available in his free time to beat carpets for his sergeant-major's wife, a strict division is to be drawn between his "service" and "free time." He will be able to wear civilian clothes outside the barracks and take weekend leave — luxuries denied his predecessors. Severe punishments are to be prescribed for officers and NCOs who treat their men in an "unworthy" manner. In each unit a "soldier's friend" (*Vertrauensmann*) is to be elected by the troops — with a right to be heard whenever a member of the unit is up on a serious charge.

The moving spirit behind the reform plans is Count Baudissin, a youngish, outstandingly high-minded idealist, and more an intellectual than a soldier. Count Baudissin outlined his views to me at length just before I left Germany. In any war against an Eastern aggressor, he explained, the Western soldier would be heavily outnumbered, and would have to depend for success on his superior equipment and mechanization. In the highly mechanized German forces, each private soldier would have to be a "technical" combatant, trained to act independently, think for himself, and use a variety of complicated automatic weapons; for this the blind, unthinking obedience instilled into the riflemen of the past would no longer do. Education would have to replace drill. More than ever before the quality of the new German soldier would depend on the quality of his officer, who would be responsible for his "education." A soldier's loyalty to his officer — bred in the old days of fear and discipline — would have to be replaced by respect based on confidence. The future officer's responsibilities would be enormous, and his selection most exacting. He would be required to serve a minimum of nine months as a private, followed by a period as an NCO before entering an OCTU; total pre-commissioning service would be at least two years.

Count Baudissin told me he was much interested in the British

Army scheme to teach a man a civilian trade while doing his service. "It will be our duty," he said, "to make a man a good citizen as well as a good soldier. While he is in the army he must not feel isolated from civilian life. And," he added, "if he encounters totalitarian methods in the army, there is a grave danger that he will take them back into civilian life." I asked if he thought that the new soldier would be as tough as the old; he replied that the men would be made tough by "practical exercises" such as marching and maneuvering in the rain — but not by "chasing" on the parade ground.

The professional soldiers surrounding Herr Blank, however, do not all favor Count Baudissin's "citizens in uniform." In November, 1952, an upheaval occurred in the Blank Office which shook Bonn in no uncertain manner, and which revealed the existence of a clique of officers, conservative in outlook, who feared that Count Baudissin's reform, if carried to its conclusion, would deprive German forces of their former striking power. At the head of this clique was a dashing Potsdam-trained ex-cavalry officer, ex-colonel Bogislav von Bonin. The son of parents who were both of Prussian military stock, his mother a von Buelow, von Bonin was a typical product of the old German General Staff. In 1944, at 36, he had been chief of the Operations Branch of the General Staff of the Army (OKH) where he gained a well-earned reputation as a brilliant staff officer. Although his loyalty to the Nazi regime was never in any doubt, in 1945 von Bonin was consigned to a concentration camp for rejecting the Führer's orders to hang on in Warsaw. In issuing instructions for evacuating the city, von Bonin was obviously motivated by operational rather than by any moral or ideological considerations. In June, 1952, the "Devil's Colonel" (as he was later nicknamed by a German newspaper), was selected by Herr Blank to be head of his Military Planning Branch—not on account of his ideological qualities but because the Blank Office badly needed somebody of his professional ability.

Von Bonin was soon at odds with the reformers whose plans he condemned as "dream dancing." (Of their leader, von Bonin remarked contemptuously: "After ratification, Count Baudissin will be sent off to a girl's boarding school for two years!") An adherent to the old school of *Kommiss,* von Bonin believed that the only way to counter Russian numerical superiority was to combine American "technical know-how" with Prussian *Präzision*. Along these lines, Herr von Bonin drafted an extremely brilliant minute, pushing to one side the Baudissin thesis, and winning a certain amount of support.

Then suddenly, in the belief that the *Kommiss* school was gaining the day, two members of the Blank Office handed in their resignations. One was a Freiherr von dem Bussche, whose background brought the dispute greater publicity than it would otherwise have had. A selfless idealist, he had devoted most of his life to combating tyranny in general and Prussianism in particular. In 1943, even before the von Stauffenberg bomb plot, von dem Bussche, a regular officer then aged 24, volunteered to "model" a new army overcoat before Hitler. In the pockets of the overcoat were to be hand-grenades which von dem Bussche would detonate, thus killing both himself and Hitler. Von dem Bussche's courage and self-dedication at this time were little short of superhuman, and such a willingness to sacrifice all for an ideal still remains today the motivating force of his character. Several times Hitler cancelled the demonstration, and after each cancellation von dem Bussche screwed up his courage for yet another attempt. In November, 1943, at last, all was fixed for the demonstration and von dem Bussche again made ready; then, by a million-to-one chance, the overcoats were destroyed in a sudden Allied air raid. The demonstration was arranged yet again to take place at Christmastime, but in the meantime von dem Bussche had returned to his regiment on the Russian front, which had suddenly flamed up, and his divisional commander refused von Stauffenberg's request to release him. Fate overtook von dem Bussche a few days later in the form of severe wounds which eventually resulted in the amputation of a leg. By a curious twist of fate the long hospitalization which followed — isolating von dem Bussche from his co-plotters — saved his life, while von Stauffenberg paid the penalty after his abortive bomb attempt on July 20th, 1944.

After the war, together with Count Baudissin, ex-Generals Speidel and Heusinger, Herr Oster (the son of another executed leading Julyist) and ex-Colonel Count Kielmannsegg, a close personal friend of von Stauffenberg's — who had all been to a greater or lesser degree associated with the resistance — von dem Bussche had become one of the founder members of the Blank Office and a staunch supporter of Count Baudissin's reform plans. His tall, distinguished figure with its heavy limp became a familiar and impressive sight in Bonn. There was something about his almost quixotic idealism that made him strike one as the very epitome of Hölderlin's "inwardly torn" German. He seemed an almost anachronistic survival of a breed nearly extinct as a result of two wars and the massacre which followed the "20th of July;" the best of the German nobility that opposed Hitler.

In the light of later events, it seems that von dem Bussche's act in resigning from the Blank Office may have been somewhat precipitate. Herr Blank made it at once clear that Herr von Bonin's proposals would not receive his support, and their author was sidetracked shortly thereafter to a position of minor importance. (In April 1955, he was dismissed altogether from the Blank Office for canvassing outside support for another equally brilliant — but rejected — plan calling for a radical revision of NATO strategy; a plan which will be discussed in detail later.) Although the anti-Baudissin faction appears to have been defeated, it still remains at large in the Blank Office and it would be surprising if nothing more were heard of von Bonin's conservative principles — especially when the Baudissin reform plans meet with their first ordeal by fire on the formation of the *Streitkräfte*. In January, 1955, another of Herr Blank's advisers, ex-Colonel von Claer, drew sharp parliamentary criticism when he told representatives of the German Ex-Prisoners of War Association that it was high time that people stopped talking about coddling the German soldier, who would have to be much tougher than his *Wehrmacht* predecessor. About the same time, a further big gun opened up in support of von Bonin in the form of a book by Herr Werner Picht, one of Germany's leading military commentators. In his book *Wiederbewaffung* (Rearmament) Herr Picht condemned the reform theories as "misleading notions" which would prove quite unworkable in practice. In his eyes the soldier "is a being whose life no longer belongs to him. He has renounced the supreme rights of humanity and of citizenship . . ."

Von dem Bussche's resignation had perhaps an even more significant aspect, for it drew outside attention to the existence in the Blank Office of a much deeper split than the Bonin-Baudissin controversy: the psychological rift between the ex-officers who had taken part in the resistance movement which culminated in the "20th of July," and the "loyalists," or those who had not. By 1952 the Office was more or less equally divided into the two camps. Even a flat denial by Herr Blank that the 20th of July had played any role in the recent "dispute" did not allay outside apprehensions. West German political leaders appealed for tolerance from both sides, and far-sighted Germans foresaw dangerous situations arising under the strain of fighting in a future war where "loyalist" Germans found themselves commanded by officers who had "broken their oaths" to the Supreme Commander in a previous war.

The whole question surrounding the moral rightness or wrongness of the 20th of July has become an issue of first importance in Germany. It goes far deeper than the question of pro- or anti-Nazi. Since 1944, Germans have tormented themselves with the same restless argument which went on in the England of Elizabethan times about the legitimacy of the Tudor succession, and which Shakespeare attempted to resolve in his series of history plays. The question is, "When is tyrannicide permissible; when is it legitimate to overthrow the State?" Some of Germany's best brains — leading moralists of both Churches, lawyers, scholars, and intellectuals like President Heuss — have striven to justify the 20th of July, and their findings have been widely publicized through such agencies as the Bureau for Home Service and its non-party publication *Das Parlament*. The findings roughly paral-

lel Shakespeare's — that tyrannicide *is* permissible when a tyrant
has transgressed all laws of humanity, and there remains no other
means for his removal. Schiller's lines from *William Tell* have
been widely quoted in this context, as by Professor Heuss in his
commemoration speech in Berlin in 1954, on the tenth anniversary of the plot:

> There is a limit to the tyrant's power.
> When justice is denied to the oppressed,
> When insupportable becomes his burden — then
> He reaches upwards, confident, to heaven,
> And fetches down his everlasting rights . . .
> And if all other means shall fail his need
> One last resource remains — his own good sword.

Some important precedents absolving the Julyists of treason
were established by the Court in the test case against Otto Remer.
The Court ruled that the men had not committed treason, because
(1) the State they sought to overthrow had already rendered itself "illegal" as a result of its persecution of the Jews, and (2)
in making contact with the enemy they had not acted to the
detriment of the German nation, but, on the contrary, sought its
salvation. Experts were also brought in to prove that the war had
already been lost, militarily, by July 1944, thus attempting to
forestall the creation of a new Stab-in-the-Back legend around
the Julyists. In his Tenth Anniversary Commemoration speech,
Professor Heuss denied that they, the conspirators, had perjured
the sacred oath of allegiance which Hitler had cunningly forced
the entire officer corps to transfer to his person. Referring to ancient Nordic lore, he declared that the Oath was a two-way affair.
It also bound the person to whom it was made — in this case a
professional oath-breaker who had relied on the German officer's
allegiance to this oath to make him carry out a countless series
of illegal orders.

But for ordinary Germans the vindications of the Julyists have
for the most part been hard for them to swallow. It is a popular
misconception that the entire resistance movement was limited to
a small class of high-born officers, belonging to a largely dis-

credited aristocracy. The prominent role played by such civilians as Mayor Goerdeler of Leipzig, Pastor Bonhoeffer, and the strong Socialist element led by Leuschner and Leber, tends to be forgotten. The Julyists' repute is further reduced by the simple fact that they did not succeed — and by German standards success often constitutes a yardstick of rightness. The various arguments in defense of the Julyists have been so complex as to be understandable only to a small proportion of the intelligentsia. It will take more than the words of President Heuss to convince a loyalist ex-officer whose belief in the holiness of the oath of allegiance to his leader is rooted in ancient legend; a factor difficult for non-Germans to appreciate. A great many educated Germans are in tacit agreement with the pretentious claim of that arch-cynic, Ernst von Salomon: "The 20th of July 1944 marked the final collapse not only of the Prussian Army but of the whole educational world of the nineteenth century."

With the growth of the post-war rift between the ex-Allies and the consequent change of Western policy towards Germany, the ground was broken for the growth of a new Stab-in-the-back legend — that Germany need not have lost the war. There are three versions which find support among Germans who traditionally look for reasons outside themselves for their own failings.

One, especially prevalent among the survivors of the General Staff, is the allegation that the war might have been won but for Hitler's constant interference with the military conduct of the war. (This runs parallel to the theme that Hitler was ultimately responsible for all war crimes.) The book *Bilanz des Zweiten Weltkrieges,* to which I referred earlier, damns Hitler as the scapegoat for the lost war in every other line:

The high qualities of troop leaders were paralyzed by bondage to the demands of total leadership of a military layman and fanatic. (Werner Picht, "The German Soldier")

It wasn't their [the Wehrmacht's] fault that the outcome of the mighty struggle brought about the destruction of the Reich. (General Guderian, "Experiences of the Russian Campaign")

It was not the German flyer, it was not the German aircraft constructor who failed; the blame lay in the false planning of the war. (Field Marshal Kesselring, "The German Luftwaffe")

It [the Eastern Front] collapsed because of Hitler's strategical conceptions. (Walter Lüdde-Neurath, "The Finale on German Ground")

It is painful for Germans to realize what astonishing achievements the researchers, engineers and technicians effected during the war, without fulfilling the hope of success, especially since the Allies could not counter these new technical weapons with anything equal. (Lt.-Gen. Schneider, "Technique and Weapon Development in the War")

The Supreme Command was not prepared to credit the carefully assessed results of intelligence work . . . Hitler . . . wanted to see the situation as it suited his own intentions. (Dr. Paul Leverkühn, "The Military Intelligence Service").

This theme is pursued still further by Kesselring in his book (published 1955) *Gedanken zum Zweiten Weltkrieg*, which concludes with the sinister summing up: "The course of the war, seen from a purely military point of view . . . could have had an entirely different ending, if . . ." The rest of the book is devoted to justifying the *if* — *if* we generals hadn't suffered from the interference of a military layman. Almost simultaneously the war memoirs of Field Marshal von Manstein appeared. His *Verlorene Siege* is nearly 700 pages long and is a much solider and more impressive work than Kesselring's. It will be rated by military historians as one of the most interesting German studies to emerge from World War II, especially as Manstein is generally considered to have been the Wehrmacht's greatest strategist. It is therefore a pity that he too should have lent his support to the dangerous idea that the German General Staff might have won the war had it not been for Hitler.

Manstein castigates the General Staff (OKW) for their unimaginative planning of the 1940 assault in the West which, proven wrong, caused them to abdicate once and for all to the

Führer's intuitions. After the collapse of France, the OKW became "no more than a military secretariat" — and from then on
everything that went wrong was Hitler's fault. Manstein blames
Hitler for leaving Britain unconquered in his rear when he attacked Russia; for dissipating his forces at the opening of *Barbarossa* in June '41 by advancing all along the 2,000 mile Russian front instead of concentrating on a drive on Moscow, as
recommended by the generals; he blames him for the Wehrmacht's
failure to relieve the encirclement of Paulus's 6th Army at Stalingrad; for the failure of the last German offensive of the Russian
campaign at Kursk; for forbidding any limited withdrawals which
might have allowed the Wehrmacht, once it was pushed onto the
defensive in Russia, to gain a local tactical advantage; and he
blames him for always providing vital reinforcements too late. To
the last, Manstein believed that, but for Hitler's interference,
Germany could have been saved by a "stalemate solution" in the
East forced upon an exhausted Red Army. If Hitler wasn't wholly
to blame, it was the failure of her Rumanian and Italian allies
that let Germany down in Russia — but, and Manstein repeats
this *ad nauseam,* it was never the fault of the German professional soldier.

For all this powerful argument, though, even a "military layman" cannot help reading between the lines and wondering if it
really was all Hitler's fault. Whose fault but Manstein's was it
that at the time of the Stalingrad relief attempts the Rumanians
happened to be located on a crucial wing of his front which was
inviting to Russian attack? And whose fault was it that the professional soldiers accepted so meekly the amateur's strategical
follies year after year? Apart from their spinelessness, the German generals seemed to suffer from a defect also common to
allied military men writing their memoirs — of being unable to
see beyond their own particular sphere of operations. Manstein is
quite oblivious to the disaster facing Germany in the West, and
Kesselring is incapable of realizing how completely outmanned
was the Wehrmacht in Russia after 1942. Discredited as is the
German General Staff in the eyes of today's young German, it is

alarming that future German generations may have to rely on the writings of blinkered generals for a version of the course of World War II.

A second variation of the Stab-in-the-back legend, one which may gain strength once the new German army is well-established and national confidence restored, runs like this: "Hitler and the Nazis may have been wrong and lost the war, but at least they were right in two things: in wanting to push the Russians back into Asia, and in believing that they and their Western Allies would soon squabble. The Russians only beat us because they had the whole of the rest of the world on their side; but if we could have held on a little longer, the British and Americans might have joined us against the Russians. We still might not have won the war, but at least partition could have been avoided." The protagonists of this notion got great satisfaction in November, 1954, out of the episode of the Churchill telegram: the telegram which Sir Winston claimed he had sent to F. M. Montgomery in 1945, ordering him to keep available the Wehrmacht's surrendered arms in case they had to be reissued to repel a continued sweep of the Red Army. The significance of the affair was certainly not wasted on Kesselring, who comments in *Gedanken zum Zweiten Weltkrieg,* "even if this step was not taken, these revelations provide a sense of vindication, and full recognition at last of the Doenitz policy which was to continue the war *only* against the Russians."

The third variation, and potentially the ugliest, leads on from the premise of the second: that the reason the Wehrmacht did not fight on until the Grand Alliance disintegrated was because it was *betrayed* from within by a disloyal and self-seeking caucus of professional officers who had for years been annulling the orders of the Supreme Command, and even conspiring with the country's enemies abroad. This specifically refers to those involved in the 20th of July affair.

If a fundamental split exists in the German conscience on this issue it will obviously damage the morale of Herr Blank's forces. In a moment of acute battle crisis are soldiers and junior officers going to wonder about the ultimate loyalty of some of their superiors? And there is yet a second psychological conflict which faces the future German soldier. This is the problem of obedience in relation to war crimes. The Blank Office planners themselves admit this has deeply affected all German military thinking.

At the top of the box-office attractions for 1954 was the play of *The Caine Mutiny* by Herman Wouk. In its review *Der Spiegel* commented: "Since Zuckmeyer's *The Devil's General* there has hardly been any play that has struck so much at the heart of the principal unresolved enigma of countless Germans; when can (or must) an order be refused? At what point — in the line which extended leads to the justification of treason — does the right (or duty) to mutiny lie?" The *Frankfurter Rundschau* greeted the acquittal of the Caine mutineers as a vindication of the Julyists: "In our eyes, there before the court stand the rebels of 20th July, who also wanted nothing more than to tear a lunatic away from the helm . . ."

Keitel's words at Nuremberg, "Every soldier in the world should reflect seriously on this question of obedience, for it concerns him closely," have come home to roost in Germany. Although the favorite plea at the War Crimes Trials of obedience to superior orders was seldom accepted as genuine by the Allied Courts, undoubtedly in a great many cases of simple soldiers the plea was made in good faith, as a consequence of the doctrine of blind obedience instilled into every German soldier under the old Prussian regime.

One of the first tasks of the Blank Office lawyers was to draft a new Military Penal Code. The earliest draft prescribed that all superior orders were to be obeyed *except* where the "conscience of the subordinate realizes that an order has no other purpose than the committing of a crime." If, in spite of his conscience having registered protest, he still carried out the order, he would render himself as punishable as the officer who gave the illegal order. In the heat of battle, where so often operational orders cannot be carried out without causing suffering to civilians, the simple German soldier, constantly searching his conscience for justification of each and every order, might well find it intolerably burdened. Realizing the psychological dangers latent in this new formula, the Blank lawyers had radically altered the draft by 1955. In the *Soldatengesetz* that went before the Bundesrat for its approval in June the relevant clause read: "An order may not be followed when it would lead to the commission of a crime or misdemeanor. If, nevertheless, the subordinate follows the order, *his guilt is excluded if he does not know,* and if it is also not apparent to him, that a crime or misdemeanor is thereby committed." (The italics are mine.) The implementing regulations to the *Soldatengesetz* carried this idea still further. It dismissed as a *"transitory phenomenon"* Allied Law 10, which laid down the theory of responsibility for war crimes that had formed the basis for all the Allied trials, and added that it "need not influence the legal settlement of the question to be made now in Germany." This ran directly counter to British law which prescribes that, where a crime is committed through obedience to an order, the recipient is responsible whether the order is manifestly illegal or not. By declaring Allied Law 10 a "transitory phenomenon," the way was opened to justification of the German plea of "superior orders," never accepted as valid in Allied Courts.

In trying to find a solution that combined legitimacy with the necessities of war, the Blank Office was by no means exaggerating the psychological impact that Nuremberg had made upon the simple German. A vivid warning of what *might* happen in a future war was provided by an incident that occurred prior to the Federal Elections in September, 1953. The East German authorities were trying to infiltrate hordes of Communist "Free German Youths" over the interzonal frontier, with the aim of sabotaging polling in the Ruhr. The 10,000-strong West German frontier force was deployed to prevent them getting over, and in many cases detachments were given orders to fire on any infiltrators who refused to halt. At least one detachment, however, refused to comply until they had received the orders *in writing* from their officer.

From the German officer's point of view, F. M. von Manstein, shortly after his war crimes' trial, made a remark to my predecessor on "The Daily Telegraph" in Bonn, Anthony Mann, that is perhaps worth repeating: "In any future war a general will be well advised to give and transmit no operational order without first taking counsel's opinion. Even then he will not be protected if an enemy court disagrees with his lawyer." If soldiers demand orders in writing and their officers appeal for legal advice in the heat of action, it is hard to imagine West German troops putting up a very good showing in face of a possible future war with the Russians.

At a foreign press luncheon in August 1952 in Bonn, Field-Marshal Sir John Harding (then C-in-C British Army of the Rhine) praised the creation of the German defense contingent, as successor to the only force which fought the Russians on their own ground in World War II. The Field-Marshal's courageous words (which provoked a storm on the Left in England) came as a welcome tonic to Herr Blank and his planners, who were beginning to feel that they were bringing a child into the world that nobody wanted. But one asks whether it is militarily realistic to gauge the future capacity of the *Streitkräfte* by the performance of past German armies. The fact that the German authorities want their *Streitkräfte* to be democratic is admirable and most encouraging — but will it work?

The contrast between old and new will be far more revolutionary than anything that has ever been undertaken in so short a space of years by any Western army. If ever there was an army motivated by the principle "theirs not to reason why," it was the old German army, and few will dispute that much of the secret of the striking power of the Wehrmacht lay in its ability to carry out orders with ruthless speed, totally without regard for civilian populations. In the event of a Russian aggression, Allied troops will have to be of the highest quality to stand up to the tremendous onslaught. The initial phases will severely test the morale and stamina of the German units which will be fighting on German ground — either East or West. Whether, shorn of its iron discipline of old, and shaken by doubts born of the 20th of July and Nuremberg, the new German army will be able to stand the test, time alone will tell. One can only hope that there will be time to steer a course between a revived *Furor Teutonicus* and complete inefficacy, and that European defense plans are not based on a myth.

When 1955 arrived bringing with it at last the prospect of realizing West German rearmament plans, Herr Blank's sea of troubles did not recede.

An important development inside the Blank Office was the outbreak of what might be called the "second Bonin offensive," launched by the presentation by von Bonin of a new strategical plan for the defense of Germany. It reflected the psychological weaknesses that lay at the base of German rearmament, and was conditioned by political expediency. In the course of his work in the Blank Office, von Bonin was deeply shocked by the implications of the official NATO defense plan for Germany. This envisaged the inevitability of the Allied forces in Germany having to make a mobile defensive withdrawal before the overwhelming impetus of a Soviet attack from East Germany. In von Bonin's eyes, NATO planning was based on the establishment of the first static line of defense behind the Rhine. There the NATO armies would regroup for a counter offensive against the Russians. Meanwhile, the area between the Elbe and Rhine would be turned into a vast "killing ground" in which the Russian spearheads would be saturated with every form of atomic missile, thus gaining the salvation of Western Europe at the expense of the total devastation of West Germany. "Am I to call upon my son to defend his fatherland on the Rhine?" asked von Bonin. As an East German by origin he found the alternative to the official NATO strategy, the so-called "Schuyler Plan" just as disturbing. The object of this plan was to halt any Russian aggression in its very initial stages, east of the Elbe, by stationing US atomic cannon along the interzonal frontier, reinforced by longer range atomic weapons farther back. Thus the communications and concentration areas of the Russian offensive would be shattered while these areas were still in Eastern Germany. If either plan had to be carried out, it would in all probability result in the total destruction of one or the other half of Germany.

The von Bonin reaction was shared by a great many Germans, but he alone thought he saw a way out. In July, 1954, he submitted a clearly thought out plan to Herr Blank, which reoriented NATO's defense plan and completely revised Germany's military participation with the West, then still awaiting French approval. After a relay of some months, von Bonin's proposals were turned down. The Devil's Colonel thereupon took the foolhardy step — somewhat recalling his earlier rebellion against Hitler — of seeking support for his plan outside the Blank Office. In April of the following year he was dismissed on grounds of "disloyalty." Nevertheless the Bonin plan provoked considerable interest among West Germans, and its author claimed to have gained a substantial following, including seven ex-generals, among them F. M. von Manstein.

An influential West German won over by von Bonin was Herr Adelbert Weinstein, co-editor of the *Frankfurter Allgemeine Zeitung,* and, at 39, a foremost military commentator. He became chief spokesman for the Bonin plan. Sometime after von Bonin's "disgrace," I sat at lunch with Herr Weinstein as he enthusiastically described the Bonin plan to me, illustrating it by means of fork marks on the table cloth. Instead of the 12 German divisions being spread over the whole Federal Republic in a defense in depth, the Bonin plan held that the great bulk should be concentrated in a 30-mile-deep "defense strip" all along the 500-mile interzonal frontier. Far from presenting a "Maginot line" form of static defense, the units would be highly mobile, and equipped almost exclusively with anti-tank weapons. Behind them would be a tactical reserve of streamlined *Panzer* divisions; still further back would be an emergency reserve, covering the whole Federal Republic, of German "militia" on the lines of Britain's wartime "Home Guard." Behind the Rhine, would be the mass of the Allied NATO armies. The West German forces themselves, excluding the "militia," would total only 150,000 men, instead of the proposed 500,000 — but it was hoped that this force would suffice to contain a Russian attack within the 30-mile "defense strip," thus saving the remainder of Germany from desolation.

As Herr Weinstein outlined the plan to me, he made little attempt to conceal his — and Colonel von Bonin's — reservations about Allied ability to stem a Russian attack. "On the very first night," he commented, "most of Allied forces, deployed as they are now, will be surprised in their beds by Russian tanks." On past performance he did not believe the Allies under present NATO strategy would be able to launch an effective counter attack until the Russians had already breached the Rhine line. The 30 available NATO divisions he thought would be "lost" in the vast space between the Pyrenees and the Elbe. But, on the basis of this argument, it was difficult to see how only 150,000 German regulars could hold the "defense strip" against the masses that the Russians could throw in. (General Heusinger, I learned afterwards, had commented that to carry out the Bonin plan effectively, it would be necessary to deploy at least 70 divisions along the interzonal frontier.) Moreover, would the defense-in-depth offered by a 30-mile strip be adequate? I pointed out to Herr Weinstein that in the first day of *Barbarossa* (the Nazi invasion of Russia in 1941), German spearheads had penetrated up to 100 miles — against defenders who were much better prepared and numerically superior to the von Bonin force. And what would happen to the German defense if the Russians threw in a large scale paratroop attack behind the "defense strip?" With the Allied forces far off behind the Rhine, and only a few militiamen available to deal with the airborne threat, the German line of defense would be completely turned.

I was not enough of an amateur strategist to come to any decisive conclusions on the military value of the Bonin plan, but I did not see how you could devise an effective defense plan when it had to be linked with such considerations as (a) not allowing Germany to become a battlefield, and (b) the politics of German reunification. The figure of 150,000 men for the West German standing army, von Bonin had selected as representing parity with the East German Barracked People's Police; anything in excess of parity he felt could only cause a "hardening" of the split between East and West. The object of having the Allies withdraw their forces behind the Rhine would be to encourage the Russians to make a similar withdrawal behind the Oder—creating a demilitarized Germany (with the exception of two opposing German defense strips on either side of the Interzonal frontier) which could gradually be reunited as tension died away. Thus vital features of the Bonin plan were based on political rather than military premises.

The political thinking at the back of the Bonin plan was distinctly neutralist, and the career of the Devil's Colonel after leaving the Blank Office illustrated this. At the Geneva "Summit" Conference in July 1955 he surprised journalists by appearing to deliver his proposals to Marshal Bulganin, accompanied by a curious selection of neutralists which included Pastor Niemoeller and Herr Artur Stegner, the ex-Free Democrat deputy who was closely associated with Naumann (see Ch. 3). On returning to Germany, von Bonin took up work in Duesseldorf with a weekly newspaper of pronounced neutralist views, the *"Rheinisch West-faelische Nachrichten."* [1] The editor of the paper, Herr Hermann Schaefer, was an ultra-nationalist who was also closely connected with the Naumann group. The Federal Government claims to have concrete evidence that the paper is financed from East Germany, and there is no reason to doubt this, since the paper manages to survive while selling only some 5 per cent of the 35,000 copies it prints weekly. Affiliated to the *Nachrichten* is a dubious body called the *Hans Seeckt Association* — a name that leaves little doubt about the association's leanings.[2] Von Bonin himself made no secret of the fact that it was his intention to go over to

---

[1] Weinstein split politically with von Bonin on his openly declaring for the neutralist camp.

[2] It was Col.-General von Seeckt who achieved Germany's post-Versailles secret rearmament through a policy of collaboration with the Soviets.

East Germany at the earliest opportunity to make contact with Field Marshal Paulus and others. Altogether the nest in which von Bonin landed represented a triangular relationship — of neutralism-nationalism-communism — which has become almost classical in postwar Germany.

In a sober assessment of von Bonin, *Die Zeit* of August 11th, 1955, commented: "It is possible that one could not trust one's life in time of war to any better military commander than Colonel von Bonin; but to give one vote in time of peace to the politician von Bonin would be dangerous lunacy." However discredited von Bonin may be, the importance of what he represents should not be underrated. German fears, of which the Bonin plan was so symptomatic, received a further goad when an Allied air exercise on a major scale, called *Carte Blanche,* took place over the Federal Republic in the summer of 1955 — unhappily coinciding with the initial debates on the new Armed Forces Bill in Bonn. In *Carte Blanche* one side played the role of a defender retaliating with massive atomic air strikes against the surprise attack of an aggressor. The results — which received much publicity in the German press — indicated that in the first five days of battle some 260 atom bombs had fallen on German territory, in which circumstances it was difficult not to conclude that the country would have virtually ceased to exist. (An aspect of the exercise which particularly upset *Der Spiegel* was a report claiming that in one instance US units had deployed with guns aimed — not at the enemy — but at the civil population, forecasting measures that would be adopted to control mass panic in the event of atomic war.)

When the Federal Parliament convened shortly after the restoration of sovereignty in May, 1955, to legislate for the creation of the first military units, West German reluctance to rearm brought Dr. Adenauer one of his most serious parliamentary setbacks. In view of the imminence of negotiations with the Russians, Dr. Adenauer was anxious to strengthen his hand by taking a concrete step towards producing the first contingents of the armed forces before the parliamentary recess. In June he presented a draft Bill to the Bundestag providing for the enrollment of the first volunteers. An unspecified number, they were to be for the most part officers, charged with receiving American arms and organizing the machinery for later large-scale enlistment. The Bill was designed purely as a temporary measure, to expire on March 31, 1956, pending preparation of the full *Soldatengesetz*. The Chancellor's Bill, however, consisting of only three brief paragraphs, drew a storm of protest from all sides of the Bundestag. Even members of Dr. Adenauer's own Christian Democrat Party joined the Socialists in criticizing it. The Bill, they feared, was so indefinite that it could be misused by the army as an "Enabling Act" under which the military could set themselves up once again as a "State within a State."

As a result of this opposition, the Bill was sent back to the Bundestag's Security Committee for redrafting, and Dr. Adenauer was forced to prolong the parliamentary session. When the new version was completed on July 9, it restricted the number of volunteers to 6,000, specified their duties, fixed their pay, and applied a number of important limitations giving Parliament increased control over the military. Before the Bundestag would pass the second reading of the Volunteer Bill on July 15, however, both sides of the house insisted on passing through all its stages a bill to establish a standing committee on officer's appointments, a committee which Herr Mellies, the Deputy leader of the Social Democrats, described as designed to "protect the armed forces against the people who have learned nothing from history." The following day the amended bill was passed by the Bundestag, and handed on to the Bundesrat. On the 22nd, a week after the parliament had been due to start its recess, the Bundesrat passed both the bills.

In refusing to be stampeded into a hasty decision over the Volunteer Bill, and in asserting its determination not to let the question *"Quis custodiet ipsos custodes?"* go unanswered again in German parliamentary history, the Bundestag gained just commendation throughout the Western world. But the discussions still left some very explosive subjects unsettled, and in some ways they had not eased Herr Blank's task of finding recruits for the new army. Still to be solved was the question of the Supreme Commander of the Armed Forces — whether he was to be the President or the Chancellor. Recalling all too vividly the catastrophe that had resulted from allowing Hitler to usurp the Supreme Command, even the parties of the Adenauer coalition were bitterly split over this issue. A subsidiary, but equally important issue was that of the oath: how should it be phrased, to whom or to what should it be? Again there were memories to be exorcised. In the latter stages of the war Hitler had abused the oath by making his officers swear personal allegiance to himself. When a draft of the new oath was made public several German newspapers asked what was to be understood by the word "Fatherland." Did it refer to all Germany of the 1937 frontiers? If so, how could a West German soldier swear allegiance to a part of Germany that was under Russian domination? Or did it mean simply the Federal Republic? By contrast, no such soul-searching has troubled the East Germans; the Barracked People's Police swears allegiance, not to the Fatherland, but to the "Party" — thus describing a full circle back to Nazi days.

Encouraging as were the signs that the German parliament was determined to keep the upper hand over the military, there were also signs that in an excess of enthusiasm the parliamentarians threatened to upset Herr Blank's plans to give the army a professional prestige it had not had before. As its last measure before the summer recess, the Bundesrat reduced by one fifth the salaries Herr Blank had proposed for his senior officers, fixing the salary of the highest general at a level below that of a State Secretary in a civil ministry — and so on down the ranks. The *Streitkräfte* would thus offer wages lower than could be obtained in industry or in other government services. In a country verging on full employment this would not help attract good men to an already unattractive profession. Giving voice to fears that such an excess of parliamentary zeal might defeat its own ends, Count Baudissin's deputy, Herr Heinz Karst, wrote in a Blank Office memorandum in August, 1955; "The 'citizen-in-uniform' has been replaced by the soldier in the ghetto, who, so that he can commit no mischief, will be bridled by severest controls, minimum expenditure, and poor pay. . . . Continuance of this development will endanger the whole thinking of this office. . . ."

Since the realization of rearmament, there has certainly been no noticeable rush of West Germans to get back into uniform. Nor did the publication of pictures of the new uniforms create any new martial ardor; comment in the German press ranged from "like South American generals" to "bellhops" and "airline stewards." On my last trip to Germany in summer 1955, I picked up on the Autobahn an unemployed old soldier who was heading for Bonn to look for work. I asked him why he did not volunteer for the army again? Looking at me with a mixture of incredulity and contempt on his face, he growled, "That bunch of drawing-room soldiers — I'd rather starve!"

In mid-1955 the Blank Office postponed the activation of the twelve German divisions to sometime in 1959. The original target had been the end of 1954. Some observers, recalling the many delays already experienced, doubted the 1959 date was reasonable. Moreover, they pointed to the H-bomb and asked if the very idea of German divisions for NATO was not in 1955 rather out-of-date. How would it appear in 1959?

5

Krupp, the Special Case

PERHAPS NO SINGLE EVENT SINCE THE END OF THE WAR
brought home to the average Briton more vividly the significance
of the full circle described by Allied policy towards Germany
than the news which leaked out in August, 1952 of the intended
"settlement" with Krupp. There was certainly none which provoked greater indignation.

In 1945, Gustav Krupp von Bohlen und Halbach, who had
helped finance Hitler's way to power and had played an important role in the secret rearming of Germany, was on the Allied
list for trial as a major war criminal. He was considered too ill
to stand trial; instead an American court (Great Britain washed
her hands of the dubious business of trying Alfried Krupp in lieu
of his father) tried his heir, Alfried Krupp, and ten of the top
Krupp executives. Krupp himself received twelve years for employment of slave labor and spoliation of occupied territories,
although he was acquitted on the more serious charges of crimes
against peace and of planning an aggressive war. At the same
time, Krupp was ordered to suffer the confiscation of all his properties — a penalty unique in the war crimes proceedings. In January, 1951, Mr. McCloy, the US High Commissioner, released
Krupp and his co-defendants. At the same time he rescinded the
confiscation order, on the grounds that such an action was "generally repugnant to American concepts of justice."

The uproar caused abroad by the McCloy decision was remarkably violent — especially in the British Press. But it was nothing compared to the furor which arose in August, 1952, when the Allied High Commission were forced to reveal with much embarrassment (as a result of some astute deductions by a Reuter's correspondent) the terms of their plan to "liquidate" the Krupp empire. Herr Krupp was to be forced to give up all his coal and steel holdings — *but* he was to receive their full value. Once again he would be the richest man in Europe.

The reaction was not entirely surprising. The name Krupp had become a synonym for everything foreigners resent about Germany and the Germans; it fitted conveniently into a newspaper headline, and was one of the three German names — with Hitler and the Kaiser — universally known. However you pronounced it, the word "Krupp" sounded like the explosion of a shell. To the French it was Krupp guns that had ravaged France three times in a century. At Sedan Krupp breech-loaders made of cast steel had outmatched the bronze muzzle-loaders of the French garrison. It was heavy Krupp mortars that bombarded Paris in 1870, and rudimentary AA cannon designed by Krupp that fired on the escaping balloons flown by Gambetta and his confrères. In 1918, it was a monster Krupp rifle, "Long Max," which shelled Paris with 452 shots from a range of seventy-five miles.[1] To the Americans, it had been Tiger tanks built by Krupp that led the slaughter at Kasserine Pass and spearheaded the Ardennes offensive. Particularly memorable to the Russians were the giant 32-inch mortars which decided the siege of Sevastopol. Originally designed to pierce the Maginot Line forts, these were the cannon king's most notable contributions to World War II. Each weighed 1,456 tons and had to be transported on a specially constructed twin-track railway.

To the British Krupp was noted, among other things, for having built the first U-boats used in 1914. In World War II most of

---

[1] Contrary to popular belief, "Big Bertha," named after the Krupp heiress, never shelled Paris. It was a 420-mm. mortar employed to shatter the Belgian fortifications at Liége.

the heavy guns which shelled the south coast were of Krupp manufacture, and one monster, called K.12, which fortunately had a
short career, was claimed by the Germans to be able to reach the
suburbs of London. Generally speaking, the average Englishman
saw Krupps of Essen as one of the prime movers in the German
militarism. Now Allied policy was "compensating" him for his
troubles. It shocked many of those who had previously accepted
German rearmament, actively or passively.

If the name of Krupp denoted abroad everything that was bad
about Germany, it conveyed the opposite at home. In peacetime,
Krupp was regarded as the emblem of German industrial prowess,
and in wartime, Prussian gunners of 1870 are said to have wept
with joy on receiving a new Krupp cannon. Since the war Krupps
had regained their place in German sympathy through the country's universal indignation at the application of *Sippenhaft* (arrest of next of kin) in the Krupp trial. The confiscation of Krupp's
property seemed to them a blatant injustice, but that the Allies
should still hold the shattered Krupp empire in such awe as to
make a special case of Krupp was viewed as a sort of inverted
honor.

The Krupps had always been treated as a special case. In 1943
Hitler enacted a special law, the *Lex Krupp,* which made the
Krupp empire indivisible, and thus limited the depredations of
death duties. In 1906 the Kaiser attended the wedding of Bertha
Krupp, then head of the family, and gave her husband, Gustav
von Bohlen und Halbach, special permission to adopt the name
of Krupp, so as to preserve the dynasty. Even in Bismarck's day
the head of the Krupp family had always had direct access to the
Kaiser. It was Krupp workers who were shot by the French in
1923, and Gustav Krupp whom the French sentenced to fifteen
years' imprisonment as being responsible for the "sabotage" which
followed their occupation of the Ruhr. It was thus hardly surprising to the Germans that the Allies should single out Alfried
Krupp for specially harsh treatment — first confiscating his properties, then forcing him to sell all his coal and steel holdings.

As an illustration of the assorted passions which the magic

name of Krupp awoke, it is perhaps worth noting at this juncture that Friedrich Flick was also forced to relinquish his coal and steel holdings. But this news raised hardly any comment — although he was to receive about $31 million from his sales.

It would, however, be unfair to imply that Krupps did not merit their special position in Germany. The fascinating story of the Krupp empire is one of technical excellence and success gained (at least until Hitler) as fairly as by any other big arms manufacturer. When the first Alfred Krupp, aged 14, took the firm over from his father in 1826, he had seven employees. By his death in 1887, they had grown to 12,674 and the population of Essen had risen with it from 5,000 to 70,000. Curiously enough, the family fortunes were founded originally on neither cannon nor the requirements of the Prussian war machine, but on the invention of a seamless railway wheel. When Alfred Krupp first displayed his cast-steel cannon at the Crystal Palace in 1851, women thought it "quite bewitching" but no orders came in. In fact, when the first orders did arrive six years later, they came from Egypt! It took another two years before the conservative Prussians bought Krupp's steel guns, and even longer before Krupp could get any assistance from the State. As Krupp once was forced to explain to the Kaiser, it was only through orders from abroad that he could finance the building-up of plant for an emergency.

By the outbreak of World War I, Krupps had turned their hand to the production of the toughest armor yet seen, with which the new German fleet was to be equipped. At the peak of the war, Krupp employees totalled 180,000, with 105,000 employed at the Gussstahlfabrik in Essen alone. During World War II, Krupp's total personnel approached the 250,000 mark.

In Germany, Krupps had always had a reputation for being the best of employers. They constantly paid higher wages than their competitors, and in periods of depression their vast resources had enabled them to keep on workers while other firms were firing them. Although Alfred Krupp had a conservative loathing of the trade union movement, he bound the loyalty of his workers with social innovations which were extremely advanced for their day.

Employees were provided with works-owned houses at low rentals, excellent retail-wholesale shops, medical services and generous pensions. That Krupps are still good employers today was indicated by the celebration in December 1952 for three brothers who had worked for Krupp for a total of 123 years. The Krupp Workers' Council were also quick to protest, most strongly, against the Allied plans to deconcentrate the Krupp empire, which they considered would jeopardize their own security.

All in all, to a great many Germans, past and present, the fortunes of "Firma Krupp" had always been associated with the national destiny. The breaking-up of Krupps on the one hand, and the granting to Alfried Krupp of funds for vast new economic power on the other, seemed all part and parcel of the contradictory Allied policy to partition and emasculate Germany, while simultaneously proclaiming intentions to rebuild and rearm her as a bastion of the West. In Germany, only the Social Democrats protested against the immorality of Krupp regaining power. They commented, "we have now arrived once more at the point where the German catastrophe began."

As seen by the deconcentration wizards of the Allied High Commission, the Krupp plan fitted neatly and logically within the framework of Allied Law 27. This envisaged the "elimination of excessive concentrations of economic power" in Germany. Under Hitler, eleven steel combines, designed to wage ruthless economic warfare, controlled 90 per cent of all German steel and 55 per cent of the Ruhr coal. As well as constituting a major political force inside Germany, they also wielded enormous power over European countries dependent on Ruhr coal. One of these combines, the vast Vereinigte Stahlwerke, in 1938 produced as much pig iron as the whole British steel industry, and nearly 50 per cent of all German raw steel. Under Allied Law 27 (by and large a brain-child of American trust-busters) the eleven combines were to be split up into twenty-six separate steel units, and twenty independent coal companies.

The Law also stated the Allies' determination to prevent the return to ownership and control of the basic industries of those who had "furthered the aggressive designs of the National Socialist Party," in which category came Krupp. But the Law had not kept pace with the times; devised in 1948 and promulgated in 1950 a month before the invasion of South Korea, by 1952, when at last it came to be enforced, it was thoroughly out of date. Once the Americans had rescinded the order confiscating Krupp's property, there was nothing in either German or Allied law which would permit expropriation of Krupp's coal and steel holdings, *without his receiving full compensation.* Although British dismantling at the Gussstahlwerk had been extremely thorough, it was curious that the Socialist Government did not seize the opportunity to bilk Krupps completely during the two and a half years that the confiscation ruling was operative. Even more curious, and highly disturbing, was the fact that the Russians came out of it best of all by receiving as reparations the complete Borbeck special steelworks. This had produced the armor for Krupp's Tiger tanks, and was considered to be one of the highest-quality armor-plate producers in the world. One shudders at the ingenuousness of the British Labor leaders responsible for consigning that particular plant to the Russians.

The Allied Plan for Krupps, as first announced in August 1952, divided the Krupp property into four parts. Groups I and II comprised the coal and steel holdings that Alfried Krupp was to sell. In Group I was placed the stock of the Rheinhausen steelworks (formerly known as Friedrich Alfred Hütte, after Alfried's grandfather) and its holding company. The ordinary shares were to be handed over to German "Disposition Trustees" appointed by the Allies, who were to sell them over a period of five years. Up to the end of the five years, the Disposition Trustees could only sell at prices acceptable to Alfried Krupp. If then any shares still remained unsold, with Allied concurrence the period could be extended, during which time Krupp would have the right to protest against the selling prices. The new, independent steel company formed from Rheinhausen was also to incorporate three Krupp coal mines, Rossenray, Rheinberg and Alfried. From their coal sales, Alfried Krupp was to receive a 2½-per cent royalty;

which, capitalized, represented 10 million DM ($2,380,000). From all the proceeds of Group I, it was estimated that Krupp would receive at least $43 million.

Under Group II were bracketed three Krupp coal mines; Hannover–Hannibal, Constantin der Grosse (Krupp holding 51 per cent), and Emscher-Lippe. These were to be set up as independent companies and sold. In addition, there was a 51 per cent holding in an iron-ore mine, which Krupp was to sell to the Rheinhausen Steel Co. At the time the plan was drawn up, the new companies had not yet been capitalized, and the value of the Krupp holdings could only be approximately assessed at $23 million.

Group III consisted of two steel manufacturing firms: Capito and Klein (value $1.5 million), and the Westphalian Wire Co. ($2.4 million). These were to be transferred in equal shares, one half to Krupp's sister, Frau Irmgard Eilenstein, and one half to a minor, Arnold von Bohlen und Halbach, the son of Alfried Krupp's brother, Klaus, who was killed in the Luftwaffe in 1940. Krupp was also to pay $3 million in compensation to each of four other members of the Krupp clan who lost sources of income as a result of the enforced coal and steel sales.

Under the Allied deconcentration order, the Lex Krupp was to be annulled and thus, nominally, Krupps ceased to be a family enterprise; although Alfried remained personally in possession of the vast rump of the Krupp empire which was left untouched by deconcentration.

The rump was listed in Group IV of the Krupp agreement. At the head of this list was the Gussstahlfabrik, the former hub of the Krupp empire, which, although now largely dismantled or destroyed, still represented some five million square meters of valuable land in the center of Essen. It also included a locomotive factory, a heavy truck factory, a machine-tool producing plant, building firms, printing shops, wholesale-retail shops, a false-tooth factory and the Widia tungsten-carbide works, which was to assume particular importance at a later stage in the negotiations between Krupp and the Allies. Outside of Essen, Krupp was to be left his shipyard at Bremen, and the completely dismantled Germaniawerft at Kiel, as well as the site of the dismantled Nord-Deutsche Steelworks at Bremen. The most important single item left to Krupp was, however, the Stahlbau Rheinhausen bridge-building and steel manufacturing company near Duisburg.

Holdings which were not taken into account in the Plan were plants lying East of the Elbe, which the Russians had already seized, as well as possessions which Krupp had acquired in German-occupied territory, now also removed from Krupp ownership. The most considerable plants in Eastern Germany were two big machinery manufacturing plants, the Berthawerk in Breslau, and the Grusonwerk at Magdeburg, now part of the Sowjetische Maschinenbau AG.

There would be many estimates at the time of how rich Krupp would become if the Allied Plan were carried through. Some claimed that he would receive as much as $140 million from the coal and steel sales alone. An accurate assessment was made particularly difficult by the fact that Krupps, unlike most firms, had a policy of never revealing their profit or turnover figures. Our estimate was 64 to 70 million dollars, and this now seems to have been fairly accurate. From this sum Krupp would have to pay $12 million in family compensations, and an estimated capital sum of about $24 million in accrued pensions. With all liabilities deducted, it could be assumed that Krupp, on liquidation of the coal and steel groups, would be worth, in terms of assets and cash, at least $120 million, if not $150 million.

Some idea of the astronomical pre-war value of Krupps can be deduced from independent German figures which put bomb damage alone suffered by the firm at $150 million — which, according to Krupps, accounted for a 30 per cent drop in capacity.

Another factor which has an interesting bearing on the future wealth of Krupps is the question of *Lastenausgleich* (Equalization-of-Burdens Tax). This was a Federal law designed to provide rehabilitation for the "have-not" refugees from the East by heavily taxing the "haves" of Western Germany on the basis of a capital levy. Other big West German industries have been hit hard under this law, but it is by no means inconceivable that in the long run Krupp may actually receive *Lastenausgleich* in compensation for the loss of his properties in Eastern Germany.

Once the plan had been drafted, it remained for the Allies to get Alfried Krupp's signature, and a guarantee from the Federal Government that they would see the agreement was honored.

While the agreement was being negotiated, in the winter of 1952, I paid several visits to Krupps at Essen. The foreign press, especially the British, were, to say the least of it, not popular. On one occasion I was told that the workers' council had passed a resolution the night before deploring references in British newspapers to the "war criminal Krupp." On another occasion I was invited to lunch, together with a French correspondent and a British colleague, by the Krupp directors. After our defenses had been rendered insensitive by quantities of superb Chateau claret, one of the directors produced a wad of newspaper cuttings from his pocket and proceeded to denounce the aberrations of the British press for some three-quarters of an hour. Krupps took particular exception to a bitter article in the *News Chronicle* of September 5th, 1952, describing in macabre detail how Krupps had allegedly produced its own torture equipment for its wartime slave labor, with the conclusion: "We must be grateful that Herr Himmler is not with us still. At current values it would cost the earth to do him justice."

The opportunity to spend a day going around what was once the greatest arms arsenal of all time filled the three of us with a perverse longing to know something more about the past achievements of Krupps. But emotions were so charged that it was seldom possible to get a straight answer without a tirade on the maltreatment of Krupp. When we asked about "Big Bertha," we were given figures on locomotive production. When we asked where the Tiger tank works had stood, we were shown a workers' latrine adjacent to the demolished plant, the construction of which in 1949 had apparently been hailed by a certain British newspaper as the reopening of Panzer production. It was explained to us carefully by Dr. Hardach, then chairman of the liquidation company, that it was incorrect to call Krupp the "cannon king," because even at the peak of the last war, no more than 42.5 per cent of production had been devoted to arms production. Krupps had, of course, produced the best cannon but never the most.

Destruction at the Gussstahlfabrik, where (at the end of 1952) 17,000 workers were balanced out by the same number of pensioners, almost surpassed description — in spite of the years of extensive reconstruction. Seen from the top of the Krupp administrative offices, it reached on every side almost as far as the eye could see. Scores of bombed buildings with their girders bent and twisted by fire had been left still standing but deserted amidst the acres of rubble. Even more terrifying were the vast areas of empty spaces, punctuated only by an occasional isolated chimney stack, or a concrete foundation, looking like a vast tombstone, where dismantlement had been carried out. The dismantling orgy, which Krupps claim provided over a quarter of a million tons of scrap iron for British blast furnaces, had removed a further 40 per cent of the Krupp potential that had survived the bombing. Our guides made sure that we should see where the British had removed such "obnoxious elements" as heavy cranes, and the site whence the Borbeck steel mill, all 84,000 tons of it, had been shipped to the Urals. They told us how systematic the British sappers had been, even dynamiting the foundations so that no future heavy industry could ever be built again on the same site. They claimed it would cost 2,000 m. DM ($476 million) to restore what had been destroyed in Essen alone. My reactions on leaving Krupps after my first visit were, "Thank God *we* were spared this."

After the signature of the Krupp agreement in March, 1953, and another effusion of vitriol abroad, the Firma Krupp became even more sensitive to the foreign press. Requests to visit plants were met with evasion, or downright refusal. Once when, after several previous attempts, I asked to be allowed to visit the Widia plant, I was put off with the excuse "We've ceased all visits, because they disturbed the workers so much that we lost production!" When at last I managed to arrange a visit to Stahlbau

Rheinhausen with the managing director himself, Dr. Herrmann, I arrived to be told that Dr. Herrmann and another director were away, and the third member of the board was ill, and therefore there was no one who could answer my questions. It was very different from the treatment one received everywhere else in the Ruhr. The Krupp press officer, Herr Wittkamp, explained to me once, "It will take a generation before the animosity passes"; which was not helpful to a journalist seeking information for to-morrow's newspaper. Those intense, overworked faces — usually the color of German asparagus grown underground — working amidst the wreckage of the Ruhr always frightened me, but the pent-up resentment at Krupp was far more disturbing, especially if it really will remain there, building up pressure, during the next twenty-five years.

Later I visited the Villa Hügel, the fantastic white elephant built for some $2,500,000 during the Franco-Prussian war by Alfred Krupp, who, according to his biographer, Gert von Klass, thought that artists were "ne'er-do-wells and daylight robbers." Both his more aesthetically conscious great-grandsons, Alfried and Berthold, found the mansion too hideous and uncomfortable to live in, and opened it in 1953 as a museum, containing a curious mixture of van Dycks, Corots and Kruppiana. As frontispiece to the catalogue was depicted one of the invaluable Krupp Gobelins, with the title *Ars deprimit bellum,* which, it duly explained, meant "War suppresses the Arts, although it is aided by them."

On the day of my visit there were many Krupp workers who, like myself (I am ashamed to say), were far more interested in the Krupp relics than in the assembled art treasures. They gazed in veneration at the 12 foot by 6 foot desk used by Gustav von Bohlen, at the framed letters from the Kaiser, at the full-length portraits of both Kaiser Wilhelms in uniform and of Bertha Krupp as a young bride, and at a British Bessemer Gold Medal won in 1902 for "great services in the development of iron and steel." As they passed a Rodin statue, each tapped it in a professional manner, as if to ascertain by what process the metal had been cast.

"Kanonenberg," as Germans affectionately call it, was built on really Wagnerian lines, and can never have been a happy dwelling-place for the Krupps. Alfred Krupp apparently had two phobias — fire and drafts. As a result, the Hügel was built entirely of stone and Krupp steel, and no window was designed to open; instead the mansion was ventilated by an enormous air-conditioner, which was apparently quite inadequate to the task, and the Krupps grilled in summer and froze in winter. A later Krupp attempted to alleviate the severity of the Hügel by fitting massive oak panels and embellishments, which included a vast carved dining-room dresser, enshrining the kitchen serving hatch — but even that contrived somehow to suggest an open-hearth furnace.

Great secrecy surrounded the final negotiations over the Krupp agreement, but as the winter of 1952 drew on, it became clear that there were some serious hitches. It was apparent from the beginning that both the French and British High Commissions were lukewarm about the whole plan, but the gravest threat to its effectiveness came from the Federal Government, who refused to accept responsibility for enforcing it. They claimed that, although they had undertaken to act as executors of Allied Law 27, they had no powers to exclude Alfried Krupp from the basic coal and steel industries. This was discrimination, they said, and contrary to the Federal Constitution, which grants every citizen the right to enter any business. The fact that the Federal Government had not objected to the Allied agreement excluding Flick from the basic industries suggested that even Dr. Adenauer's industrial advisers were aware of the "specialness" of Krupp's position in Germany.

The recalcitrance of the Germans caused the French to boggle, and demand that the agreement be made more watertight so as to ensure that Krupp would be bound during the whole of his life-time. The French also believed that the definition of the basic steel industries, from which Krupp was to be excluded, should be more closely defined so as to include in addition the Widia works.

Under American pressure, however, their objections were over-ruled, and in late February, 1953, a draft agreement was flown out to Alfried Krupp in Davos by his American lawyers, Earl J. Carroll and Joseph S. Robinson. It left unspecified the duration of validity of Krupp's undertaking not to re-enter the coal and steel industries.

Then the astonishing occurred — Herr Krupp refused to sign the agreement! Supposedly alarmed by the past attitude of the French, Krupp wanted to make quite sure that his continued ownership of the Widia should be unchallengeable. The agreement was referred back to the High Commissions, who quickly consulted their respective governments. A statement which Mr. Eden was to make in the House of Commons on the completion of the Krupp settlement had to be postponed. Eventually the Allies agreed upon a compromise, and, upon Herr Krupp's request, undertook to amend the text of the agreement and to annex to it a "letter of definition" on what was meant by basic steel industries. At last, on March 4th, the agreement was signed in the Allied High Commission at Mehlem with Herr Krupp's lawyers, and embarrassed officials published its contents after consistently refuting leakages which had appeared in the *Daily Telegraph*.

The financial details concerning the sales of the coal and steel holdings remained essentially unchanged from those announced the previous August, as did the list of assets that Krupp was allowed to keep. Herr Krupp agreed not to buy himself back into, or to attempt to regain control, directly or indirectly, of the "steel or iron producing industries *in Germany* or in the coal-mining industry *in Germany*." Thus there was no restriction placed on Krupp's participation in basic industries abroad.

But the most significant features — and weaknesses — of the Krupp agreement lay in the "letter of definition." This defined the "steel or iron producing industry," from which Alfried Krupp was to be barred, as including (my italics) "the making of *alloy steel by any method except in small quantities incidental to the enterprises which will remain in the possession of Alfried Krupp von*

Bohlen und Halbach on the effective date of this plan, and the *hot rolling of steel except as incidental to the enterprises which will remain in the possession of Alfried Krupp von Bohlen und Halbach* on the effective date of this plan. *The production of Widia is not regarded as part of the steel producing industry.*" The implications of this escape clause were staggering. As Brigadier Oxborrow, the head of the British deconcentration branch, confirmed to me, should Krupp be given an EDC order to build tanks he could, within the letter of the agreement, rebuild his steel mills to provide the armor plate "incidental" to his requirements. The only stipulation was that he would have to buy his raw steel ingots, instead of making them himself.

As for the Widia works, what in fact was its importance that had caused Krupp to delay his signature at the last moment? It was a small plant, with less than 1,500 employees, valued at not much more than $4,500,000, and described in the Allied release as "specializing in production of tungsten-carbide material." But, apart from producing diamond-hard cutting tips for engineering tools, Widia had a far greater potential importance. At one point in the last war Widia had been the only plant in Germany able to produce alloy steels sufficiently heat-resistant for use in fighter jet engines. British steel experts also firmly believe that capture of the Widia steel secrets at the Magdeburg Grusonwerke gave the Soviets the indispensable technical knowledge for designing the MIG jet fighter engine. Thus the significance of the Widia works in a Germany, armed or disarmed, with its own aircraft industry, can hardly be exaggerated.[2] Nor is it by any means clear how the Allies propose to limit Widia production to the vaguely defined "small quantities."

While the bulk of the British press, I felt quite unfairly, continued to choose Krupp as the main object of acrimony, it was really the Allied Planners who deserved the greatest blame for

[2] Since the above was written, Krupps in April 1955 announced themselves to be the first firm in Europe (including Great Britain) in commercial production of titanium, a rare metal of particular value in the construction of modern jet aircraft.

producing a plan so farcically unrealistic, and which was unworkable for at least five major reasons:

1. Enforcement by the German Government was uncertain.

2. The escape clause in the letter of definition left Krupp wide powers to build up a steel-*processing* combine without violating his pledge.

3. As a result of the acute limitations of the capital market in Germany, the disposal of over $65 million worth of coal and steel shares would present very serious difficulties. As several German industrialists told me subsequently, there existed a sort of gentlemen's agreement in the Ruhr not to buy Krupp's coal and steel shares. Up till the time of writing, Krupp has only sold two coal mines; one was bought by a foreign consortium, the other by a Federal-owned company.

4. It did not bar Krupp from the manufacture of arms in the future, which to the simple-minded, might once have seemed to be the point of any settlement with Krupp. No doubt Alfried Krupp is quite sincere in his own declared aversion to making arms again, but once German rearmament becomes a fact, Krupps, like any other big German industry, will obviously receive its share of arms contracts.

5. It has left Krupp still a major economic power, both in Germany and the world at large. There is nothing to prevent Krupp building and owning basic industries abroad.

The specialness of Krupps was reaffirmed in 1953 when, following in the steps of previous German heads of State, the Federal Chancellor paid an official visit to the Villa Hügel. The following year the flag of Ethiopia flew above the Hügel, next to the Krupp banner of three black rings on a white field, when Alfried Krupp took up once more the unofficial role of ambassador of the Ruhr to entertain Emperor Haile Selassie; a reception on a scale worthy of Wilhelm II.

As for the economic prospects of Krupps once the agreement was concluded, a recent German book [3] on the Ruhr commented:

[3] *Die Nachfolger der Ruhrkonzerne*, by K. H. Herchenröder, Joh. Schäfer and Manfred Zapp (Econ Verlag, Düsseldorf.)

The restraints imposed by the Allies force the Firma Fried. Krupp to take an increasingly active part in the world market. They constantly seek and find new trading areas. Great projects in Greece, Pakistan, India and South America are being won today for the Firma Fried. Krupp, Essen. It is a paradox that, through the policy of the Allies, especially of the English, the Firma Fried. Krupp is forced to wage successful competition against the British in their very oldest markets, for example Pakistan and India. This is a result of the deconcentration policy that its originators had not foreseen.

The truth of this paradox has indeed been demonstrated time and again in the past two years as news of one Krupp foreign conquest after another startled British exporters. That Krupp could offer such competition all of a sudden was not really very surprising. Against the prospective sale of his $65 million coal and steel shares he has been able to raise considerable loans, which have enabled him to offer longer and better terms of credit for export than his British competitors.

Within a few months of signing the Allied agreement, Krupps gained the lion's share of a contract to build a $140 million steel plant in India, in which they are to receive a portion of the stock as part of the contract. Here, once again, Krupp was treated as a special case when the Federal Government in 1953 promised him allocation of ERP funds to help finance the deal. In the same year Krupps gained a $3 million contract to develop the Greek nickel mines, with a proviso guaranteeing them a substantial proportion of production in part payment. In considering this extension of Krupp power abroad, caused by restraints at home, one cannot help recalling the pattern followed after World War I. Forbidden to produce arms at home, Krupps gained control of shipyards in Holland and Spain, where U-boats were actually produced. By 1925, according to J. W. Wheeler-Bennett, in his *The Nemesis of Power,* Krupps had acquired a controlling interest in Bofors, the Swedish arms manufacturers, and was producing there tanks, heavy guns and other weapons.

After the Allied agreement had been signed, Krupps wasted no time in setting about the reorganization of the firm. For the first time since the war, on March 12th, 1953, Alfried Krupp, at the age of 46, once again took over the control of the firm. Up to the war, he had had little to do with the management of the firm, and was generally considered to have been something of a playboy — principally interested in leading the good life and driving along the Autobahn in his twin-engined motor car of special design. According to his friends, the war and particularly his experiences in jail had a sobering effect and he threw himself into the work of reconstructing Krupps with great seriousness. One of his first actions was to appoint a new general manager, Herr Berthold Beitz, the chairman of one of Germany's biggest insurance companies. Herr Beitz, who was only 40 when he took over the Krupp empire, is very much one of the new generation of German big business men — vigorous and breezy with American ideas of business efficiency, he held little brief for the fusty conservatism left over from Krupps' past.

His plan, as he outlined it to me, was first to concentrate the scattered and diverse industrial functions remaining to Krupps around the bridge-building and engineering firm of Stahlbau Rheinhausen. This factory had originally been constructed as the repairs shop to the neighboring Rheinhausen steel plant, now removed from Krupp control. Since the war it had built nineteen of the new Rhine bridges between Koblenz and the Dutch border. It had projected plans for a bridge across the Bosphorus which was placed in abeyance only because of lack of funds on the part of the Turkish Government. Its personnel has already been nearly doubled since 1950, and the plan is to incorporate within it eventually all the former machine-building and steel-construction functions of the lost Krupp Grusonwerk and Berthawerk in the Soviet Zone, and of the wrecked Gussstahlfabrik in Essen. Already plans have been laid to expand the factory area by another third. Exports comprise currently about two-thirds of production, and the whole framework of Stahlbau Rheinhausen is to be welded into a weapon for waging aggressive export war in a field which already accounts for the greatest value of German orders from abroad. Without forgetting the possibly greater potential of the Widia works, as mentioned above, British heavy manufacturers will do well to keep a close eye on Krupp's Stahlbau Rheinhausen.

In early 1955, Krupps granted the public a rare glimpse at their balance sheet. The Krupp empire was shown to embrace once again sixty companies in West Germany alone, with a turnover the previous year of some $230 million. It was not bad going for a man who, little more than five years ago, was in prison with all his properties forfeit.

The failure of the Allied deconcentration scheme has not been limited to its abortive efforts to break up the Krupp empire. Although the scheme has had some successes, notably with IG Farben and anti-cartel legislation, between 1952 and 1955 its results have come to resemble the severed worm that joins itself together again. Ruhr industrialists are unanimous in claiming that the separation of steel plants from their coal ancillaries has made many formerly prosperous concerns run at a loss. They point to reverse developments in France, where rationalization of French heavy industry has led to the creation of five big vertical trusts. At the same time the Germans note resentfully that many units forcibly divorced from parent companies have been scooped up by foreign interests because of the shortage of capital in Germany. Nearly 25 per cent of all German steel production and 20 per cent of coal production is now under foreign control, and the trend continues.

The High Authority of the Schuman Plan, in whose hands the continuation or reversal of the Allied deconcentration policy now lies, has been under heaviest pressure from German industry to allow re-concentrations to take place. (Under its charter, the Schuman Plan can permit creation of vertical combines, providing a case of assisting *rationalization* of industry can be proved.) Mannesmann, Germany's biggest steel tube manufacturers, have already received permission to reabsorb their old coal holdings, with the result that they are now larger than ever before. Similar plans are also afoot to merge three of the separated holdings of the gigantic Vereinigte Stalhwerke, which, if they succeed, will lead to the creation once again of the strongest single concentration of economic power in Europe.

If the High Authority does not apply the brakes on this development, it is difficult to believe that Krupps will not somehow follow with the tide.

6

Occupiers and Occupied

WHILE THE SOCIAL DEMOCRATS WERE CASTING ABOUT FURI-
ously for any weapon with which to defeat the Treaties with the
West, in the autumn of 1952 a windfall came their way.

Rising dramatically in the *Land* Diet on October 8th Herr
August Zinn, the Socialist Minister-President of Hesse, unfolded an extraordinary tale which even many of his own supporters could hardly credit. He had concrete evidence, he claimed,
that the American authorities in Hesse had been training and
financing a force of young Germans to play the role of stay-behind
partisans in the event of a Russian invasion of Western Germany.
Some 1,000 to 2,000 members of an organization called the
"League of German Youth" (BDJ) had been formed into a
"Technical Service," which was being coached regularly by US
officers in the art of sabotage and guerrilla fighting.

What really aroused the predominantly Socialist Diet was Herr
Zinn's disclosure that the police had discovered "liquidation" lists
compiled by the Technical Service, consisting of "unreliables"
who were to be put out of action in the event of a Russian invasion — by shooting if necessary. The lists contained the names of
fifteen Communists — and eighty prominent Social Democrats,
including not only the Hesse Minister of the Interior, Herr Zinn-
kann, but also Herr Ollenhauer, leader of the West German So-

cialist Party, and Herr Kaisen and Herr Brauer, the much respected Bürgermeisters of Bremen and Hamburg.

The US High Commissioner, Mr. Donnelly, at once vehemently
denied all knowledge of the activities of the partisan group. There
was a major uproar in the German press, and the authoritative
Frankfurter Allgemeine demanded that a thorough and speedy
inquiry be held. A special sub-committee of the Bundestag was
formed, followed later by a joint German-American investigatory
committee. Some confirmation of Herr Zinn's allegations was received when the Hesse police unearthed a secret cache of some
hundred rifles in the Odenwald hills, and amidst much feet-
shuffling the US authorities eventually admitted that a "stay-
behind" organization had at one time been formed in the US
Zone during the dark days following the invasion of Korea. The
American body responsible was apparently the cloak-and-dagger
Central Intelligence Agency, of the activities of which the High
Commissioner appeared to be genuinely ignorant. Through some
lapse or other, orders were never given to abolish the Technical
Service as the international situation altered. Whence the instruc-
tion to compile the liquidation lists originated was never quite
made clear; all in all it seemed to have been an appalling case of
the right hand not knowing what the left hand was doing.

With the crucial second and third readings on EDC and Bonn
Conventions in the offing, and Federal elections scheduled for
the following year, the Socialists swiftly turned the attack on the
Adenauer Government. Dr. Menzel, leading the Socialist attack
in the Bundestag debate on October 23rd, described the affair
as West Germany's "greatest political scandal since 1945." Dr.
Adenauer solemnly relayed to the outraged Bundestag a pledge
of the US Government not to form any more partisan groups, and
the episode was eventually relegated to limbo; but it was sufficient to delay the ratification of the EDC in Germany while the
Chancellor once again rallied parliamentary opinion.

If the episode was soon forgotten, the grave damage it did to
American prestige was not; and with it, in German eyes, fell also
the prestige of the other two Western occupying powers, in spite

of pious French and British protestations that "this couldn't happen in our zone." The German press comment was virulent; *Die Welt am Sonntag* chastised the US for its "ignorance and simplemindedness."

The wane of US prestige did not stop there. In pursuit of its re-education program, which in many ways had had a most enlightening and beneficial effect among German youth, the US High Commission had in the past generously subsidized the production of many books and texts for German schools. One of these was a world history done in a novel tabular form, whose authors were a German school teacher, Herr Arno Peters, and his wife Anneliese. The book — called the *Synchronoptic World History* — had been financed by the Americans to the extent of $50,000, and 28,500 copies were ordered for German schools. Then at the beginning of November, 1952, a probing American correspondent disclosed that the US High Commission had suddenly discontinued its support on the grounds that it showed a "pro-Communist bias," and that its authors were allegedly Communist Party members.

A few days later Herr Peters and his wife held a press conference, hotly denying the allegations, and producing excerpts of the book for examination. Although the excerpts did not cover the controversial twentieth century, which was, in fact, purely Marxist (of the Communist persuasion) in jargon and choice of events and personalities, the Peters' interpretation of history did, indeed, seem to be a curious one. (Judas Iscariot was described as a "Jewish freedom fighter who wished Jesus to revolt against the occupation troops." The downfall of Robespierre was attributed to his having "sought to achieve political revolution without, however, altering the laws of private property. Thus his rule strengthened the moderate bourgeoisie, who liquidated him.") The US High Commission admitted, somewhat shamefacedly, that the partially completed book had actually been submitted for their approval in 1949, and received the official OK. But once again, it seemed, somebody had slipped up somewhere. Needless to say the episode was again not wasted by the German press, who, like any vanquished nation, were ever eager to note the follies and shortcomings of their conquerors.

American prestige had barely recovered from these two incidents when, in April, 1953, Senator McCarthy's two traveling tragi-comedians, Cohn and Schine, arrived in Western Germany. They had an impressive brief: they were to pinpoint wastage of public funds and ferret out "commies" in US Government services throughout Europe — for which they allowed themselves twenty-six hours in Paris and three days in Western Germany, including Berlin.

The ground in Germany offered them much promise. The US had a vast but efficient information services network in Germany — there were a number of American-licensed periodicals, still run in many cases by left wing Liberals, left-overs from the days when anti-Nazism had constituted the principal qualification for employment with the Occupation authorities in Germany — and there was the *Synchronoptic World History,* and doubtless other projects of the same order. There were also such objects of McCarthyist ire as the brilliant John Paton Davies (finally harried out of the State Department in 1954), Charles Thayer, the gifted US Consul-General in Munich, and Theodore Kaghan, the capable and courageous deputy chief of the US Information Services in Germany, staunchly and effectively anti-communist.

It soon turned out that Kaghan was the McCarthy "Committee's" principal prey in Europe — Cohn and Schine had only been sent like Zulu witchdoctors to drag him forth from the tribal circle for the sacrifice. Kaghan, the "investigators" revealed, had written a "pro-Communist" play as an undergraduate in the 1930s — therefore by the articles of McCarthyism he was still a dangerous Communist. At a press conference in Frankfurt, Schine when asked what had been the name of this play, replied he thought "Hullo Franco" — then after being prompted by Cohn, amid much mirth from the correspondents, added that on the other hand it might have been "Franco, Goodbye!" Unlike most victims about to be consumed by McCarthy, Kaghan counter-attacked violently; "I have," he said "supervised anti-Soviet radio stations, newspapers, news agencies, pamphlets and other operations here and behind the Iron Curtain for more years than Senator McCarthy's two junketeering gum-shoes have been out of school. When they have made half the record I have in Central Europe in the field of psychological warfare against Communism, then perhaps the money this trip is costing the US taxpayer might begin to pay off." For his defiance, however, Kaghan was recalled to Washington and forced to resign his job. Having despatched Kaghan, Cohn and Schine turned to nosing out books with Communist tendencies in the US Public Library in Munich. Then they moved on to London, leaving behind them a wake of wreckage and ridicule in Germany. Their "book burning" activities in particular provoked most quizzical comment in the German press, with its vivid memories of the Hitler period. The Allied re-education program, designed to eradicate the teaching of the Nazis, seemed to many Germans to have come a very full circle indeed.

Between 1953 and 1954, what with the combined effect of the McCarthy purges and the Republican economy drive, the numbers of both the US and German staffs at the US High Commission in Mehlem were halved, with corresponding reductions throughout the US Zone. Employees who had been in Germany for eight years and had made their lives around the High Commission were suddenly put on a month's notice. With typical American wry humor, the High Commissioner's staff began to greet each other with "See you next week, come Cohn or Schine!" Morale sagged sharply and with it went much of the ambitious American educational and cultural program, including the influential and highly regarded *Neue Zeitung* the US High Commission's overt German organ — and down went American prestige in Germany.

At the same time, although the British High Commission was spared the degrading experience of the McCarthy purges, the change in relations with Germany and the demands of the British taxpayer resulted in similarly drastic reductions in the British administration. The British Land Commissioners, men of the highest qualities, combining a vast experience of German affairs with administrative ability reminiscent of the best tradition of Empire servants, had once had a finger in nearly every aspect of German local life. They included men like Dr. Dunlop, the Land Commissioner of Hamburg, whose almost patriarchal interest in Hamburg resembled that of a British country squire towards his village, who had composed a standard British history of Hamburg and given the proceeds to Hamburg University. His efficient administration, the Hamburgers themselves admitted, was largely responsible for the harbor regaining its old reputation as one of the world's fastest ports. Now the Land Commissioners' staffs were being reduced to a minimum, and their powers on the German scene diminished correspondingly. Similar slashes in personnel and expenditure went on in the French Zone.

Parallel to these changes in jurisdiction, a profound change was taking place in the relations between the occupying forces and the Germans, leading up to the point when, upon the ratification of EDC, they were to be no longer troops of conquering nations but allies with equal privileges and restrictions. An example in miniature of how radically this relationship had altered since 1945 was provided by the new arrangements about shooting and fishing, which came into force in the summer of 1952. In the first post-war days, the forces had simply requisitioned land from the Germans who were then not allowed to possess a gun. Later, the forces were permitted to invite the German owner to shoot or fish on his own land while paying him compensation for the rights at 1939 rates. In April, 1952, all the land was handed back and the position completely reversed, German syndicates being able to invite — or not, as the case might be — neighboring Allied troops to partake of their sport.

With the agonizingly slow metamorphosis from occupying to defending forces, relations between the Allied troops and the Germans have not worsened. Considering the proud and contentious character of the occupied, the long time that the occupation has lasted, and its unsettling shifts of policy, the German attitude to the Occupation on the personal level is still remarkably favorable. Incidents are surprisingly few and far between, and generally stem from most trivial issues. In the two and a half years that I was in Germany, as a British correspondent officially accredited to the High Commission, with a car bearing occupation number plates, I cannot recall any occasion in Western Germany or Berlin where I encountered open hostility or resentment.

In 1951–52, EMNID (the West German public-opinion poll) asked a cross-section of Germans which of the four occupying Powers they considered the most "sympathetic." 33 per cent voted for the Americans, 8 per cent for the British, 2 per cent for the French and 1 per cent for the Russians (although 44 per cent chose no occupation Power at all). In a second poll, EMNID asked, "How do you find the behavior of these soldiers towards the German public?" Of those in West Germany as a whole who expressed opinions, some 41 per cent said "good" or "very good," as opposed to 24 per cent "moderate" and "bad." (No doubt to the average German with memories of how Hitler's legions behaved, both at home and abroad, most Allied troops must have seemed angels by comparison.) The breakdown into the various nationalities was highly complimentary to the British. Of the inhabitants of the British Zone questioned, 48 per cent thought the behavior of the Occupation troops was either good or very good, and only 22 per cent moderate or bad. The US Zone came next with 34 per cent "good" to "very good," 46 per cent "moderate" or "bad"; and the French third: 26 per cent "good" and "very good," and 53 per cent in the less creditable categories.

The two polls presented a fairly accurate report of German opinion. The relative popularity of the Americans in West Germany, as indicated by the first poll, is probably no exaggeration; in spite of the unfortunate errors referred to earlier in the chapter, I would say that a poll taken in 1955 would show little change. The repute of the West as a whole may have declined, but the popularity of the various occupiers relative to each other has probably remained fairly constant.

The US Army is certainly less unpopular in Germany than anywhere else in Europe. The most obvious reason for this, of course, is that in the eyes of many West Germans the United States is the senior partner and guiding power behind the Western Alliance, which still offers the surest defense against Russian expansionist designs. But there is also a surprising degree of genuine gratitude for what the USA has done to help Germany, and a wide realization of how much it helped the country's remarkable recovery — which reaches down even to the working-class German, and is certainly far wider spread than in some other European countries. In the earliest days the US occupation treated German civilians far more harshly than the British, but in later years carried the "be nice to the Germans" swing a great deal farther. The initial US harshness was something the Germans could understand — indeed expected — as being the natural treatment of a conquered nation.

On the whole, the "Amis" (as the US forces were nicknamed) have been better at getting to know the locals than the British forces; and the sentimental Germans appreciate their open-handedness and hospitality. A typical US project was the army's Operation Friendly Hand in summer 1954, which brought some hundreds of German children from poor homes and refugee camps in Berlin for a holiday as the guests of families of American forces in the US Zone. There was a report in the US Army newspaper which happened to catch my eye, of a master sergeant with six children who applied to join Operation Friendly Hand, with the explanation that his own large family prevented him from traveling, so that a German child in his house would be his only chance to learn something about the country.

The Germans tend to sneer at what they consider American naïveté; on the other hand they admire and have a fellow-feeling for the material efficiency of the "Amis," and their brisk way of getting things done. The Americans are also sufficiently non-European to be psychologically still something of a curiosity to many Germans — and sufficiently far away both geographically and commercially not to be rivals in the sense of the British and

French. Conversely, it might well be argued that the very remoteness of the Americans from the European scene gives them less cause for retaining any deep-seated prejudices against the German people. The US military authorities in Germany have also been meticulous in seeing that good relations have been maintained and discipline has been most strict, ranging from frequent curfews on offending units to recent prohibitions of blue jeans and bare backs among forces' dependents.

If there has been a vast transformation in treatment of the German population by the Americans, a great many Americans feel — rather aggrievedly — that any change in the attitude of the British towards them has been almost undetectable. In 1945 the occupying British forces treated the Germans coldly, fairly, and without hatred; in 1955 they still treat them coldly, fairly, and without hatred. In 1945 non-fraternization was an order; in 1955 — at least in the officers' messes of a great many regiments in BAOR — "fratting" is still regarded somewhere between a mess joke and a social lapse. Although BAOR is rated as a "home posting," one has the impression that the majority of British officers in Germany might just as well be in Korea or among the Mau-Mau. After a tour of three years they return with little more knowledge of Germany than they have gleaned from the British press. There are certain factors which obviously militate against fratting on a large scale, such as the language barrier; and without doubt a great many Germans are reluctant to appear too friendly with the Occupation forces.

The British forces' aloofness to the Germans must be in part conditioned by that air of insularity which so often seems to accompany them in most foreign places. On the other hand, there is no doubt that in the background lurks that instinctive, inbred distrust of the average Englishman for the German, as the traditional enemy — added to the vexation of discovering so many of the more irritating features of his own race, such as "queuemindedness," mirrored and enlarged in the Germans.

A British correspondent in Bonn once summed up the instinctive approach as "the glandular reaction," thinking perhaps of

D. H. Lawrence's curious heroes who seemed to have both their thought and emotional processes centered around the solar plexus. The prototype of the glandular reaction has never been more brilliantly portrayed than by Nancy Mitford's "Uncle Matthew," who mentally reached for the 1914 entrenching tool that hung on the wall each time anyone with a German-sounding name entered the house. It is the glandular reaction which can transmute a brass band playing on a Rhine steamer into a vision of goose-stepping, grey-clad hordes; or turn an aggressive motor-cyclist wearing a square-shouldered shiny black coat into a relentless Panzer thrust; or evoke the image of a V-2 from the back of a fat German professor's neck. The glandular reaction was typified in a remark made to me, when I was writing this book, by a senior naval officer whom I had met for the first time only five minutes earlier: "I don't mind anyone knowing it — I hate the damn fellows, and I'm damned if I'm going to hide it if I have to train with them."

It would perhaps be remarkable if anybody who had spent six years of his life fighting the Germans should not still experience some sort of glandular reaction — but what was less easy to understand in Germany was the impression one frequently got that it was the younger officers, commissioned since the war, who showed the strongest and most ill-concealed dislike of the Germans. A great many of them, who could barely have reached their public schools by the time the war ended, still adopt a most overbearingly arrogant attitude towards the Germans, as if they themselves had just led in the conquering troops. There was a particularly flagrant case in the summer of 1952, when a second lieutenant drove his tank into the garden of a restaurant proprietor in Lower Saxony because the proprietor refused him a drink — thereby doing some three thousand dollars worth of damage. The officer concerned was severely reprimanded by his divisional commander, and sentenced to suffer a twelve-months loss of seniority; although unconfirmed reports had it at the time that he had been subsequently congratulated by his commanding officer for showing "initiative."

What they consider the "superiority" of the British has long filled the Germans with a mixture of admiration and resentment — years before the Occupation started. Even that amateur philosopher, Hitler, in one of his dissertations on the British character, commented: "The British are superior to the Germans because of their self-confidence." In German eyes today, the stand-offishness of the British is symbolized by the doors in former German-owned buildings of German towns marked "No Germans allowed here." On the main Berlin–Frankfurt Autobahn, there is a much-frequented British rest house, still with separate conveniences, marked "Officers," "Other Ranks" — and "Germans." To Germans, with their immense national pride, this sort of apartheid treatment is intolerable ten years after the war.

With the commitment now to keep the four British divisions at present in Germany on the Continent for the remainder of the century, relations between the British forces and the Germans will become increasingly important. Since the signature of the EDC in 1952, progressively more elaborate precautions have been taken by the British Army Command in Germany to avoid friction between the local inhabitants and the forces. German observers are now taken along with the exercising troops to assess all damage to property on the spot. At the same time it was recognized that something seriously needed to be done to counter the "glandular reaction" and modify the forces' attitude towards the "new allies." Special pamphlets explaining the changing role and status of the British troops in Germany were issued down to unit levels in 1954 by the C-in-C of BAOR, General Sir Richard Gale, combined with frequent notes to Commanding Officers on how to improve relations with the Germans. This was later followed by distribution of an excellent 100-page history of Germany composed by Dr. Dunlop to improve the British Forces' knowledge of the country in which they were serving. In June, 1954, General Gale told the Foreign Press Association that Anglo-German relations were now good and steadily improving. One fears, however, that the glandular reaction will still be an unconscionable time a-dying.

Then one turns to the French — least popular of the three Western occupation forces, according to the EMNID poll. It is really hardly to be expected that the French — after all their country has suffered from three Teutonic invasions within seventy years — should have made themselves particularly beloved by the Germans during their occupation. Unlike the British or the Americans, they had a score in kind to pay off, and were determined to make their occupation felt — and to squeeze every penny out of occupation costs up to the very moment when the occupation regime should end with the enforcement of the Treaties. The Germans of the French Zone are, for the most part, sufficiently realistic to appreciate that whatever they may suffer at the hands of the French occupation is but a small token of what France suffered under the yoke of the Wehrmacht, and harbor little resentment against the occupation for that. Where the resentment does lie — particularly among the various stab-in-the-back apostles — is in France having a zone at all, or possessing a third and equal voice on the Allied High Commission and in all discussions concerning Germany. Added to the humiliation of being occupied there is the — to the Germans — far greater humiliation of being occupied by a power once beaten to the ground in a three-weeks campaign by weight of German arms alone. In reverse, they argue, French arms contributed nothing effectual to the overthrow of Germany five years later, and thus the French owe their "sub-tenancy" in Germany to the grace of the big Allies. As, in the course of the months which followed German ratification of the Treaties, German sovereignty became more and more hopelessly bogged down in the mire of French political uncertainty, so naturally did resentment wax at France's occupation rights which provided her power of veto. The Yalta revelations of March, 1955, can hardly have lessened this resentment.

The biggest single point of friction between the Germans and the French occupation has been the large-scale recruiting for the Foreign Legion which has gone on in the French Zone since the end of the war. At one time there was a French Foreign Legion recruiting center in almost every French garrison town within the zone, with its doors constantly open to lure in fugitives from justice and any young Germans in search of more adventure than the dull Federal Republic could offer them. Once inside the recruiting station, they were outside German law and were shipped to France by a virtual underground railway protected by occupation privilege. Imaginative stories circulated in West Germany of university students, "pressed" when drunk, or even doped by Foreign Legion agents, regaining consciousness in Marseilles aboard a trooper bound for Indo-China. German protests reached a peak at the time of the siege of Dien Bien Phu in 1954, when the Social Democrat youth organization published a virulent attack on the Foreign Legion recruiting, claiming that nearly a quarter of a million young Germans had been inducted in this way since 1945, and that 46,000 of them had been killed in the fighting in Indo-China. A military spokesman in Paris at once declared that the German figures were "grotesque" — but went on to admit that 60 per cent of the Foreign Legion troops then serving in Indo-China were "of German origin."

Apart from this, the French Zone has been deceptively quiet during the past two and a half years. This is partly due to the fact that, although covering a vast territory, it is one of the least populated — and certainly the least industrialized — areas of Germany, comprising principally the Black Forest and the vineyards of the Palatinate. Had the French occupied the Ruhr — as they did in 1923 — post-war Franco-German relations might have taken a much more savage turn than they have.

There is another aspect: In the post-war years there has been a very widespread feeling in Germany — not just limited to the supporters of Dr. Adenauer — that Germany's first responsibility in foreign affairs lies in effecting a reconciliation with France. No doubt many of those who share this feeling do so because they realize that France was both the key and the stumbling-block in the all-important issue of Germany regaining her sovereignty. One of the survivors of former times, now in a prominent position in the German Foreign Office, once commented with admirable frankness to me:

"In my younger days in the *Auswärtiges Amt* we spent our lives longing for a crisis in France — now we live with our fingers crossed hoping there won't be one."

On the other hand in the early 1950's (the honeymoon period of the Schuman-Adenauer *entente*), a powerful wave of sincere idealism swept Germany, particularly among the youth, founded on the dream of a United Europe as envisaged by those two great internationalists. In line with political trends, individual Germans took it upon themselves to be "nice to the French." The attempts often resembled the love overtures between a bull mastiff and an agile and untrusting cat, and the results were not always felicitous. A favorite German conversational gambit — I have heard it countless times — runs somehow as follows: "You come from Paris? Ah, yes — Paris is the most beautiful city in the world. I am so fond of it; you see, *I knew it in 1942*." It is, of course, disastrous; yet the German is doubtless sincerely and genuinely of the belief that he could have paid a Frenchman no prettier compliment.[1] There are times when one cannot help feeling sorry for the Germans for the perpetual disadvantage which they suffer in relations with the French, both on a personal and national level; because, with their immense native charm the French will always be able to get away with murder — and with their equally immense lack of charm, the Germans will seldom draw full credit for even their most high-minded and honorable acts.

[1] There is no doubt that tact is not one of the Germans' strongest points. With the advent of the German economic recovery, busloads of exuberant German tourists set off for holidays abroad — often with banners bearing the slogan, "We're back again!" Yet they were surprised that European countries that had been occupied during the war did not greet them with the same degree of enthusiasm with which they had set out. German tactlessness reached a peak at Easter, 1954, when some 200,000 tourists swarmed over into Holland, many of them drawn by a sense of nostalgia to revisit their wartime billets — coinciding with the date of the anniversary of the country's liberation from the Nazis. Many Dutch innkeepers, enraged by the grossness of some of the German tourists, erected signs "Germans keep out" and "No Germans here." The following year, the tenth anniversay of the Dutch Liberation, the German press was wise enough to advise German tourists to keep away from Holland over Eastertime.

As it was, the Franco-German honeymoon of the early '50s was to have unfortunately all too short a life. By the latter half of 1952 major political storms were arising which would severely shake this delicate *amourette,* as will be seen shortly.

7

Saar Tug-of-War

IN THE LATTER PART OF 1952 A SHADOW BEGAN TO CREEP across the face of Western Europe, already unsettled by the disquieting delays in ratification of the Treaties. The shadow was the reviving spirit of Franco-German animosity, a specter which, it had been hoped in the days of common danger in 1950, was on its way to final interment.

As in so many Franco-German disputes of past and present, the thirty-miles-square territory of the Saar was the root of the trouble. On January 25th, 1952, the French Government promoted M. Gilbert Grandval, former French High Commissioner to the Saar, to the rank of Ambassador, thereby establishing the Saar as an autonomous Republic. At the same time France assured the survival of its puppet regime run by Herr Johannes Hoffmann, a Saar miner's son, by refusing to license any of the three pro-German political parties of the Saar. As Mr. James Warburg mildly commented in his book *Germany — Key to Peace,* it was "a bit of old-fashioned provocative chauvinism." That France should with one hand offer Germany equal rights in a new European Community and with the other deny her sympathizers rights in the new, and predominantly German, "autonomous" state, seemed a curious interpretation of "Europeanism." On February 8th, while the Treaties were still in the drafting stage, the Bundestag replied by a resolution taking "the strongest exception to the French Government's attempt to pre-judge the political fate of the German Saar population before the conclusion of a peace treaty." In March, the Federal Government decided to refer the Saar dispute to the Council of Europe. The decision was in fact deferred, because in the meantime Dr. Adenauer and his good friend and German-speaking fellow Europeanist, M. Robert Schuman, had agreed to try to hammer out differences *unter vier Augen*. Their talks began in August of the same year.

The conversations were to continue sporadically over the next two years, poisoning Franco-German relations because the discussants could not find common ground. Their seemingly endless inconclusiveness provided little incentive for correspondents to become engrossed in the problem, especially in the certain knowledge that those infallible yardsticks of public interest, the sub-editors, would reduce the most penetrating analysis to a matter of two lines, generally with the caption: "Saar Talks Resumed." But as the Saar issue was to play such a central role in great European problems its background is sketched here that later developments may be intelligible.

The country itself, a grubby land packed with coal mines and factories, contains just under one million inhabitants, in one of the most densely populated areas of the world. The vast majority of the population is of German origin, speaks German, and feels cultural bonds with the Germans. It produces annually some 17 million tons of coal and over three million tons of raw steel, representing 8 per cent of the total resources of the Schuman Plan countries. Economically it is closely tied to the iron-ore fields in Lorraine, which fact has provided the double-edged argument that prompted Bismarck in 1871 to seize Lorraine for Germany, and the French in 1945 to claim the Saar for France. Neither claim has any moral justification, but France in 1945 — backed by Great Britain and America — felt that the Saar, as an integral part of Hitler's Reich from 1935 onwards, should be made to deliver its production as reparations for the havoc the Nazis had caused to French industry. After the initial period of occupation and reparations, the French proceeded to consolidate their *de facto* grip on the Saar's economy by concluding a series of economic conventions with the Hoffmann regime. These granted France a fifty-year lease on the Saar coal mines, and provided for the use of French currency, and the removal of all customs barriers between the two countries — while at the same time requiring duties on German products entering the area.

With the swing of Allied policy on Germany, followed by the release of controls on the Ruhr and the rapid return of Germany as a major heavy industrial power, fears grew in France that, if the Saar ever returned to Germany, she would find herself once again outmatched by the Teutonic industrial colossus. In French eyes — as M. François-Poncet, the French High Commissioner, once commented — France without the Saar would lead to a "lean France and a fat Germany." Within the Schuman Plan, France plus Saar shared 32 per cent of the Community's total coal and steel resources compared with Germany's 45 per cent; whereas the transfer of the Saar to Germany would have given her 53 per cent of the total resources, compared with only 24 per cent for France. In addition to this, the Saar has been contributing more than 10,000 million francs ($30 million) annually to France's shaky foreign exchange reserves, and has provided an important market for French agricultural and consumer goods. France's demands, advanced at the Schuman-Adenauer talks, were that the Saar Conventions be maintained, that the Saar's political autonomy, in respect of Germany, be assured, and that any settlement should be final.

While French claims were based almost exclusively on economic interests, German claims had a largely cultural and ethnic — and emotional — basis. In all the discussions the Federal Government's main interest was the granting of equal rights for the pro-German political parties in the Saar. This the French were apparently afraid to do lest it should enable the Germans once again to whip up the *Deutsch ist die Saar* emotions among the Saarlanders which Hitler had so successfully utilized. More than being concerned at just the material implications of the unilateral and preferential French ties with the Saar, the Germans saw them as a form of discrimination against them, which would be unacceptable in a European system which promised equal rights to all its member States. They demanded that the Saar frontiers be opened to German goods without payment of any discriminatory duties.

Another vital difference of opinion was that the Germans considered that any final settlement on the political future of the Saar would have to await the conclusion of an All-German Peace Treaty. Here they were motivated by a fear that renunciation of the Saar, prior to a Peace Conference, might give the Communists a precedent for permanent annexation of the Oder-Neisse area.

In brief, the Saar is economically non-essential to Germany, and racially and politically alien to France. The happiest solution yet arrived at was the van Naters Plan. This was a scheme produced by a Dutch lawyer, Mr. van der Goes van Naters, at the request of the Consultative Assembly of the Council of Europe, which proposed establishing the Saar as the first "European Territory." The Saar would thereby retain initially its autonomy and parliament, while gradually moving towards the status of a European Territory which would make it independent from, but economically equally accessible to, both claimants. At its head would be nominated a European High Commissioner (not a German, Frenchman, nor Saarlander) who would receive his orders either from the High Authority of the Schuman Plan or from the Council of Europe. One of the van Naters proposals to start the Saar off with a "European" function was to transfer the seat of the High Authority from Luxemburg to Saarbrücken. The existing unilateral economic union with France, so bitterly resented by the Germans, would be modified gradually to bring about liberation of trade with the Federal Republic. But much gall was to flow before the van Naters Plan was even adopted as the basis for Franco-German discussion.

Meanwhile, the rather relevant question of what the Saarlanders themselves wanted was almost entirely obscured. In fact, in 1952, what the average Saarlander wanted — if he was vocal enough to express it — was a continuation of the *status quo,* because he was then enjoying very much the best of both worlds. Because of France's interest in wooing the Saarlanders, they were receiving the economic plums of the French system, and few of its crab apples. Their claim to cultural bonds with Germany (e.g. the teaching of German in schools) was by and large satisfied by the French. They would have liked greater freedom of trade with Germany, but on the other hand were terrified that a completely open frontier would leave them to be swamped by German competition, and especially the higher-quality Ruhr coal. Post-war severance from Germany had saved the Saar from the fearful fate of dismantlement which overtook German heavy industry, and they did not want reunion and the disadvantages which would be brought them, such as higher taxes, higher unemployment and lower wages, and the almost certain influx of East German refugees in search of jobs. Moreover, there was much to be said for waiting in hopes that the Saar might be chosen as the permanent headquarters of the Schuman Plan.

However, if German prosperity continued its astronomic ascent, and left France far behind, the Saarlanders might well think again. In 1952, this consideration undoubtedly lent urgency to the French demand for a once-for-all decision.

At the Saar talks, which began in August of 1952, the mounting pressure of nationalist feeling at his rear prevented M. Schuman from making any major concessions on the previous French position, and Dr. Adenauer's hands were tied by his slim majority at home. Although both parties for the first time endorsed the principle of Europeanization as a possible basis for a Saar solution, the French would not retreat from their veto on the German political parties, and the Germans would not relinquish demands for the cancellation of the Franco-German Conventions. By October the talks had reached a deadlock, and were broken off. These were the last to take place between Adenauer and Schuman. On October 27th, the *Daily Telegraph* correspondent in Paris reported a "crisis in Franco-German relations and in the growth of a European union."

In the teeth of bitterest criticism from Germany, the Saar Government — prompted by France — decided to go ahead with elections on November 30th, without licensing any of the pro-German parties. The Free Democrats accused Herr Hoffmann of "daring to attempt a ballot-box putsch." In a speech at Cologne on November 2nd, Dr. Adenauer expressed fears lest European integration "be destroyed by the machinations of Herr Hoffmann." On November 16th the Bundestag resolved by acclamation not to recognize the results of the Saar elections.

A few days later an incident occurred in Saarbrücken which raised German emotions to a new pitch of indignation. Saar Government agents raided the house of Herr Georg Geiger, a functionary of one of the banned pro-German parties, in search of illegal pamphlets. During the raid there was a scuffle, and Herr Geiger, who was 70 and had a weak heart, was seized with a heart attack and died. Herr Blücher, the mild and usually restrained Federal Vice-Chancellor, received the news of the incident at the Free Democrat Party Congress at Bad Ems. He at once jumped to his feet and declared impassionedly to the Congress that Herr Geiger had been "ruthlessly murdered." The 200 delegates rose and stood in silence for two minutes. Herr Blücher's accusation was most indignantly refuted in both Paris and Saarbrücken. There was a further emotional scene at the burial of Herr Geiger, when the leader of his party, Herr Becker, declaimed: "I can speak only when my country is free again. You were faithful unto death. We shall never forget it."

On the day of the elections, a German butcher stabbed a French soldier with his slaughtering knife in a wine parlor altercation at Ockfen, on the Saar frontier. The score was even, and blood was up on both sides.

During the election campaign, massive pressure was exerted on the Saarlanders over the German radio and in the German press. The various German political parties poured pamphlets into the Saar, some of them extravagantly claiming that work vacancies there were being filled by Moroccans, and telling the Saarlanders not to vote for "the separatists and traitors." Highly melodramatic speeches were made near the frontiers of the Saar, at places redolent of German nationalistic mystique, such as Deutsches Eck at the confluence of the Mosel and the Rhine. The aim of the German efforts, which were concerted by Herr Kaiser's Ministry for All-German Questions (known more ribaldly as the Ministry for all German Answers), was to get the maximum number of Saarlanders either to spoil their votes or abstain from voting as a protest against the Saar regime and a declaration of pro-German solidarity. If this was done the elections would constitute a plebiscite favoring the Germans. The Kaiser Ministry was backed up by no less a person than the Catholic Bishop of Trier (in whose diocese the Saar lies), who circulated a pastoral letter to the Saar clergy absolving Catholic parishioners (comprising three-quarters of the Saar population) from the duty to vote.

But it was all to little avail. Out of a total poll of 93 per cent, only 24 per cent of the votes were spoiled and only 7 per cent abstained — and this on a dismally rainy day. It was a major defeat for Pan-Germanism, and made it clear to the world that the majority of Saarlanders — at least in 1952 — did not want to go back to Germany. If the matter had stopped there it would not have been so serious; but unfortunately the crude and clumsy campaign waged by Herr Kaiser, and the intensity of the German propaganda, must have made many a Frenchman think "this has all happened before." As members of the German Foreign Office now freely admit, the agitation had done the greatest harm to Franco-German relations, and the results were soon to be seen.

Within a month of the Saar elections, the European-minded Pinay-Schuman Government fell in France and was replaced by a more nationalistic regime headed by M. Mayer, with M. Bidault as Foreign Minister. The new Government at once reflected the alarm which had been mounting in France at the thought of German rearmament and France's national submersion under the EDC. Apart from international considerations, the Mayer Government was obviously influenced by such recent developments in Germany as General Ramcke's outburst, the Saar agitation, the uncompromising opposition of the Social Democrats to the Treaties, and the endless delays in ratification by the Germans — capped by a threat of constitutional crisis in Bonn (referred to in the next chapter) which had broken out just before the Mayer Government entered office. The bitterest memories were also being aroused by the Oradour trial.[1] In his inaugural speech, M. Mayer now produced his *conditions préalables* (preliminary conditions), which were to strike at the very heart of the EDC. First and foremost of these conditions was that France would not ratify the EDC before a settlement had been reached on the Saar.

In return for the Gaullist support which brought him to power, M. Mayer was also induced to make a promise that would safeguard the national identity of the French army. This gave rise to a second *condition préalable* — later to take the form of "Additional Annexes" to the EDC Treaty. They incorporated the following demands:

1. In the event of crises in her overseas territories, France should be allowed to withdraw contingents from the EDC forces *without* the need for the approval of the Supreme Allied Commander, as was required under the EDC Treaty. (The Supreme Commander would be able to refuse consent *only* if it was established that the withdrawal of French forces would endanger the security of the Community, and that in such an event a meeting of the North Atlantic Council and the EDC Council would be necessary to decide that the Community would be imperilled by the withdrawal of French forces from Europe.)

2. Regardless of the extent of her withdrawals from the EDC to meet overseas commitments, France's voting powers on the EDC Defense Board must remain constant, and equal to Germany's.

In a third condition, M. Mayer demanded closer British association with the EDC as an additional safeguard against the es-

---

[1] In June 1944, the SS massacred 624 people in the French village of Oradour as a reprisal against the Maquis. Twenty-one Germans and Alsatians were later brought to trial — but the trial did not open until January 1953.

tablishment of a German hegemony, before he would submit the
Treaties to the Assembly.

The Additional Annexes met with instant opposition from all
the other five EDC signatories — as well as Germany. The original EDC Treaty had already gone as far as possible to provide for
France's special position, and the new French demands tore great
holes in the whole conception of the European Army. It was
militarily ludicrous to imagine the NATO and EDC Councils
sitting down to discuss whether France could send a division to
Morocco at a time of some future emergency when Russian T34s
might already be pouring over the Elbe. Under the Additional
Annexes the way was opened for France to leave at her own
will as little as one token division with the EDC, while still claiming full rights in the EDC command. It was gross discrimination
against the Germans and the other members of the Community.
On top of this, the French were urging that Britain be represented
on the EDC Defense Board as a further counter-balance against
German domination.

During the tense days in Bonn which followed delivery of the
Mayer terms, I had several conversations with members of the
French High Commission. One senior official consistently threw
the blame for French hesitance squarely upon the British for refusing to contribute forces to the EDC. He was remarkably frank.

"Frenchmen," he said, "have always at the back of their minds
the fear that Britain, with no stake in a European Army, may
once again confront them with a Dunkirk. Secondly, they are re-
sentful that you ask us to do something you are not willing to do;
to give up the sovereignty of our army. We too have old regi-
mental traditions, and an Empire to defend!"

The Annexes were widely resented in Germany for the distrust
of her goodwill they revealed, and the discriminatory conditions
they contained. On the eve of departing for the Rome EDC conference in February 1953, Dr. Adenauer branded them as a "serious threat" to the Treaty's ratification. His attitude seemed to be
shared by the representatives of the other member countries.
Nonetheless, in an earnest attempt to obtain French acceptance

of EDC, the Annexes were approved in substance at Rome, and appended to the Treaty. Complying with French requests, in March Great Britain stated that she was prepared to extend her guarantees from twenty to fifty years and to send a strong, permanent mission to the Defense Board of the EDC — but no forces. In the same month, Dr. Adenauer told his Cabinet that he was ready to make wide concessions on the Saar, in spite of the risks at home, in order to clear the way for French ratification. The Schuman-Adenauer talks were now resumed on a State secretary level.

The Additional Annexes really sounded the first note of the death knell of EDC. Their acceptance by the five other countries apparently did nothing to assuage the Treaty's opponents in France — on the contrary, they had the effect of drilling a hole in a boat to drain the water out. To the average German, the *conditions préalables* attached to an already concluded Treaty smacked of something as nasty-sounding as blackmail. They came at a time when the Germans were aroused by the banning of the pro-German parties in the Saar and the sentencing of Germans for war crimes so long after the war had ended. Franco-German relations had reached a low point for the post-war period.

8

Germany Ratifies

BETWEEN THE SAAR ELECTIONS AND THE ANNOUNCEMENT OF THE
Mayer conditions, the Bundestag, after many delays, had taken
up the second and third readings of the Treaties. The Committees
having finished their work, Dr. Adenauer had wanted to forge
ahead with the debates at the end of November, but an unexpected
defeat in the Bundestag on November 18th caused him to drop
the idea. Reacting against the French refusal to license the pro-
German parties in the Saar elections, some twenty coalition rebels
voted against the Government timetable, while fifty-six abstained,
to give Dr. Adenauer his first major parliamentary defeat. The
stern old Chancellor managed to restore order in his ranks the following week, and December 3rd was fixed as the date for the first
of the ratification debates. On the basis of that trial of strength,
which brought Dr. Adenauer a majority of 220 to 160, he seemed
assured of an easy victory in the debates themselves.

On the day of the debates, an atmosphere of tremendous tension hung over Bonn. The whole of the Bundeshaus enclave, including the press houses, and all the roads leading to the Parliament buildings, were cordoned off with barbed-wire barricades
as precautions against a possible Communist assault. About 400
police reinforcements, armed with truncheons and *Wasserkano-
nen* (an invention resembling an armored car, but with two fire

hoses in its turret instead of a gun), were drawn from neighboring districts to man the defenses. Several bus-loads of Communist supporters imported from the Ruhr, consisting mostly of women, made one or two half-hearted attempts to reach the Bundeshaus. A few Communists suffered split heads, and several journalists inside the perimeter — including myself — got wet. A group of some forty Communists, armed with passes supplied by Communist deputies, did in fact achieve a Trojan Horse penetration of the Bundeshaus, and actually reached the doors of the chamber while the debate was in process, causing some consternation in the Bundestag.

The debate was opened with a two-hour speech by Dr. Adenauer, an impassioned warning of the perilous consequences for Germany should the Bundestag reject the Treaties. Amidst constant interruptions by both Communists and Socialists, he declared with slow and deliberate emphasis which underlined the high seriousness of the occasion:

> We must at least learn our lesson from history. After 1870 Germany was always trying to find friends and allies, because it was realized that Germany, in spite of her strength, could not exist without strong friends. She did not find them, mainly through her own fault, through blindness and failure to appreciate what was offered, and through too great confidence in herself.
>
> Germany's position is today more perilous than it has ever been before throughout her long history. Germany is divided and torn, disarmed and defenseless, bordered by a colossus who is trying to enslave and swallow her . . .
>
> I call upon the whole German people to become conscious of the weight of this decision. It is the fateful hour of Germany. We are at the crossroads of slavery and freedom. We shall choose freedom.

If Parliament rejected the Treaties, he warned, "the gradually brightening future of the German people, and of Europe, would be plunged into darkness again. The unification of Europe into a Federal body would be nipped in the bud. The Soviet Union would be done the greatest imaginable service." There was, he emphasized, no third choice to accepting or refusing the Treaties. Refusal meant exposing Germany to the danger of being swallowed up by the Communist giant, or of becoming a battlefield for the two great powers. Rejection of the Treaties by Germany would cause the other powers to come to an arrangement with Russia. It was unnecessary for him to tell the Bundestag, who knew of the stories of the refugees from the East, what a settlement with Russia at Germany's expense would mean.

His warnings about the menace of the Red Colossus were backed up by the timely release in London that morning of a Foreign Office statement revealing that 100,000 East Germans were now under arms, and equipped with heavy guns and Russian T34 tanks. This represented an increase of between 35,000 and 40,000 since the signature of the EDC Treaty six months ago.

Opening for the Social Democrats, Herr Willi Brandt of Berlin countered with the argument that the Treaties represented only one half of Germany. "The Treaties are not designed to lead to a reunification of Germany, and we are afraid that they will prevent it," he said. On the following day, Herr Ollenhauer, the Social Democrat leader, demanded vaguely the creation of a "world security system" as an alternative to EDC. In his rebuttal, Dr. Adenauer commented acidly: "There exists already a world security system — its name is the UN." In noting French hesitance towards German rearmament, Herr Ollenhauer struck a chord which was very true at that time: "The EDC lacks the one essential for defense — *confidence.*"

Division was due to take place on the second reading late on the night of the 4th, to be followed with a vote on the third and final reading the next day. A Government victory seemed a foregone conclusion. Then, on the afternoon of the 4th, some disquieting rumors began to circulate in the lobby. Dr. Adenauer, it was said, had decided to postpone the third reading because he had run into constitutional difficulties. An atmosphere of utmost confusion prevailed in the Bundeshaus, reminding one rather of crash night on the stock exchange. I would never have thought that such an essentially phlegmatic and dour race as the Germans would be prone to stampede, but there was certainly a feeling of near-panic detectable among the coalition deputies and German journalists that evening. Late that night Herr von Brentano, parliamentary leader of the Christian Democrats, rose to confirm the Government's intention to adjourn the third reading of the Treaties. In the meantime it would apply to the Supreme Court at Karlsruhe for a constitutional ruling on whether a simple majority in the Bundestag would be sufficient for ratification of the Treaties.

The constitutional issues which surrounded the EDC in Germany had become hideously complex, and almost impossible to explain within the space of a chapter. It was therefore not surprising that the new German hesitation — arising as it appeared from the most legalistic of hair-splitting — should have caused new misgivings in France. The trouble dated back to May, 1949, when the new Federal Constitution was first approved by the Western Allies. World peace had yet to be disrupted by the invasion of South Korea, and there was no intention of rearming Germany. As a result, the Constitution contained no provisions for raising an army. As soon as the EDC project, and German participation therein, was broached, the Social Democrats at once seized on this loophole and filed a brief with the Constitutional Court alleging that ratification of the Treaty would be unconstitutional. If their point was upheld, an amendment to the Constitution would have to be passed, requiring a two-thirds majority in both Houses, which everybody knew the coalition Government could not then achieve. Thus the Treaties would perish, and German rearmament be placed in limbo until a new German Government could muster a two-thirds majority. It was clever politics on the part of the Socialists, but not particularly honest, for — as they had often admitted — they were not themselves opposed to rearmament in principle.

At the end of July, 1952, however, the Constitutional Court from its seat in Karlsruhe rejected the Socialists' brief on the grounds that it could not pass judgment on what was still only a draft bill. They told the SPD they could try again once Parliament had ratified.

Meanwhile President Heuss, apparently disturbed by the Socialist accusations, asked the Court for a private counsel to assist him in deciding whether or not he could sign the Treaties when they had passed through Parliament. The luminaries at Karlsruhe were nearing completion of their work on this counsel at the beginning of December, when the Bundestag embarked on the second reading of the Treaties. According to well-informed reports at the time, in the middle of the debate Dr. Adenauer received word from his legal rapporteur in Karlsruhe that the Heuss counsel was likely to go against the Government; in which case the President would undoubtedly feel himself bound by it, and refuse to sign the Treaties until the Constitution was amended. The net result would have been the same as if the SPD plaint had succeeded. As a result, Dr. Adenauer's legal advisers urged him strongly to postpone the third reading and put in his own case to Karlsruhe.

The innocent mind might well ask what was the point of Dr. Adenauer consulting the Court when the SPD's application had already been turned down, and the Court's counsel to the President was likely to be adverse. The answer lay within the Court's structure, which enabled it, like the Oracle of Delphi, to give more than one answer to the same problem. It consisted of two chambers, each of twelve judges who were politically appointed. The two chambers were popularly dubbed the "red" and the "black," because the judges of the first were reputed to incline preponderantly towards the Socialists, and the second towards the Government. Each chamber had competence to deal with a specific form of constitutional issue. The SPD legalists had phrased their brief in such a way as to be a litigation *by a political party against a law,* and thus it came before the "red" Chamber — which the Socialists considered friendly to their interests.

Now the Coalition brief devised by Dr. Adenauer's legalists was drafted in terms challenging the right of the SPD to insist that ratification of the Treaties would require more than a simple majority. As a result it became a dispute *by a party against another party,* and thus fell within the competence of the second, or "black" chamber. President Heuss's case before the Court, as an *advisory council,* was dealt with in yet a third way — by both chambers sitting jointly. It was an incredible situation, and showed most dangerous flaws in the German Constitution which now enabled sparring politicians to degrade the Supreme Judiciary of the land to a weapon of partisan politics. For being persuaded to stoop to the same unsavory practices of his opponents, Dr. Adenauer brought upon himself most stinging criticism within the country.

But the Constitutional Court, apparently disgusted at the slur cast upon its reputation by all the talk about its red and black chambers, reacted to the Government's maneuvering in an unexpectedly independent fashion. It decided that whatever ruling the full court reached in its counsel for President Heuss would take precedence over any ruling issued by either chamber sitting independently. This threatened at once to bring the Government back to the point where Dr. Adenauer had felt himself forced to postpone the third reading.

Dr. Adenauer promptly challenged the validity of the Court's decision, on the grounds that no purely *advisory opinion* could be binding over a definite *ruling,* such as the Government had asked the Court to provide. The situation had got completely out of hand; the Court seemed to have gone as much astray as the contesting parties, and a major constitutional crisis threatened.

The Cabinet held an emergency meeting to decide what to do next. There was in fact only one State organ that had as yet remained unsullied throughout the dispute, and alone could offer a way out. This was the President himself. That night Dr. Adenauer called upon Professor Heuss. The two were closeted together for a long interview, during which time the Chancellor brought all the power of his forceful personality to bear upon the President to save the situation by withdrawing his request for counsel. The President, an elderly, easy-going Swabian intellectual with an unimpeachable liberal record, finally gave way.

The following day President Heuss broadcast to the nation, explaining his reasons for withdrawing his request. He had, he said, wanted advice and not a definite ruling. But now, because of its decision that its advisory counsel would be binding over any other ruling, there was a danger that the Constitutional Court might become involved in political responsibilities. He strongly denied that he had withdrawn under pressure from Dr. Adenauer. "I have the habit of making decisions myself. No one can relieve me of this responsibility before history and my own conscience."

The Social Democrats were, however, not satisfied and accused the Government of "exerting massive pressure on the President." Dr. Adenauer followed up the President's withdrawal with a further attack on Karlsruhe, asserting, "The Government is convinced that the Supreme Court's decision of December 8th is supported neither by the Constitution nor by any other law."

Thus ended a pretty dismal episode, in which all the guardians of the infant West German State had damaged their reputations — including the highly respected President. It had shaken confidence both at home and abroad in the responsibility of the new German Parliamentary democracy. Dr. Adenauer's view was that in the long term the damage done to the Federal Constitution would be soon forgotten, and repaired, while if the Treaties had been allowed to founder on the rock of German constitutional bickering, the damage might be irreparable, and the world less likely to forget or forgive. When one considers the havoc wrought to Western unity over the next eighteen months by the ditherings of successive French Governments, one is perhaps less inclined now to criticize Dr. Adenauer's actions of December, 1952.

As far as the immediate future was concerned, Dr. Adenauer had won a round in removing from the board all other constitutional petitions on the EDC save the Government's. Following the Government's decision to postpone the third reading, a vote on the second reading had been taken amid stormy scenes, bringing victory to the Government. There was, however, absolutely no indication of how the judges of the black chamber, piqued by the treatment of the Court as a whole, would now adjudge the

Government's case. Meanwhile droves of legal experts from the opposing parties decamped for Karlsruhe to press their various cases, supported by more droves of university professors of law revelling in the prospects of a protracted session of legalistic casuistry so dear to the German intellect. Reflecting on the time it had taken the Court to deliberate both the SPD brief and the President's counsel, the German press gloomily predicted another interminable delay before the Treaties could be ratified, possibly making them an issue of the Federal elections due to take place the following autumn. In some alarm, Washington dispatched Mr. William Draper, the US ambassador-at-large in Europe, on a fact-finding mission to Bonn at the end of December.

At last, on March 8th, 1953, the luminaries of Kalsruhe gave an answer to the Government's plaint concerning the procedural treatment of the Treaties. In a 50-page exposition, the Court backed the Government, ruling that it was impermissible for a party to hinder passage of a bill through Parliament because it considered it to be unconstitutional. Until the bills had become law by passing through both Houses, the Court itself would not pass judgment on their constitutionality.

Their decision marked the final defeat of the Social Democrats' attempts to thwart German ratification of the Treaties by obstructionist tactics; but in the long run their delaying action resulted in victory for them, although they could hardly have foreseen it. The time they had wasted had been sufficient to sow the seeds of doubt in France, which a year and a half later was to strangle the EDC.

On receiving the Court's answer, the Government accelerated its plans for the third and final reading of the Treaties. There was particular urgency as at the end of the month Dr. Adenauer was to fly to America, and he wanted to take the offering of German ratification with him. The final division, which Dr. Adenauer described as "Germany's hour of destiny," took place at 9:40 p.m. on the night of March 19th in an atmosphere remarkable for its calm, compared with the stormy sessions of December.

The Treaties sailed through by 226 to 166. Russian threats of the previous month — obviously aimed for the Bundestag's consumption — to complete the sealing-off of Berlin in the event of "ratification of the Western war treaties" did not materialize.

The Federal Government heaved a sigh and passed the Treaties on to the Bundesrat for its approval. In one last feeble jab, Herr Ollenhauer, apparently acting entirely on his own initiative, applied to the Constitutional Court for an injunction to prevent President Heuss signing, and thus completing, the Treaties until the Court had pronounced on their constitutionality. The other leaders of the SPD were incensed at not being consulted by Herr Ollenhauer, and critical of the slight which his action cast upon the President. Five days later the injunction was withdrawn, although Professor Heuss later promised Herr Ollenhauer that he would not append his signature to the Treaties while there still remained any doubt about their constitutionality.

On April 1st Dr. Adenauer set forth on his voyage to the United States. As the first European premier to achieve parliamentary ratification of the EDC Treaty, he went as "the best boy in the European class," and moreover as one of the few European statesmen in the post-war period not to accompany his visit with a request for money.

His reception, as the first German Chancellor in office ever to visit America, was tremendous. Dr. Adenauer's tour of the States evidently made a deep and important impression upon the US Government, and indeed upon Adenauer himself. On his return he said with some emotion: "I shall never forget the visit to the Arlington Cemetery. There, before the tomb of the American Unknown Soldier, the *Deutschland Lied* was played together with the Star-Spangled Banner for the first time." The American visit had an immeasurable effect, too, upon Dr. Adenauer's prestige inside Germany, and undoubtedly contributed greatly to his subsequent election successes.

When Dr. Adenauer returned to Bonn in mid-April, he found, to his disquiet, that the political scene had become dominated by a new figure, Dr. Reinhold Maier, the Prime Minister of Baden–Württemberg and President of the Bundesrat. The Bundesrat, which represented the *Land* Governments, had a total of thirty-eight seats allotted to the various *Länder* in blocs according to their size. Although most of the *Länder* Governments were made up of coalitions of different parties, in the Bundesrat each *Land* contingent voted as a unit. Thus it was calculated that eighteen of the Bundesrat votes were a certainty for the Treaties, and fifteen certain to vote against. In the middle were the five votes of Baden-Württemberg, controlled by Dr. Maier, which could tip the balance either way and were anything but certain. This uncertainty was dictated by the fact that Dr. Maier, although a member of the Free Democrats, who were partners in the Bonn Coalition and supported the Treaties, ruled in Baden-Württemberg by means of a tenuous coalition with the Social Democrats. The Socialists had made it plain that if Dr. Maier followed his own party's line and cast his five votes for the Treaties, they would destroy his coalition Government. To a statesmanlike leader, the choice would have presented no difficulty, but Dr. Maier, although a personality of greatest charm and in other ways a public figure of a stamp all too rare in Germany, was no statesman. For nearly a month the whimsical and waggish old Swabian held the limelight, manifestly with the greatest relish, while all the Bonn pundits attempted to divine which way he would jump. During that short period, he held within his hands the most terrifying power: if he decided to cast his votes against the Treaties, they would have to be presented anew to the Bundestag and the whole tedious process of ratification started all over again.

Eventually Dr. Maier dithered, and in an attempt to save his Government he found a compromise acceptable to his Socialist partners, and decided not to decide. It was an unworthy action. On April 24th the Bundesrat voted by twenty ballots (of which five were Maier's) to eighteen to postpone a final vote until the Constitutional Court had given a ruling on the Treaties. A complete deadlock threatened, since the Court had already stated that it would not pass judgment until the Treaties had passed through all the stages of legislation and become law. Dr. Adenauer was furious at the irresolution of Dr. Maier, and threatened at a press conference held the same day to by-pass the Bundesrat and send the bills direct to the President for his signature. Under the Constitution, he said, the Bundesrat had fourteen days from the time in which its debates opened, either to approve a bill or submit objections. However, Professor Heuss, still apparently smarting from the Chancellor's treatment after the second reading in December, would not this time be moved. He insisted on honoring his promise to the Social Democrats and persuaded Dr. Adenauer that any attempt to secure ratification without approval of the Bundesrat would undermine the moral force of the Treaties. Once again confusion reigned in Bonn.

Dr. Adenauer's next move was to get into touch with the leader of the Refugee Party (BHE), Herr Waldemar Kraft, whose party, although not yet represented in the Federal Parliament, played a key role in the Socialist-controlled coalition Government of Lower Saxony. Herr Kraft had spoken up in favor of the Treaties, and now Dr. Adenauer was prevailing upon him to abandon the Socialists and form a new coalition with the Christian Democrats in Lower Saxony. Lower Saxony's five votes would thus swing the issue for the Government, regardless of Dr. Maier. Herr Kraft's fee for this switch of allegiances, *Der Spiegel* reported at the time, was two seats in the Federal Cabinet in the next Government. It was a fee he subsequently collected, but for another service related to the Treaties (see Chapter 14).

Meanwhile Dr. Maier, somewhat alarmed by the commotion he had caused and under heavy pressure from his own party, was now finding the limelight a little uncomfortable. Making a second compromise, which remarkably enough satisfied both sides, Maier decided to take a vote on only two parts of the Treaties — those dealing with finance and Allied troops — and let the rest by-pass the Bundesrat. The Government was appeased because its legal pundits had all along insisted that these were the only two parts which came strictly within the Bundesrat's competence, insofar as they affected the various *Länder*. The Opposition were pleased because their legalists were certain that the Constitutional Court would eventually rule that the Treaties had to be passed in entirety by both Chambers, and so, like "snakes and ladders," the Government would have to start all over again.

On May 15th the Bundesrat ratified by twenty-three to fifteen. Only President Heuss' signature remained to complete the work; Western Germany was still the first of the six EDC countries to get the Treaties through its Parliament, and Dr. Maier still ruled in Baden–Württemberg.

Dr. Maier's reputation, however, suffered severely from the episode and he was widely attacked for bringing pettifoggery to national politics. His government, and with it his post of *Land* Prime Minister which he had held uninterruptedly since 1945, survived only until the September elections, when Dr. Adenauer's Christian Democrats surged in.

It was the greatest pity that Maier had ever found himself in a position of having to make a decision of national importance. His undoing came about because the affairs of the *Land,* to which he was devoted, were of more importance to him than the Federation. In Baden–Württemberg he had reigned for eight years like a benevolent emperor, and he was probably the most beloved *Land* Prime Minister of post-war Germany. He is one of the few genuine Liberals of the old school left in the Free Democrat Party, and a true independent, a nearly extinct breed in Germany. His independent spirit, combined with strong anti-clericalism, brought him into bitter conflict with Dr. Adenauer. He resented the Chancellor's autocratic manner, and was one of the very few German politicians who not only dared to cross swords with him, but often came off best with his pointed shafts of Swabian wit. On one occasion when he was being brow-beaten by Dr. Adenauer for his Bundesrat stand, I attended a banquet given by Dr. Maier (a renowned *bon viveur*) at his official residence, the Villa Reitzenstein, in Stuttgart. We were amused to discover that the excellent wine our host produced was called "Poor Konrad." In his speech later, Maier explained that "Poor Konrad" was a historical Swabian figure from the Peasants' War; a tyrannical and autocratic farmer who had oppressed his contemporaries. The parallel to a living namesake was fairly pointed. One felt that Maier had allowed his personal hostility to Dr. Adenauer to influence his decision in the Bundesrat. It was a regrettable interlude, but in the long run perhaps a healthy sign that there are such independent-minded Liberals as Reinhold Maier in the Federal Republic, especially within the nationalist-inundated Free Democrat Party.

Meanwhile events of greatest moment to Germany were taking place in the outside world. On April 19th the East German Parliament heralded a new Soviet gambit on Germany in a letter to the House of Commons urging it to join in demanding the prompt summoning of a Four Power conference to consider "the German question." Noting this, and encouraged by the series of small conciliatory gestures made by the Soviets since the death of Stalin in March, Sir Winston Churchill, on May 11th, delivered his famous "Locarno" speech in the Commons. Recalling the original Locarno Treaty whereby Great Britain undertook to come to the help of either Germany or France if attacked by the other, he threw out the hint that this might be the way to tackle Russo-German relations. At the same time he advocated Four Power talks "at the top" to take place at the earliest opportunity. The proposals were received with little enthusiasm in the States, although the notion of an "Eastern Locarno" was taken more seriously than Sir Winston probably intended at the time.

In the Federal Government the speech, in spite of Sir Winston's moving assurance to the contrary, reawakened old dormant fears that the Western Allies might just conceivably make a deal with the Russians one day at the expense of Germany. The *Rheinische Post,* which represents Dr. Adenauer's views, commented, "We Germans naturally react more soberly and skeptically than the House of Commons. We experienced the failure of the first Locarno Treaty, and, as a result of our special position, we are bound to be suspicious of negotiations between East and West."

Dr. Adenauer's two-day visit to Sir Winston later in May went further to reassure him, but when plans for calling the Three Power Bermuda Conference were announced, the Federal Government wanted something more concrete. At the end of May, the Chancellor sent his special emissary, Herr Blankenhorn, on a secret mission to the US. It was a form of diplomacy which attracted Dr. Adenauer, and which reminded one of the muffled and mysterious envoys employed by another great Catholic statesman, Cardinal Richelieu. While the Bonn Foreign Office was denying all knowledge that he had left the country, Herr Blankenhorn was in Washington requesting that Western Germany be permitted to send an observer to attend the Bermuda Conference. The request was further pressed by Dr. Adenauer himself in Bonn in a talk with Dr. Conant, the US High Commissioner, on the eve of his departure for Washington. It was refused, but a week later President Eisenhower cabled Dr. Adenauer the assurance that no decision would be taken at the Bermuda Conference concerning Germany without prior consultation of the Federal Government. Professor Hallstein, Dr. Adenauer's State Secretary in the Foreign Office, hastened to qualify that the assurance would presumably be valid not only for the coming conference, but also for all future talks on Germany. It was a notable victory for Germany and an important principle had been established.

9

The Naumann Plot

IN THE MIDST OF DR. ADENAUER'S ATTEMPTS TO HAVE THE treaties ratified, a bomb exploded in Western Germany that set off a powerful shock wave abroad. On January 15, 1953, the British authorities had arrested seven ex-Nazis in the small hours of the previous night. They were stated to be the ring-leaders of a group plotting to seize power in Federal Germany. They were:

Dr. Werner Naumann, 43, secretary of state in the Goebbels propaganda ministry, and nominated to succeed Goebbels in Hitler's testament. A Nazi party member since 1928 (then aged 19), captain in the SS and currently in charge of export department of Firma Lucht, an export-import firm in the Ruhr.

Dr. Gustav Scheel, 45, former "Reich Student Leader" and Gauleiter of Salzburg, nominated in Hitler's testament as Minister of Culture. When arrested, a physician in a Hamburg clinic.

Herr Paul Zimmermann, 57, former SS "Brigade-Führer." As an official in the SS economic and administrative department, dealt with the operation of Nazi concentration camps. Currently an adviser to the Iron and Steel Industry Association in the Ruhr.

Dr. Heinrich Haselmeyer, 46, an early member of the Nazi Party, who took part in the abortive Munich Putsch of 1923. Head of the Nazi Student's League in Hamburg and ranked as an expert on "racial science" and sterilization of the unfit.

Herr Heinz Siepen, former Nazi district leader and provincial councillor, currently part-owner of the Punktal steelworks in Solingen.

Dr. Karl Scharping, 44, former official in the broadcasting department of the Goebbels Ministry.

Herr Karl Kaufmann, 52, former Gauleiter of Hamburg; joined Nazi Party in 1921, interned by Allies from 1945–8.

At the same time a warrant was issued for an eighth man, *Dr. Karl Friedrich Bornemann,* editor of the "Independent German Newspaper Service," who happened to be on holiday in the American Zone, where he prudently remained until the British handed over the other seven men to the German authorities.

The operation was planned and carried out in a most clandestine fashion, equalled only by the school-boyish secrecy observed by the British High Commission on the activities of the Naumann group long after the details had appeared in the German press. Only a handful of people in both the High Commission and the German Section of the Foreign Office knew of what was afoot. The US and French High Commissioners — and, worse still, Dr. Adenauer himself — were only informed of the action a few hours before the arrests were due to take place, and after all orders had been given. Dr. Otto John, the chief of the Western German security service, who was then still held in high esteem, and had provided the British with most of the material on Naumann, was not informed until after the arrests had been made.

The first official statements on the arrests were somewhat vague. In the Commons, Mr. Eden explained that, while the information possessed so far was not such as to establish that the activities of this small minority of unrepentant Nazis was an immediate threat to the democratic order in Germany, their potentiality for the future could not be ignored. The arrests had been carried out by the British, rather than the German authorities, because the Occupation Statute provide Britain with wider powers than the Germans. The law invoked was No. 14, concerning the safeguarding of the "security and prestige of the Allied Forces." The security of the British Occupation forces was threatened, because, the British authorities were led to believe, Naumann's plans aimed at the expulsion of the Allied Forces from Germany, once he had gained power.

In his first press conference in Bonn, Sir Ivone Kirkpatrick, the British High Commissioner and the man who had advised the Cabinet of the necessity for the arrests, explained that the arrested men had had bad political pasts and were obviously still "in cahoots together." They were also in touch with "dubious Germans abroad." Their aim, said Sir Ivone, was to gain power by infiltrating existing political parties. They were like "Chinese pirates," he thought, who "entered ships in the form of harmless looking passengers, and later stormed the bridge and put the captain in irons." But he added, "We really don't know what Mr. Naumann and his friends are up to. We've arrested them to find out." It was not very convincing, but the fact that an essentially *laissez-faire* British Government, should have viewed the Naumann danger so seriously as to take the action they did was sufficient to cause the very greatest alarm abroad.

On the morning of the arrests, I was on my way back from a holiday, via London. I rashly paid a visit to the *Daily Telegraph* buildings in Fleet Street, where I was questioned from all sides about Naumann and Co. I had to admit that until that day I had never heard of any of the arrested men. The atmosphere was somewhat cool; if a correspondent had for months been sitting virtually on top of what at first appeared to be a major plot to overthrow the German government, without knowing anything about it, obviously he could not have been very alert.

On returning to Bonn the following week, I found with some relief that none of my colleagues had been any better informed than I. (That is, with the exception of the correspondent of a small Danish newspaper, who had noted in a dispatch printed in November an account of the nefarious activities of a certain Dr. Naumann in Düsseldorf.) And there was little to be gleaned from the British High Commission, whose reticence on the whole subject had been intensified by a most regrettable lapse in press ethics. The arrests had received a bad press — in England as well as in Germany — so Sir Ivone decided to convene an intimate group of three "responsible" British correspondents, two from newspapers plus the BBC man, to "correct misapprehensions" in an *off-the-record* briefing. Ill-advisedly, he excluded the *Daily Express*. According to a correspondent who was there, Sir Ivone contributed singularly little new light to illuminate the arrests, but just contrived to "look wise and mysterious," while making remarks in a rather sophomoric vein about "not wanting to be hit on the head by an ex-Nazi." A disappointed correspondent, who of all people should have known better, inexcusably "leaked" to a news agency — with the result that a somewhat distorted version of the whole briefing appeared in the next day's *Daily Express*. Some embarrassing questions were fired at Mr. Eden in the Commons. From that time until his departure in the autumn Sir Ivone retired into a shell well nigh impenetrable to the press at large.

The lamentable handling of publicity by the British High Commission throughout the Naumann affair provoked the weirdest and most dangerous misconstructions in the German press. The reasons for the arrests given out by the British were almost universally not accepted at their face value. The fact that business documents of the Firma Lucht had been seized in evidence at once gave rise to the theme of "British commercial jealousy" — a favorite one in all Anglo-German disputes. The refrain was even taken up in the DUD, the official commentary of the Christian Democrat Party. German public opinion was widely hostile to the arrests, largely because it felt that eight years after the war the occupation authorities had no right to haul German citizens out of their beds, and fling them into prison for months without a trial. Unfounded allegations of "brutality" by the British security policemen increased their indignation, which was mingled with a certain ridicule when an eye-witness reported that Dr. Scheel, Naumann's No. 2 man, had "just sat down and laughed" when the British came. No Germans were convinced of the need for the arrests, and their doubts were not diminished by Dr. Adenauer's first comments.

"Doubtless," said Dr. Adenauer on January 19, "the activities deserved closest observation," but, he added, "what immediate cause led to this arrest is not known to me. Up till now I have received no material about the activity of this National Socialist group. I am personally of the opinion that a conspiracy of seven people, behind whom stand at the most another few dozen others, as yet signifies no threat to the security of the Federal Republic . . . I can only promise that the German authorities would themselves have intervened if there had been enough material for an arrest." Dr. Adenauer felt deeply incensed that he, as head of a government trusted in all other matters by the Allies, had not been informed by Sir Ivone of the intended action in advance — especially as it might well have had a vital effect on the coming Federal elections. He was further angered by the results of a public opinion poll put out a few days after the Naumann arrests by the US High Commission — again without his knowledge. According to the American findings there had been "a significant rise in nationalism among the German public in the last 18 months." Out of 1,200 Germans questioned, in May, 1952, 34 per cent had thought there was "more good than evil in Nazism," whereas in December, 1953, the total had risen to 44 per cent. It was not clear whether the 1,200 people had been the same in each case. The report deduced sweepingly that "attitudes have shifted from preponderantly internationalist in the middle of 1951 to preponderantly nationalist in late 1952." To both the British and the American actions, the German Chancellor replied coldly and prophetically, "Even in the forthcoming elections, any party that sympathizes with National Socialism in any form, should such a party emerge, will suffer a decisive defeat." Dr. Adenauer's view was at first shared by all the West German leaders except the Socialists, who, quick to make a little political capital, claimed that the arrests showed the "pronounced internal danger for the Federal Republic from the subversion by neo-Fascist elements of parties to the right of the Social Democrats." But they added that it was "regrettable that the measures had to be taken by an occupation power."

Far and wide other anti-Nazi voices were highly critical of the net effect the "martyrdom" of the seven men by the Occupation Powers might have in Germany. Paul Sethe in the *Frankfurter Allgemeine* of January 22 scoffed: "Kirkpatrick has created more Nazis in eight days than Naumann and the seven have been able to do by the sweat of their brow for years." The *Düsseldorfer Nachrichten* refused to believe that the Naumann plot was more than a "political tea party" until "hard proof" could be produced.

At the time of writing, no "hard proof" has yet been produced by the British authorities, although nearly two years have elapsed since the original arrests. Feeble reasons, such as the case being still *sub judice,* have been adduced, but such considerations have not hindered the Germans from airing the evidence minutely both in the press and on the radio; and indeed a lengthy British White Paper on Naumann was all ready to be issued in August, 1953, when it was withdrawn at the last moment on Cabinet instructions, for reasons which never have been made quite clear. In fact the fullest account of the Naumann "conspiracy" yet made public appeared in the *Frankfurter Rundschau* in a series of five articles in June, 1953. The author, Fried Wesemann, mysteriously had access to the documents handed over to the German government when the British passed on responsibility for prosecuting the case on April 1st. The *Rundschau* articles can thus be taken as presenting a reliable account of Naumann's activities, and I consider them worth referring to in some detail.

Naumann first re-emerged on the political scene in 1950, on joining the Firma Lucht in Düsseldorf. From Hugh Trevor-Roper's "The Last Days of Hitler," one learns that Naumann had been one of the Nazi courtiers remaining in the Berlin *Führerbunker* up till the last minute. He was one of the last to take leave of Hitler on the afternoon of his suicide, and then made his way through the street-fighting in Berlin, together with Martin Bormann [1] and Artur Axmann, the leader of the Hitler Youth. Bormann — on Axmann's testimony — was killed, but he and Naumann escaped through the Russian lines. During the intervening five years, Naumann lived quietly, in semi-hiding, at Tübingen in the French Zone, and later at Frankfurt in the US Zone. For a good part of this time, he worked as a bricklayer. Miraculously — but without trying unduly hard — he escaped the Allied denazification net, which caught far smaller fish than he.

Naumann found his way to Düsseldorf through an old acquaintance of former times, Herr Herbert Lucht, who had worked as cultural adviser in the Propaganda Ministry detachment in France, and had now gone into business. According to the *Frankfurter Rundschau,* both Herr Lucht and his Belgian born wife "Silky" Lucht (She had been a member of Leon Degrelle's fascist "Rexist" movement.) shared Naumann's political views. Following the death of Herr Lucht, Naumann went to live with Frau Lucht in the house which was also the firm's business headquarters. It was apparently at this time that the idea of forming the "Gauleiter Group" began to take shape in Naumann's mind.

It was Naumann's habit to jot down his thoughts in the form of a diary. In one of the earliest entries, in August, 1950, Naumann described how a Nazi monumental sculptor, Arno Breker, warned him to be cautious in his plans, and not allow himself to be "driven along." Later in the same month Naumann recorded a conversation with Dr. Ernst Achenbach,[2] an Essen lawyer who had been on Otto Abetz's embassy staff in occupied Paris. "In order to provide the National Socialists, in spite of everything, with influence in political life," Naumann said, "they must join the Free Democrat Party, undermine it and take over the

[1] Martin Bormann was Hitler's private secretary and executor, the third man in the Nazi hierarchy. His body was never found, and the exact circumstances of his death remain a mystery.

[2] Achenbach later became a deputy for the FDP in the Land Diet, as well as chairman of the foreign affairs committee of the party. He was expelled from this post following disclosures made in the Naumann case. He acted as Naumann's lawyer in the first part of the judicial hearings.

leadership." He believed that no more than 200 men would be required to "inherit" the whole of the party's largest and most important regional branch: North Rhine Westphalia. According to the entry, Achenbach had urged Naumann to take over the post of secretary-general. Naumann, not being a Remer or a Ramcke, had no desire for the time being for a place in the open. His plan was first to regain contact with old friends, gain a foothold in an established party and in the ex-soldiers' organizations, while at the same time rallying together the various extreme nationalist factions.

The nucleus of the "old friends" association was called the "Gauleiter Group." It met periodically, generally in Düsseldorf or Hamburg, with about 30 members. Greatest care was taken to conceal these meetings and on at least one occasion rooms were booked in a hotel under a false name. Naumann was the undisputed head of the group, with Dr. Scheel as his second in command, and the SS administrator, Zimmermann, number three and responsible for organization. Zimmermann was useful to Naumann for his relations with heavy industrialists in the Ruhr, and also for his contacts with General Neguib's German advisers, Dr. Wilhelm Voss, and ex-Major General Muenzel. Scheel was in charge of the Gauleiter Group branch in Hamburg; one of his close contacts there was Frau Dönitz, wife of Grand Admiral Dönitz (now serving a twelve-year sentence in Spandau for war crimes but still regarded by many ex-Nazis as Hitler's "legal" successor). Scheel had taken part in the founding in 1949 of the *Brüderschaft* (Brotherhood), the first Nazi manifestation to arise after the war. Its president was the former Gauleiter of Hamburg, Karl Kaufmann, who through Scheel, now also attached himself to the Naumann group. Other leading members were Artur Axmann (Naumann's old friend from bunker days), and Herr Beck-Broichsitter, later to be arrested by the German authorities as a leader of the Freikorps (see below). The "incorrigibles" moved in a tight circle. The *Brüderschaft* itself had been riven by internal disputes and collapsed in 1951; its founder, Alfred Franke-Grieksch, ex-SS colonel, disappeared to the Soviet Zone and has not been seen since. Such is the eternal intimacy between Nazism and Bolshevism; it is remarkable that Naumann's group appears to have been the only neo-Nazi organism not to have received financial assistance from the East.

The roll calls of the ex-Gauleiters and high SS officials present at the various meetings of the Gauleiter Group read like a page from some nightmare Who's Who of the Third Reich. The object of the group was eventually to form the general staff of the "National Opposition," the new political party which Naumann intended to create by infiltration and consolidation out of the existing parties of the right; the FDP, the DP and the BHE, and the various small extremist groups. At two big meetings of the Gauleiter Group in November, 1952, Naumann unfolded his program. Apart from infiltration within the political parties, loyal ex-Nazis were to get positions in local councils; "Try to become Councillors and Mayors, and then all join hands in a new Office for Local government . . . in short, penetrate into public life in all its branches, and when these — either all or only some of them — have been won over, then the hour for a united front will have arrived; then we should come forward and declare that, in addition to the parties licensed by the Allies, there is also an independent Germany." Naumann continued, "Let us form a dedicated company of a few hundred men and we shall become a power which, though as yet in the background, will one day achieve, before the eyes of the world, those ideals for which we once stood and for which our comrades fell." For this purpose, "political leadership cadres" were to be formed. Naumann saw great hopes for the future in the ranks of the "disgruntled and non-voters" (meaning those ex-Nazis who had lost their electoral privileges through denazification laws), who had supported Remer's SRP as "a lesser evil." Urging caution upon his followers, he admonished: "To prepare the field, sow and reap, cannot be done in one labor. Let us first cultivate the soil."

To Naumann, as erstwhile henchman of Dr. Goebbels, the dissemination of propaganda was to play a large role in "cultivating the soil." The group's principal organ was the news service put out by Dr. Bornemann, "Commentaries, Reports and Information." Articles by Naumann and others, often under aliases, were also printed in "Nation Europa," a Coburg periodical. This organ seems to have had special importance to Naumann, who went to considerable lengths to assure its solvency. To this end, the *Frankfurter Rundschau* states, "Naumann received help in greatest secrecy from a Paris fascist group, to which belonged . . ." a series of names . . . including that of Prof. Maurice Bardeche. According to a statement made by Dr. Adenauer after he had seen the documents, Naumann had received "not inconsiderable" sums from "French, British and Belgian sources, including Leon Degrelle and Sir Oswald Mosley." This was promptly denied by Mosley.

Naumann also had his tentacles on the rabidly nationalist newspaper of the North Rhine Westphalia FDP, *Deutsche Zukunft,* run by Siegfried Zoglmann, an area leader of the Hitler Youth, and Dr. Drewitz, a former official of the Propaganda Ministry. The *Frankfurter Rundschau* published two intercepted telephone conversations between Naumann and Drewitz. In one Naumann proposed a Dr. Josef Mahlberg, an ex-employee of Goebbels, for an editorial· post on the paper. The *Rundschau* commented "the conversations show the absolute submissiveness of Dr. Drewitz to Naumann," his former chief. It added, "It is also clear that these National Socialists regard the FDP paper as being completely in their pockets." Another contact from old times, now also in the FDP, was the late Hans Fritzsche,[3] Naumann's immediate superior in the Goebbels Ministry, whose *Sword in the Scales* had just been published, more or less whitewashing the defendants at the Nuremberg Trial.

The immediate propaganda aim of the group was apparently to correct current notions on Nazism held in Germany. In addition to the above means, Naumann arranged for the distribution privately to Ruhr industrialists and selected political figures, of the first 8,000 copies of a book called *Auch du warst dabei.* This was

[3] Fritzsche was one of the three top-ranking Nazis to be acquitted at Nuremberg.

a clever and extremely plausible apologia for Nazism, interpreted as an inevitable manifestation forced upon Germany by the crassness of pre-war European politicians, and justified by post-war trends. Its author, Dr. Peter Kleist, and publisher, Kurt Vowinckel, were also in touch with the Gauleiter Group.

In explaining the new line to be propagated, Naumann warned his disciples against trotting out "the old records," which "no longer play accurately." "For this reason," said Naumann, "we are no neo-Fascists, because for us the past is past. We have progressed from the theories of National Socialism . . . the Badenweiler March and new banners are not for us. We need a new style, new slogans, new conceptions, a new language, if we want to give our people another political shape. This style will not be over-emphatic, propagandist or extravagant, but strictly matter-of-fact and serious-minded." In his diary, Naumann left no doubt as to his own personal bonds to the past, "one cannot betray an ideal to which, from youth, one was so dedicated as we were. Perhaps there lies hidden in the debris of the Reich Chancellery more of value to us than our hasty critics to-day can imagine." He appears to have been genuinely opposed to the "mistakes" committed by the Nazis, such as the concentration camps and anti-semitism, and felt that German public opinion would have to be reassured on these scores before the "National Opposition" could sweep to success. He thought it would be impossible to replace the figure of Hitler in the present century, but believed that leadership would have to be exerted by a "central elite." In foreign affairs, Naumann presented the issue between East and West as a striking justification of Hitler's anti-Bolshevism. But he was afraid of Germany being used by the West. He favored European integration (on his terms): "We feel ourselves, as a people, to be strong enough and intelligent enough to enforce our claim to leadership in a Europe freed from national barriers." With regard to the present democratic order in Germany, Naumann commented, "The forthcoming Bundestag is a transitional parliament — let's hope the last."

Naumann had a fear of a monkey-wrench which might be

thrown into his political works: "In only one respect can our foes at home and abroad strike at us; if they succeed in persuading our people that we are wild men, radicals, not in earnest, and striving only to precipitate Germany into some new adventure." It was dangerous to tell the world, "You think we are dead? Not at all — here we are again!" For this reason he was contemptuous of the loud-mouthed Remers, and highly critical of the Verden outburst by General Ramcke, whom he warned, "next time, proceed more carefully and I shall be pleased to give you assistance." Before launching out into the open, Naumann felt that the "National Opposition" would have to be assured of 20 per cent of the German vote.

The sharpest rebuff Naumann received was from the ex-soldiers' associations. He had started off well in 1951 by becoming "a sort of political adviser" (*Frankfurter Rundschau*) to General Heinz Guderian, the famous wartime tank general, and SS General Paul Hausser. Through Guderian, Naumann hoped to infiltrate into the newly formed "Association of German Soldiers," but Guderian fell ill and Naumann's plans were thwarted by the ex-soldiers themselves. He met with similar failure in the *German Soldiers Newspaper,* which exerted considerable influence over the veterans, but whose editor, Uhlig, swung over to moderation and the support of Adenauer in the summer of 1952. Naumann's best contacts among the veterans, the *Rundschau* noted, were the ex-SS elite, and such heroes abroad as Otto Skorzeny (the man who carried off Mussolini) and the Luftwaffe ace now in Argentina, Hans Rudel. It was through Naumann's influence and clever flattery that Rudel returned to the Federal Republic to fight without success the election campaign in September.

But the ground which offered most promise to the Gauleiter Group lay within the North Rhine Westphalia branch of the FDP, headed by Dr. Friedrich Middelhauve. At its annual congress held at Bielefeld in July, 1952, the regional branch had launched its unashamedly nationalistic *Deutsches Programm* which was to split the nominally "liberal" FDP from top to bottom.

No vote was taken on the program at the national congress of the FDP at Bad Ems in November, 1952, but Middelhauve won a notable victory by forcing the congress to elect two deputy chairmen instead of one — the second being himself.

The *Deutsches Programm* proclaimed its intention to "overcome Germany's deepest humiliation through new thinking and determined behavior." Laws which had brought about "inequality between German citizens" were to be repealed and compensation granted equally to those wronged by "National Socialism, [and] oppression by the victors and denazification. We absolve ourselves of the Allied judgments, which have discriminated against our people, and in particular its soldierhood. Germany can and never shall renounce the right of the expellees to regain their homes," but the Western world, which "shared responsibility for these expulsions," must help the over-burdened West German government to finance the temporary rehabilitation of these expellees. In industry, the *Programm* required the "responsible cooperation of the workers and the moral subjection of the individual to the common good." Finally, the aim of the *Deutsches Programm* was a "fatherland united in freedom and bound together in peaceful work that *heute Deutschland ist und morgen Europa sein soll.*" The words seemed familiar and the whole program frighteningly regressive. It would seek to place on a par those who had been persecuted for being Nazis with those whom the Nazis had persecuted, which would undoubtedly prove attractive to many of the 6-8 million ex-party members. The *Deutsches Programm* was certainly the sort of "soil" Naumann was seeking for "cultivation," and its conceiver, Dr. Middelhauve, provided an ideal cover behind which the ex-Nazis could operate.

Dr. Middelhauve described the political meanderings which had led to the *Deutsches Programm* at a Foreign Press Association lunch three weeks after the Naumann arrests, which cast a shadow on his reputation. His intellectual vanity was enormous: "I was educated by one of the greatest stylists in Germany," he said. "In 1931 I associated with the Nazis, but purely out of intellectual curiosity." To ascribe to him neo-Nazi tendencies now would be "utmost madness." From his experiences in the Weimar Republic, he considered the Federal Republic should become a "military democracy" with three duties:

1. To assimilate the ex-soldiers into politics.

2. To assimilate the ex-Nazis: "otherwise the young ex-Nazis will be forced towards the Remers and the Dorlses, where they could become a real danger."

3. To avoid splitting the parties. Thus there should be three big parties, CDU, SPD and an expanded FDP to combine "liberal and conservative elements to the right of the CDU."

The second idea was undoubtedly a praiseworthy one in theory and probably quite sincere, but one questioned whether Dr. Middelhauve was the right man to carry it out. At this same lunch, Rix Loewenthal of the *Observer* told Dr. Middelhauve (much to the latter's amusement) "in my opinion, you are far more dangerous than Dr. Naumann." In the *Rundschau* revelations, Middelhauve appeared more as a fool than a knave. (The *Rundschau* described Middelhauve as a "strange mixture of audacity and naïveté.") Referring to conversations between Naumann and Drewitz, the *Rundschau* commented: "It leaves no doubt that the Regional Chairman was nothing more than a man-of-straw to these National Socialists." But, as such, as the revelations showed, Middelhauve did assume a potentially far more dangerous role than if his post had been filled by a discredited ex-Nazi such as Remer, or Naumann himself.

The *Rundschau* thought that "the greatest success" for Naumann came with the infiltration of "his intimate political friend and former subordinate Wolfgang Diewerge" into the post of private secretary and "political adviser" to Middelhauve himself. Within a short space of time, Diewerge had gained sufficient influence over his new chief to effect the entree of a second Naumann candidate, Herr Lindner, as second assistant to Middelhauve. Through the offices of Diewerge, the draft of the *Deutsches Programm* was on Naumann's desk a week *before* it was announced at Bielefeld. The *Rundschau* commented, "From the list of the principal organizers of the Düsseldorf regional branch of the FDP, it is to be noted that, with very few exceptions, nobody was employed who had not held a post in Nazi administration." Further, such ex-Nazis as were in touch with Naumann "took no step within a democratic party without consulting the former Goebbels State Secretary and his collaborators." Middelhauve seems to have been genuinely oblivious of the degree to which his personal staff had been infiltrated by Naumann. He told the FDP commission of inquiry: "Herr Diewerge sits in the office next to mine. He writes no line that I do not read, he speaks no word that I do not hear, he does nothing I do not know about."

Another important figure in the FDP regional branch, the extent of whose association with the Gauleiter Group still remains something of a mystery, was Dr. Ernst Achenbach (see footnote [2] above), the extremely clever lawyer who took up Naumann's defense, later to relinquish it because of the "international press campaign" he said had been waged against him. According to the British evidence, Achenbach had effected a direct contact between Middelhauve and Naumann at the end of 1952. He had also kept up useful contacts in departments of the Federal Government which enabled him to promise Naumann that a German visa might be granted to Otto Skorzeny in Madrid. As friend and legal adviser to Hugo Stinnes, Jr., the industrialist, he was able to provide Naumann with links to the Ruhr. On the day Naumann and Co. were handed over to the Germans, Achenbach told me that he viewed his relationship to them as "a missionary who goes among the Africans to teach them the real religion"; his mission was to teach the ex-Nazis the "free thoughts" of the FDP — that was all. Nevertheless, the FDP later found it wise to dismiss Achenbach as chairman of the party's Foreign Affairs committee, although he remained in the party, and regained his seat in the local Diet in the following year's Land elections.

According to the *Rundschau,* Naumann had a valuable ally in the Lower Saxon FDP, in the shape of its obese and unattractive chairman, Artur Stegner — although he later did a Simon-Peter on Naumann, denouncing him as an "incorrigible element." Stegner was reported to Naumann in May, 1952, by one of his talent scouts as "the only opponent of Dr. Adenauer" within the FDP. A meeting between the two took place in Naumann's flat on June 11th of the same year, after which Stegner claimed (the *Rundschau* stated) "he was in contact with a number of former high National Socialists, including Naumann and the ex-Gauleiter Kaufmann, with the purpose of setting up a National Opposition Party." The aim of it, said Stegner, would be "to combat the one-sided dependence of the Chancellor upon the West."

Naumann further established close contact with the various right wing splinter groups, which, although holding little brief for the ability of their leaders, he hoped one day to draw into the "National Opposition." These included organizations with such fanciful sounding names as the "League of Germans True to the Homeland," "The German Community," "The Working Community of the National Groups," and the *Deutsche Reichspartei*. For the latter Naumann eventually stood, *faute de mieux,* as candidate in the 1953 Federal Elections. But Naumann contemptuously referred to Remer's outlawed SRP as a "short circuit," and refused to associate with its leaders.

Another Nazi organization worthy of note was the *Freikorps Deutschland,* which was attached to Dr. Scheel's branch of the Gauleiter Group in Hamburg. A month after the Naumann arrests the Freikorps was banned by the Germans and four of its leaders, including Herr Alfred Frauenfeld, the former Gauleiter of Vienna, were arrested. The Freikorps took its name from those bands of thugs who had roamed Germany in the chaotic days immediately after World War I, and had to their credit such deeds as the murder of Rathenau and Erzberger. Its modern namesake had as its patron Col. Rudel; it recognized Dönitz as legal head of the German state; approved Nazi persecution of the Jews; and aimed mystically at the creation of a *Grosses Reich* which was to be a combination of those races in Europe which still possessed vitality — the Germans and the Slavs! It was considered by the British authorities to "compare to the Naumann group in intent, but not in importance." Nevertheless, as a Nazi cosmos in miniature, its activities were most revealing. According to a German journalist friend of mine, who had made it his business to get closely in touch with such movements, the Freikorps consisted of about 1,000-2,000 adherents, divided into *Freischaren* (volunteer companies) of 113 members each. "Members are filled with an ineradicable Germanic mysticism and blurred phantasies of valor in the cause of the German race. They undergo training to imbue toughness, enduring long marches carrying 50 lbs. of stones in a knapsack, silent marches, nocturnal war games, the waving of flags in the breeze, etc., etc. Theirs is the urge to lead and command, even if the group consists of only 6 men who seek to submit themselves to a 'Führer.' It is impossible to eliminate such tendencies among certain varieties of Germans," my friend concluded sadly.

Toward the end of 1952, Naumann began to show great interest in the BHE (Refugee Party) which had won considerable successes in the recent Land elections, and had good prospects in the coming Federal elections. By December he had managed to hold two meetings with the head of the party, Herr Waldemar Kraft himself. Whatever success Naumann might have achieved in penetrating the BHE was cut short by the British arrests, as was his infiltration of the DP. And here the tale in the *Frankfurter Rundschau* ended.

One of the most unfortunate secondary effects of the Naumann affair was the damage it did to notions of British justice in a country where it has been a major aim for eight years to establish an impartial and democratic judicial system. In a further explanation as to why the British had arrested the ex-Nazis, in preference to the German authorities, Mr. Eden pointed out on January 28th that the Germans did not hold powers to detain for interrogation without preferring a charge. The House gasped when he told them that the material seized filled 30 crates, each measuring 4 ft. by 2 by 2. There were only a handful of British Intelligence officers left in Germany whose German was good enough to help sift the information. Although Herr Heinz Siepen broke down and gave a full "confession" of the Gauleiter Group's activities, Naumann himself proved a hard nut for the interrogators to crack. (At one point, Naumann audaciously asked his interrogator to make an offer to Sir Ivone: "Release me quietly, and I will not exploit it politically or complain about the personal injustice I have suffered.") The conspirators were held incommunicado for over two months before they were even allowed to meet their own lawyers.

Shortly after the arrests, **Dr. Achenbach**, who had taken up Naumann's defense, tried to obtain his release on habeas corpus from the British authorities. The High Commissioner replied that, under Occupation Law, neither habeas corpus, nor the German law which required prisoners to be produced before a judge for the preferring of charges within 24 hours of arrest, were applicable. Thus the ex-Nazis could, in theory, be held indefinitely at the High Commissioner's pleasure. This was not designed to encourage Germans, now in the toils of trying to ratify the EDC and Bonn Conventions. It made them realize that these immense powers, contained in the reserve rights to be retained by the Allies under the Conventions, could still be applied to Germans.

Eventually Achenbach employed Mr. Scott-Henderson, QC, who had defended Sir Oswald Mosley during the war, to force a show-down on habeas corpus rights for Naumann. A hearing was arranged at a High Commission court in Bielefeld for February 20th. There were lively exchanges between the High Commission judge, Sir Norman Edgley, QC, and Mr. Maurice Bathurst, the chief legal adviser to the High Commission. On the first day, Mr. Bathurst said he had "definite instructions" to oppose any meeting between Naumann and his lawyer. The High Commission later explained, "It was essential that none of the detained men should have access to an outsider, particularly his own German counsel, and given an opportunity to discuss matters which were not within the limits of the hearing." Sir Norman Edgley, however, countered sharply, "Do you suggest that I have no jurisdiction to make such an order?" On the following day, Sir Norman overruled

the High Commission ruling, in spite of Mr. Bathurst having received further "categorical instructions" from London overnight.
An appeal against the court order was lodged by Mr. Bathurst.

This display of independence by a High Commission judge
seemed to bewilder Germans following the case. One remarked
to me, "If Kirkpatrick is prepared to go to such authoritarian
lengths to prevent Naumann seeing his lawyer, why didn't he
'organize' the judge as well?" Such was the disrepute into which
British justice had fallen.

The High Commission appeal against Naumann meeting Achenbach was not heard until March 15th, which gave the interrogators further time for their work. The appeal was denied by two
High Commission judges of appeal, Sir Edward Jackson and Mr.
Rogers, who thereupon gave Naumann permission to meet both
his German and British counsels. The meeting took place on the
following day, when Naumann was produced for the first time
in the courtroom at Bielefeld. He said that he had been told nothing about the habeas corpus action. "It was only when I came
through this door and saw the honorable judge that I realized that
some kind of proceedings were afoot." On the same day, Sir Norman Edgley who had resumed the habeas corpus hearing, dismissed the petition by Naumann's lawyers and Naumann was
returned to Werl prison. Sir Norman commented that he found
that the petitioner's arrest and detention were quite legal. The
British High Commissioner had acted by virtue of discretionary
powers to arrest persons engaged or about to engage in activities dangerous to the Allied Forces. "He alone is in a position to
say whether circumstances exist which make it necessary for him
to take this action." The discretionary authority was similar to
that given to the Secretary of State in England under emergency
regulations in wartime.

Petitions by the other ex-Nazis followed, and were dealt with in
a similar manner.

Ten days later, on April 1st — by which time the interrogations
had been completed and all the material collated — the seven
men were unexpectedly handed over to the German authorities,

on the "request" of Dr. Adenauer. Mr. Eden explained in the House, "Our intention from the beginning has been to frustrate a serious potential danger, to bring the facts to light, and to enable the German people to form their own judgment on it." He trusted this purpose would now be served. In Germany, many papers considered the British decision to hand over the cases a tacit admission of failure. Having seen the full evidence, however, both Dr. Adenauer and his Minister of Justice Dr. Dehler of the Free Democrats, modified their earlier skepticism. Dr. Dehler described Naumann as a "cool superior man with a penetrating mind and a remarkable power of speech." Dr. Adenauer said that although "it was ridiculous to think that they could have intended to march on Bonn and arrest all of us," they had "definitely been drawing up plans in the hope that West Germany would face economic and political disintegration some time during the next four years and they hoped to take over at that time."

The release, and acquittal, of the minor members of the Gauleiter Group followed shortly afterwards. Kaufmann had already been released by the British on grounds of ill health; Siepen, Sharping, Haselmeyer, and later Zimmermann and Scheel were set free by the Germans. Meanwhile, Bornemann, cocksure of his acquittal, surrendered himself to the German authorities after his three months sojourn in the US Zone. He would, he said, stand trial as one of the Naumann group, before a German court, but not a British court. Ironically, together with Naumann, he was the last to be released. The release came a year later, June 29, 1954, by which time it was felt that there would be no further prosecutions of the Naumann group. Bornemann and Naumann were charged by the Federal Supreme Court with being "ringleaders of an organization whose aim was hostile to the constitutional order of the Federal Republic." The charges could not be conclusively proved in the hearing before the Supreme Court. On December 3, 1954, proceedings against both Naumann and Bornemann were discontinued. The episode itself seems to have completely disappeared from German thoughts.

Ever since January, 1953, controversy has raged as to the wisdom of the High Commissioner's action against the Naumann group. Were the arrests justifiable, did they achieve their objectives, or did they do more harm than good? There is no doubt that certain facts have emerged from the evidence gleaned by the British. One is that Naumann undoubtedly presented, as Dr. Dehler put it, "a most acute danger" to German democracy. All his utterances showed him to be an unrepentant Nazi, and his activities within the nationalist wing of the FDP were extremely sinister. The British action was effective in (at least temporarily) diminishing the potential danger of Naumann by exposing him, and thus disrupting his carefully planned time-table so that he was forced in the 1953 Federal elections to associate himself, a discredited figure, with one of the splinter extremist parties he so despised, instead of being able to emerge, in his own time, as a powerful figure in an established major party such as the FDP. The really big question was how deep did an essentially retrospective "neo-Nazism" as Naumann's was, really penetrate among the German people? So far, the only convincing answer to this question is found in the results of the 1953 Federal elections.

In spite of the subsequent change of heart by Dr. Adenauer and Dr. Dehler, the British action failed in its secondary objective of convincing the German people that their security was really threatened by the Gauleiter Group. I have already pointed to the deficiencies of British publicity, but there now seems to have been an even graver deficiency in the evidence passed on to the Germans. In the first short British summary of the case given the West German cabinet, the following conclusion was drawn: "When seen as part of the overall West German political scene, then the group was still only a small power, *hardly a direct danger to the security of the Basic Law*." On this basis, and taking account of the material published in the *Frankfurter Rundschau,* it is difficult to believe that a British court would have found sufficient evidence to convict Naumann on grounds of "conspiracy," let alone a court in Germany where the law tends to be somewhat less stringent than the British. To most Germans, the British decision to hand over prosecution of the ex-Nazis was simply "passing the buck." A German lawyer commented to me, "You have put us in the gravest embarrassment; we want to prosecute Naumann, but you have not given us enough evidence; and if a German Court acquits him for lack of evidence, just imagine what your *Daily Express* will say."

If the evidence has turned out to be inadequate, one asks why Sir Ivone ordered the arrests to be carried out when he did. Was the action too premature? Apparently Sir Ivone's intelligence advisers themselves had advised against action at that time. The *Frankfurter Rundschau* reports give the impression that the infiltration activities of the Gauleiter Group had barely got under way and that, if "conspiratorial tendencies" had indeed existed, they would have become far more incriminating over the next few months. Here one cannot help recalling with some disquiet that a very large part of the information on Naumann had been provided by Dr. Otto John. The tragic events following July 20th, 1954, have revealed that he suffered from an extreme "Nazi phobia," and one is forced to wonder how accurate were some of his reports on Naumann's activities. Sir Ivone himself served for a long time under Sir Nevile Henderson, who in March, 1939, had told the Foreign Office, "I believe the Germans want peace very badly," and later wrote, "History will judge the press to have been the cause of the war." Sir Ivone had watched at first hand the terrifying machinations that brought the Nazis to power, and one can well appreciate the alarm he must have felt on reading the reports of Naumann's activities, and understand his instinct not to repeat the errors of his former chief.

The British objective of curing the nationalistic aspirations of the FDP has met with little success. It is true that the FDP suffered a setback in the Federal elections because of the Naumann taint, but the North Rhine Westphalia branch still remained powerful and unrepentant, its leaders unchanged. Herr Diewerge and other minor officials were dropped. Dr. Achenbach was dismissed as chairman of the FDP Foreign Affairs Committee. Herr Stegner was expelled from the party — but for profligacy with party funds, and *not* because of his associations with Naumann. Dr.

Middelhauve survived a party "Court of Honor" and was re-elected vice-chairman of the party. *Deutsche Zukunft,* the organ of the FDP in North Rhine Westphalia, became even more outrageously nationalist, its editorial staff unchanged. Should Dr. Adenauer's European policies suffer further reverses, the nationalist wing of the FDP can be expected to provide a powerful breeze to fan the smouldering disappointment of the population — and if things get really bad, the Naumanns and their followers might well have a better chance the next time.

10

Tightening the Screw

SINCE THE BRUTAL COMMUNIST STEPS TO SEAL OFF THE INTER-
zonal frontier in May, 1952, the misery of the East Germans had
been steadily intensified. The decisive turn of the screw was given
in July of that year by Walter Ulbricht, Secretary-General of the
Socialist Unity Party (SED)[1] — known, unlovingly, as the
Saxon Lenin because of his goatee beard. In a seven-hour speech
at the second party congress, he announced the SED program
for the "building-up of Socialism" in Eastern Germany. It was
made clear that the regime intended within the next twelve
months to hammer East Germany into total and final conformity
with Soviet structure.

The new measures included the speeding-up of an industriali-
zation closely integrated with the Russian economy, ruthless collectivization of agriculture, a judicial reform designed to render
prosecution against "class enemies" yet more Draconian, an administrative reform (or purge of the governmental structure),
and the creation and equipment of the new National Defense
Forces. More power was to be granted to the State, which had,
as one aim, the total liquidation of such private property as had
hitherto remained immune.

[1] A shotgun marriage between the East German Communist and Socialist
parties.

It very soon became apparent that Herr Ulbricht and his Russian overlords were flogging a dead donkey — or if not a dead donkey, at any rate one that threatened to die very soon under its new burden. The Soviet zone economy was in no fit state to accept any new loads.

Since 1945, Eastern Germany had been systematically bled white by the Russians. Twenty-two per cent of the industrial potential had been destroyed in the war. Russian destruction and promiscuous demolition of plants had followed. Then came carefully planned dismantlement and removal eastwards of whole industries. A total of 45 per cent of the East German post-war industrial potential is estimated to have been eliminated by Soviet dismantling. On top of this came astronomic Russian demands for reparations and occupation costs. Although the Russians had, up to December 31st, 1953, acknowledged receipt of only $4,292 million worth of reparations, these are conservatively estimated to have valued in fact $13,570 million, excluding occupation costs, thus far exceeding Russian demands put forward at Yalta for $10,000 million of reparations.

The earliest post-war Soviet plan for their zone appears to have been a sort of Morgenthau Plan for the East, aimed at creating a desert buffer, devoid of both industry and communications, between Russia and the West. Some of the most devastating dislocation caused by the Russian occupation was suffered by the East German railways. Immediately after the war, over one-third of the total railway track length was torn up. Nearly all multiple-track stretches were reduced to single tracks. Under the new Ulbricht program, new stretches of line urgently needed had to be constructed from line scavenged from other parts of the country. Every year, reparations claimed 12 per cent of locomotive production, and no new rolling stock was produced — except for the Soviet occupation forces. By the end of 1952, there were some 1,000 locomotives left to the East Germans, and most of these required constant repair. Fearful accidents caused by worn-out rails and rolling stock were frequent occurrences. In January, 1953, Herr Wollweber, then Secretary of State for transport, took

Konrad Adenauer—Chancellor of the German Federal Republic.

(left) Dr. Adenauer inspects one of his prize-winning roses with the same impassive composure with which he faces all of his accomplishments.

(right) This photograph appeared on a political postcard which carried this inscription: "Have you ever thought about what Konrad Adenauer has done for Germany in the last four years? Think about it on election day, September 6!"

Theodor Heuss—President of the German Federal Republic.

Heinrich von Brentano—Foreign Minister of Germany.

Theodor Blank—Minister of Defense.

Adolf Heusinger—Inspector-General of the German Army.

Ludwig Erhard—Minister of Economics.

Campaign posters of four of Germany's major political parties are displayed on a billboard across the street from the Bonn railroad station.

The Bundestag in session. Its functions approximate those of the House of Representatives.

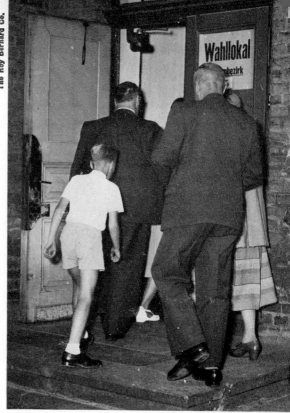

One German family believes their son can learn some of the mechanics of democracy by accompanying them to the polls on election day.

On Sunday, September 6, 1953, more than 28 million West German voters (86 per cent of those eligible) cast their ballots.

(right) East Berlin, June 17, 1953—Rioters raided and set fire to Communist offices, smashed pictures of Stalin and Ulbricht (the "Saxon Lenin"), tore down Communist slogans and burned government files and furniture in the streets.

Leipzig, East Germany, 1952—A rally of the FDJ (Communist Youth Organization) unfortunately reminds one of Hitler's Youth Movement of the Thirties.

Breslau, East Germany (Polish Sector), 1953—The market place is surrounded by the rubble and ruins created during the fighting in 1945.

(below) East Berlin, June 17, 1953—Unarmed, but defiant, East Berliners were finally subdued by the deployment of T34 tanks of the Soviet First Mechanized Division. In Leipzig some 275 tanks (twice the number Rommel had at el Alamein) were called up to quell the rioting.

The Bavarian Alps near Oberau.

The beautiful Moselle valley. The town of Bernkastel is in the foreground and across the river is Kues, the birthplace of Cardinal Cusanus.

The City Hall of Staufen in the Black Forest area dates from 1546. Legend has it that Faust died in Staufen in 1539.

The city gate at Traben-Trarbach, an import town in the Middle Ages, still stands six centuries after its construction.

An example of post-war church architecture in Gmünden am Main. The architect is Hans Schädel.

Reconstruction in Hambu A school is shown bef and after its rebuildi Every usable part of the g ted ruins was salvaged a incorporated into this ha some modern structure.

A modern apartment house in Bonn.

During the 76th Catholic Conference held in September, 1954, over 10,000 children attended Holy mass in front of the famous Fulda Cathedral.

Bayreuth—The Wagner Festival. Kurt Edelmann as Hans Sachs in "Meistersinger."

the traditional line of blaming sabotage by enemy agents for the fact that 10,000 railway trucks were idle — despite the transport crisis — but the real reason was that there were no locomotives and no coal to move them.

In spite of every sort of encouragement to "Stakhanovism," the coal mines in the Soviet zone had proved quite incapable of meeting normal demands, let alone the production now called for by Herr Ulbricht. Long periods of power cuts were already enforced, by the autumn of 1952, on both private consumer and industry alike.

Since the war, approximately two million inhabitants of the Soviet zone had fled west. Many had been technicians, driven from their places of work by Soviet dismantlement. By mid-1952 there was already an acute manpower shortage, and the new National Army, the "voluntary" labor service, the new arms industries, and the extra demands of "socialization" would impose further strain. Agriculture was crippled by labor shortage, and a lack of fertilizers — which were being shipped to Russia as reparations. As an additional blow, the 1952 harvest had failed. All of this hardly provided a sound basis for the Socialist Utopia dreamed of by Herr Ulbricht.

By October, it was clear that the population of Eastern Germany was going to be faced with a winter of semi-famine unless the regime would drop its plans and import food. The following month, deficiencies in food supplies were officially admitted. The Soviet Zone Prime Minister, Herr Grotewohl, castigated the Ministry of Food and Supplies for the shortages. Taking a hint, the Secretary of State in the Ministry, Herr Handke, fled to West Berlin, where he blamed the food crisis on stockpiling for the new army. His Minister, Herr Hamann, was less fortunate and was dismissed, and later sentenced to ten years' hard labor. At the same time, trusted party "activists" were allotted the task of leading brigades through the countryside to force farmers to deliver more. These so-called brigades, which resembled marauding bands from the period of the Thirty Years' War, had powers to dispossess big farmers (those owning fifty acres or more) who had not fulfilled their quota. As the *Berliner Zeitung* boasted, the activities of these brigades had resulted in "open class warfare."

During that winter, the situation became comparable to the desperate days following the end of the war in Germany. There were frequent reports from the Soviet zone of frantic housewives being trampled to death in food queues. Most East Germans — except, of course, the privileged supporters of the regime — were reduced to a diet of bread and frost-ruined potatoes. In East Berlin, a few hundred yards from the luxurious restaurants of the Kurfurstendamm in the western half of the city, State shops were offering carrots blackened by frost at $1.40 a bunch. Hunger drove people to suicide, to the West, or, lured by promises of priority rations, to the National Army.

Meanwhile the State shopping centers (the HO) continued to run a most scandalous national swindle at the expense of the workers, by charging them between four and eight times the price they paid the food producers. This was estimated to have brought the State in nearly 3,000m. DM ($714 million) a year. With a State swindle of such proportions, it was hardly surprising that the *Tägliche Rundschau,* the official organ of the Soviet High Commission in Eastern Germany, in February, 1953, discovered that private embezzlement in the HO had amounted to $3,500,-000 during the first nine months of the previous year.

Far from relinquishing its grandiose planning because of the catastrophic food shortages, the Government used the famine as a pretext to accelerate collectivization. Only in its smaller scale did East German collectivization in 1952-53 differ from the tragic liquidation of the Ukrainian kulaks in the 1920s. Between June, 1952, and May, 1953, the number of collective farms increased from 59 to 4,381. What happened to farm owners will be seen shortly.

The food crisis, the fuel shortage, and the accompanying collapse of overworked and worn-out machinery in the factories also gave the regime pretexts for carrying out wholesale purges envisaged in its "administrative reforms." Purging brigades, similar to those sent out into the country, were dispatched to haul out

"saboteurs of production" from the coal mines and industrial administration. As the identity of prominent victims began to appear in the columns of the East German press, it became increasingly apparent that the underlying slant of the purges was political.
Most of those purged belonged to one or other of the so-called
bourgeois or non-Communist puppet parties — the Christian
Democrats, the Liberal Party (LDP), and the National Democrat Party (NDP). The Socialist Unity Party had already purged
its own ranks of about a million members from 1951, and now
it was determined to consolidate, once and for all, its grasp on
the puppet parties. The arrest of Herr Hamann (chairman of
the LDP) was followed in January by the arrest of Herr Georg
Dertinger, the Foreign Minister and Deputy Chairman of the
East Zone Christian Democrats, for "hostile activity in the service
of the imperialist espionage services." He was sentenced to fifteen years' hard labor.

An unprecedented increase in the numbers of refugees pouring westwards was the immediate and obvious result of all these
concurrent oppressive factors. In April, 1952, refugee figures for
the month totalled 7,700, of which just under half had arrived
directly over the interzonal frontier. By mid January, the rate of
flights had reached 2,000 in one day. Because of the "death
strip" which now stretched along the interzonal frontier, all but
a handful of these came over into West Berlin, where, as yet, the
sector boundaries were still open.

The refugees presented the most tragic and pathetic figures as
they straggled into West Berlin. Most of them had left everything,
not even daring to bring a suitcase or paper parcel for fear that
the People's Police, the hated "Vopos," would see through their
excuse of "visiting relatives in the west." Often families would
split up and come over separately, so as to avoid the attention of
the police.

They included small farmers, driven out of their holdings by the
Communist brigades, youths fleeing from military service or work
in the uranium mines, small shopkeepers and a host of other victims of Communism. As they queued up to register at the Kuno-

Fischerstrasse, the West Berlin refugee center, there were those who seemed set apart, and treated with loathing and suspicion by the rest. They were the party functionaries and small-time State bosses, driven like chaff before the purging wind of the regime they had served.

There were occasionally cases where an enterprising private contractor would crash through the Communist barricades with his truck, towing a trailer with all his possessions. Not all such attempts were successful. On one occasion, West Berlin was nauseated by an account of how a Vopo had run alongside an escaping vehicle, firing repeatedly at point-blank range at the driver, his wife and child. At the reception center in the Kuno-Fischerstrasse, there was a sign warning refugees, "Beware of spies: beware of abduction: don't stray across the sector or zonal boundary." Here the refugees, after waiting hours in a six-deep queue, were given meal tickets and allotted accommodation. This — the best that overtaxed Berlin could provide — usually consisted of a straw palliasse in a hall with 500 others, in what had previously been a bombed-out factory. Families were separated into their male and female contingents, and here, under leaky roofs in bitter cold, and the most primitive conditions, the refugees stayed up to three months until their cases had been thoroughly investigated by the Berlin authorities. Eventually, those fortunate enough to be "recognized" under the rigid West German regulations [2] were either found work and accommodation in West Berlin, or, more often flown to the Federal Republic. The first to go were the easily employable, the able-bodied. For those whom the authorities refused to recognize, who totalled a third of those who fled, the prospects were nearly as grim as if they had remained in the Soviet zone. They were doomed to hover precariously between worlds, like figures out of Dante's *Purgatory*. They became "illegal" residents of West Berlin, re-

[2] The regulations prescribed that only those who "had to leave the Soviet zone because of direct danger to life or limb, to personal freedom or on other urgent grounds" could be recognized. "Urgent grounds" were not considered to include economic oppression, or detestation of the regime for moral reasons.

fused rights to accommodation and work, and denied a *Zuzugs-genehmigung,* or residence permit, without which it is virtually impossible to exist in bureaucratic Western Germany.

This might have been considered fair treatment of the asocial elements who left the Soviet zone because of some offense committed against the civil laws, but it seemed appalling injustice to the farmers and small business men who had been driven out of their private holdings — especially when those granted official asylum also included the despised former toadies of the Communists, who now felt their "life and limb" threatened. As these wretched "illegals" roved through the neon-lit opulence of West Berlin, feeling hungry and unwanted, they became utterly disillusioned and began to wonder whether they had not jumped from the frying pan into the fire. They could not leave Berlin, and thus were forced to find "black" work at starvation wages in a city that already had one-quarter of its total workers unemployed. Many of them, in their despair, fell prey to their old oppressors, the Communists, who inveigled them as "double-agents" into the ranks of one or other of the forty-two Western intelligence agencies in West Berlin. One of the most notable of these was Ruth Schramm, who found a job in the League of Free Jurists, played Judas to her chief, Dr. Linse, and prepared the ground for his kidnapping (see page 39). By March, 1953, the number of "illegals" in West Berlin had passed the 100,000 mark. It raised a first-class security problem.

Although the peak of 58,000 in one month was not to be reached until March, the flood of refugees reached panic proportions by the end of January. To the already existing categories had been added 800 Jews, representing nearly one-half the surviving Jewish community in Eastern Germany, who had been forced to flee because of anti-semitic purges set off by the Slansky trial in Czechoslovakia. The situation for Berlin had become critical — she could no longer handle the refugees with her own resources. Professor Ernst Reuter, the inspired Oberbürgermeister of Berlin, warned that the "lighthouse of freedom" was in danger of being "smothered" by the refugees. Dr. Adenauer, broadcasting a "stay at home" plea to the Eastern Germans, cautioned: "If hundreds of thousands flee, the same number of Russians or Asiatics will be sent in from the East to take their places. Every German who remains defends a piece of Germany, a piece of the Western world."

The attitude of most other Germans to the plight of their countrymen was incredibly apathetic. When individual Western Germans clamor for reunification, one gets the impression that they are prompted chiefly by an abstract, nationalistic emotion, rather than by any sentiment of brotherly love. I remember the despair of my secretary, who, when she wished to bring her 80-year-old mother from East Berlin to live with her in Bonn during that terrible winter of 1952, was refused the vital countersignature to the *Zuzugsgenehmigung* by her Rhenish landlady, who "did not want any refugees in her house." In December, 1954, the Senate of Hamburg — West Germany's most prosperous city — decided to organize a "good neighbor" Christmas campaign, in which the 1,700,000 people of the city might "adopt" 25,000 occupants of hutted camps and 10,000 East German refugees. But less than forty prospective "hosts" volunteered to take people in, and some of them made it a condition that their "guests" did housework. To most Western Germans, understandably, a Prussian refugee, willing to work twice as hard for half as much, was a threat to his own employment. Nevertheless, the Federal Government succeeded in inducing the reluctant *Land* Governments to increase their intake of refugees. Appeals were also made to the Allies for assistance. The answer was prompt, and a small airlift was set up by the civil airlines to bring refugees out from West Berlin at the rate of 1,000 to 1,500 a day — or rather by night.

It was not only the West that began to take notice of the East German migration. At last, when over half a million acres of farmland lay deserted by its farmers, the Russians realized the extent to which the exodus was paralyzing the tottering Soviet zone economy. Something had got out of hand. On their instructions, barricades and check points were erected at all the crossing points into West Berlin, and on the inter-sector railway stations.

Wooden lookout towers were hastily built on the Soviet zonal frontier with West Berlin. A large number of Vopo officers, suspected of conniving at the escape of refugees, were arrested (which in itself but served to increase the rate of flight from the Vopo ranks). Identity cards were issued, allowing travel only within a thirty-mile radius, and eventually identity cards of would-be refugees were withdrawn, rendering them liable to arrest on sight. All these measures only had the effect of intensifying the panic to get out.

It was significant that the Russians never employed the one trump in their hand with which they could have stopped all flights — the complete blocking of West Berlin from the Soviet zone. There was no doubt at all that they could have done so at any time, had they wished. On the contrary, there was considerable evidence for believing that, at first, the East German regime had cynically anticipated the refugee exodus, and actually assisted it by cracking the whip of terror. In many ways it served the aim of complete subjection of the East Germans. Those who fled were, for the most part, those who had resisted, or would resist — elements unlikely to prove reliable for the "build-up of socialism." Driving the farmers west made collectivization of their properties much easier. Furthermore the floods of refugees served as a dangerous embarrassment to the tightly stretched West German economy. The keeping open of Western Berlin as a neutral spy island, a sort of Switzerland of the cold war, was also of paramount importance to Soviet Intelligence.

It was clear, though, that by February the Communists realized that the exodus had attained proportions which were proving disastrous to the East German economy. The Soviet ambassador, Pushkin, was even forced to deliver a sharp protest at the failure of Eastern Germany to fulfil her reparations for 1952. No figure for the deficit was given, but it must have been considerable, as on the basis of it the Soviets then levied a fine of about $200,-000,000 on the wretched East Germans. Whether at this juncture the Soviet zone authorities intended to go all out to stop the refugees can now only be surmised. Meanwhile an event had

taken place in Russia which placed a temporary check on all
Communist policy.

When the world was rocked by news of the death of the Red
dictator, western crystal-gazers tried every permutation, combination and probability in their prognostications for the future.
As on the death of Genghis Khan, they said, the vast empire
would now crumble; or there would be a period of conciliation
towards the West now the harsh Stalin was dead; or the Soviets
would harden their line still more now the restraining hand of the
benevolent Stalin was removed from the wheel; or there would
be no change.

Among the East German puppets the first reaction was one of
uncertainty. Herr Ulbricht flew at once to Moscow, and no
member of the regime was willing to make any decision without
written orders from above. With the succession of Malenkov, the
old self-assurance began to return. For the first time the refugee
wave showed signs of slackening off: now that the old cat was
dead, the mice may have hoped for chances of a better deal from
his successors. The East German press for days on end poured
out nauseous eulogies on the "great Stalin," enlivened only by a
lapsus linguae in the *Tribüne,* which referred to the "leading fighter
for the maintenance and strengthening of war." Whether it was
sabotage or simply unconscious humor, the unfortunate proof
readers were flung into jail for "sabotage and deliberate slander
of the dead Comrade Stalin."

During the period of indecision, the Soviet forces themselves
acted like an angry dog at bay with its hackles up. On March
10th a US jet fighter was shot down by MIGs just on the Bavarian side of the Czech frontier. Two days later a RAF Lincoln,
with seven members of its crew, was shot down near Lauenberg
on the interzonal frontier. On the same day a BEA Viking was
fired at in the Munich–Berlin air-corridor. A few days later the
Russians attacked a US weather plane off Kamchatka in the
Pacific. A horrid, cold fear gripped the vitals of the western world
that the shootings presaged a new policy of aggressiveness by

the Soviets. Later it became apparent that the Russians had been genuinely frightened that the West might have seized the occasion of the death of Stalin to "start something." Major Ronzhin, a Red Army officer who defected from the Soviet zone on April 23rd, revealed that all Soviet units had been recalled from leave on Stalin's death, and all forces alerted for an emergency.

As is so often the case when Communist regimes realize they have gone too far, the Russians at once followed up the shooting down of the Lincoln with a wave of conciliation. Press attacks on the Allies were largely dropped by the East German press, and the Russians proposed air security talks. The offer was seized upon with high expectations by the Allies, and the British High Commission became so responsive to Russian requests for secrecy that newspapers had to consult the Soviet news agency, Tass, for the name of the British delegate. The talks dragged on for over a year, with little material gratification, except for those Western diplomats who feel that any conference with the Russians represents progress.

Before new orders came from Moscow, the interregnum period did not bring Eastern Germany, as Professor Reuter put it, "any gentle spring zephyrs from the East." In April, the regime turned its attention to the powerful Protestant Church. About 100 of its pastors and lay-clergymen were arrested, and in some areas the Christian "Young Community" organization was declared illegal; State stipends for the clergy were withdrawn, and churches desecrated and services broken up by thugs of the Free German Youth. In a display of fearless defiance, which recalled Luther's act of resistance to the Catholic Church at Wittenberg in 1517, Bishop Dibelius (leader of the Protestant Church in both East and West Germany) pinned his protests against the Communist measures to the noticeboard of the Marienkirche in Eastern Berlin.

At the beginning of May ration cards were withdrawn from some two million independent business men (i.e. small shopkeepers etc.), and refugee figures rose again. Finally, Herr Rau, the Five Year Plan chief, ordered a 10 per cent increase in the work norms on which wages were based, to force up lagging production; there were to be pay reductions and harsher penalties for those who did not fulfil their norms.

The spring had now been wound nearly to breaking-point. Then, on May 28th, Moscow announced the appointment of Vladimir Semeonov to be Soviet High Commissioner in Eastern Germany. The post was a new one; formerly the Soviets had governed their zone through a Control Commission, under the supreme authority of General Chuikov, the C-in-C of the Russian occupation forces. Now General Chuikov was to return to Russia, his authority taken over by a civilian who had previously been his political adviser and his junior. The new C-in-C, the unknown Lt-Gen. Andrei Gretchko, was to have his powers limited to purely military matters. It was a step equivalent to that taken by the three Western Allies in 1949. Semeonov himself had a reputation as a moderate and an expert on German affairs, and had established good relations with non-Communist politicians in both East and West Germany. In May, even before his promotion to High Commissioner, Semeonov had been making attractive hints to visiting West German politicians that the Soviets might be prepared for a revision of the Oder–Neisse line, as well as reunification, once EDC was dropped.

The appointment of Semeonov brought with it what at first blush seemed like the most radical change of Soviet policy in Eastern Germany since the war. It was apparent that the new regime in the Kremlin had realized that the harsh Stalin policy was ruining the country economically, and assisting America's task of rearming Western Germany. The plight of the Eastern Germans and the seeming finality of the dividing line along the Elbe had only pushed the West Germans farther into the arms of the West. Promoting the Soviet representative in Germany to par with the Western Allies portended the Malenkov regime's intention to open up a new diplomatic offensive on Germany. But, like Soviet disarmament proposals, the new policy on Germany had two levels to it — the *propaganda* and the *actual*. The *propaganda* level was aimed at the millions of susceptible inhabitants of the Federal Republic and the West prepared to believe that Russia's initiative for Four Power talks on German reunification *might* really mean that she was ready to give up Eastern Germany. Meanwhile, on the *actual* level the objectives remained roughly the same; to prevent West German rearmament and to hold on to Eastern Germany. Seen now in retrospect the Malenkov "new look" brought no more permanent change of heart than Lenin's NEP. Methods in Eastern Germany may have changed but there was no evidence that the steady course towards complete political and economical integration within the Eastern block was ever relaxed for a second.

Semeonov's first measures were designed to repair the havoc caused to the Eastern German economy during the preceding nine months. Until this was achieved, it would be impossible to bridge the vast material gulf now existing between East and West Germany, imperative before diplomatic negotiations could be opened.

Within a fortnight, the Politburo of the SED was required, on orders Semeonov had brought from Moscow, to announce startling details of a "New Course." It was a complete reversal of the policy of ruthless socialization announced at the Party Congress of the previous July, and Western observers at once surmised that it could but presage the fall of Herr Ulbricht.

1. Collectivization was to be halted.

2. State Bank credits were to be granted to private businessmen, so that those who had been driven out of business under the "building-up of socialism" might start up again.

3. Refugees who wished to return would not be penalized and would be handed back their property.

4. An amnesty was to be granted to all those sentenced to no more than three years' imprisonment "for sabotage" of public property.

5. The Government was to provide greater freedom of travel from East to West Germany.

6. By agreement with leaders of the Protestant Church, attacks on the Church and its members were to cease, and sentences on pastors were to be reviewed.

In the announcement the SED criticized itself for "grave errors" in the past, which had made the reforms necessary. At the same time a significant admission was made in a rider that these reforms aimed at "facilitating the rapprochement between the two parts of Germany."

The regime showed that it intended to carry out the reforms in at least temporary good faith. Within a few days 4,029 prisoners were released — an indication of the scale of the earlier wave of arrests. In East Berlin Dr. Dibelius held a service of Thanksgiving. In Western Germany shares of companies with properties in the Soviet zone took a sharper upward leap than at any time since the end of the war. At once many West German politicians snapped with great relish and speed at the bait of reunification talks dangled by the Red concessions, but the sceptical and sober-minded Chancellor cautioned that the West should not let itself be deflected from its goal of rearmament.

To the government toadies in Eastern Germany, the sudden reversal of policy caused as much consternation as that provoked in the British Communist Party following the Ribbentrop–Molotov Non-Aggression Pact. The members of the brigades which had plundered the farms now feared for their necks. Herr Ebert, the Mayor of East Berlin, pleaded for discipline on the part of "good, honest friends who are seized with doubt and grave concern at the new political course." To soften the blow, *Tägliche Rundschau* admitted nobly that "the former Soviet Control Commission is to a certain extent responsible for the mistakes which have been made."

The reaction of the East German population, of the working proletarian masses — the foundation of any Marxist Utopia — was very simple, and typically Prussian. For the concessions made by their Red oppressors they felt no gratitude: the concessions had been made out of weakness, and when an enemy showed weakness it meant that he was ripe for attack. That the Russians should have been such inept psychologists was incredible.

But even more incredible was the fact that amid all the concessions to the oppressed bourgeois classes, no move was made to rescind a measure which angered the workers more than any other—the increased work norms recently initiated by Herr Rau.

On June 12th, two days after the announcement of the New Course, builders in the much vaunted Stalinallee housing project of East Berlin were informed that their norms were to be raised, retrospective to June 1st, thus involving them in a loss of pay of as much as 30 per cent. During the next two days the workers' fury and agitation mounted steadily. On Monday, June 15th, the builders employed on Block 40 decided to send a two-man deputation personally to Herr Grotewohl to protest against the raising of the norms. On the following morning, an inflammatory article appeared in *Tribüne*, praising the norm increases. This put steel in the Stalinallee workers' resolution. From past experience, the two-man delegation were apprehensive lest they might not return from their interview with Herr Grotewohl. Instead, the workers of Block 40 decided to go *en masse*.

At about 8 o'clock on the morning of Tuesday, June 16th, eighty angry workers left Block 40 in the Stalinallee for Goering's old Air Ministry, which now housed the East German Government.

11

The Snapping of the Spring

AS THE BLOCK 40 DEMONSTRATORS MARCHED DOWN STALIN-allee they were joined by other workers from the building sites. At the end of Stalinallee their strength had already reached 300. The vanguard had provided itself with a banner with an SED slogan struck out and the words "We demand a reduction in norms" painted on the back.

By 1 p.m. the demonstrators reached the East German Government HQ on the Leipzigerstrasse, their ranks by now swollen with large numbers of excited East Berliners who had joined the column as it marched down Unter den Linden. Officials of the regime looked out of the windows of the Government building with incredulity at the demonstrators. Not for twenty years had such a spontaneous demonstration occurred. Eventually Herr Selbmann, the Minister for Heavy Industry, appeared, but the crowd shouted, "We don't want small fry, we want Grotewohl and the *Spitzbart* [Ulbricht]." Workers at the front of the crowd made Herr Selbmann get on a table and address the demonstrators. When he began with the words "I am a worker myself," he was at once shouted down with "That's so long ago you've forgotten it! You're no worker — you're a traitor to the workers!"

The remainder of Herr Selbmann's speech was drowned by the shouts of the demonstrators, and one more daring than the rest thrust him off the table to begin a revolutionary speech, "Comrades, I spent five years in a Nazi concentration camp and I'm not afraid of spending another ten years in the prisons of this lot for the sake of freedom."

His place was taken by a rugged stonemason with a bare chest, who took the refrain a stage further: "Here stand not only the workers of Stalinallee; here stand the workers of all Berlin and the whole Soviet zone. This is a people's uprising — we want free, secret elections!"

At this juncture, the demonstration took on an entirely new aspect, for the Stalinallee demands for norm cuts were replaced by much more general slogans: "We don't want a People's Army, we want butter!" "Free elections!" "Down with the Siberian goat!" [Ulbricht again.]

When the workers realized there was no prospect of seeing Grotewohl or Ulbricht, they decided to march back through East Berlin, calling out other workers to join in a general strike the following morning. The temper of the crowd was rising, and Communist officials who tried to disperse them were beaten up. An SED loudspeaker van which attempted to pacify the demonstrators was seized and used to broadcast the news of the strike. No effort was made by the Vopos to restrain or break up the crowds, who by the evening were already tearing down Communist emblems and slogans from building fronts. The news spread rapidly, and workers in the outlying areas of East Berlin sent in word that they would join in the strike planned for Tuesday morning.

At 7 a.m. on the morning of June 17th, several thousand workers assembled in the Strausbergerplatz in pouring rain, and started a second march on the Government quarter. This time the old Goering Air Ministry had been cordoned off by Vopo detachments, but the strikers burst through the Vopo barricades and hand-to-hand fighting broke out. Attempts were made to break into the Government buildings. With a few exceptions, the Vopos still withheld their fire. By 10 a.m. the strikers had been swollen by some 12,000 workers from the Hennigsdorf rolling mills outside Berlin. The demonstrations in Berlin had now attained the proportions of an uprising. Things had gone much too far for the enraged East Berliners to accept the offer of the regime to make the norm increases "voluntary." Numbers of anti-Communist West Berliners began to come over to join in the fun, and, egged on by the crowd, a young East Berliner climbed the Brandenburger Tor to tear down the Red Flag. After three attempts, during which he was under fire from Vopo snipers, the courageous fellow threw the flag down to the crowd, who promptly ripped it to shreds.

By midday, the rioting workers appeared to have gained control throughout East Berlin. No Communist functionaries were to be seen and the Vopos made only half-hearted attempts to intervene. The crowds became intoxicated with their success, and felt there was no end to it — they raided and set fire to Communist offices, smashed up pictures of Stalin and Ulbricht, tore down Communist slogans, and hurled Government files out of windows. Herr Nuschke, a deputy prime minister (he led the East German deputation to Bonn the previous September) was dragged out of his car and pushed over the frontier into West Berlin, where he was detained and later made to broadcast over RIAS, the American station in Berlin. There were several instances of Vopos who, feeling that the day belonged to the strikers, threw off their jackets and joined forces with the workers. An old woman of eighty, living in East Berlin, wrote jubilantly to her daughter whom I knew in Bonn: "Isn't it wonderful, at last *Der Tag* has come when we shall be delivered from these terrible people!"

The supremacy of the rebelling workers was, however, destined to be short-lived. After 10,000 Vopos in East Berlin had shown themselves unable or unwilling to cope with the situation, the Soviet authorities, acting with great alacrity, dispatched the whole of their First Mechanized Division into the trouble centers. By midday the first T34 tanks made their appearance, charging recklessly into the crowds in the Potsdamer Platz, to take up positions near Government buildings. At 1.30 p.m. the Military

Commandant of the Soviet sector of Berlin, Major-General Dibrova, proclaimed a state of martial law, banning assemblies of more than three people and imposing a complete curfew from 9 p.m. to 5 a.m. The uprising was broken, for a totally unarmed population could not resist armored cars and 30-ton tanks. Nevertheless the crowds did not disperse, and acts of rebellion continued until the streets were cleared by the curfew that evening. There were acts of incredible, desperate courage — one of the most memorable was that of the East German youth who hurled a rock at a Russian T34 at twenty yards. A West German newsreel camera recorded this bit of defiance.

One of the last actions of the East Berliners was to burn the Communist restaurant Haus Vaterland, in the Potsdamer Platz, while under heavy Russian fire. By 9 p.m. and curfew the streets were completely empty — except for the Soviet tanks and troops and battered Vopo patrols. An angry silence hung over East Berlin. In one empty street was a rough wooden cross on top of a West German flag to mark a bloodstained patch where a worker had been run down by a Russian tank.

Meanwhile, the uprising had spread like wildfire throughout the Soviet zone. At Brandenburg strikers seized and handcuffed the public prosecutor and a notoriously brutal judge, who were saved only by the advent of Soviet troops. At Halle, the HQ of the dreaded State Security Service was raided and its entire index system carried off to West Berlin. As the Soviet tanks rolled into the town, some 60,000 strikers gathered in the market place and sang *Deutschland Über Alles*. At Magdeburg, workers from the former Krupp Grusonwerk stormed the prison and released about 100 political prisoners. The fighting in Magdeburg reached a far more savage pitch than in East Berlin. On the 17th at least forty workers were killed, and several Vopos lynched by enraged crowds.

Outside Berlin, the focal point of the uprisings was Leipzig and its environs, including the Leuna synthetic oil works, and the traditionally socialist area of the brown-coal industries. In Leipzig and its immediate neighborhood alone, the Russians deployed

some 275 tanks — twice as many as Rommel had at the Battle of
Alamein. A letter received in West Germany from a Leipziger,
dated June 19th, read:

> You can't imagine what Wednesday was like. These masses on the
> streets. In Ritterstrasse a fully-manned police car was tossed on
> its side, in the market the pavilion was set afire. The prison in the
> Beethovenstrasse was raided, the prisoners set free. The rage and
> despair was beyond all example. The big sliding grille in front of
> the District Court was literally lifted out and taken to pieces with
> bare hands. Files and furniture thrown out of the windows, the
> gate pushed in. Then our "People's Protectors" shot out of the
> windows. Popular rage turned into a hurricane. The crowd went
> over to the attack. There were dead and wounded. A young girl
> was shot in the abdomen and screamed dreadfully . . . There
> are dead and wounded, nobody knows how many. But the people
> are moving. With rage and bitterness we read in the rags of
> newspapers the allegations that Western provocateurs are respon-
> sible . . .

Once the Russians had restored order in their zone, the grim
and inevitable work of reprisals began. It was only remarkable
that they were so relatively light: according to West German
Government figures forty-two death sentences were carried out
after June 17th and 25,000 people arrested, but most of them
were released shortly afterwards. With a brutal arbitrariness
typical of the system, the Russians selected as an example in Berlin an unemployed West Berliner, Willi Goettling, who was arrested while crossing the Soviet sector of the city on the 17th.
Although he appears to have been no more than an innocent by-
stander, he was sentenced to death by a Soviet military court on
the 18th and immediately executed. The charge was that he had
"acted on the orders of a foreign intelligence organization and
was one of the active organizers of the provocations and disturbances in the Soviet sector of Berlin." An Allied note of protest to
the Russians described the condemnation and execution of
Goettling as a "travesty of justice" and "acts of brutality which
will shock the conscience of the world." Nevertheless, the episode

fitted neatly into the thesis developed in a written statement by Herr Grotewohl, which asserted that the riots had been caused by "provocateurs and Fascist agents of foreign powers," aimed to "make more difficult the reunification of Germany." This became the official Communist version of June 17th, but none believed it and it only further increased the contempt of the East Germans for the Grotewohl–Ulbricht regime.

For some time afterwards commentators in the West, always ready to ascribe the utmost Machiavellian cunning to the Soviets, expressed belief that the uprisings had been started as a planned putsch, stimulated by the regime, in the same way that the Tsarist secret police were thought to have provoked the Russian revolution of 1905. There were arguments to support this case: the initial non-interference of the Vopos, the unusual restraint which the Russians exercised once they had intervened, and the fact that the arrest of the riot leaders was a crushing blow against resistant elements.

Nevertheless this case was not sustained by later evidence. Soviet timing was severely thrown off balance by the uprising, which interrupted plans for smoothing the way towards quadripartite talks, begun by Semeonov's "New Course." This was confirmed by statements of German prisoners of war released *en masse* by the Russians just before the Berlin Conference. Many of them said that at the beginning of June, 1953, they had been ordered to move from their prison camps and told that they were shortly to be sent home. After June 17th their westward movement was halted and they were transferred to new camps, where they waited another six months until the Russians felt their release would be a useful diplomatic gesture. It is now also quite clear that the Soviet forces and the Vopos received orders to exercise restraint in order not to spoil the much bigger game — the defeat of EDC by Four Power negotiations, and the eventual neutralization of all Germany.

The behavior of some Soviet soldiers during the uprising, as well as German Vopos, must have created an icy chill within the Kremlin. There were countless cases of Vopo desertions for which

Herr Zaisser (the chief of the State Security Service) was later blamed, but nothing was more frightening for the Soviets than what happened at Magdeburg. Here Russian soldiers guarding the prison refused orders to shoot at the workers attempting to liberate their comrades. Eighteen of them, including NCOs, were later executed. The Russian leaders must have recalled that in Petrograd in 1917, a similar refusal to fire on unarmed workers had precipitated the Russian Revolution.

The Soviets' immediate aim was to get their forces out of Berlin and the other East German cities at the earliest possible moment so as to get ahead with the reconsolidation. But obviously they did not dare withdraw while there was still any likelihood of a fresh outbreak. Up to June 20th there were still reports of the Russians being forced to break up groups of workers meeting in defiance of General Dibrova's edict. The curfew was not lifted until a fortnight after the uprising, and the tanks rumbled back to their bases a day later. On June 22nd, the East German Government announced new measures to improve life in the zone: the norm increases were to be withdrawn, electricity cuts abolished, social services expanded and about $150,000,000 provided for the building of private houses. It was not enough, but the workers' will to resist had been temporarily broken. When, on July 1st, correspondents from West Berlin could re-enter the Soviet sector, they found red banners flying at the Stalinallee over sullen workers, proclaiming, "Our government has fulfilled our demands. We are back at work." The Communist Press kept up its barrage against the "capitalist instigators," but their attempts to convince exceeded the ludicrous. One issue of the *Tägliche Rundschau* described how posses of American youths, wearing Texas shirts and armed with lassoes, had been sent into East Berlin to stir up trouble.

In West Germany the first reaction to the uprising was a mixture of indignation and exhilaration, followed quickly by a feeling of hopelessness when it became clear that nothing would or could be done to help the East Germans. Particularly significant were the spontaneous expressions of solidarity made by West German workers — acknowledging that the uprisings had been a genuine workers' rebellion. Some 60,000 miners in Essen supported a resolution declaring themselves to be "100 per cent behind the workers of East Berlin and the Soviet zone." The left-wing Metalworkers' Union put up $12,000 as "preliminary assistance" for the East Berliners.

A somber memorial service for those killed in the uprising was held in the Bundestag, and that day flags throughout Bonn were hung at half-mast. The 17th of June was decreed a national holiday, to be entitled "Day of Unity." For a short time, the unemployed Berlin house-painter, Willi Goettling, achieved the same kind of unintentional fame as Horst Wessel. On the Tuesday after the uprising, Dr. Adenauer and most of the West German leaders flew to Berlin to hold a service there for Goettling and the seven other West Berliners who had lost their lives. With that dramatic solemnity that Germans know so well how to affect, Dr. Adenauer pledged 500,000 West Berliners standing before their Town Hall:

"I swear in the name of the whole German people that we will not rest or desist until Germans behind the Iron Curtain are free and united with us in freedom and peace."

There was no doubt that the East German uprising was an embarrassment to Dr. Adenauer's policy of "first EDC, then unification." No West German leader could at this moment ignore the urgency of the call for reunification, and, with the impending elections, it provided the demagogues with dangerous fuel with which to inflame the emotions of the German masses. On June 22nd Dr. Adenauer sent telegrams to the three Allied heads of government, appealing for their help to "re-establish the unity of the whole German people." This was interpreted in Bonn as an indirect recommendation to the Allies that they propose a Four Power conference at an early opportunity while the Russians were still off balance. There was obviously no other help the Allies could be expected to provide. Thus, nine days later, enraged Social Democrats accused Dr. Adenauer of gross insincerity when the Bundestag voted by 178 to 146 against a Social Democrat motion to request the Allies to "hold a Four Power conference immediately after the Bermuda Conference." Dr. Adenauer stated after the division that, although he would work for any Four Power conference which offered the slightest promise of success, he had in no way deviated from his previous view that any conference held on terms not destined to bring success would be a disaster for the West.

It was courageous of the Chancellor to stick to his guns with the elections coming up, and the results of the Berlin Conference to a large degree confirmed his fears. Nevertheless, it was a pity that the West could not have taken this once-in-a-lifetime opportunity to seize the diplomatic initiative when the Russians were reeling back on the defensive. Unfortunately, just at this moment, Fate seemed to be acting against the West with an incredible unkindness. There had been no French Government for five weeks, and the Bermuda Conference had to be postponed twice because of the crisis in France. On June 27th Sir Winston Churchill's unexpected collapse, since revealed as a slight stroke, caused the indefinite postponement of the conference. As a substitute, a Foreign Ministers' conference was called in Washington for the second week of July. Mr. Eden was still *hors de combat* and had to be represented by the Marquess of Salisbury. Thus in these vital weeks both Britain and France were leaderless, and the Americans were themselves divided as to what course to take. Finally, on July 15, at the end of the Foreign Ministers' meeting in Washington, notes were sent to the Russians cautiously proposing that a Four Power conference "might begin about the end of September." The Russians' delaying tactics managed to postpone it until the end of the following January, by which time they were so firmly in the saddle again in East Germany that they could dare to propose Berlin as the site of the conference. The Allies had by then lost all the advantage offered them by the East Germans' courageous revolt.

After the suppression of the 17th of June uprisings, the morale of the East Germans badly needed a boost. To those who had risked their lives in the streets of Berlin, Halle, Leipzig, Magdeburg and the countless other areas of insurrection in the Soviet zone, the apparent refusal of the Western Allies and the West Germans to come to their help evoked unpleasant comparisons with the Warsaw rebellion of 1944, when the Russians had waited outside the city until the destruction of General Bor-Komorowski's forces was complete. Their morale was not improved when Mr. Selwyn Lloyd, in the House of Commons, commended the Soviet troops for their restraint in suppressing the uprising. During Mr. Semeonov's absence in Moscow at the end of June, the East Germans hoped that he would return with instructions to liquidate the hated Ulbricht–Grotewohl regime. They were thrown into deepest despair when it transpired that, not only had Herr Ulbricht survived, but that by August 21st his confidence had returned to such a degree that he could safely venture to re-impose some of the norm increases — the very cause of the revolt. At the same time, an auxiliary force of 150,000 to 200,000 men was to be formed to co-operate with the police in stamping out "resistance to the regime" and to help purge "petty bourgeois deviationists" who had supported "hostile groups of cowards and traitors." The drive for collectivization was also to be renewed, and many of the prisoners amnestied under Semeonov's New Course were to be re-tried. Herr Max Fechner, the East German Minister of Justice, was replaced by the dreaded Frau "Red Hilde" Benjamin, a former chief justice of the Soviet zone. The East Germans could derive little satisfaction at the liquidation of Beria's henchman, Herr Zaisser, for the failure of the MVD apparatus before and during the uprising. Meanwhile the food shortages were again as desperate as they had been during the previous winter.

At this juncture the West embarked upon its one single act of initiative following the 17th of June. The American Government made an offer of $15,000,000 of food aid for the Soviet zone. It was both a humanitarian gesture, so typical of the Americans, and an important propaganda move aimed at restoring the morale of the East Germans. Not surprisingly, it was indignantly refused by the Russians, who promptly promised to send the Soviet zone over $50,000,000 of food during the remainder of the year. Then Herr Willi Kressmann, the mayor of the Kreuzberg suburb of Berlin, launched his own food scheme from private donations. Stalls were set up on the inter-sector boundary, and food coupons worth $1.20 each were distributed to the East Berliners. The scheme was an instantaneous success, and 5,000 East Berliners came to collect food packets on the first day. The Communist authorities were so embarrassed that they went so far as to flood the market with forged coupons. The scheme was promptly taken up by other districts of West Berlin, and the food supplies were augmented by the Federal Republic, who were in turn receiving from the US the food which had been offered to the Russians, and which was now put at the disposal of the West German Government.

The food deliveries were on an enormous scale, with hungry East Germans traveling from farthest ends of the Soviet zone to collect the food packages. The regime took the most desperate and brutal measures to halt the traffic, but with even less success than when they had tried to halt the determined refugees. When the first scheme came to an end in August, the Federal Government, with American support, decided to continue the action until East German rations were supplemented by the harvest at the beginning of October. This was resisted by the British High Commission, which took the rather cautious line that the first food scheme had made its point, and that any continuations might cause trouble (presumably a Russian reprisal against West Berlin). The American view, however, prevailed, and the second food distribution was carried through without any threats from the East materializing. All in all, some 4½ million food parcels were delivered to the East Germans. It was a notable American victory, and did something towards raising East German morale. It also coincided with a Russian admission of defeat in their attempts to re-establish the "friendship bonds" between their occupation forces and the East Germans, which Russian armed intervention of June 17th had shaken. Soon afterwards the strict "non-fraternization" ban had been lifted, but abruptly reimposed again in August after some fifty murders and numerous rapes and robberies had marred the new friendship campaign.

In France the 17th of June and the subsequent German unity appeals had the unfortunate effect of aggravating the fears of those who felt that the EDC would one day necessitate *mourir pour Königsberg,* as *Der Spiegel,* the German weekly which had always opposed the treaty, hastened to point out. M. Hervé Alphand, France's permanent representative to NATO, was cited (in *Der Spiegel* of July 8th) as having warned that it could not now be expected that the German EDC contingent would be used *only* for the defense of the West. On August 5th, a leader appeared in *Der Spiegel,* posing the question, "If half a million West Germans had stood under arms on June 17th, who would have wanted to guarantee that they would not have hurried to the help of their rebelling brethren?" Indeed, there is no doubt that the reacquisition of the lost territories has become the supreme goal of a great many Germans. In July, 1952, a year before the uprising, EMNID (the West German public-opinion poll) asked 2,000 representative Germans what they considered to be the most urgent task before the Federal Government. Over half were most concerned with various problems of living conditions, but the largest single faction, numbering 16 per cent, declared for reunification of West and East Germany. Another poll showed that no less than 41 per cent of the inhabitants of the Federal Republic had relatives or friends living in East Germany.

The reunification urge has been constantly stimulated by the presence in Western Germany of over ten million expellees and refugees, augmented by the most recent exodus from the Soviet zone. The hopes of the expellees that one day they would return to their former homes have been kept alive by the efforts of Herr Jakob Kaiser's Ministry for All-German Questions and Professor Oberländer's Refugee Ministry. Reunification claims fostered by these two ministries extend considerably beyond the area covered at present by the Soviet zone. While providing a valuable and generally accurate picture of conditions and events in Eastern

Germany, these ministries also provide a somewhat exaggerated picture of the incompetence of the Polish "colonization" in the ceded areas. Reports are produced of thousands of acres of farmland reverting to desert because of insufficient population — reports designed to encourage the German expellees in the dangerous belief that the Poles regard their tenancy as only a temporary one. In fact, as *The Times* pointed out in an authoritative article on April 1st, 1954, Communist planning probably intended "the deliberate neglect of the less fertile areas in a part of Europe where farming had always yielded poor returns." At the same time, *The Times* concluded, the highly industrial regions of Upper Silesia now had a higher population under the Poles than in German days. Vast sums of money are being expended in the reconstruction and expansion of Silesian industry, and it seems most unlikely that either the Poles, or the Russian planners behind them, look on tenancy of the Oder–Neisse area as being anything but permanent.

Nevertheless, no West German cartographer would dare put out a revised map of Germany showing the Oder-Neisse as the frontier with Poland: instead, the area of 1937 Germany to the east of the Oder is always shaded in and marked "under Polish administration." Herr Kaiser's Ministry goes further and has produced maps entitled "The Lands we must not forget," which include all the 1937 territories, as well as East Prussia. No wonder the fear of *mourir pour Königsberg* has fixed itself in the minds of Frenchmen when they see on maps Prussian pincer-claws reaching out into the East again!

Of all the various expellee groups, by far the most vocal and organized are the nearly two million Sudeten German expellees, mostly concentrated in Bavaria, who for one reason or another have found assimilation in Western Germany more difficult than other expellee factions. To avoid provoking foreign public opinion, their leaders talk in elaborate cyphers about the "meaninglessness of frontiers in the future Europe." Conversations I have had with Sudeten rank and file show them, however, to be in no doubt that what the leaders really mean is the return of the Su-deten–Czech lands to their former tenants and German rule. At the 1954 Whitsun rally of some 500,000 Sudeten Germans in Munich, the bombastic Federal Minister of Transport, Dr. See-bohm (himself a Sudeten German), made a complicated speech which was interpreted by the reliable *Neue Zürcher Zeitung* as follows: "In Seebohm's opinion, Bohemia, Moravia and Silesia must always be united to the Reich."

As has so often been pointed out, one of the gravest dangers in rearming the Germans is that one day they may use these arms to regain by force the lost territories. As the lessons of the East German uprising indicate, the danger threatens to be more pro-nounced if a time comes when the Germans decide the Soviet colossus is weakening, and their own power is increasing. The stimulus of *Lebensraum,* of which Hitler made such adept use, is acuter than ever: the population in the West German rump is now 48.5 million compared with 39.4 million in 1939.

As against this, irredentism among the expellees and refugees has, up to now, been kept to a remarkably low level by the al-most unbelievable achievement of the Federal Republic in assimi-lating these extraneous ten million within its own strained econ-omy; a project on which about $300,000,000 have already been spent. Entire refugee industries, such as Gablonz glass and the Leitz Leica works, have been re-established in the Federal Re-public. The mildness of the expellees' discontent was well illus-trated by the unexpectedly poor results of the Kraft–Oberländer Refugee Party (BHE) during the 1953 Federal elections. It won only 5.9 per cent of the votes, and its strength appears to have been declining ever since. In the course of the next thirty years the Federal Government intends to redistribute $14 billion for the benefit of the expellees through *Lastenausgleich*. Eventual-ly many of the former expellees will be so well established that the *Drang nach Osten* will hold little attraction for them.

Furthermore, there is little doubt that the German reunification urge has been presented in greatly inflated proportions abroad —

largely as a result of the incessant emotional utterances of German politicians. As an issue of internal politics, reunification has been built up to be the *sine qua non* of all West German political parties, which none dare be accused of soft pedalling. But although in the open they react to the emotional stimuli of their leaders, in private a great many West Germans are several laps behind the politicians. Especially in the Catholic strongholds of Bavaria and the Rhineland, many hold doubts on reunification that verge on apathy. In their heart of hearts, materially-minded West Germans feel that reunification at this time would almost certainly bring to an end the remarkable period of economic prosperity the Federal Republic has been enjoying — if nothing worse. In dispassionate moments, most intelligent Germans admit to themselves that, with the present conflict of world forces, reunification "in peace and freedom" is fated to be a distant mirage for a very long time. But as a highly emotional race, the Germans do not always think things out dispassionately. Nevertheless, in 1953, it was hard to discover any indigenous West German possessed of a crusading zeal to use the EDC for the sort of *mourir pour Königsberg* adventure the French so feared.

In a last message to the French people before the EDC debate in the Assembly, Dr. Adenauer, on August 6th, 1954, gave the assurance:

"All German political parties — even the expellee organizations — are united in their wish to effect reunification *only* by peaceful means."

This utterance may not have been sufficient to allay French qualms, but it was certainly quite genuine. Under the present balance of power, it is quite ludicrous to think that the exposed rump of Western Germany could create a modern war machine powerful enough for a war of liberation in the East — even in the absence of Western occupying forces. As to the distant future, one would have thought that the EDC would recommend itself most strongly to the realistic Frenchman, as being by far the safest means of preventing Germany from ever getting herself into an aggressive position. Certainly the system of integrated staffs, a common arms budget and control of equipment allocation provided for under EDC would have made it virtually impossible for the West Germans to undertake any "independent operation" in the East.

12

West Germany

Prepares for Elections

BARELY HAD THE ECHOES OF THE STUPENDOUS EVENTS IN BER-
lin died away when the West Germans were faced with the task of
electing a new Federal Parliament to replace the first post-war
Bundestag, which had nearly reached the end of its allotted span
of four years. For many reasons, the 1953 elections were to be
of particular historical importance to Germany. They would be
the first genuinely free national elections to be held since Weimar
days, the 1949 elections having taken place under the strong influence of Military Government. A generation of young Germans who had grown up under post-war conditions would be
voting for the first time, as would a large number of ex-Nazis who
had been banned from voting in 1949. The success of German
democratization was to be very much on test.

One of the last bills to be handled by the expiring Bundestag
was a new Federal electoral law. After lengthy negotiations in
committee a compromise draft was approved by a large majority
of all parties, except the Communists. The law provided in the
first place that the Bundestag should be increased from 402 deputies to 484, so as to give the forty-eight million West Germans
a more proportional representation. Of the 484, half were to be
elected directly from constituencies and the other half indirectly.
The latter would be elected from party lists in each of the *Länder*,

according to the proportion of votes received by the party. Each German was thus provided with two votes: one to be cast for a particular candidate and the second for a party. An elector could cast his first vote for Herr Schmidt of the Free Democrats, because he was an upstanding figure in local politics, and vote with his second ballot for the Christian Democrats in approbation of the party's foreign policy. It was a fair but complicated system.

By far the most important feature of the new law, however, was the 5 per cent anti-splinter clause, which was Dr. Adenauer's special rider to the draft. Unless a party gained direct election of a candidate from a constituency, it would be required to get a minimum of 5 per cent of all votes cast throughout the Federal Republic in order to obtain any representation in Bonn. The provision was designed, nominally, to avoid the danger of a multiplicity of splinter parties, which so enfeebled the Weimar Republic. In addition, Dr. Adenauer aimed at ridding the Bundestag of both the Communists and the right-wing extremists. The 5 per cent limit had been carefully calculated on the basis that the Communists had gained just 5.7 per cent of the votes in 1949, and their popularity had been waning steadily ever since. The memories of the brutal repressions which followed the June uprising in Eastern Germany were still fresh in the minds of all deputies, and a plea by a Communist, Herr Rische, that the new law was undemocratic was greeted with loud derision.

On July 4th, the Bundestag dissolved. It was singularly unfortunate that what may well be described in future history books as a good parliament (at any rate by comparison with its predecessors) should have been marred by an extraordinary lapse in its final legislative act. The incident is worth recounting if only to illustrate the sort of triviality on which so much of present Franco-German mistrust is founded. It was occasioned by the ratification of the London Debt Agreement, signed by Germany in February, 1953. During the course of a remarkably dull day's debating, all voting had gone smoothly until the eighth and final item — the treaty on debts claimed by France for post-war aid. By this time it was approaching the lunch hour, and many bored deputies, succumbing to a very national foible, had gone off to the Bundeshaus restaurant. When the division bell rang, none of them stirred, confident that their presence was not required. Meanwhile, a number of coalition deputies had been won over by Socialist diatribes on French occupation rapacity — which resulted in a Government defeat of 148 to 153. Over 100 deputies did not vote.

Because of the imminent dissolution of Parliament, this meant that the French Debt Agreement would have to be abandoned until the next Bundestag. Reaction in France was immediate and astonishingly violent. In Bonn a hasty council was held to find a way of deleting the unintentional slight at the eleventh hour. On the last morning of the Bundestag, a group of deputies appealed to Dr. Ehlers, president of the Bundestag, to take the division again. With about as much dignity as penitent schoolboys, they claimed they had acted in error in leaving the Chamber the day before. Despite objections from the Opposition, this remarkably unparliamentary request was accepted and the Treaty ratified.

The first Bundestag bore a certain resemblance to Dr. Johnson's preaching female; it was not brilliant, but one was surprised that it worked at all. In 1949 the newly created parliament had some mountainous disadvantages to overcome. Only eleven elder members had had any previous experience since the last elected parliament came to an end in 1933, and that had been no great success. Nor had the Germans any historical parliamentary tradition on which to draw, as have most other European states. Owing to the completeness of the administrative breakdown in 1945, the Bundestag had to pass the most basic legislature to get the country going. At the same time it had to struggle with a jungle of laws carried over from both Weimar and Nazi times, as well as Allied occupation legislation.

A considerable drawback to normal parliamentary life lay in the choice of Bonn as capital. The sleepy Rhineland university town of about 100,000, famous only as the birthplace of Beethoven, did not make for the ideal capital. It could not have been less suited to receive the influx of diplomats, deputies, officials and correspondents. There is still an acute housing shortage. Deputies for the most part were housed in small, speedily run-up government flats adequate neither for work nor entertaining. This was the result of hesitation on the part of both the Government and private enterprise lest the temporary capital might one day move back to Berlin. The dank, enervating climate of Bonn too seemed to have its depressing effect on the deputies. Only Dr. Adenauer, a born Rhinelander, appeared to thrive on it. Some 30 per cent of the members of the first Bundestag were said to be suffering from some form of heart complaint, aggravated, if not directly induced, by the climate (twenty-seven actually died from various causes).

There were many jokes at Bonn's expense—most of them seeming to originate with Americans. Certainly nothing summed up Bonn better than a remark attributed to an American diplomat, who described an assignment in Bonn as "capital punishment." Another described Bonn as "half as big as the cemetery back home, and twice as dead." Yet a third apocryphal tale told of an American soldier on leave who approached a Bonn policeman with the simple request: "Say, where are the girls in this town?" "I'm sorry, sir," the answer came, "but she's visiting her aunt in Cologne today."

The Bundeshaus building itself was not exactly designed to lend the Parliament either character or dignity. A soulless, square, white structure on the bank of the Rhine, it had started life originally as a school for teachers. Owing to the parochial limitations of Bonn the Bundeshaus achieved more the air of a small town community center than the seat of government of forty-eight million people. The large chambers were often leased out for such unparliamentary functions as auctions and balls, and on one occasion for a fashion show.

Several summers ago young Germans on Rhine steamers inevitably used to sing *Wer soll das bezahlen?* (Who's to foot the bill?) as they passed the Bundeshaus. The average German was inclined to be distrustful of the new Parliament, and somewhat contemptuous. Anything to do with the word *Politik* smelled bad to him after the Nazi era, and the Federal Government seemed at first to be just a costly puppet of the Allies. The point of a Parliament was difficult for him to grasp. A German farmer said to me once: "I wouldn't like to see the Nazis back, but why do we need 402 men to do what one man did?" Again, the average German was remarkably ill-informed as to how democracy actually functioned. A survey of the Allensbach Institute (a German public-opinion poll) concluded in 1951 that only 8 per cent of all West Germans knew what role the Bundesrat played, and only 12 per cent knew what happened in the Bundestag.

In spite of the scepticism of the electorate, the first Bundestag established a noteworthy record of mature legislation. In its four years' life, nearly 500 laws were passed in the course of 281 plenary sessions, and some 25,000 petitions were dealt with. In comparison with the House of Commons, much more work on draft bills is carried out in committee, and no less than 5,300 Bundestag committee meetings were held. That so much of the workings of the Bundestag went on removed from the public eye did not help the task of "selling" democracy to the populace. By the time bills reached the Bundestag for the second and third readings, they had been well thrashed out in both party and committee sessions, thus there was little new to be said and often little genuine debating was done. Instead, with an eye on home consumption, speakers tended to dreary demagogy — always a German weakness. As a result, a casual visitor to the Bundestag usually witnessed the disheartening spectacle of a speaker haranguing a half-full chamber, most of whom would be reading newspapers, or holding private conversations. The first Bundestag also suffered from drones, sixty of whom never spoke in all four years, and colorful speeches from the back benches were non-existent. That there were a few stimulating debates was largely due to the forceful personalities of Dr. Adenauer and Dr. Schumacher, and the dignified control of the President of the Bundestag, Dr. Ehlers.

Apart from spectacular debates like that on the EDC treaty, which received utmost publicity, legislation did include such solid achievements as a law organizing revenue administration, a general railway law, and a law setting up a Federal criminal police. Two particular successes were the Housing Bill, which paved the way for the industry to build at the rate of 520,000 units a year by the end of 1954, and the Co-determination in Industry Law. This was evolved as a compromise solution between all parties, and laid down the principle that workers in heavy industry should be given their own representation in the management of their plants. It was remarkable as distinctly social legislation passed by a right-of-center Government, and contributed materially to the industrial peace which prevailed in German industry after the currency reform. The Coalition role in its inception also undoubtedly cut much ground from underneath the Socialists' 1953 election platform.

One of the early defects of the Bundestag was the length of time required to dispatch each law, largely a result of inexperience. In the first years, the average time for passage of a bill was five months: by 1953 this had been reduced to eighty-four days. Such delays further detracted from the repute of the Bundestag in that the Germans often felt it was "doing nothing."

By 1952 the Federal Government feared, with good reason, that the Bundestag had not been getting its message over to the people and that if democracy was to stick in Germany, Germans would have to be better informed about parliament. As a result an unusual body called the Federal Bureau for Home Service, to which I have already referred in passing, was set up in Bad Godesberg to publicize the Bundestag. It was a non-party organization run by a handful of young men of unimpeachable political antecedents and some psychological training. They attacked the problem with great drive and ingenuity. Factories were asked to include in their house organs articles reporting on the doings of Parliament and describing its workings. General knowledge tests on the Bundestag were circulated to all schools, prizes for which were free outings to Bonn, including a reception by Dr. Adenauer and President Heuss. The Bureau devised a game similar to Monopoly called Let's Play Governments, which contained such injunctions as "One of your assistants intentionally

opened the letter of an opponent — move back five spaces,"
"You accepted a bribe — move back ten spaces." During the
election campaigns the Bureau distributed masses of literature
exhorting the people to vote and describing the complicated two-
vote system in simplest terms. It even composed a jazz record
which went somehow as follows: "With politics as with girls, it's
a man's duty to choose the right party."

The efforts of the Bureau for Home Service certainly contributed to the remarkably high poll on September 6th (86.2 per
cent) and in the last months of the first Bundestag one began to
sense a deeper respect among the Germans for their Parliament.
By 1953, the material benefits of its legislation were already making themselves felt. Under Dr. Ehlers' own program of "putting
the people in touch with democracy" nearly one million visitors
had been conducted on tours through the Bundeshaus. In June,
Professor Carlo Schmid, the Socialist deputy president of the
Bundestag, told me: "At least I have heard nobody sing *Wer soll
das bezahlen?* this year."

Selling democracy to a people who had spent twelve years of
their lives under a dictatorship (and many of them had welcomed that after a period of unstable parliamentary rule) is a
slow business, but in 1953 it seemed to be gradually succeeding.
Dr. Ehlers summed it up for me in an interview: "These four
years have been just a learning period, but we have already succeeded in constituting an organ of State with definite features."

The election campaigns began very slowly. Until the release
and subsequent candidature of Naumann, there were to be no
"sensations." The policies of the various parties were by now well
known to the electorate, and no party had any surprises to offer.
For this reason the Germans gave a deceptive appearance of
apathy during the campaigning. From the start it was clear that
the election would be fought on foreign policy, with the EDC
as the focal point — although, since the East German uprisings,
every party had found it politically expedient to declare reunification as its *principal* aim. Dr. Adenauer's personal appeal of

June 22nd to the three Allied heads of Government for their help in re-establishing German unity had been backed up at the beginning of September by concrete Allied proposals for a Four Power conference on Germany to take place in Lugano in October. Together this had had the effect of firing a deadly shot against the Social Democrats. Their charges that Dr. Adenauer was prepared to sacrifice reunification for integration of a "Little Europe" now carried much less weight. Henceforth, to a large section of the population, Dr. Adenauer, and *not* the Social Democratic Party, was the true champion of German unity.

Dr. Adenauer's greatest asset in the elections was, as it always had been, his unflagging persistence. Again and again, at every major West German city, he steadfastly hammered in the same theme, which by constant repetition in his strikingly simple words had become a slogan: "Reunification can only be achieved by arguing with the Russians from strength; strength can only be achieved by Western European integration; EDC is the only way for Germany to contribute to this strength."

This was positive, and a policy that Germans could understand, while the program outlined by the Social Democrats was negative and vague. Much of this party's efforts were directed to non-constructive criticisms of the Schuman Plan and the Bonn Conventions in that they embarrassed the aim of German reunification. The best alternative to EDC that it could offer was its vague hypothesis of a security organization of apparently unlimited membership.

Many young Germans with whom I spoke during the elections deeply feared that the Social Democrat policy of neutralization would leave a weak, truncated West Germany like a nut between two gigantic crackers.

Like other German leaders in the past, Herr Ollenhauer found himself in the disagreeable position of having to fight a war on two fronts — with a shortage of weapons. On the home front the Christian Democrats had a line firmly anchored in material achievements. They could point to solid facts that the average German could see and feel: unemployment down from over two million to well below a million, the cost of living pegged, and standards of life higher than most German workers could remember; the vast majority of ten million post-war refugees had been assimilated, nearly six million people had received new houses, the workers had been granted "co-determination" in industry. The Socialists could not breach this line with vague promises of higher wages and nationalization which were not even whole-heartedly backed by the trade unions. Nor, on the second front, could Herr Ollenhauer counter-attack against the tremendous new world prestige which Dr. Adenauer had gained for Germany. Sir Winston Churchill's statement that Dr. Adenauer was "the wisest German statesman since Bismarck" had made an incalculable impression in Germany. The CDU election propaganda found fertile ground when it distributed postcards showing Churchill and Adenauer in conversation, with the comment "Have you ever thought of what Konrad Adenauer has done for Germany in the last four years?"

The dice were, from the start, loaded against the Socialists, and it was never clear what prompted the British High Commission to inform the Foreign Office that the SPD was likely to emerge the largest single party after the elections. (The same dispatch concluded that the right wing, which by then numbered Naumann as chief candidate of the German Reich Party (DRP), would also be strengthened at the cost of the CDU. As events turned out, the High Commission's forecast could hardly have been more wrong.)

Some of the election posters were highly revealing of the plan of battle of the various parties. The most popular Christian Democrat poster bore just the head of Dr. Adenauer, without words. A similar Social Democrat poster portrayed Dr. Schumacher, the leader who had died a year before. The BHE (Refugee Party) depicted the Brandenburger Tor as the symbol of German unity. The Free Democrats relied almost entirely on the German Eagle to connote national dignity, although the sinister black bird must have made many a German shudder from memories as he passed under the hoardings.

The FDP did in fact enter the lists badly shaken and divided as a result of the Naumann case. Its patchwork character showed more clearly than ever through great cracks in the respectable "liberal" façade. The attempt to house old-school liberalism within the same party that championed big business and nationalism had never seemed likely to succeed, and the Naumann "infection" caused even a number of the leading Ruhr industrialists to withdraw their support in 1953. As September 6th approached, it became increasingly clear that the elections would develop into a straight fight between CDU and SPD.

The German Party (DP), the junior partner of the coalition, was just inside the limits of right-wing respectability. It contained the only monarchists in German politics, and claimed direct descent from the Hanoverian Guelphs who had opposed Bismarck because he rejected an *Anschluss* of Austria within the new Reich.

As with the FDP, the DP fully supported Dr. Adenauer's foreign policy, although its motives for backing European integration may be somewhat questionable in view of the chauvinistic tendencies of most of its leaders.

The BHE (League of the Expellees and Disenfranchised) was essentially a party for refugees. (Of the twenty-seven deputies elected on September 6th, fourteen originated from territory behind the Iron Curtain.) Formed in 1950, it had not stood in the first Federal elections. Notable successes of the party in the 1952 Landstag elections had, in view of its irredentist tendencies, caused Allied observers grave misgivings as to the power it might obtain in the new Bundestag. Furthermore, of its leaders, Herr Waldemar Kraft had been an officer of the Waffen SS, and Professor Theodor Oberländer a prominent member of Nazi Minister Rosenberg's infamous *Ostministerium*. Of the party's chances, Dr. Adenauer punned, badly but prophetically, before the elections, "I do not believe it will constitute a *dritte Kraft* (third force)." But although the voting strength of the BHE was an unknown quantity, the party offered obvious attractions to the ten million refugees and angled assiduously for the votes of the "persecuted" ex-Nazis. As well as demanding better terms for these elements, its program called for the restoration of *all* German territories, not restricted to 1937 frontiers, and the granting of land to propertyless farmers. It attacked the decentralized Federal system and urged the restoration of the "Prussian tradition" in the civil service.

Two other new factors in the elections were the All-German People's Party (GVP) and the League of Germans (BdD). Both parties were avowedly neutralist, and under the guidance of Moscow were welded into a united front to fight Dr. Adenauer at the polls. Their activities formed a fascinating revelation of Soviet political intriguing, as will be seen later.

The news of the sudden and totally unexpected release of Dr. Werner Naumann, just five weeks before polling, fell like a bomb among the electioneering parties. On July 28th he was released by order of the West German Supreme Court while charges against him were still pending. Two days later Herr Adolf von Thadden, leader of the German Reich Party (DRP), announced that Naumann had been invited to stand as a candidate. (The DRP was a violently nationalist party centered — like Remer's Socialist Reich Party — in Lower Saxony, with only five members in the Bundestag. It stood for the re-creation of a strong, rearmed Reich, independent of both East and West.) Naumann's candidature was soon followed by the news that Colonel Hans Rudel, Germany's most famous fighter-bomber pilot of World War II, was to return from the Argentine to stand for the Reich Party in Lower Saxony.

On August 12th, Naumann's short-lived election campaign reached its peak at a meeting in Bonn — attended largely by foreign correspondents. He accused the British of "absolutely inhuman treatment" while he was in Werl prison, and heaped ridicule on Sir Ivone Kirkpatrick and his interrogators. It was the common theme of all his election speeches. Naumann received some applause at the meeting from his small following of scarfaced ex-Nazis when he exclaimed, "Why should we deprecate that which we once stood for?" and again when he attacked Dr.

Adenauer: "He should be careful lest he be called once again 'the Chancellor of the Allies.' "

This was the first time I met Naumann in person. There was no doubt that he was a most forceful personality. His eyes had a disconcertingly fixed and fanatical stare which made you think he was looking straight through you and at someone behind. He was a magnetic speaker and possessed qualities shared by few other contemporary German politicians — poise and stature. With scornful deliberation he opened his speeches with the phrase Hitler had always used: *"Deutsche Männer und Frauen . . ."*

At a press conference afterwards he handled a distinctly hostile German press in an authoritative and impelling manner that showed he had not been Goebbels' right-hand man for nothing. An incident occurred which is worth repeating if only to illustrate how many Germans reacted to all that Naumann conveyed. Several of Naumann's scar-faced henchmen (a most unpleasant and sinister crew) had sprinkled themselves among the journalists, and one rebuked a German radio correspondent, Heinz Kerneck, for laughing aloud at some statement by Naumann. Kerneck, who won the German equivalent of the Congressional Medal of Honor for wartime valor, at once protested with the words, "Laughter is the privilege of the free press — the times when you could prevent our laughing are now past!"

On August 14th the Federal authorities began to rally against Naumann. The steel city of Dortmund banned a Naumann meeting on the grounds that it would have "promoted the expression of opinions the subject of which was either a crime or an offense against German law." The Hesse Minister of the Interior also issued a ban on Naumann meetings. In Munich, Dr. Adenauer warned the outside world "not to take these things too tragically"; if a law was required to counter the Nazi "manifestations," one would be passed.

In Lower Saxony, as might have been expected, Naumann had a little more success. At Hanover on August 16th he drew his biggest audience — but even so, it numbered little more than

1,000. There were reports, though, that the extreme right-wing groups in Lower Saxony were rallying to the DRP. Former members of Remer's outlawed SRP deserted another party (Dr. Loritz's Economic Reconstruction Party) to join Naumann. Contemporary historians began to recall Hitler's early efforts in gathering about him all the right-wing splinter groups. Herr von Thadden boasted to the press that his party, with Naumann as a candidate, would get about twenty-five seats in the Bundestag. But meanwhile, Naumann was meeting with more and more bans on his meetings. In Hamburg he was taken in custody by the police after ignoring their warning not to hold a political rally. Even in Lower Saxony two meetings were banned. The rats began to leave the sinking ship; Dr. Bornemann, the last of the Gauleiter Group to be released with Naumann, commented to our German assistant, "I fear the long imprisonment may have had its effects on a sensitive soul."

On August 24th, the Germans struck a crushing blow against Naumann. The *Land* Government of North-Rhine Westphalia, where Naumann was nominally resident, received powers from the British authorities to "denazify" categories 1 and 2 of ex-Nazis (major offenders) — previously a reserved right of the High Commission. Naumann was at once classified as category 2, which debarred him from standing in the election; he was also forbidden to hold public office, engage in any public activity, enter the legal profession, or join any professional organization; or carry on any journalistic or literary activity for five years.

These draconic measures spelt the doom of both Naumann and the DRP in the 1953 elections. Blow followed blow; on the 25th, twenty-four candidates of the DRP were struck off the North-Rhine Westphalia electoral lists after some of their sponsoring signatures were found to have been forged. The ace Colonel Rudel, who was to have been DRP star candidate after Naumann, had no sooner arrived in Germany from the Argentine than his candidature was disqualified on the grounds that his period of residence in Germany had been too short.

Interest in Naumann and the neo-Nazis waned with quite remarkable speed once the DRP bubble had been pricked by the denazification edict, and this fact seemed to me at the time to show very clearly how shallow an impression Naumann had made on the German masses. That the vast majority rejected Naumann and his ways was conclusively proved by the very poor showing of the DRP at the polls (1.1 per cent of the total votes). There was also absolutely no case for arguing that these results were entirely due to official hindrances; even in the DRP strongholds of Lower Saxony, where candidates had not been banned, the party lost ground — and there was no evidence of abstentions on a large scale. Furthermore, the swing away from all the right-wing parties (Free Democrats, German Party and Refugees) completely disproved DRP claims that their supporters had rallied to one or other of these parties in areas where the DRP itself was banned. The whole movement was indeed a bubble and it had truly been pricked, not merely by either the British or the German official action, but by the sound common sense of the German people.

Whether the German people will continue to resist as vigorously such manifestations of neo-Nazism must remain an open question — but so far the omens are good. Nothing was more encouraging than the reaction of the *ordinary* West Germans in June 1955 to the appointment of Herr Leonhard Schlueter as new Minister of Education in Lower Saxony. Schlueter was a member of the ultra-nationalist wing of the Lower Saxon Free Democrats, in which Naumann had once shown a great interest, and had an unsavory reputation on account of his pro-Nazi sympathies. Immediately upon the announcement of his nomination, the rector and 18 senior professors of Goettingen University resigned in protest, and 3,000 students "struck" in support of their professors. Their stand touched off a powerful chain reaction in Germany, and Herr Schlueter was placed "on leave" and later resigned the post altogether under the pressure of popular opinion. Commenting on the Schlueter affair, Dr. Robert Birley, the headmaster of Eton, wrote a letter to the *Times,* which is perhaps worth quoting in part: "The details of a political controversy may not be the concern of those who belong to another nation, but we, who belong to the academic tradition of Western Europe, will be false to that tradition if we do not recognize — and say that we recognize — the courage and the sense of responsibility which the University of Goettingen, both professors and students, has shown. Perhaps one who is deeply interested in Germany may add that, in his view, it would be impossible to imagine a more hopeful augury for her future than the immediate reaction of German education during these days in support of Goettingen."

One person who in 1953 never over-estimated Naumann or the right wing threat as a whole was Dr. Adenauer himself. His personal feelings towards Naumann were composed more of contempt than of fear, as was illustrated by the following remark: "If I had been State Secretary under Goebbels, I would try to hide in the darkest corner out of shame over all the evil that the Nazi regime brought upon the world." I remember vividly being tackled by the Chancellor at a reception at the Palais Shaumburg about an article which had appeared in the *Daily Telegraph* shortly before the elections, entitled "Old Dangers Revived in Germany." It was written by Edgar Stern-Rubarth, an ex-German. Adenauer looked very grave and said: "I am extremely disturbed by this article in the *Daily Telegraph*. The right-wing danger in Germany is much exaggerated; Herr Rubarth's fears are completely without ground."

As always, the Chancellor saw Germany's greatest danger coming in the East. While the Naumann election campaign was petering out, the Soviets loosed a broadside timed to deflect the eyes of the West German voter from the attractions of Western integration that Dr. Adenauer was offering. Preceded by a new Note to the Allies proposing a German peace conference within six months, a delegation of the East German Government was invited to talks in Moscow. They returned with a whole series of concessions designed for *West* German consumption: among them, the cutting of occupation costs in the Soviet zone to the deceptively low figure of 5 per cent of the national revenue.

Unmoved by the Russian blandishments, Dr. Adenauer wound up his election campaign with a triumphant whistle stop tour of northern Germany. The Chancellor's train, financed by massive CDU election funds, carried special radio and teleprinter apparatus to keep in constant touch with Bonn, and two Mercedes 300s to reach remote localities without loss of time. The Chancellor was in high spirits at his prospects, and in spite of his seventy-seven years, seemed utterly untired after making four two-hour speeches in three days. To exhausted correspondents on the last day he quipped: "Gentlemen, how can you be so tired? Why, after my meeting last night I read half a detective novel and finished it before breakfast this morning! I fear you eat and drink too much."

In his final speech before the elections, Dr. Adenauer made a last eloquent appeal for European unity: "The barriers must fall between the countries of Europe, and Europe must be united so that Western civilization can survive. There is no other way to ensure that our children shall have a brighter future and be spared the sufferings that our generation went through. It will be a long road, calling for unending patience and the overcoming of a world of prejudices."

13

The Chancellor's Victory

OVER MOST OF WESTERN GERMANY, SUNDAY THE 6TH OF SEP-
tember, 1953, was a day of unusually glorious late summer sunshine. The dank Rhenish air of Bonn was permeated with a rare
breath of freshness. As I drove up the Autobahn to observe polling in the Ruhr, streams of excursionists passed me in the early
morning on their way south for a day's pleasure in the Rhineland.

In the grimy, battered cities of the Ruhr, the streets were as
deserted as any English steel city on a Sunday. Only the ubiquitous election posters and the remnants of pamphlets in the gutters
gave the impression that it might have been anything but an ordinary Sunday. By a most felicitous choice, the majority of the
polling booths had been set up in beer *Lokalen*. In several of these
I watched as coal miners and steel workers came to cast their
votes, usually within the privacy provided by a beer barrel sawn
in two for the purpose. After going through the motions in a calm
and nonchalant manner, they sat down at tables in the *Lokal* to
discuss football results over a glass of beer before returning home.
They came, by ones and twos, in a slow trickle. Throughout the
Ruhr one got the impression that morning of the same deceptive
indifference that had seemingly prevailed during the election
campaigns. All the omens seemed to point to a poor poll, which,
by British experience, generally worked to the disadvantage of
the conservative forces.

In Essen, however, an electoral inspector explained the morning's disappointing results to me: "You see, most people here go to church first, then lunch, then sleep, and vote last — but they will all vote." He added that he had been gratified to find that nearly all the voters, including the older people, fully understood the complicated two-vote system. The inspector apparently knew his electorate: by four p.m., when I reached Wuppertal in the South Ruhr, there were long queues outside each polling booth and some 65 per cent of the listed electors had already voted. At his home in Rhöndorf on the Rhine, Dr. Adenauer followed the example of many of his countrymen by quietly going to church and then casting his vote — amidst the flashing of cameras — in the village polling center.

At 6 p.m. the booths closed their doors, after a day of quiet and orderly polling.

In Bonn, the Bundeshaus had made elaborate plans for some 350 German and foreign journalists to receive the election results that night with speed and accuracy in the comfort of the Bundeshaus restaurant. At one end a screen had been erected to flash results by lantern slide, and special forms were distributed for the annotation of results constituency by constituency. Unfortunately, as so often happens, the super-efficiency of the German planning defeated itself. The slides turned out not to fit the machine, so the projection scheme broke down, and the forms were so cumbersome and complicated that it was almost impossible to keep up with the loudspeaker announcements. After the Bundeshaus had made a merry profit in alcoholic refreshments, many journalists drifted back to their offices, where they found that the German radio was getting out the results quicker. For the rest of the night, rumors and counter-rumors of landslides and defeats swept back and forth across the Bundestag restaurant. The defeat of the DRP chief, von Thadden, drew cheers from German journalists, and a subsequent reprimand over the loudspeakers, with the reminder that *Unparteilichkeit* was the sole condition under which they could avail themselves of the Bundeshaus facilities.

One of the first results to give some indication of the election trends was the victory of a Christian Democrat woman candidate, Frau Pretorius, who won the Ruhr city of Mühlheim in spite of heavy Socialist pressure. Although the full extent of the CDU victory was not realized until much later, the news that they were back in power was brought to journalists in the Bundeshaus at about 2:30 a.m. on Monday. The harbinger of good tidings was the President of the Bundestag, Dr. Ehlers, whose chubby features were fairly aglow with satisfaction. Shortly after dawn, Dr. Adenauer was roused to get the news of his victory by his Secretary of State, Dr. Otto Lenz, who had also gained a seat. Dr. Adenauer acknowledged with a laconic "Thank you, Herr Lenz."

When the final results of the elections became known, even the party executives of the CDU were taken aback by their triumph, which surpassed their most optimistic expectations. The CDU had increased its lead in the Bundestag over the SPD from eight seats to ninety-four — giving them for the first time an absolute majority of 1 over all other parties. By comparison with the 1949 Federal Elections, the 1953 results showed a striking shift in the political structure:

1953 FEDERAL ELECTION RESULTS (1949 RESULTS IN BRACKETS)*

	VOTES CAST		PERCENTAGE OF TOTAL	SEATS WON
Electorate	33,390,098	(31,207,620)	—	—
Votes cast	28,468,054	(24,495,614)	86.2 (78.5)	—
Christian Democrats (CDU/CSU)	12,440,799	(7,359,084)	45.2 (31)	244 (139)
Social Democrats	7,939,774	(6,934,975)	28.8 (29.2)	150 (131)
Free Democrats	2,628,246	(2,829,920)	9.5 (11.9)	48 (52)
Refugee Party	1,614,474	(did not stand)	5.9 (——)	27 (——)
German Party	897,952	(939,934)	3.3 (4.0)	15 (17)
Communist Party	607,413	(1,361,706)	2.2 (5.7)	Nil (15)
All-German Party and League of Germans	318,323	(did not stand)	1.2 (——)	Nil (——)
German Reich Party	295,615	(429,931)	1.1 (1.8)	Nil (5)

* Regional parties, e.g. the Bavarian Party, excluded.

At the SPD headquarters, the Socialist leaders had watched with gloom as their dwindling returns were set out on tables beneath a bronze bust of Dr. Schumacher. In the early morning hours a functionary who had seen the writing on the wall surreptitiously removed the large red banner outside the building which bore the words "Instead of Adenauer — Ollenhauer!" The SPD showed themselves to be surprisingly poor losers. Herr Ollenhauer's first comment on the party's failure was that the CDU's successes were indubitably founded on the support of "restorationist and authoritarian" elements of the extreme Right. Later, his press chief, Herr Fritz Heine, bemoaned, "This is the beginning of the end of democracy in Germany."

In the long-term view of German democracy, the seats that the CDU had won from the Socialists were dwarfed in significance by their successes at the cost of the extremist and splinter parties. The Communist Party had suffered a shattering defeat and lost over half of its following. Gone was its bridgehead on the left of the Bundestag from which it had hurled abuse at Government and Opposition alike, and contributed nothing to the work of legislation. Gone also was Herr von Thadden and his boast that the German Reich Party would gain twenty-five seats; with or without Naumann's help the party could cull little more than one per cent of the votes. Even that unknown quantity, the Refugee Party, which it was thought might have gained some of the DRP support after the Naumann ban, just scraped over the 5 per cent line to get twenty-seven seats in the Bundestag, instead of the estimated fifty the Cassandras had allotted them. The Free Democrats had also had their wings clipped as a result of their embroilment in the Naumann affair, and the right-wing German Party would never have survived but for its directly elected deputies in Lower Saxony. Another party to disappear completely from Federal politics was the parochial Bavarian Party, with its slogan of "Save the Homeland." Its Bavarian voters who had previously sent seventeen deputies to Bonn to represent purely local interests had now switched their support to the CSU, the Bavarian wing of the Christian Democrats; all the Bavarian Party could muster was 1.6 per cent of the total votes. The Federalist Union and the Economic Reconstruction Party had also disappeared; the Center Party had been taken under the wing of the CDU. In removing the splinter party threat to stable government, Dr. Adenauer had fulfilled his promise made in the US earlier in the year: "We are firmly resolved not to repeat the mistakes of the Weimar Republic, which, by its exaggerated liberalism, permitted the enemies of the country to destroy its democratic institutions."

In the passage of time and events, the significance of the 1953 election results has become somewhat obscured. But whatever interpretations may be made *ex post facto,* there can be no doubt that it provided a most reassuring display of the common sense and moderation on the part of the German electorate. The enormously high poll of 86.2 per cent had, contrary to all the deceptive omens, shown the Germans to be extremely aware of the high political issues at stake and of the duty a democracy requires of its citizens. Soberly they had, over three-quarters of them, voted for one or other of the two major parties which stood for decency and democratic standards.

They had resolutely dispersed the fears provoked by the Naumann affair that Nazism resuscitated was at large among the German masses. Particularly encouraging was the fact that millions of the refugee and expellee "have-nots" had rejected the attractions of the BHE in favor of one of the more stable parties. Neither the BHE nor the FDP "German Program" of Dr. Middelhauve had succeeded in drawing any considerable proportion of the embittered elements of the one-million-odd penalized ex-Nazis who were now voting for the first time. As a sign of the healthy state of the average German's political thinking eight years after Hitler, the importance of the 1953 elections could not be overstressed, and their results were certainly more convincing than any number of public-opinion polls. It is interesting to note that Adenauer won a considerably higher percentage of votes than ever Hitler did in any election held under reasonably democratic conditions. Hitler's best was 37 per cent, against Adenauer's 45 per cent.

The election results were a most resounding endorsement of the EDC and Dr. Adenauer's European policy. The *Neue*

Zürcher Zeitung went so far as to declare: "Adenauer's policy of European integration will not be challenged in the future with the claim that the German people want to give the question of German reunification precedence over all others."

Of immediate importance was the fact that, with the help of the BHE, whose leaders had already pledged themselves to support the EDC, Dr. Adenauer could now muster in the Lower House a two-thirds majority, if it should be required to amend the Constitution to legalize conscription. Moreover the CDU conquests in Hamburg and Württemberg presaged changes of government in those *Länder* which would eventually ensure Dr. Adenauer a two-thirds majority in the Bundesrat as well. The road to the final ratification of the Treaties now seemed quite open.

Abroad, the CDU victory was greeted with great jubilation by the apostles of EDC and the Adenauer followers. *The Economist* wrote: "If there is a single moral to be drawn from the events that led up to Dr. Adenauer's decisive victory it is that doggedness pays . . . It looks — one hardly dare say it — as if the clumsy Americans have been right and the pessimistic experts on Europe wrong." The New York *Times* rejoiced: ". . . the Kremlin has lost. West Germany is a corner-stone in the new European order."

The rejoicing in the West was, however, not free from misgivings as to the potential dangers inherent in the great concentration of power which Dr. Adenauer and the CDU had now inherited. The *Manchester Guardian* wondered whether many of the German millions who had voted for Dr. Adenauer had not done so simply because he was a "strong man," thus arousing echoes of the old cry *Ein Volk, ein Reich, ein Führer*. In France, the neutralist *Le Monde* pointed out with concern that, of the original three great proponents of European integration, Adenauer alone remained, and he was stronger than ever before. "From this realization, it is only one step to the conclusion that the Washington Government will reckon more and more on Western Germany and less and less on France and Italy."

Inside Germany, Jens Daniel in *Der Spiegel* was one of the few West German columnists to take a gloomy view of the election results: "The Chancellor's victory in the Federal Elections was too complete. It was an inverted Pyrrhic victory; instead of receiving too many wounds, the victor received too much power. Another victory like this and German democracy is doomed." At the opposite extreme, the Naumann – DRP organ, *Das Ziel,* grieved that the Adenauer landslide spelt a "deathly danger for the *Reich* ideal."

Misgivings abroad, particularly in France, were heightened after the very first post-election speech by Dr. Adenauer, through the unfortunate selection of one word — *Befreiung*. It was a dramatic occasion — in the gathering dusk of Monday, September 7th, the re-elected Chancellor was to appear on the balcony of Bonn's 18th-century Rathaus. The market place was densely packed with expectant Bonners, about to experience one of the rare excitements in the life of the town. Preceded by a torchlight procession of boy scouts and three white-clad outriders, Adenauer arrived in a Mercedes 300, accompanied by his daughter Lotte. His face was drawn and unusually fatigued, but he waved cheerfully in answer to the wild applause as he mounted the steps of the Rathaus. The Bürgermeister of Bonn, Herr Busen, presented him as "*Bundeskanzler* and Deputy for Bonn." In a quiet, rather tired voice, Dr. Adenauer thanked his supporters for their votes, then said: "My friends, it was a decisive day yesterday." He outlined his aims for his new term of office as "a happy, more prosperous future for Germany," the furthering of European integration plans to provide "a better Europe for our youth," and reunification for Germany.

Here the Chancellor paused momentarily, and amidst sustained cheers qualified his last statement, "But instead of reunification, let us rather talk of *Befreiung* (liberation) — the liberation of our brethren in slavery in the East. That is our aim, and that we shall achieve, but only with outside help." It was fuel for the *mourir pour Königsberg* Frenchmen, who at once associated the word *Befreiung* with the *Befreiungskreig* that Blücher and

Scharnhorst had waged so successfully against Napoleon. It was splendid copy for the Hunhaters of Great Britain: here, once more, was the voice of unmitigated German militarism — and coming from the mouth of the old Chancellor who had previously pretended to be such a good, peaceloving European! Now, with his new-gained power, he felt it safe to hoist his true colors. In Germany it was seized upon by Dr. Adenauer's adversary, Jens Daniel of *Der Spiegel,* who commented: "This was the first time for fifteen years that a German Chancellor had pledged *Befreiung* to Germans outside his jurisdiction."

The Federal Press Office at once pointed out in answer to the queries of foreign correspondents that, in their complicated language, *'Befreiung'* also meant a *deliverance,* which was what was intended by the Chancellor — and of course the Federal Government had in no way deviated from its former policy that reunification could only be effected by peaceful means. It was obvious to all who heard the speech — except those totally dedicated to squeezing Dr. Adenauer willy-nilly into a Procrustean bed of Prussianism — that *Befreiung* in this context had no more sinister meaning. Nothing was more absurd, or more contrary to the background of the man, than the notion of the 77-year-old Catholic Rhinelander planning a forcible *Befreiung* of the Protestant East Germans, either in September, 1953, or at any other time, and the German explanation was accepted unreservedly by the Allied High Commission.

As soon as the dust from the elections began to settle, the Social Democrats set about a serious post-mortem to examine the causes of the party's dismal failure at the polls, and the serious plight in which it now found itself. Barely a fortnight after the elections, fate contributed another unkind blow to their misfortunes by the tragic and unexpected death of Professor Ernst Reuter, the Oberbürgermeister of Berlin, who, since the death of Schumacher, had been the party's most impressive and influential figure. Although, as indicated in the previous chapter, the negativeness of the party's policy had been the chief cause of its downfall, the ineptitude with which the party leaders had conducted the election campaign had undoubtedly contributed significantly to its weakness. To the public, the Socialists attributed their failure to such factors as unfair methods employed by the Christian Democrats in their campaign; and indeed, as for instance when the CDU accused SPD candidates of receiving funds from the Soviet zone, on evidence which they later admitted to be spurious, the SPD often had a case. But in private, they, like Cassius, admitted that the fault lay within themselves. Had their Marxism been as rigidly orthodox as that of the parties of Eastern Germany, there would undoubtedly have been some unpleasant purges within the party ranks. Professor Carlo Schmid, the SPD's leading intellectual and party theorist, furiously attacked the executive for their mistaken election tactics of concentrating the attack on rural and suburban districts — which were generally staunchly CDU — while ignoring the industrial areas which they felt to be firmly in their own hands. In this way, Professor Schmid contended, the SPD had lost in such traditionally workers' constituencies as Hamburg, Frankfurt, and Mühlheim in the Ruhr. Indeed, from what one had seen of it, the SPD campaign in the big cities appeared to have been organized on a most casual basis.

Shortly before the elections, Herr Ollenhauer told the Foreign Press Association that he would welcome a bi-partisan foreign policy. But the Socialists' enfeebled condition after the elections certainly did not enhance their case for a bigger hearing on foreign affairs, or improve their prospects of being taken into a *Grosse Koalition* in Bonn or the *Länder*. Nor did they show any willingness to compromise in their opposition to the Bonn Treaties, which any conjoint foreign policy would have required of them. As Dr. Adenauer remarked after the elections, "You cannot make foreign policy by mixing two entirely different liquids. It becomes cloudy." And SPD foreign policy was certainly cloudy enough on its own. That the SPD influence in Germany should have been so weakened, through nobody's fault but their own, was in fact very much to be deplored. Potentially the party is one of the foremost stabilizing forces against any threatened revival of Nazism, and could render democracy in Germany the very greatest service. Many of its leaders had suffered in Nazi concentration camps, and one, Herr Willi Brandt, had actually borne arms against the Nazis in the Norwegian underground. Individually, and as a party, it had better cause to suspect and detest any form of resurgent German nationalism than many of its opponents; yet it had allowed itself to be led by Dr. Schumacher into a cul-de-sac of nationalism as virulent as that of any other party. A sad fate for what, between the wars, probably had been the most internationally-minded of all socialist parties.

If one could weep over the decline of the SPD, it was difficult to find tears for the demise of the Communists — especially after the 17th of June. On the Tuesday after the elections a small crowd watched in silence as obese Herr Rische, acid Herr Renner and sibilant Herr Reimann, and their twelve cell-mates, packed up their belongings in the Bundeshaus and collected their last salary payments from the cash office. Many of them were exchanging the comfort of the Bundestag which they had so incessantly abused for the uncertainty of the court room; with their parliamentary immunity removed, they now faced more than forty charges ranging from libel to treason.

As the chief of police at Solingen in the Ruhr commented to me on the night of Max Reimann's final election speech there, "The Communists have had their day in Western Germany" — at least temporarily. In Germany, Communism meant Russia; and it has always struck me how very similar are the German and Yugoslav attitudes to the Russians. Both had had intimate relations with them, which had turned to hate and fear — one, the result of a love turned sour, the other, of a forcible ravishment. And to both the hated one was still so very close. With a realism unfortunately not shared by their confrères farther off in England, the heads of the principal West German trade unions have virtually barred Communists from their executives, through the ruling that no official may accept orders from outside. Once the German workers had themselves seen through Communist intentions, there was little hope that the Communist Party or its allies could find fertile ground for expansion in Western Germany.

But the Russians most patently did think they had a chance in the 1953 elections, and their enormous failure gave reassuring signs that the Kremlin's German experts had misinterpreted trends in Western Germany just as grossly as they had misjudged them in their own zone. Perhaps since these experts had to read every day in their own press elaborate polemics about "mass demonstrations against the Adenauer terror regime" by West German workers, their optimism was hardly surprising.

The Soviet campaign formed roughly a three-pronged offensive, comprising, first, the infiltration of Free German Youth agitators from Eastern Germany to disturb polling; second, the organization of "travelling voters" to beat the 5 per cent clause by gaining one direct seat to the Bundestag; and third, the formation of a cover "front" of the All-German Party and the League of Germans, designed to draw the neutralist voter who would not vote Communist.

The large-scale infiltration of FDJ agitators, ironically dubbed Operation Lorelei by its organizers, first came to the notice of the West German authorities exactly a week before the elections. Some 2,000 young Communists were stopped on the interzonal frontier, equipped with West German passes bearing crudely forged stamps of cities in the Ruhr. They all brazenly stated that they were on their way to visit relatives in the Federal Republic. When searched, they were found to be carrying masses of Communist propaganda in their suitcases and very large sums in West German marks. These were hidden in such unlikely places as inside toothpaste tubes, soap containers and the linings of jackets and neckties. This novel form of influx from Eastern Germany continued throughout the next week.

At first the West Germans simply turned them back, until they found that the same would-be infiltrators were coming back again and again. One youth admitted under interrogation that he had been supplied with money and ordered to get over into the Federal Republic "at all costs." He and his comrades had been granted leave from their work to attend "party education outside the district." If he failed in his mission he feared that he would be severely penalized. Eventually the infiltrators gave up using the obvious routes of the interzonal trains and crossing-points, and tried to slip over in small groups through unmanned parts of the frontier. The entire 10,000-man strength of the West German Frontier Force was mobilized to meet this threat, and thenceforth all infiltrators were not sent back, but detained in emergency camps until after the elections. The West German authorities calculated that, by the end of the action, over 8,000 illegal attempts to cross had been made. Of these, some 4,500 passed the elections in West German custody. At the same time Operation Lorelei was backed up by energetic party scribes in Eastern Germany who dispatched some 50,000 letters to West Germans during the week preceding the elections, trying to persuade them by cajolery or threats to vote against Dr. Adenauer.

Over $75,000 in West German marks was confiscated; on the current rate of exchange, Operation Lorelei is estimated to have cost its organizers, the *West Kommission* of the Socialist Unity Party, over $420,000 and this had to be found from the scanty East German foreign trade funds. For this outlay, out of the 20,000 Free German youths nominated for the operation, it is doubtful if more than a handful of agitators could have slipped through the West German net, and their efforts had no noticeable effect. A number of the FDJs indeed took the golden opportunity to seek asylum in the West. The Russians could hardly have expected that the results of the elections would have been influenced even if the "Lorelei" youths had succeeded in penetrating to the Ruhr. But the disturbances provoked by them would have given the Russians the "proof" they wanted to claim that the Communists were being ruthlessly suppressed in Western Germany; an excuse for strengthening their line on free elections to reunite Germany.

The second part of the Communist election offensive took place on polling day itself. The aim was to bring Communist voters from various parts of the Ruhr to cast their votes in Solin-

gen, by tradition the reddest town in Germany, where Max Reimann, the party chief, had the best chance of getting elected on
the direct ticket. By an extraordinary loophole in the new electoral law, on presentation of a good case, an absentee voter could
cast his vote in any constituency of his choosing. At one election
Lokal in Solingen, I watched as a block of some twenty youths
self-consciously registered as "absentee voters." By a curious co-
incidence, all appeared to come from a small Ruhr town called
Cösfeld. The electoral officer shrugged his shoulders resignedly:

"What can we do? Their community authorities give them the
certificate to vote in Solingen and we can't challenge it. They're
supposed to have a good excuse, such as a sick relative in Solingen, but they can't all have sick aunts here!'

Outside, discreetly parked in a side alley, I found the buses
which had brought the "travelling" voters. One of them had not
even bothered to remove its Communist Party banner.

But apparently the party could not find sufficient supporters to
make even this stunt succeed, although it had worked well in
Czechoslovakia in 1948. In spite of the travelling vote, Herr
Reimann came a poor third in the elections, drawing only 20,120
votes in a vastly increased poll, compared with his 29,760 in
1949. For his efforts he was summoned to Moscow for a severe
castigation, which he duly passed on to the rank and file on his
return.

The third prong of the Communist offensive was just as unsuccessful as the other two, but it revealed much more grandiose
and tortuous long-range planning. Its carrying out was also the
responsibility of the *West Kommission*. That every detail of this
Communist plot should be made known to the West subsequently
was largely due to the defection of two of its originators, Georg
Jost and Georg Wieber, who held a press conference in Bonn on
August 27th, 1953.

The plot had its origin in 1950, when the Russians were preparing their first overtures to Western Germany for reunification
— on Russian terms. With finance from the *West Kommission,*
an organization was created in Western Germany entitled the

"Working Circle for German Understanding and a Just Peace."
Its best-known supporter in Western Germany was Herr Wilhelm
Elfes, an ex-Mayor of München-Gladbach, but the *West Kommission* was meanwhile busily searching for a West German personality of greater weight who could rally bourgeois support for
the Russian proposals. Acording to Jost, at the end of 1951 the
Kommission submitted to the Soviet Control Commission the
name of Dr. Josef Wirth, aged seventy-four, one-time Chancellor
of the Weimar Republic. His qualification was that in 1922 he
had signed the Treaty of Rapallo, formally launching the first
Russo-German *entente* of the post-war period.[1] Now feeling his
age, and somewhat doddering, he was lured from his retirement
to East Berlin where the Communists courted him with every
form of oily flattery until he agreed to take over leadership of the
"Working Circle." On his return to the Federal Republic, the
"circle" was transformed into a new political party with the title
of the "German Rally," of which Elfes now became a leading
executive.

At the first public meeting of the party on June 30th, 1952, Dr.
Wirth was surprised to discover at the last moment that the chief
speaker was to be Herr Reimann, the Communist Party boss.
Apparently nobody had bothered to notify Dr. Wirth, a foretaste
of the way in which he and his movement were to be treated
throughout. His first audience consisted of 6,000 Communists
transported from all over the Ruhr, and, of course, financed by

[1] I have already commented in several places on the curious triangular relationship that is almost invariably shown to exist between post-war German
"neutralism," ultra-nationalism and Communism. As background to Dr.
Wirth, a report which I came across in the course of research is perhaps
worth quoting in part. It came from the Swiss *Luzerner Tageblatt* dated
August 9, 1937, which quoted Dr. Wirth as boasting: "As to the rearmament of Germany, Hitler has only continued the rearmament that had been
prepared by the Weimar Republic. I myself deserve great credit for this
preparation. . . . The great difficulty was that our military efforts had to
be kept secret from the Allies. I therefore always had to appear polite and
harmless . . . when Hitler came to power he no longer needed to concern
himself with the quality of the German army but only with the quantity. The
real reorganization was our work."

Communist funds. During the meeting, Dr. Wirth launched the bogus "National Referendum," soliciting signatures of those opposed to the EDC. By April, 1953, it was claiming that fifteen million had been gathered in Western Germany alone. The figure may be somewhat open to question, as, after a brief period of counting actual signatures, the organizers adopted the simpler and much more satisfying course of just counting heads at anti-EDC meetings, regardless of duplication!

At this juncture the party ranks were joined by Frau Charlotte Fleischmann, the disaffected Chairman of the Munich branch of the Christian Democrats. Like Jost and Wieber, she too saw the light later, and gave an account of her experiences in the Wirth movement. At first, she said, her duties had been to canvass for followers, accepting an "expense allowance" for the work. In 1953 she began to notice with some vexation that manifestoes were appearing over her name, without her knowledge or permission, which were verbatim repetitions of current Communist propaganda. About the same time, an unknown "fairy godmother" provided the party with sumptuous offices in Düsseldorf, tenanted by a mysterious staff. Neither she nor Wirth nor Elfes knew who they were, whence they came or what they did, but each time she entered the office "there were more of them there." According to Frau Fleischmann, "far from having been appointed by us or by any responsible organ of the Rally, they usually did not even bother to tell us their names."

In May, 1953, the party once again changed its name — now to the League of Germans (BdD). Under this cover were amalgamated such fellow-travelling organizations as the Leadership Ring of German Soldiers, the Democratic Women's League, the Principal Committee against Remilitarization, the Democratic Culture League, all of which had links with the *West Kommission* in East Berlin. By this time, however, the Communist infiltration within the party had become well publicized in Western Germany. So as to give the BdD a more respectable façade for the coming elections, the *West Kommission* decided to ally it with another West German party which had previously remained free from Communist infection.

They chose the neutralist All-German People's Party (GVP) formed by Dr. Gustav Heinemann, who had been Dr. Adenauer's Minister of the Interior until 1950, when he had resigned in disagreement with the rearmament policy. He enjoyed considerable prestige among German Protestants as a senior lay functionary of the Evangelical Church, and had frequently criticized the Communists. But his party lacked the funds needed to fight an election campaign on a Federal level. Hence, Dr. Heinemann was willing to sell his soul to the Mephistophelian backers of Dr. Wirth in return for apparently unlimited financial support. It must have seemed an attractive agreement to him; with noble selflessness, the BdD agreed to put up no candidates and leave propaganda to the GVP. A number of BdD candidates would be incorporated in the GVP lists, but the party would go to the polls under the title of the GVP. The BdD's financial support meant that the GVP could now put up candidates for the fantastically high number of 229 constituencies out of a total of 242.

In actual practice, of course, its alliance with the BdD worked out quite differently from GVP expectations, and the whole campaign was in fact manipulated by the mysterious personages in the BdD Düsseldorf HQ, many of whom were in fact visiting Communist doctrinaires from the Soviet zone. Frau Fleischmann said that at a meeting at Aschaffenburg she had found that of the six GVP officials on the platform, four were Communists. To each GVP candidate, the BdD attached a full-time "adviser." These were all known Communists and complete foreigners to the constituency, and indeed often political "instructors" detailed from Eastern Germany. Frau Fleischmann, who resigned in disgust at these antics, stated that she had conclusive evidence that all the BdD's massive election funds had come from the East. The BdD was described by Jost as a "marionette of Communist policy inside the Federal Republic."

As a study in infiltration, the Communist conspiracy made the activities of Naumann look like a lower-school intrigue. Its cost must have run into millions, and yet it gained the joint GVP/ BdD barely more than 300,000 votes, was a gigantic fiasco, and exposed the Russians to great ridicule. Nevertheless, although this time it failed, it gave a frightening pointer to what would have happened if All-German elections had taken place at that date on Russian terms — i.e. the total withdrawal of all occupation forces, and the absence of any UN election arbitrators.

14

Shaping the New Government

THE FIRST MONTHS OF THE NEW GOVERNMENT WERE A VAST disappointment to the gloom-bound Cassandras of the SPD, who had forecast that the Adenauer landslide would bring with it a new era of "authoritarianism." Quite the contrary, Dr. Adenauer's authority over the various components of the coalition — even weakened as some of them were by the elections — showed itself at once to be somewhat more tenuous than in the days when the coalition had been bound together by the peril of a slim majority.

Dr. Adenauer's new difficulties were first revealed in the deliberations over the make-up of the new cabinet, which took the inordinately long time of six weeks. It was clear from the start that Dr. Adenauer's main consideration here would be his need to be assured of a two-thirds majority in the Bundestag. He had to make quite sure of the support not only of his previous collaborators, the FDP and the DP (who together now disposed of 12.8 per cent of the Bundestag seats, compared with 15.9 per cent previously), but also of the new BHE's twenty-seven seats. The price of assured collaboration was seats in the Federal cabinet, and the three parties were making their fee a high one.

The Chancellor himself was from the start willing to grant them stakes in the cabinet well in excess of their relative strengths, but he reckoned without the personal ambitions of some of his own cohorts and the demands of the CSU (the Bavarian branch of the CDU). This faction had contributed very materially to the Adenauer victory, gaining fifty-two seats on their own account, and they now felt, as a reward for their efforts, that they should be allotted at least as many cabinet posts as the FDP with forty-eight seats. On the other hand, the influential Finance Minister, Herr Fritz Schäffer, also a CSU member, was strongly opposed to an enlarged cabinet on financial grounds. The undignified scramble for seats which ensued had a certain element of comic opera about it, and many minor injuries were sustained. A cartoon in *Die Welt* at the time showed Dr. Adenauer and his daughter Lotte on vacation in the Black Forest, surrounded by figures disguised as peasants or beasts of the forest. The caption read: "Don't look round, Lotte — they're only foolish people who want to become ministers!"

One of the first casualties was the unfortunate Dr. Heinrich von Brentano, the extremely loyal and hard-working parliamentary leader of the CDU. Dr. von Brentano had led the Federal Government delegation at the Council of Europe, and he was generally regarded as West German foreign minister-elect — pending relinquishment of the post by Dr. Adenauer. A chain-smoker, extremely nervous and not over-endowed with charm, Dr. von Brentano seemed to lack the personality required for so exacting a post. Nevertheless, before the elections Dr. Adenauer had expressed the intention of surrendering the Foreign Office, and on September 9th Dr. von Brentano let correspondents know at his press conference that his appointment was all but decided. But at the very moment that Dr. von Brentano was saying with blushing modesty, "It is, of course, no secret that my name has been mentioned in this connection," the Chancellery was issuing a statement to the effect that it was not yet considered "opportune" for Dr. Adenauer to give up the post. It was never quite clear what caused this embarrassing crossing of the wires, although it was understood at the time that the Americans had urgently prevailed upon Dr. Adenauer at the eleventh hour to continue to represent Germany abroad. The badly snubbed Dr. von Brentano was consoled by the Chancellor with the promise that he would get the job once the Treaties were ratified. (He did not in fact get it until mid-June 1955.)

Meanwhile, Herr Blank, the "shadow" defense commissioner, was becoming exceedingly worried by the manifest ambitions of Herr Franz-Josef Strauss. Herr Strauss, a thirty-eight-year-old deputy of the CSU, who had played a vocal role in the first Bundestag, was covetous of the post of Defense Minister, which would be established once the EDC Treaty was ratified. He was one of the CSU's principal candidates for a cabinet post, and their insistence finally prevailed upon Dr. Adenauer to take Herr Strauss as a Minister without Portfolio. Herr Blank hitherto had only an advisory position in the cabinet, and he feared that Herr Strauss' appointment would give him an advantageous foothold for pressing future claims. In extreme agitation he wrote the Chancellor an impetuous letter (which he rashly published), demanding a voice in the cabinet for himself. It was, he claimed, necessary that his office become an independent organ, instead of a satellite of the Chancellery, and have full representation in the cabinet. He backed up his demands with a hint at resignation if they were not fulfilled.

Although this palace revolt was something quite unheard-of in Bonn, the Chancellor was not to be flustered, and he made it clear to correspondents at one of his periodic "tea parties" that Herr Blank's requirements were not to be accepted. At this moment, Dr. Adenauer explained, a promotion of Herr Blank and his office could only cause an unfavorable reaction in Paris among circles who were now wavering on ratification. He hoped however that Herr Blank would be encouraged to stay in office. Herr Blank *was* encouraged to stay in office, apparently by assurances of his priority over Herr Strauss for the future Defense Ministry.

In addition to the clamorers without, Dr. Adenauer also had to contend with the "wild men" within the previous cabinet, Dr. Thomas Dehler (Free Democrat), the Minister of Justice, and Dr. Hans-Christoph Seebohm (German Party), Minister of

Transport. Dr. Dehler had frequently worried the Chancellor by his fiery displays of independence in the first cabinet, but he was a genuine spokesman of the Liberal element of the Free Democrats, his vigorous personality commanded a strong following within the party, and Dr. Adenauer would have liked to have him safely under his wing in the cabinet. Dr. Dehler, however, was determined not to place himself within the restricting confines of the front bench again. He was seriously concerned at the loss of prestige his party had suffered as a result of the Naumann episode, and feared that another four years of amorphousness within the coalition would result in the FDP entirely losing its identity as a party. Thus he felt that his prime duty was to the party, of which he was soon elected Chairman. In his maiden speech from the floor Dr. Dehler drew much mirth from the Bundestag when he said, "You will perhaps understand the feelings which creep over me as I mount this dais for the first time as a completely free man." To Dr. Adenauer, however, it was a warning of the independent line along which Dr. Dehler now intended to lead his party, and indeed, in the difficult months of 1954, Dr. Adenauer was to experience far more opposition from the FDP than from any other faction within the coalition.

From the point of view of ensuring uniformity of foreign policy within the coalition, subsequent events certainly proved the soundness of Dr. Adenauer's method of controlling his more questionable allies by muzzling their strong men with cabinet jobs. One of these was Dr. Seebohm, whose polemics had caused Dr. Adenauer much embarrassment in the past four years. Few people considered that he would be recalled to the cabinet, and up until the tenth "authentic" cabinet list drafted by the lobby journalists of the Bundeshaus, his name was absent. But Dr. Adenauer's view was that it was much safer to have Seebohm under his eye within the cabinet, and kept busy in the Transport Ministry, thus leaving the manipulating of the German Party to the more moderate and restrained deputies, Hellwege and von Merkatz.

Dr. Adenauer let the same principles guide him in his choice of the two ex-Nazi BHE leaders, Herr Waldemar Kraft and Professor Theodor Oberländer, as Minister without Portfolio and Refugee Minister respectively. Dr. Adenauer never made any secret of the fact that he held little brief for the Refugee Party, its policy or its personalities. Nevertheless, he had to have their support for the completion of EDC ratification, and this was the price. As it turned out, of the three coalition juniors, the BHE have proved more loyal partners than the senior member of the former coalition, the liberal-nationalist Free Democrat Party. At the same time, the party, bereft of its leadership, markedly lost ground within the country. It was a calculated political risk, and it seemed to be entirely justified. The great pity was that the political necessities imposed on Dr. Adenauer in his cabinet selections were never fully appreciated abroad, and the hue and cry against the "ex-Nazi" ministers was never abated. Professor Oberländer, more perhaps than any of the others, aroused considerable misgivings, especially when he subsequently began to bring into his Ministry "old friends" from the Nazi *Ost Ministerium*. None of this could, however, be justly blamed upon Dr. Adenauer. Under the Federal Constitution drawn up by the Allies, the personnel policy of each Ministry was entirely the affair of the Minister and sacrosanct even from the stern tutelage of the Chancellor. But there could be little doubt — and those Ministers held no illusions as to their future — that as soon as the Refugee Party has fulfilled its role, or lost its national position at the next poll, Dr. Adenauer would replace Prof. Oberländer with another who would soon scour out his protégés from the Refugee Ministry.

Before the final formation of his cabinet, Dr. Adenauer had one last consideration — he must avoid all suspicion of having formed a Catholic cabinet. His own party was split down the middle into a Catholic and Protestant wing, and his allies were essentially non-Catholic. To provide the balance which he considered desirable, eleven Protestants to eight Catholics, Dr. Adenauer wanted to replace his not very successful Catholic Minister of Posts, Dr. Hans Schubert, with a Protestant. To please his Bavarian followers, he also had to be a member of the CSU. Further-more, he had to have technical qualifications. Such a man was not readily available; nevertheless the formation of the cabinet could be delayed no longer, so the post was left vacant for the time being. It was not filled until Christmas.

By the night of October 19th, the eve of the first Government declaration, the cabinet at last seemed complete. It was to con-sist of eight Christian Democrats, three Christian Socialists (four with the Minister of Posts), three Free Democrats, two German Party and two Refugees — a total of nineteen compared with the fourteen of its predecessor. Far too many for Herr Schäffer's liking.

At the last moment there was one further hitch, due to the dissatisfaction of a coalition partner: Herr Martin Euler, par-liamentary leader of the Free Democrats, threatened that the FDP would "either have four seats or none" in the new cabinet. There were hasty consultations. Finally, on the very morning of the investiture of the cabinet members by President Heuss, the unfortunate Dr. Paul Nerreter of the CSU, who was to have been Minister of Justice, was informed that his place had been taken by Herr Fritz Neumayer of the FDP. Legend has it that Herr Neumayer had to do a hasty change into his morning coat in his car on the way to the investiture.

One of the new CDU ministers, Dr. Franz Joseph Würme-ling, a Catholic, had a novel and thankless task. He was to take charge of the newly created Ministry for Family Affairs. This was a special project of Dr. Adenauer's, who, in his Government Declaration, had expressed gravest fears that the low German birthrate threatened to make Germany a *Raum ohne Volk,* as op-posed to the converse slogan of the Nazis. The statistics did in-deed give Dr. Adenauer some cause for alarm. By 1952 the birth-rate had dropped to 15.7 per thousand inhabitants — the lowest in Europe except for Austria. Nearly a quarter of the population was over 65. As a result of the war there were three million widows and the women greatly outnumbered the men — in the ages of 25 to 35, the proportion was 1,342 women to every 1,000 men. The upset economic and moral standards of the post-war period added 380,000 divorced women to the total number of disrupted families. Divorces were currently at more than twice the pre-war level. Uncertain conditions provided young Germans with little incentive to marry.

Dr. Würmeling's job was to increase the *Wille zum Kind* — the desire to have children. On the assumption that a successful business man makes a good Minister of Economics, a father of five was unquestionably the right man for this difficult task. Devoid of any executive powers, his role was to co-ordinate legislation of the other Ministries which touched upon the family; to see that the Housing Minister built more multi-room flats and fewer bachelor establishments; to wring tax concessions for families from the Finance Minister. He also bravely suggested that he would like to do something about the low moral tone of German films.

All these were excellent intentions, but it scarcely seemed to warrant the creation of a special ministry. The scheme met with stinging criticism from all quarters, especially when it implied any form of film censorship. Dr. Würmeling himself became the butt of every dirty joke for several months. His enemies accused him of planning to revive the Nazi tradition of the "Mother's Medal," and Bonn students ridiculed the poor man by making a trophy of his ministerial plaque during the Carnival.

Although the attacks on Würmeling were mostly frivolous, they had a far graver undertone — the question of religion in German politics. To anyone who has not lived in Germany, it is extremely hard to appreciate the extent to which animosity between Catholicism and Protestantism plays a role in both public and private life. Even among the impoverished remnants of the German aristocracy, whom, one would have thought, adversity would have welded into unity, the Catholic and Protestant families are so sharply divided that, in many cases, they are barely on social terms with each other. The fact that the gulf between the two religions in Germany is today so much greater than in Great Britain can be traced back historically to the fearful savagery of the Thirty Years War, followed later by the regional loyalties that accentuated the rivalry between Protestant Prussia and Catholic Bavaria. It is also abetted by the equality of forces in the West German rump, where there are 23.9 million Protestants to 21.6 million Catholics, and by the character of the German Protestant Church — a far more militant organization than the Church of England.

The issues have been accentuated in politics by the mere fact that the CDU/CSU is first and foremost a "Christian" party. Its cultural policy of confessional schools — that is, separate schools for each creed — is constantly under hot attack from the other, non-confessional parties. There was also bitter criticism at election time of the instructions put out from Catholic pulpits to vote Christian Democrat.

No one could seriously accuse Dr. Adenauer, staunch Catholic though he is, of deliberately fostering the religious war in Bonn politics. But even some of his own followers were critical that, on the contrary, by leaning over backwards to avoid any such stigma and granting the Protestants a considerable preponderance in the new cabinet, he had only made people more conscious of the problem than ever before. A non-confessional CDU deputy commented to me, "If I had to build a cabinet, I would not choose ministers because of their religions, but because they were competent men."

The fact that Dr. Adenauer should have laid so much emphasis on the confessional issues in selecting his Cabinet pointed to one of the most gravely disquieting problems of the future — what will happen within the CDU, that vast and ungainly concentration of power, when Dr. Adenauer fades from the scene? In spite of its brilliant victory at the 1953 polls, the CDU's appearance of outward strength is perhaps deceptive. In contrast to the SPD the CDU has no pre-war tradition or ideology to provide it with a central welding force — nor is it, like the SPD, a homogeneous political body. A Christian Democrat deputy once described it to me as "a coalition of its own, bound together by common interests and one strong man. If either should go, the results will be disastrous." The common interests, broadly speaking, have been anti-Marxism and a policy of alignment with the West. As a "coalition," the CDU contains a number of radically different components, some of them possessing latent forces of disintegration. First and foremost as a "Christian" party, the CDU, as I have previously noted, is in fact an alliance between the two principal religious antitheses — Catholics and Protestants. Until November, 1954, the Protestant wing of the CDU was headed by Dr. Hermann Ehlers, the extremely able President of the Bundestag, who was generally considered as the natural heir to Dr. Adenauer. Ehlers was a man of outstanding personality whom the majority of Catholics would have followed with the same loyalty that the Protestants have accorded Dr. Adenauer. But Ehlers died, exhausted, at the premature age of 50. His death was a shattering blow both to West German political life and to his own party. He was succeeded by Dr. Eugen Gerstenmaier, a notable survivor of the 20th of July and a staunch democrat — but not endowed with the personality needed to weld the two factions together on the retirement of Dr. Adenauer. Among the candidates for the sucession there are indeed few who could command unconditional loyalty from both confessional wings.

Another factor of considerable significance in the party's fortunes is the strongly federalistic structure of Western Germany. In sharp contrast to each other are the regional parties of the two Länder that give the CDU its strongest support — North-Rhine Westphalia and parochial Bavaria. The Bavarians, with their extreme federalist attitude and incessant internal feuds are still regarded as something of a joke in other parts of Germany; and inside the party — as I have already indicated earlier in this chapter — they have provided Dr. Adenauer with some of his greatest headaches. Something of the historic animosity between Bavaria and Prussia remains in the aloofness with which Bavarians regard the other *Lands* of the West German Federation.

Politically the Christian Democrats also have distinct left and right wings with a wide gulf between the two. In the Ruhr the party draws strong support from both ends of the industrial scale; as a Christian party it has the backing of Catholic workers, as a party of free enterprise it has the backing of the heads of industry. The strength of this mixed support has so far derived from the enormous success of the policies of Professor Erhard which have benefitted both employer and employee, and this strength is undoubtedly conditional upon the continuance of the current boom in Germany.

Yet another considerable group now attached to the CDU is the "floating voters" who were largely responsible for giving the party its greatly increased vote in 1953. Among them were large numbers of refugees who, at the time, saw in Adenauer's foreign policy the only chance of returning to their homes in the East. Their future support for the CDU will depend largely upon the outcome of future reunification talks with the Russians.

One of the most depressing features of the German political scene is that there is no one ready to take over as Chancellor at a moment's notice. No figure approaching the stature of Dr. Adenauer has yet emerged as a candidate for either of the two posts involved: party leader and Chancellor. One reason is that 12 years of Nazi rule and a further 4 years of military government have made it all but impossible for men of political talent to gain experience. But a fair share of the blame must also be laid on Dr. Adenauer and his way of ruling. Like the Turk, Dr. Adenauer has borne no brother near the throne — let alone a crown prince. He has been so determined to enforce his policies himself that he has devoted no thought to a successor. It was only under considerable party pressure that he was persuaded in June 1955 to relinquish at last the foreign ministry in favor of Herr von Brentano. At that time, Dr. Adenauer confided to a member of his party that he hoped to be at the helm for at least another six years! But the fact that there is no crown prince or heir apparent is frightening when a leader is approaching eighty, even though he enjoys such miraculously robust health as does Dr. Adenauer.

For the role of Chancellor and party leader, many "possibles" have been named, notably Herr Fritz Schäffer, the Bavarian, and Catholic, Minister of Finance in both Governments. Herr Schäffer has been brilliant in his post and noted for being the only cabinet member who could, and frequently did, resist the "Old Man's" decisions. In talks over occupation costs, he had made his mark on the Allies as a hard bargainer and able negotiator. But he is not popular with many members of the Protestant wing — nor is he popular in the Ruhr where industrialists have resented the restraint he has shown in granting tax-reductions. Herr Schäffer is a rather wizened and melancholy little man, who eschews any form of publicity and is essentially a "back room" administrator. In the two and a half years that I was in Bonn, I cannot recall having seem him at any public reception. It is somewhat difficult to conceive of Herr Schäffer weaving through the maze of diplomatic intrigues that surround a Premier, or exhibiting the degree of statesmanship that has been shown by Dr. Adenauer in dealing both with foreign leaders and his own supporters. But this may be an unfair prejudgment. He is, moreover, already 67 and suffering from bad health, which might preclude a long stay at the Chancellery. Of the other senior ministers, Professor Ludwig Erhard, 58, the ebullient Minister of Economics, has shown great administrative flair and success on the international scene, but is dismissed as a future Chancellor by the party pundits as being "too whimsical" and limited to his own specialist sphere — economics. Among his greatest advantages are the facts that although a Bavarian he is not an ardent particularist, and, though a Protestant, he is not a militant "confessionalist." Herr von Brentano, 51, is also considered to have a claim to the leadership as a loyal party man of long standing. He is a Catholic and a lawyer. He made a name for himself as chief of the German delegation to Strassburg, and is an avowed supporter of the Adenauer policy of West European integration. In his short term of office he has impressed political observers in Germany by maintaining a surprising degree of independence from the Chancellery. But as a highly nervous personality and uninspiring speaker he seems to lack the gift of commanding popular support.

Another Strassburg figure who certainly has an important political future is Dr. Kurt-Georg Kiesinger, 51, a Catholic Berliner, who is at present chairman of the Foreign Affairs committee of the Bundestag. Dr. Kiesinger, also a staunch supporter of Adenauer's European policy, is one of the most popular figures in the party, and also has extremely good relations with the SPD. He has become the party's principal TV star as well as its leading debater in the Bundestag. It is generally reckoned that his possible path to the Chancellery would first lie via the Foreign Ministry. He belongs to the group of able younger men not regarded as candidates for the immediate succession. Among others in this group are Dr. Eugen Gerstenmaier, 49, Dr. Gerhard Schroeder, 44, the Minister of the Interior, Herr von Hassel, 42, the new Minister President of Schleswig Holstein and next President of the Bundesrat in Bonn, and Herr Erik Blumenfeld, 40, the highly capable organizer of the Hamburg CDU, of Jewish origin, who survived three years in Buchenwald and Auschwitz during the war.

No chapter of the intrigues which surrounded the formation of Dr. Adenauer's 1953 cabinet would be complete without reference to the aspirations of the Chancellor's former Secretary of State, Dr. Otto Lenz, which provoked so much disquiet abroad. A plan of Dr. Lenz's to create a super Ministry of Information was revealed by the resourceful journalists of *Der Spiegel*. According to the *Spiegel* of September 23rd, 1953 the new Ministry was to include:

1. The Federal Press and Information Office.

2. The propaganda section of the Kaiser Ministry for All-German Questions.

3. An information service for foreign consumption.

4. Powers for control of broadcasts directed abroad.

5. The Bureau for Home Service, which (see Chapter 14) was responsible for explaining the workings of parliamentary democracy to schools and factories. This body would now have the more particularized task of "enlightening" the German people on the work of their government, thus obscuring its hitherto supra-party character.

6. A Film Censorship Board.

The Ministry, which of course was to be headed by Dr. Lenz himself, was also to be charged with the drafting of a new and rather more restrictive press law. According to the *Spiegel,* the proposals for the creation of the Ministry of Information had been submitted to the Chancellor in the form of a memorandum, which he had taken away to study in the Black Forest during his post-election holidays.

The *Spiegel* report was at once recognized as authentic and received great attention in the press, both in Germany and abroad. In the German press, the reaction was almost unanimously hostile, and many of the senior officials of the Federal Press Office, including Herr von Eckardt, made it known that they would resign if the plan were carried through. On September 25th, the German Press Association in Bonn passed, with an overwhelming majority, a resolution to protest against the creation of such a ministry. They also appealed to the Bundestag not to support any legislation for it. Meanwhile, the senior members of the CDU were giving Dr. Lenz very little encouragement. The Allied High Commissions, risking the accusation of interference in a domestic issue, also pronounced themselves unfavorably inclined towards the scheme. (The French High Commission commented bluntly that if such a ministry were to be created "it would undoubtedly be viewed with concern by the French Government, because it would give rise to disquieting memories of the earlier Nazi Propaganda Ministry.") In face of all this pressure, and especially because of the severe criticism abroad, Dr. Adenauer could not but give way. On the same day that the German Press Association passed its resolution, Dr. Adenauer announced from his Black Forest retreat that he had "right from the beginning adopted a negative attitude to the formation of a Federal Ministry of Information."

Bonn journalists heaved a sigh of relief, and in their minds the sinister project was disposed of. The theory was advanced that the Machiavellian Chancellor had merely "lured on to thin ice" his State Secretary, in the same way that he had treated other over-ambitious members of his entourage. Dr. Lenz tactfully took a long holiday in Morocco, and then quietly assumed his place as a rank and file CDU deputy in the Bundestag. Dr. Adenauer wrote him a formal letter of thanks for his services during his time in the Chancellery, wished him well in his future parliamentary career, and then concluded, "I would be grateful if, in the future as well, you would place yourself at my disposal for the fulfilment of *special tasks*." For the time being, so complete seemed Dr. Lenz's defeat that this last remark passed without comment.

Then, nine months later, when people were beginning to forget Dr. Lenz and his scheme, a bombshell was burst in the form of a terse announcement from the Chancellery to the effect that a "Co-ordinating Committee for the Distribution of Information by the Federal Government" was to be set up forthwith. The committee would comprise one member of each of the Coalition parties, and representatives of the various ministries; chairman of the committee — Dr. Otto Lenz. The object of the committee would be to "keep the population currently in touch with measures of general political significance planned by the Government, and to co-ordinate the allocation of financial and other resources to the information of the public." The big difference this time was that the plan had the signature of the Chancellor, and was presented as a *fait accompli*. The "second Lenz offensive" had been prepared in complete secrecy; the Press Office, the Coalition leaders and the Allies had none of them been informed in advance. The members of the cabinet had themselves only been notified by letter of the Chancellor's autocratic decision.

Although the "Co-ordinating Committee" was in fact a considerably watered-down version of the original Lenz plan, the opposition it aroused in Germany was far more violent and universal than on the first occasion, although the Allies refrained from comment. Dr. Dehler, the leader of the Free Democrats, stated categorically that his party would have nothing to do with the committee and warned the press to keep watch on it. This time it was much more the personality of Dr. Lenz that the German press feared than his proposals. One paper caricatured Lenz as the djinn in the bottle, another showed him calling out the time to a column of marching newspapers. *Die Zeit* topically depicted a beaming Dr. Lenz obscuring the sun with the caption "Total eclipse over Bonn." Once again the Chancellor was forced to retreat before public sentiment. On July 8th, 1954, he informed the coalition leaders that the "Co-ordinating Committee" plans had been dropped because of "misunderstandings" in the press. Dr. Lenz once again went on holiday, and this time it seemed that his public career had received a very severe check. But even then, Dr. Adenauer showed that he had still not entirely dropped the idea; after the parliamentary recess, he said, another body for improving dissemination of information to the press might be evolved.

What caused Dr. Adenauer to persist in encouraging such a scheme, in the teeth of most severe criticism both at home and abroad? The answer perhaps lies in his excessive sensitivity to public opinion. He had seen how every discreditable manifestation in Germany, however insignificant, had been seized upon and magnified to her disadvantage abroad. At the time of the launching of the "Co-ordinating Committee," an anti-German campaign was reaching its climax, led in Great Britain by the *Daily Express*. Moreover, the Chancellor felt bitterly that a large section of his home press — which he held in little esteem — completely and unceasingly misinterpreted his policy through being uninformed.

In spite of all these mitigating circumstances, Dr. Adenauer at times displayed a remarkable misconception of the role of a free press at the end of the 1953 election campaign. After an important speech at Dortmund, he was furious with his press chief,

Herr von Eckardt, because the German press had not reported his speech *in full*. No wonder then that he was receptive to Dr. Lenz's ideas embodying a "guided" flow of information. Dr. Lenz himself had undoubtedly rendered notable services in the field of publicity, both as a founder of the Bureau for Home Service and as publicity consultant to Dr. Adenauer during the elections. Moreover there is no reason to suspect that he was not motivated by quite genuine concern about the political ignorance of the average German. He once told a member of the British High Commission that, in his opinion, Germany was not yet ripe for democracy in its broadest sense; what was needed to begin with was a "guided democracy." As a democrat, Dr. Lenz himself had an unimpeachable career and had suffered persecution by the Nazis; as he pointed out bitterly after his second *débâcle,* "I sat in prison while many journalists who are now attacking me were writing for Goebbels's Propaganda Ministry." As a personality, Dr. Lenz always seemed to me much less sinister than his German critics made him out to be, and not specially well informed. On at least one occasion, Dr. Lenz showed himself to be singularly ignorant of similar developments abroad, when, during his press conference on the "Co-ordinating Committee" in June, 1954, he described the British Council (an agency sponsored by the British government to acquaint foreigners with British culture and way of life, in some functions similar to the United States Information Agency) as being responsible for co-ordinating the British Government's information services! Another Lenz creation, *Deutsche Korrespondenz,* a Government propaganda service for foreign consumption, produced a series of most dull and clumsy reports, almost entirely devoid of any propaganda value. They were certainly not the emanations of a potential Goebbels.

What was sinister about the Ministry of Information plan was that it could provide a menacing weapon in less desirable hands than Dr. Lenz's. Apart from the sheer concentration of authority, it would have at its disposal vast sums of money, which could be used by an unscrupulous regime to purchase support of press organs, and drive hostile papers to the wall. The existence of such a weapon could be a serious danger in a country where "professionals" like Dr. Naumann are still around.

Moreover, it is not only such creatures as Naumann that the German press have to keep an eye on. At the time of the "second Lenz offensive," a dubious supporter was found in the ranks of the CDU, one Dr. Rudolf Vogel,[1] former chairman of the Bundestag Press Committee, who solicited some fifty-odd deputies to favor the Lenz scheme. Dr. Vogel also gained attention in the columns of the *Spiegel* for a letter he wrote to the editor of the *Bremer Nachrichten* suggesting that the paper "reconsider" the appointment of its Bonn representative, who had written a report unfriendly to Dr. Vogel. The editor promptly sent the letter to the German Press Association, whence it reached the *Spiegel* who queried, "what sort of letters . . . would deputies write once they became members of the Co-ordinating Committee?"

Nevertheless, one should in all fairness attribute these manifestations to growing pains in a country which has had to create a free press from nothing. In fact the net result of the super-ministry project is more heartening than disheartening, for at least two good reasons: it has shown that the Adenauer Government, despite accusations of its excessive authoritarianism, will readily yield to public opinion; and it has revealed that the German press itself is determined to resist all threats to its independence.

[1] According to the *Spiegel*, Vogel, who was a journalist by profession, wrote during the war that he would follow Hitler "through thick and thin."

15

Hard Work

and a Hard Currency

ONCE THE CABINET HAD BEEN FORMED AND THE WOUNDS within the coalition healed, there followed a period of political consolidation and watchful tranquillity in Western Germany for the remainder of 1953. The focus of attention which for most of the year had been concentrated on Germany now moved to a higher international plane. Important meetings, first of the three Western Heads of State in Bermuda, and later the Four Power Foreign Ministers' conference in Berlin, were in the offing. The West Germans could do no more than adopt an attitude of wait-and-see. For the same reasons, all work in Paris on the ratification of the Treaties had once again been suspended, while the opponents of German rearmament and the waverers hoped that something might emerge from talks with the Russians to solve France's dilemma.

Amid all the political delays and disappointments since the signature of the EDC in May 1952, there was one aspect of West German life that had by no means remained static. This was her economy. The remarkable economic recovery has been well named the "German Miracle." In spite of the switch to a buyer's market following the end of the Korean War boom, which had made trade more difficult for most other countries of the West, in 1952 and 1953 the graphs marking Western Germany's economic progress continued their vigorous upward movement. As the political doldrums of the end of 1953 were also a time when complaints in Great Britain against German export competition were reaching a climax, it may be timely to review here the achievements which had brought Germany back into the ranks of the world's first industrial powers.

The "German Miracle" really began in 1948 with the enactment of the currency reform in the three Western Zones, under which the new Deutschmark in a ratio of one for every ten of the old devalued Reichsmarks was issued. The reform wiped out the life savings of millions of Germans, but by providing a stable currency it prevented a repetition of the fearful inflations of the Weimar period, when a suitcase full of bank notes would hardly buy a loaf of bread. It laid a sound foundation without which the revitalization of German industry could not have taken place; prior to 1948–49 attempts at economic recovery had been little more than peckings at the main problem. The currency reform of 1948 was far more than just a monetary measure; it marked the radical revision of the Western Allies' economic policy in Germany — a transition from Morgenthau to Marshall. The cost of keeping a West Germany with a permanent and enormous trade deficit and the realization that the rest of Western Europe could not recover without German coal and steel had forced Britain and America to abandon the policy of reducing Germany's industrial potential to that of a third rate nation's. From currency reform onwards the re-industrialization of West Germany became a foregone conclusion. In his book, *Germany's Comeback in the World Market,* Professor Erhard admits: "Until the currency reform our economy was like a prisoner of war camp; the inmates were partly kept by the Allies. . . ."

Shortly after the new mark was issued, its value on the open market was 100 to 29 Swiss francs. On a trip to Switzerland at Christmas 1952, I found that with 100 DM I could buy 94 francs; a year and a half later, the mark had already exceeded the Swiss franc for hardness, and the exchange rate had risen to 100 DM = 105 Swiss francs. As a further sign of confidence in their own economic strength and as a measure to gain foreign investment by restoring confidence in German credit abroad, the Federal Republic took the important step, in the London Debt Agreement of February 1953, of acknowledging both her pre- and post-war debts. The total agreed upon was $3,600,000,000, which the Federal Government undertook to repay over a period of years.

By 1954, the mark had become so hard that Western Germany had already gone ahead of Great Britain towards the common goal of convertibility by instituting convertible bank accounts for resident foreigners. The German export drive had by then piled up a vast credit surplus of nearly $1,000,000,000 within the European Payments Union, and a "D-mark Gap" seriously threatened Germany's unhappy debtors within the EPU — particularly Great Britain and France. It was a curious relationship for victor and vanquished. When Mr. Butler hurried to Bonn to seek a solution in personal talks with the corpulent Professor Erhard, he remarked aptly to British correspondents afterwards: "EPU is getting too tight for its clothes — one might almost say that Professor Erhard was bursting out of them!"

From currency reform to mid-1954, Western Germany increased her over-all industrial production by over 230 per cent. In spite of the devastations of war and dismantlement, nearly every branch of industry has already exceeded the peak achieved by Hitler's pre-war economy. At the Moscow Conference in 1947, the West expressed its belief that it would be impossible to increase German steel production to 10 million tons in the foreseeable future. Yet, in the seven years to the end of 1955, German annual production of crude steel rose from 6 million to almost 23 million tons, and coal from 97 million to 145 million tons. West German steel production (exclusive of the Saar) outstripped that of France, and at the end of 1955 her dynamically expanding steel-producing capacity (which even now is some 15 per cent ahead of her production) had overtaken the lead gained by Great Britain in the early post-war years when Allied controls paralyzed the German industry and dismantlement delivered German plant as scrap to feed British blast furnaces.

(Paradoxically enough, dismantlement has by and large turned out to have been a blessing in disguise for the Germans, in that it scrapped obsolescent equipment of a vintage still being used in many British steel plants. Much of the dismantled machinery has since been replaced by some of the most modern and cost-cutting equipment in the world — and to a large degree purchased with American relief dollars!)

Another remarkable achievement (for which the revival of the steel industry was essential) was that of the West German shipbuilding industry. By the end of 1953, Lloyd's Register revealed that Western Germany had reached second place in world construction; a place she retained during 1954. At the end of the war, her merchant fleet, which once boasted over 4 million gross tons, was reduced to less than 144,000 tons of battered and obsolete shipping; its flagship, a vessel commissioned in 1899. The majority of her foremost shipyards, such as Hamburg's Blohm & Voss, had been totally dismantled. By superhuman efforts, well over half the pre-war tonnage had been replaced by 1954 — in addition to substantial orders fulfilled for foreign ship-owners, including the world's biggest oil-tanker, the *Tina Onassis*. In 1955, when orders were still swelling, 104 vessels to a total of 344,883 GRT were completed during the first five months of the year alone. At the end of May the yards had ships totalling 857,336 GRT under construction at one moment — more than a fifth of the whole of her own pre-war merchant fleet. The German shipyards were certainly much helped in their first successes by the fact that British yards were glutted with orders, and offering unfavorably long delivery dates, but nevertheless the speed of construction at Hamburg and the other North Sea ports was breathtaking. British shipbuilders were given a particularly rude shock in February, 1954, on the arrival at Southampton of the m.v. *Schwabenstein* (12,000 tons), the first German ocean passenger liner to call at a British port for fifteen years. The keel of the *Schwabenstein* had been laid only *six months earlier*. A shipbuilder was quoted in the London press as saying that it would have taken about three times as long to complete a ship of similar size on the Tyne. On a tour of the Hamburg shipyards in 1953, amid all the tremendous activity of rebuilding the war-shattered port, I came across a sight that struck me as typical of the German recovery; a British merchantman was being repaired in a half-finished German dry-dock, while at the same time another gang of workers were still welding plates on to the dock itself.

In the field of chemicals, traditionally one of Germany's strongest industries, the West Germans had succeeded in winning one-sixth of the world trade by 1952. In spite of the splitting up of the vast IG Farben complex and the dismantlement of its elaborate overseas sales network, its successor firms have established themselves in the world market with remarkable speed. Somewhat reminiscent of old times was the news in December, 1954, that Farbwerke Hoechst, one of the principal IG Farben successors, had set up a $5,600,000 company in Brazil in partnership with a group of American chemical firms. It seemed a far cry from the pre-currency reform days of 1946 when all foreign trade was carried on through Allied agencies and a German exporter was allowed no contact with the foreign importer; when German exports had consisted of pencils, fountain pens and glassware.

With an expanding economy, the over-all standard of living in Western Germany improved vastly and great inroads into unemployment had been made. In 1952, unemployment figures were still little below the two million mark; by 1955, this was reduced to 570,000 — of which probably at least half were people on part-time work of one sort or another and thus not strictly unemployed. Thus had Germany to all intents and purposes reached the state of full-employment. Between 1950 and 1954, real wages had risen by 47 per cent, compared with a drop of 1 per cent for Great Britain (although German wages are still pathetically low in comparison with British scales), and during the same period the cost-of-living index rose only seven points in the Federal Republic compared with twenty-three points in Great Britain.

In March 1954, Herr Schäffer forecast large-scale tax reliefs, based on the boldly confident postulate that the Federal Republic

would increase her gross national product by a further 5 per cent
during the year (it actually increased by 7.5 per cent); an increase he claimed that "no other country in Europe dare count
upon at present." In fact the Schäffer tax cuts paid dividends;
during 1955 the Federal treasury lost nothing through the substantial cuts granted at the beginning of the year because the increase in the gross national product outstripped Herr Schäffer's
concessions. Herr Schäffer's reforms included radical reductions
in income tax rates — especially for the top income brackets —
making West Germany a veritable taxation paradise for the very
rich. Although the disparity between the Ruhr big business man
and the threadbare West German worker has become alarmingly
great, by 1954 the signs were that the workers were also bene-
fitting from the wave of prosperity; between 1951 and 1954 savings accounts had risen from a total of 4 billion DM to 11 billion
DM, and in 1953 the sums paid into these accounts had already
exceeded the equivalent rate in the best pre-war years of 1926–28.
At the same time purchases of furniture and household goods on
the installment plan attained proportions that were something
entirely new to Germany. Typical of the new wave of material
prosperity was a large sign displayed one day in the Bonn *Kauf-
halle* (a sort of super 5 and 10 cent store) advertising that it was
— "full with goods right up to the roof!" In the void left by the
economic collapse of the 1930s, a new solid middle class was
already springing up.

Before industrial expansion could take place on any large
scale, the West Germans were faced with the Herculean task of
providing accommodation for the workers in the war-shattered
cities. At the end of the war one in every five houses in Western
Germany was totally destroyed, and another one in five so badly
damaged as to be uninhabitable. On top of this came more than
eleven million uprooted refugees from the East, all requiring accommodation. In 1950 the Adenauer Government's first housing
bill laid down a "Six Year Plan" in which 1.8 million housing
units were to be built at a rate of 300,000 a year. But by the end

of that same year the rate had already reached 350,000, and by 1954 Dr. Preusker, the new Minister of Housing, could claim to be building the staggering total of 520,000 finished units per year, far exceeding even Government estimates.

To achieve this remarkable feat, no less than one fifth of the country's total investment was spent on housing between 1950–53. During the peak seasons, the building industry employed over one and a half million men, making it the second biggest industrial group in the country. But at the foundation of the national achievement was the astounding rate at which the German bricklayers and joiners were willing to work. Watching, from the Parliament restaurant, work on the extension of the Bundestag building during the summer recess of 1953, one could identify the same workers working by arc light at 9 p.m. who had been on the site in the morning hours. There were no constant breaks for cups of tea. Almost every day as I drove into Bonn from the village where we lived five miles out, I would pass some new building site. A month later, the complete shell of a building would have sprung out of the hole in the ground, with the *Richtfest* tree fluttering aloft to show that the roof was about to be laid.[1] The drilled teamwork of German builders on the job, working with an almost mesmerized intensity, is something fascinating — but frightening — to behold.

As against the German construction claims, the British housing industry may justifiably claim that the average German unit is distinctly smaller than its British counterpart — more are two-room flats and fewer are detached houses — and the diagonal

---

[1] A delightful custom dating, I believe, from pre-Christian times. A small fir tree — supposedly "garlanded by the hands of maidens" — is placed on a pole above the about-to-be-roofed building as an augury of the fertility of the future owner. The master carpenter reads a dedicatory verse from the top of the building, drinks a toast, and then hurls the glass to the ground — the shattering of which seals the good omens of prosperity. (Glum glances were exchanged at the *Richtfest* of the new British Embassy building in 1952, when after falling three floors the glass just bounced!) After the ceremony, the workers are given the rest of the day off and, at the owner's expense, lavished with wine — no doubt an additional incentive to speedy completion of a building!

plaster cracks in nearly every new German house testify to the speed of construction. But, whatever the origin of the expression, new German housing is not "jerry-built." Architectural standards are high, and with their traditional high-peaked gables the new housing estates tend to fit far more gracefully into the surrounding scene than many of the ribbon-development horrors built in post-war Britain to fulfil political pledges.

The Federal Republic's housing record, however, cannot be explained purely in terms of the energy of the German workman — or in the high degree of standardizing of components and rationalization achieved by the industry. It would not have been possible without heavy Government subsidies applied in a most intelligent manner. In the three years 1950–52, about half the cost of the country's housing bill was financed from Federal or *Länder* public sources. The biggest, and most successful, housing subsidies were granted in the form of tax exemptions and interest-free loans to industrial employers as an incentive to build for their workers. Private companies could deduct as much as 50 per cent of the cost of construction from their income tax. The scheme [2] was extremely attractive to private enterprise; it helped them increase their capital property from profits that otherwise Herr Schäffer would have grabbed, and enabled them to supply their labor with really first-class accommodations at low rents (10 per cent of income or less compared with between 15 and 30 per cent at pre-war German rates). On a visit to Henkels (the makers of "Persil") at Düsseldorf in June, 1954, Mr. Harold Macmillan (then British Minister of Housing) revealed the profound impression that had been made on him during his tour of Ruhr housing estates: "I feel that if in our country we had more of those who would undertake this sort of development for their employees, it would make my job a lot easier." By the following year, the West Germans reckoned that their housing task was

[2] A parallel scheme of tax reliefs was instituted to subsidize the West German shipbuilders; both ended in December, 1954. In Herr Schäffer's view the two industries should now be able to find the necessary finance from private sources.

about three-fifths completed; provided that it was not further increased by a new exodus of refugees from East Germany.

The German industrial recovery was for me always the most dramatic and exciting of the many scenes on which I had to report, and I devoted much of my time to visiting factories in various parts of the country. In March, 1954, I made a protracted tour of the northern industrial area, including the Ruhr, and returned with my mind reeling from the vast new projects that I had seen everywhere, and exhausted by the vitality of my hosts. The Ruhr is run by a new generation of young industrialists in their early forties, who drive themselves at such a rate that one doubts whether they will last far into their fifties. Their day in the office begins at eight and they leave at eight; after that they are prepared to stay up into the small hours discussing their difficulties and achievements with a burning enthusiasm, and often when they begin to flag, their wives intervene to take up the tale with an incredible knowledge of their husbands' affairs. In most West German industries, management works a six-day week, as do the workers, and the directors look upon Sunday as a day of peace at home — so that they can mull over problems that have arisen at the factory during the week, undisturbed by the whirr of machinery.

On my way through the Ruhr, the expansion of the steel industry first struck me forcibly when I noted the new steel bridges conveying roads over the Autobahn, where only a few months earlier there had been just the gaps left by the war. In a space of some ten miles I counted no less than thirty, then gave up. At the Bochumer Verein, a steel plant in Bochum which had suffered heavily from both bombing and dismantlement, I was proudly shown a brand new $21,000,000 rolling mill, which had just rolled its first ingot. It was claimed to be the most modern in Europe; all manual handling of the ingots had been eliminated, and it was staffed by less than half the number of men required by the dismantled mill it replaced; the vital control bridge was air-conditioned with ice-cold air, and instructions were issued by ultra-short-wave radio. At the former IG Farben subsidiary of

Chemische Werke Hüls, I saw West Germany's one and only post-war synthetic rubber plant turning out *Buna* from waste gases piped from the Ruhr coal mines — the process without which Hitler could never have undertaken a mechanized war. Again, all the machinery for making *Buna* had been dismantled, but in May, 1951, the Allies gave Hüls permission to start up again with 560 tons per month. To everybody's amazement, the first consignment of *Buna* left the factory by November of that same year.

Two factories where one came most dramatically face to face with the saga of modern industrial Germany were not in the Ruhr at all, but lay on either side of the Berlin–Frankfurt Autobahn, some ten miles from the interzonal frontier — almost within sight of covetous Russian eyes. These were the Volkswagen works at Wolfsburg and the Reichswerke steel complex at Salzgitter, both of which had started as fabulous dreams of the Nazi industrial emperors. Construction of the Reichswerke (once known as the Hermann Goeringwerke after its sponsor) began in 1938 in the middle of a barren plain in Lower Saxony. Its reasons for existence were the presence of a vast field of low-grade iron ore, and Nazi fears that the coming total war might sever Germany's vital supplies of Swedish ore. Under Goering's plans, the combine was to have eventually no less than thirty-two blast furnaces and produce 4½ million tons of steel annually — nearly a quarter of Germany's total pre-war production. A steel city for 250,000 inhabitants was to have sprung out of nothingness. Its model was Corby steelworks, built on the iron-ore fields of Northamptonshire in the early 1930s.

A part of the Goering dream was in fact fulfilled during the war. Twelve of the thirty-two furnaces were brought into production, and in 1942 — its peak year — 2.8 million tons of crude steel were actually produced. At one time the Reichswerke also controlled a vast steel empire employing 400,000 workers in the conquered territories of Poland, Austria and Czechoslovakia. Then came the end of the war and the combine was doomed by Allied ordinance to be almost completely dismantled, on the grounds that it was "uneconomic" and superfluous to post-war German needs. That anything of Salzgitter survived was thanks largely to the vastness of Goering's project, which required three years to make an inventory alone — by which time Allied policy had already begun to change. Nine of its twelve blast furnaces were however removed, and the British occupation authorities were preparing to dynamite the main housing when ugly strikes broke out in Salzgitter, with workers and their wives and children declaring a sit-down strike inside the condemned building. The Allies relented, and this marked the turn of the tide of the crazy dismantlement policy, which had so nearly ruined the rest of Europe by depriving it of German steel.

When I visited Salzgitter in March, 1954, it was manfully trying to fight its way back to the surface. Its natural hinterland — middle and Eastern Germany — was gone, and it could hardly compete in prices with the Ruhr. But it had gained a new significance as an industry to give employment to the thousands of refugees pouring in from the Soviet zone, and as a producer of vital steel plate for the shipyards of the equally isolated port of Hamburg. The first sight that greeted me at Salzgitter was a row of vast concrete saucers, some thirty feet in diameter, with great spouts protruding from a center island — for all the world like Brobdingnagian goldfish ponds. They were, I discovered, the bases of Goering's nine dismantled blast furnaces. Farther on, an immense crane was in the act of lowering a blast furnace back into position; it was one that had already been dismantled and was on its way to Hamburg, consigned as reparations to Greece, when the dismantlement order was rescinded, and it was turned back to be re-installed at Salzgitter. One brand-new rolling mill had already sprung out of the wreckage, and another went into operation a month after my visit. In 1955 the biggest slabbing mill in Europe entered production at Salzgitter. By the end of 1954, the combine was already giving work to nearly 60,000 men and turning out 950,000 tons of steel — which put it among the largest single steel producers in the Federal Republic. Three years ago it had been virtually at a standstill.

The story of the Volkswagen works is a more familiar one. It all began as a gigantic Nazi swindle when some 336,000 trusting Germans were duped into investing $225 each to finance construction of the plant in return for a "people's car" which never materialized. The money went on the production of vehicles of war, and until the Allied Occupation began not a single Volkswagen reached the civilian market. With possibly more fairness than commercial good sense, the Control Commission and the British car manufacturers between them ignored the golden opportunities offered them in the first post-war years of either liquidating or buying up a potentially dangerous competitor. In fact, it was the British authorities who got the Volkswagen works (which had been 65 per cent destroyed by bombing) going again to supply the Occupation with vehicles, initially at a rate of twenty a day.

In order to restore standards of commercial efficiency to the plant, the British Occupation authorities began to search around for a German with some previous experience of manufacturing automobiles to run Volkswagens. In 1947 they discovered a Dr. Heinz Nordhoff, who had been trained by General Motors in the US and later became Managing Director of the Opel works in Brandenburg — where he remained until the Russians arrived in 1945. When found by the British, Nordhoff was living in penury in Hamburg with his wife and daughter, and with a suit and two ties to his name. At first Nordhoff demurred, because like most German car manufacturers he had held a low opinion of Hitler's Volkswagen. Eventually Nordhoff was persuaded, and the new managing director of Volkswagens moved, with a cot, into his office at Wolfsburg.

With his forceful personality Nordhoff succeeded in overcoming the acute shortage of raw materials that was crippling production. Through the eyes of a man trained in American methods of mass production, he watched in horror as workers hand-tooled their products, taking 400 man hours to finish one car. "If we continue like this we shall be ruined," he commented. "We must cut it down to 100 man hours per car." The factory hands thought

Nordhoff was mad, but a few years later cars were being produced at rather less than 100 hours a unit. With the installation
of a highly efficient production line system, and the most modern
automatic machinery, much of it obtained from America under
Marshall Aid, Nordhoff turned Volkswagens from an ugly
duckling project into one of the world's most successful industries; from a bomb-ridden shambles into the cleanest and most
rationally laid out automobile factory in Europe. From 20 a day
in 1946, production rose to 1,200 a day in 1955 and is expected
to reach 1,500 within the next year or so. Although the astonishing pace of the Volkswagen success story is largely due to the
unique circumstances that give the firm no shareholders to eat
away at its profits (for reasons that will be seen later), that it
succeeded at all is almost entirely thanks to Nordhoff. Now 56,
Nordhoff is undoubtedly one of the most brilliant men, perhaps
the most brilliant, on the German industrial scene today. A slim,
bronzed and handsome figure, Nordhoff at once strikes one as a
far more typically American than German executive. His appre-
ciation for things American reaches deep, however, and he has
brought to Volkswagens an atmosphere of practical democracy
and an informal "boss-worker" relationship such as has seldom
been seen in Germany. The resounding applause which greeted
Nordhoff's conferment of the *Grossverdienstkreuz* [3] at the ceremony marking production of the millionth Volkswagen in 1955
left one in no doubt of his immense personal popularity with the
workers. Later that day at a press conference for 1,200 journalists
invited from every corner of the globe, Nordhoff personally answered all questions — bilingually — with a combination of
charm, good humor and good sense that one does not often en-
counter in Germany. It was a remarkable performance — a German correspondent sitting next to me commented: "They should
bring that man to Bonn and make him a Minister."

One of Nordhoff's favorite mottoes is an old Prussian saying:
"Work hard, don't boast, and be bigger than you appear." He

[3] West Germany's highest award.

practices what he preaches; in spite of now being head of one of Europe's most prosperous concerns, he still appears as a man of great personal modesty leading an unpretentious middle-class existence.

Volkswagens now employs some 30,000 workers at the highest wages in Germany. The vast factory, which stands like a buttressed fortress in the midst of Lower Saxon wheatfields and pinewoods, moated by the Mitelland Canal, comes close to the British ideal of a garden factory and is the veritable epitome of the new German prosperity. Out of the Lower Saxon wilderness a smart modern town of over 50,000 inhabitants has sprung up. Over every inch of it prevails the ubiquitous spirit of the golden goose; the main street with its luxurious shops is called Porsche Strasse after the designer of the Volkswagen; even in the churches and schools the little beetle-like car appears incorporated in mosaics or murals. Most modern, well-appointed housing is provided for its employees, every worker with more than a year's service automatically receives a 100 DM bonus ($25) on getting married, and 50 DM for each child — even if illegitimate. (It is also the only industry I have visited as a journalist that insists on paying your hotel bill!)

High-power salesmanship has played a leading role in Volkswagens' successes, as it has in the "German Miracle" as a whole. Scores of bright young "customer consultants" from Wolfsburg are sent around the world without let-up to explain to dealers the secrets of "How to Win Friends and Influence People." They are subjected to intensive psychological training and equipped with multilingual manuals breaking down the human race into forty-one basic types which the car salesman is likely to meet — e.g. "the Brute," "the Knowall," "the Credit-No-Good," "the *ingénu*," and "the Hesitator." The manuals explain, with high German seriousness and detailed illustrations, how best to break down the sales-resistance of each category. The accent of Volkswagen salesmanship is very much on persuading the potential customer that his robust little car would be guaranteed cheap and first-class servicing throughout its life and throughout the world. This is not an empty promise. By 1954 the company could claim to have a repair depot bearing the increasingly familiar VW sign at an average of every twenty miles throughout Europe and to have handed out some 30,000 gold watches to owners completing 100,000 kilometers without a major overhaul. It also claimed to be the only manufacturer in the world to provide owners with a list of standard charges for each and every repair job. The VW facilities have justifiably become the envy of many a British car owner upon the Continent.

In spite of its many austere features by comparison with competitive small cars (you have to get out and use a dipstick when checking the gas and the makers seem unable to banish that smell of hot oil that comes up through the heater), Volkswagens have seized the market in five European countries where British products used to hold sway. Assembly plants have been set up in Canada, South Africa, Belgium, Ireland — and now New Jersey. Similar plants are planned for Brazil, Australia, and New Zealand. More than 50 per cent of production is devoted to the export markets. Nor has the Volkswagen threat fully developed yet. Because of its anomalous origins, the plant is in the curious position of having no owners — thus no profits have to be set aside to pay dividends to shareholders. Although the cost price of a Volkswagen is a closely guarded trade secret, it has been assessed by reliable German industrial sources to be as much as $280 below its selling price. During the past five and a half years, the company is said to have made profits of almost $120,000,000. These have, for the most part, been put to reserve to meet the eventuality of having to refund, or provide a new Volkswagen, to the original pre-war investors. After years of litigation over a test case put up by two investors, the Federal Supreme Court at the end of 1954 finally ruled, however, that the investors had no claim against the present Volkswagen company. Thus the company's hands are now free to devote their emergency reserves to expanding and rationalizing production still further, and no doubt they will soon strike even harder at the export markets by price reductions that the British exporters may find hard to meet.

In mid-'55 British car manufacturers suffered a nasty shock when it was revealed that VW sales to Sweden had trebled over the past year, while all British car sales had decreased.

Perhaps no single occasion was more symptomatic of the German recovery than the fantastic ceremony at Wolfsburg to celebrate production of the one millionth Volkswagen. For two days the company entertained journalists and Volkswagen agents flown at its own expense from the far ends of the earth. The organization was flawless. The millionth VW — gold plated, studded with industrial diamonds, and upholstered in gold damask — was in itself a symbol of national recovery. On the second day we were taken to see the new plant for constructing the VW miniature buses near Hanover. Designed to employ another 7,000 workers, the factory was built from scratch in 190 days! Later that day we were guests at the VW festival, in a stadium specially built just to house the *160,000* workers, guests and journalists that had been invited by the firm. At this festival, performers — and first-rate performers — had been assembled from every part of the far-flung Volkswagen empire; they included the band of the Irish Guards from Great Britain, Zulu dancers from South Africa and the entire ballet of the Vienna State Opera. For sheer "spectacle," I doubt if one will see its like again. Working out what the party must have cost our hosts, some Scandinavian journalist independently arrived at a figure of $3,500,000 spent for two days entertainment. In some German newspapers commentators remarked cynically that, since they had won the case against the VW "investors" the company were getting scared of their steadily mounting profits; thus they were too glad of any way of reducing them so as to remove from the Federal Government's path any temptation to nationalize Volkswagens.

Some weeks before Volkswagens held their extravagant jubilee, *Der Spiegel* published a report on a project in the East Zone of Germany that made an interesting comparison. According to the *Spiegel,* shortly after the crushing of the June 17th uprising of 1953, Herr Ulbricht ordered production of a "people's motor scooter" as a sop to the embittered East Germans. Two former engineers of the Junker aircraft plant were put to work dissecting three models of West German scooters, to copy parts for Herr Ulbricht's project. Before a prototype could be produced, however, some 1,700 modifications had to be made so as to adapt parts for machining by the limited East German industrial resources. On May 1, 1954, two prototypes were at last ready to take part in the May Day march-past in front of President Pieck. Neither started. Finally, in November of that year, 75 trial models were produced by hand, and sold at cut rates to workers at Ludwigsfelde, who were to act as test pilots for the new "People's Scooter." This time badly welded front-forks collapsed, and within a matter of weeks all 75 were back in the factory. One of the designers himself broke an arm when pitched over the handlebars by a defective fork. Only one of the original batch reached the 4,000 mile mark.

In June, 1955, the managing director of the scooter plant, Karl Roske, lost his nerve, and, seeing the red light, made a quick getaway to West Berlin, bringing the story of the "People's Scooter" with him. At last a few "redesigned" versions have appeared for sale at the state "HO" shop in East Berlin at 2,300 DM each. But according to Roske the actual production cost is between 4,000–5,000 DM — or approximately the *retail price* of the West German "People's Car." If nothing else, the story provided a graphic illustration of the economic gap that still exists between the two parts of Germany.

Although it was the foreign conquests of the Volkswagen that first brought the shock of revived German competition home to Great Britain, with the return of the buyer's market it was not only the British motor car industry that began to feel the pressure of the German economic recovery in the export trade. In every corner of the globe, German salesmen were popping up and grabbing contracts with enticing offers of quicker delivery dates and lower terms. In Brazil, Egypt, Pakistan and India, German engineers captured orders to build great new steel plants. In the Middle East, British exports during the first six months of 1953 dropped by nearly a third compared with the same period of 1952; German exports rose 40 per cent. In trade with Greece, by 1952 Great Britain had lost her place at the top of the list to the Germans; and there was scarcely a country where the name of Krupp was not in the vanguard of the German trade invasion. Nor were the Germans idle in their efforts to trade with the Eastern bloc; between 1952 and 1953 exports to China jumped from just over $2,800,000 to $25,200,000. In spite of fears of world recession and a slowing down of the rate of German economic expansion at the end of 1953, German exports continued their upward trend with another staggering increase of 20 per cent in 1954, while exports from the chemical industry alone rose from 2 billion DM to 3 billion DM in the course of the year.

To assist the export drive, a special government office for Foreign Trade Information was set up in 1951, publishing its own daily newspaper containing commercial "intelligence" for the benefit of exporters. By 1953 fourteen joint chambers of commerce had been set up in foreign countries.

The sharpness of the German export challenge in the first instance, coming as it did in markets where Britain had held undisputed sway since the end of the war, provoked apprehensions that were often as exaggerated as they were uninformed on both the extent of the German trade threat and the manner in which it was being promoted. In pre-war days, Germany (even prior to the era of Nazi territorial expansion) had an almost balanced foreign-trade budget. But the descent of the Iron Curtain deprived Western Germany of the richest agricultural areas east of the Elbe — with the result that she could satisfy only 55 per cent of her own food requirements, as compared with 83 per cent in 1937. Thus, like Great Britain, she was faced with the same grim necessity to export more than ever before to pay for the increased food imports, and to a very large degree the goods that she could offer and the markets open to them were similar — thus competitive — to those of Great Britain. What in fact has really been happening is that Western Germany has not been conquering new markets, but winning back old markets lost after her collapse in

1945; and as this table shows she has still not regained her 1938 share of the world export trade.

	1938	1950	1954
Germany	9½ %	3½ %	6½ %
G B	10½ %	11%	10%

The German export drive in its initial phases was much aided by a series of fortunate circumstances which could not all be attributed to the ingenuity of the German manufacturers: In the Korean war boom, the Federal Republic profited from the improved "terms of trade" more than any other Western country; at the same time she had no defense industry to sap her resources in the way that the expanded defense budgets necessitated by the Korean war had set back British and French recovery programs. In spite of the heavy financial burden presented by her refugees, occupation costs and reconstruction, for the year 1952–3 the overall level of West German taxation was in a proportion of 5:8 to that of Great Britain. While Great Britain's economists, in order to stimulate exports, had to apply artificial sanctions, such as stringent import restrictions, the almost non-existent buying power of the home consumer permitted the Germans to devote the maximum to the export markets. A further vital factor which greatly aided the West Germans was that in areas where Great Britain — and other colonial powers — were stormily embroiled, the Federal Republic was looked upon as a "neutral"; thus a more desirable trade partner. This was particularly the case in the Middle East. At the same time, in order to get their foot back in the door, some German exporters resorted to practices considered somewhat dubious in normal trade relations, such as vicious price-cutting and the offering of excessively long terms of credit. With such an acute shortage of capital in the country price-cutting tactics often boomeranged; at one time a monthly average of 400 firms (not only in the export trade) were going bankrupt in the Federal Republic. Both Professor Erhard and the West German banks were, however, strongly opposed to the risky policy of extending very long credits; Federal fingers had already been badly burned this way in post-war trade with Brazil. Moreover, the firms themselves were as a whole reluctant to embark upon long credit extensions, because beyond the limit of four years available under the regulations of the West German Export Credit Company they had to pay the full bank credit rate of 7½ per cent to 8½ per cent — nearly twice the British rate of interest. Nevertheless, from the isolated instances of German malpractices in foreign trade, British competitors tended to draw the somewhat overhasty and dangerous general conclusion that *all* German trade successes had a similar background. The cry of "unfair" was all too often sent up by British firms who had lost foreign contracts to German rivals; although it was the common experience of both British correspondents in Germany and the Commercial Department of the UK High Commission that specific complaints of British business could but seldom be confirmed.

Comment among the home producers grew so acrimonious by the beginning of 1954 that the Foreign Office became worried that a serious deterioration in Anglo-German relations might ensue. As a result, Mr. Butler made alleged discriminatory trade practices one of the principal points of the agenda of his visit to Bonn in May, 1954. His findings that there was little to choose between the export techniques of the two countries had the effect of pouring much cold water on the contentions of the home producers. By agreement with Professor Erhard, the one official discriminatory practice that Mr. Butler was able to unearth — the granting of profits-tax exemptions to German exporters — was abolished in 1955.

Mr. Butler's findings were later reinforced by a sober pamphlet entitled "German Competition," issued in October, 1954, by the Credit Insurance Association Ltd. of London, which issued some sharp criticism of the vigor of British export promotion. The Association found that claims that German firms were offering excessively long terms of credit were grossly exaggerated, and had frequently been propagated by foreign buyers as a bait — which appeared often to have been swallowed hook, line and sinker by

British exporters. "The Germans themselves are somewhat surprised," the pamphlet commented, "that they have not had to
face stronger competition." In Europe, it complained, "many
British exporters have failed to make a thorough investigation of
the market and therefore have not seen its possibilities."

The Association's indictment of the lethargy of some British
firms, who seem to cherish the notion that the paradise of a
seller's market still exists, unhappily rings rather true. Much of
the German trade success has been due to the great emphasis laid
on Trade Exhibitions and the good publicity gained thereby.
Such exhibitions are — it must be admitted — usually heavily
subsidized by the Federal Government as a form of "invisible export." In 1954 the Germans were prepared to spend a million
dollars on their industrial exhibition in Mexico. It outstripped
the efforts of all other countries there since the war, and was
widely attended by Pan-American trade representatives. The
German exhibitors were clever enough to take with them a quantity of units of each exhibit, so they could offer sales on the spot.
At least three-quarters of their products were sold, exclusive of
the numerous long-term deals concluded during the exhibition.

By comparison, only twenty-two British manufacturers deemed
it worth while to send exhibits to the 1954 Hanover Industries
Fair, which has now become one of the great show-windows of
Europe — and in that year drew many potential buyers from the
Eastern bloc. At the Düsseldorf "Hunting, Shooting and Fishing"
exhibition in the autumn of 1954, there were numerous demands
for British sporting products, but only one solitary British ex-
hibitor to accept them. Of the Vienna International Fair of 1954
(where Great Britain had 122 exhibitors to Western Germany's
758) the *Times Review of Industry* had this to say about British
participation: "Frequently the existence of the British firm was
indicated merely by name — together with perhaps a dozen or
two others — on a signboard over the stand. Often in these circumstances no British product was exhibited . . . the manufacturer had not taken the trouble to send any samples. The activities
of the agent seemed to be confined to handing out literature (usu-

ally in English) and taking orders." In contrast, German firms had sent their own personnel from Germany, equipped with list prices in Austrian schillings and empowered to offer credit terms on the spot. On the basis of these facts, it seemed hardly surprising that Germany had pushed Great Britain out of first place in the Austrian car market.

In the excellent series of export surveys from countries throughout the globe published by *The Times* in early 1954, the indictment that British exporters failed to meet delivery dates appeared with monotonous regularity. Another clue was provided by the *Bank deutscher Länder* (the German Central Bank) in their 1954 annual report: "German industries were the better able to take advantage of their opportunities because they try as far as possible to meet the industrial needs of customers . . ." This was very much along the lines of the motto prescribed by Professor Erhard: "trade follows the engineer" — whereby the foreign trade drive should be more the responsibility of technicians than Government or company bureaucrats. The *Bank deutscher Länder* comment might well have been thinking of orders German radio manufacturers had won by default in the Middle East, where certain British firms had offered sets with wavebands ideally suited to Great Britain, but which would pick up none of the major Arab broadcasting stations.

In Düsseldorf there is a famous hotel which proudly advertises that it was burned down before the war, bombed to its foundations during the war, was twice rebuilt and now claims (not unjustifiably) to be one of the top hotels in Europe. Its service is impeccable. Once on the way to Germany I stopped overnight at one of the leading hotels in Dover. With my key, I was handed a small card containing the following apologia: "We ask you to take into consideration that it has not been easy for Dover (known during the war as 'Hell Fire Corner') to get this hotel inaugurated under the present difficult conditions, and we pray your indulgence if every detail is not as right as we should desire and eventually intend that it should be." This was in December 1953 — nearly ten years since the last shell landed in Dover. How on earth, I thought, can we, the victors, complain about German competition when we're not prepared to fight back?

What factors account for the fabulous German recovery from the abysmal wreckage of 1945 to the prosperity of ten years later? Confronted with such a complicated economic scene as the German it was not easy for a non-specialist like myself to place a finger on the really basic forces behind the recovery — especially as by the time I took up my post the Federal Republic had already completed the first, most desperate stage of its economic struggle. But, in addition to factors that I have already touched on *en passant*, there were certain fundamental essentials without which the "German Miracle" would probably not have occurred. First, and most fundamental of all, was American aid. This was made available to Germany initially through G.A.R.I.O.A. funds (Government and Relief in Occupied Areas) in pre-Marshall Aid days, and later in the form of E.R.P.-M.S.A. assistance. G.A.R.I.O.A. aid reached its peak between 1947–9, with an annual expenditure of some $580 millions. Its primary purpose was the safeguarding of West Germany from famine and disease. Then came currency reform and the change in Allied economic policy towards Germany. Once a stable currency had been established, Marshall Plan aid began to pour into Germany. Up to mid 1953, when aid started to tail off, West Germany had received a total of $3,500,000,000, or sufficient to buy the vital imports of food and raw materials needed to get the economy going again. Professor Erhard has described US aid as the vital "pump priming" without which the dried-up pump of the German economy could not have started up again.

In the English edition of his book mentioned earlier, Professor Erhard points out that in 1948 nearly two thirds of West Germany's total imports were financed by foreign aid, in 1952 no more than 3 per cent. "These figures," he says, "show how much German reconstruction owes to the American Administration's far-sighted policy of foreign aid, and to the understanding and altruism of the American taxpayer who had to foot the bill."

Later he comments, "For every German it is therefore axiomatic, a fact forming a permanent element in his historical consciousness, that it was the United States whose foreign aid put into our hand the chief key to open the gates to world markets." (But, since there are many Germans who tend in the long run to ascribe all their successes to nothing but their own qualities, it is perhaps a pity that the chapter including these remarks could not also have been included in the original German version of Erhard's book!)

Right after American aid, comes the man and the policy that made the "German Miracle" economically possible — Professor Erhard and his "Social Market Economy." There is little that can be added here to what has already been written about Erhard and his unshakeable faith in free enterprise, at a time when most of the other European economies were guided by believers in state planning and controls of every sort. A 58-year-old former university lecturer in economics, Erhard has served in both Adenauer governments as Minister of Economics. His cheerful, owl-like features, amplitude of figure and perpetual cigar make him the very symbol of West Germany's regained prosperity — his ebullience synonymous with the energy of its export drive. In Professor Erhard's belief, all governmental controls are evil, only to be used in times of extreme emergency. His policies represent a complete antithesis to the Schachtian formula of economic autarky, adopted by the Third Reich. "Economic nationalism" says Erhard, "tends towards the throttling of world trade: its instruments are protectionism, foreign exchange control and, in the end, the control of the whole economy. . . ." On the other hand, "a genuine market economy cannot stop short at the national frontiers; it tends to abolish its own frontiers and thus provides powerful inducements to others to reciprocate." . . . it "cannot flourish as an island in a sea of controlled economies." Elaborating on his policy to the Foreign Press Association at a lunch in April, 1954, Erhard commented, "I don't view competition as annihilation, but as the most satisfying means of stimulating relations between countries." In putting into practice what he preached, Erhard, confronted with a vicious black market that was throttling the German economy, ended all rationing and price controls almost as soon as the Federal Government was established. His theory was that once true competition was established, prices would find their own level and shortages solve themselves. They did. In foreign trade he set about abolishing import quotas, reducing tariff barriers and steadfastly opposing schemes for boosting of exports by artificial subsidies. The liberalization of imports would, he believed, induce competition on the home market that would keep prices down, which in turn would help German exporters lower their prices, thus making German exports more competitive, etc.

With regard to the pronounced tendency of German big-business to protect itself by setting up powerful price-rigging cartels, as in the German economy of pre-war days, Erhard has repeatedly stressed to US HICOG's "trust-busters" that their anti-cartel policy "represents my thinking over the past 20 years." In this field Erhard has met with the strongest opposition from the vested interests of industry. After nearly five years of preparation, his anti-cartel bill has not been passed through the Federal Parliament.

The approach of full employment and accompanying inflation have not made Erhard flinch from his liberal policies — on the contrary. At a time when Britain's Chancellor of the Exchequer, Mr. R. A. Butler, was attempting to stem an adverse balance of trade and inflation by raising the bank rate to cut consumption and thereby reduce imports, Erhard was doing just the opposite. To counter claims for higher wages, he proposed to encourage imports of special categories of cheap goods for the consumption of the lower income groups, and to lower import tariffs still further so as to drive down prices of home products yet another notch. To boost consumption still more, the liberal-minded Minister is now suggesting that such household equipment as refrigerators, dish washers and laundry machines should be deductible from income tax, partly as an incentive for wage earners to earn more, partly to free more housewives for industry, now beginning to feel the pinch of a labor shortage. In the summer of 1955, when asked what he would do in the eventuality of a slump, Professor Erhard replied: "As long as I am Minister of Economics, there will be no crisis. I will mobilize 50 million consumers." These words of extreme confidence were based on a formidable record of past successes that had brought the West Germans their greatest prosperity in living memory.

Essential for the success of Professor Erhard's policies was the close collaboration of Herr Fritz Schäffer, the Finance Minister, who both in physical shape and outlook was the opposite of Erhard. Some of Erhard's more radical ideas made the conservative Schäffer shudder, and often the two were reported at loggerheads over an important issue. But it was basically Schäffer's finance policy that channelled West Germany's very scarce capital into its most useful applications. I have already mentioned the tax exemptions that provided such valuable boosts to the shipping and housing industries; in a similar way Herr Schäffer went all out to help an industry prepared to pull itself up by its bootstrap by self-financing. Corporation tax was deliberately fixed at a very high level — once at 60 per cent, recently reduced to 45 per cent, but special concessions on self-financing and very generous amortization charges are allowed so that companies are encouraged to plough back profits into plant expansion. As a result, self-financing plays the second largest role in West German industrial investment, next to Government funds. Some investment comparisons with Great Britain are perhaps interesting: between 1948 and 1953 the Federal Republic doubled its rate of investment — by 1951 the country was already investing more in fixed assets than Great Britain, although British industry is approximately one-third greater in size. In 1952 the proportion of the gross national product absorbed by consumption was 57 per cent compared with as much as 25 per cent directed to investment; at the same time consumption in Great Britain reached the rate of 70 per cent of the GNP.

Re-establishing the stock exchange in Germany has been a slow business as a result of the havoc that the war and currency reform caused to private savings, but private investment is at last beginning to make headway. In 1952–3 total investments in West Germany were of the order of 16,000 million DM, of which only 2,000 million was raised by the capital market. The lion's share of investment still comes from Government and US aid sources, but more and more is coming from private sources. Dividends are still low — returns are only 3–4 per cent — but between December, 1954, and August, 1955, share prices of a cross section of leading industrials rose on an average by 15 per cent. The recovery, plus West Germany's recognition of her debts in the London Debt Agreement, have also begun to attract foreign capital back to Germany. Prominent among foreign businessmen with new interests in Germany is the Swedish millionaire, Axel Wenner-Gren, the founder of Electrolux. He has invested several million pounds in the development of a monorail near Cologne and has also bought a majority holding in the $17 million (nominal capital) Bochumer Verein steel company.

Paradoxically enough, the delays and wrangling over EDC that provided Dr. Adenauer with so great a headache have given Herr Schäffer valuable assistance in expanding investment in German industry. The postponement (by nearly three years) of the first rearmament bill had saved Herr Schäffer perhaps as much as $250 million during a time when money was extremely scarce in Germany. This enabled him to forego issuing any new government loan in 1954 as anticipated, thus leaving all the more for industry.

Another factor which has played an important role in the German recovery, and one which no one could possibly have expected to turn out a blessing, has been the refugee influx. On one hand the incursion of 11 million homeless and impoverished refugees represented a staggering economic burden; on the other hand they included 3 million eager workers. With this extra reserve available, the West Germans have been able to increase their total labor force at a rate four to five times as rapidly as Great Britain or the US. But for hordes of young refugees desperate for any job, West Germany would have found it extremely difficult to man her coal mines. There are now estimated to be some 128,000 purely "refugee undertakings" operating in West Germany, mostly assisted initially by "Equalization-of-the-burden" funds provided by the government. In addition to unskilled labor, thousands of the finest and most industrious craftsmen in Europe have come from the East. In the early days they brought with them the staffs, designs and patent processes of whole industries to set up anew in the West. One of these was the Zeiss camera and binocular works from Jena, now re-established near Stuttgart and another was the Sudeten German Gablonz glass works, now located in Bavaria. *Neugablonz,* as it is now called, is perhaps the most remarkable of the refugee enterprises. Started in 1946 by a group of 17 semi-starving expellees from the Czech Sudetenland working in primitive shacks, it now comprises over 550 workshops in the area employing 8,000 workers. In 1954 *Neugablonz* glass ornaments, jewelry and buttons reached a record export sales of $12 million, of which more than half went to the United States.

But, in spite of all the important contributory factors I have set out above, the "German Miracle" would still not have been but for one fundamentally German "invisible asset" — the capacity for work of the average German. German hard work is legendary, but it is certainly no myth. Everywhere one came across evidence of it; in the cacophony of pneumatic drills working at night by arc-lights on a new building site, in the frenzied automatic movements of the 17-year-old assembly line workers at Volkswagens, in the set white faces of the Bundeshaus restaurant waiters feeding deputies round the clock. Most of the time one admires them deeply for a virtue that seems nearly extinct in one's own country; but sometimes one came close to despising them for their inability to get anything out of life but work. It was easy to understand the intensity of their labor in terms of earning money to recreate property and happiness destroyed by defeat, but it was more than that; work seemed to have a semi-religious significance to the German. I was brought a degree nearer the truth by a chance remark made to me by a Krupp employee: "Work to a German is like art; to look back on a day's work well done is as uplifting to him as the painting of a good picture to an artist." To the healthy Englishman, the "good picture" is the life that begins after work, and work is purely the means to buy that "good picture." Even the language a German uses to refer to his holidays is revealing; instead of asking "did you have a good holiday?" — or — "did you enjoy yourself?" he asks "sind Sie gut *erholt*?" — meaning, literally, "are you well recovered?" Thus are holidays looked upon not so much as a pleasure in themselves but as a period of "recovery" needed by the human machine between two sessions of work. It is thus not surprising that most big German firms have their own holiday centers for workers and tend to make holidays a highly organized, integral part of the firm's activities.

In February 1955, the *Manchester Guardian* ran a story which evidently impressed it, and which certainly struck me as typical of the German approach to work. A German textile firm near Hamburg had ordered a $9,000 loom from a British firm in the Midlands. To avoid delay in installing it, two drivers fitted out a truck with a bunk and drove non-stop, sleeping in turns, until the machine was back at their plant. They started on Wednesday, collected the machine from Burton-on-Trent on Thursday, and the machine was installed over the weekend — starting production on the Monday. That was the German way.

To a world accustomed to the irresistible onward march of egalitarianism — whether the egalitarianism of Marx, Ford or Shaw — one of the most astonishing attributes of the German worker is his almost complete lack of class resentment. The worker sees his boss come in at 8 a.m. in the morning, and often sees him still working in the evening as he leaves. He notes with approval the installation by the Federal Railroads of "travelling secretaries" on express trains so that busy executives can get through some of their correspondence instead of reading a western. Because his boss does not go off on a golfing weekend on Friday afternoon, the worker feels he is justly entitled to what he earns — however much larger it may be than his own pay packet. Because inherited wealth in Germany has been virtually annihilated by events of the past 20 years, because of the great levelling process of the war and the occupation, Schmidt, the German worker, tends to admire Herr Steinreich who gets to be director of a big factory and runs a Mercedes 300 on the proceeds; the fact that he *has* got there means that he must have *worked hard*, because there was no other way. Therefore, conversely, if Schmidt works hard enough long enough he too may become a Herr Steinreich. With the beginnings now of a new class of West German *nouveau riche,* flashing their recently gained wealth in the face of the still poorly paid German worker, his attitude towards the boss class may gradually alter, but at present the worker has no resentment against manifestations of wealth; wealth equals success, and success means hard work. I remember vividly how every summer Sunday evening in the small Rhine village where we lived, workers from the poorish industrial quarter nearby would line the streets to watch as the streams of cars returned from outings up the Rhine. A particularly elegant Porsche or Mercedes sports car would almost invariably draw a series of admiring "ohs" and "ahs." Similarly at German garages — quite the opposite to England, where the garagehand is generally the staunchest of democrats — the most expensive of cars always gets the best and quickest service. Nor is it because the attendant expects a fat tip — he doesn't; and the surprise and gratitude with which a German garagehand or hotel employee accepts a tip is one of the pleasantest things in the whole country.

But for all the very real virtue in the average German's capacity to work and in his balanced attitude towards wealth gained as a result of hard work, there is a lot that is not so good. However foreigners may jibe at the Englishman's leisurely approach to work, at least he finds time for himself in which to reflect on, and even partake of, what to him seem the important things of life outside his work. In the extreme, the German worker understands no life outside his work (I shall have something to say about his attitude toward spare time later on) and thus when a moral or political crisis confronts him, he is unequipped and tends to follow the line of least resistance. It always alarmed me to see German university students white with fatigue from midnight study combined with doing a job by day, worrying constantly about finding employment on leaving university instead of contemplating the less empiric truths for which university is designed. The fact that so much energy was being spent on material reconstruction and so little on moral reconstruction was perhaps one of the most depressing fundamental defects in the "new Germany." There is absolutely no doubt that, if the Federal Republic has a philosophy, that philosophy is materialism. But this is a digression, as it was not intended to speculate on current German philosophy in this book.

The basic German attitude towards work and his employer has undoubtedly helped sustain one other vital factor in the German recovery — the enviable state of peace between labor and management which has prevailed since the end of the war, only interrupted by the strikes of the summer of 1954. Serious as they were, the Federal Republic has still had only one strike on a national level — and that lasted twenty-four hours. In the four years following the formation of the Federal Republic in 1949, loss of working days due to strikes averaged about 700,000 annually, compared with Great Britain's post-war average of nearly two million a year. Much of the credit for this was due to the responsible and patriotic attitude adopted by both sides in subordinating all demands to the necessities of reconstruction. The DGB (German Federation of Trades Unions) accepted the fact that industry could not afford large-scale wage increases until after reconstruction was well on the way and the capital market had been re-established. Under both the Nazis and the early Allied administration wages were frozen. In their policy of stabilizing wages, and co-operating in general with management, the DGB was much helped by the almost total absence of Communist agitators in its ranks. There is now not one Communist functionary on the executive of any single trade union, although party membership in Western Germany is still more than twice as high as in England. The three biggest (and traditionally most left-wing) German unions — Metal, Mining and Building — now make

their officials sign an undertaking strictly to observe their constitutions; these expressly forbid the acceptance of instructions
from "outside."

On the other side, management in the earlier stages kept distributed profits down to the bare minimum required to attract
private capital. German shareholders still have to content themselves with a low return on their money, although their shares
steadily appreciate in value. A Düsseldorf industrialist, Dr. Ernst
Schneider, told me in 1954 that it was only the second year since
the war ended that he had drawn a salary in his capacity as
chairman of a large bridge-building firm. Ernst Schneider, aged
55, is typical of the new generation of German industrial leaders
— a generation of which he is one of the most able and influential members. As well as being chairman of either the board or
supervisory council of a dozen of the foremost German industries, he is also president of the Düsseldorf Chamber of Commerce — the most important in Germany. An extremely cul-
tured man, Schneider owns one of the most famous collections
of old Meissen china in Europe — most of which he managed to
save from his home in Eastern Germany in 1945. In spite of the
elevated offices he holds, he, like Nordhoff of Volkswagens,
leads a simple existence and is tied to his work. On being invited to lunch with him, I was astonished to discover that he
actually lived right above his bridge-building factory. There,
with the hum of the works clearly audible, he had set up a most
tastefully decorated small apartment — complete with his Meissen. When I asked him why he chose to live so close to his work,
he replied, "So I am in better contact with my workers."

Broadly speaking, both the Adenauer Government and management pursued the same highly intelligent aim of giving the
workers what they wanted almost before their unions had time
to shout for it. It was taking a leaf out of the book of Bismarck,
who, in 1881 when most other European countries were suffering from a bout of acute industrial unrest, had assured himself
of the German worker's allegiance by giving him the first Social
Insurance system in the world — before he could demand it.

After World War II, the German trade unionists, many of whom had spent years in Hitler's concentration camps, were demanding — even more urgently than wage increases — a share in the management of industry. (Strangely enough, this was something not entirely new in Germany, as a start had been made under Wilhelm II.) One of the first tasks of the Federal Government was to prepare a "Co-Determination in Industry" Law. This was finally passed in 1951 as a unique compromise between all parties, and gave labor almost everything it was asking. The most important feature of the law was that in the basic coal and steel industries it gave organized labor and representatives of the workers of each plant a 50 per cent representation on the factory board of management, with a neutral to mediate in disputes.

One of the chief protagonists of co-determination was Herr Ludwig Rosenberg, a German Jew who spent thirteen years in England as a refugee, and is now a leading member of the DGB executive. He once expressed to me his deep disapproval of a dictum of John L. Lewis: "I don't care what you (the employer) make — I only know the workers want $1 a day more." In line with his belief in moderation, Rosenberg thought that co-determination had given the workers a feeling of having a stake in the works and a confidence in the management that had hitherto been lacking in Germany. Through being kept informed by their own representatives of works decisions, they were "psychologically better prepared to take big shocks." So far, in the continuing German boom, there have been no big shocks, and by and large this unique experiment seems to have been a great success; at least there has been no dispute so serious that a mediator has had to intervene. In a crisis, however, co-determination would seem to contain within it seeds of conflict for the representatives of labor on the factory boards. Herr Rosenberg himself is in the anomalous position of being simultaneously a union executive and deputy chairman of the big Deutsche Edelstahlwerke steel plant at Krefeld. In the event of the plant being faced with economies necessitating the laying-off of several hundred union members among the personnel, he would no doubt find himself in a most awkward position of divided loyalties. Co-determination, just like the "profit-sharing schemes" that are now all the rage in England, seems to be all right as long as a boom prevails.

In almost all the factories I visited in Western Germany, I was at once struck by the deep sense of loyalty that existed between employee and employer, which could not just be dismissed as sheeplike German veneration for the boss, and which was bred of more than the worker's respect for his very hard-working directors. It was the harvest of the policy of going to very great lengths to satisfy the workers. The basic wage of the average German worker may be 25 per cent lower than his British counterpart's, but (especially in a big concern) he makes up a great deal on so-called "fringe benefits." I have already mentioned the advanced housing schemes, providing workers with works accommodation (although by no means in every case yet) the rent of which costs them a rather lower portion of the monthly wage packet than in Great Britain. Most big concerns have excellent holiday and convalescent resorts for their workers in the Black Forest or elsewhere. Although there is no health or national insurance scheme on the State level as in my country, individual employers are estimated to spend rather more on social security contributions than in Great Britain, and all but the smallest industries provide their own first-class medical service for workers and their families. Such fringe benefits, welfare and bonuses, comprise over 30 per cent of the total German wage bill. Bayer, the former IG Farben monster chemical works at Leverkusen, have been known to spend about $350 per year per head on "welfare" for their thirty thousand workers. This expenditure includes hiring such internationally famous artists as Yehudi Menuhin to perform at workers' concerts.

As part of the Adenauer-Erhard policy of "giving the workers a stake in prosperity," many industries have inaugurated profit-sharing schemes. At the big machine-building factory of Demag in Duisberg, the scheme has been so successful that the time-clock has been abolished, with the workers themselves dealing with absentees who threaten their expectations of profits. With its motto of "machines are expendable, but good men irreplaceable," Demag is typical of many German factories which put satisfaction of the workers as task No. 1. It is also one of the most efficient plants in Germany, with a remarkably high annual turnover of over $6,150 per capita for each of its 12,000 workers. Herr Schäffer's wise taxation policy has given every assistance to such profit-sharing schemes as Demag's and welfare programs such as Bayer's. Profits are normally soaked up under income, corporation and profits' taxes, but profits diverted into fringe benefits can be written off as supplementary wages. At the same time, in direct contrast to Great Britain, overtime is tax-free under the German PAYE system; thus the industrious German worker is fully rewarded for his labor.

German management's success in making the workers content is not unnaturally resented by the unions, who see their members being seduced away from their control by what they scathingly dub "works egoism." By the end of 1953, the DGB found union membership (which already could only lay claim to rather less than 40 per cent of German labor) dropping seriously, and decided to mount an offensive. The first prong of the offensive was aimed at a reduction in working hours, from the 48-hour week [4] of most German industries (including steel-making) to the 40-hour week. German hard work is often carried to physically and psychologically damaging extremes. There is an old German adage: "Others work to live, the German lives to work." In campaigning to give him spare time to develop some interest outside his job, and no doubt by degrees develop a more amiable approach to life, the DGB had a good cause. However, the proposals were resisted not only by the Government and management, but also in many cases by the workers themselves. The German attitude to the 40-hour week was revealingly displayed in the many articles that appeared in the German press in the spring of 1955, expressing doubts as to how the workers would

[4] In fact, according to Federal Statistics of August 1954, the average industrial week totalled 49.6 hours, with an average basic wage of $21.00.

spend the extra spare time. It was feared that they would either become ruined by alcohol, or else lured into unsavory political meetings. In the *Handelsblatt,* one of Western Germany's principal economic journals, an industrial psychologist voiced fears that the workers would either kill themselves on the roads or strain their hearts bicycling, and thus make themselves increasingly unfit for work. He noted that more suicides occurred on Monday than on any other day of the week, and that many of them were due to Sunday tiffs between man and wife — implying that they would no doubt increase if the German husband had more time at home over the weekend. As for hobbies, he commented gloomily, they were just a way of killing time "with endless patience and industry." In his speech at the Volkswagen millionth-car jubilee a year later, even that sensible man Dr. Nordhoff pursued the same train of thought. "No doubt," he said, "a Saturday off would for many be a nice gift, but for many others a curse. *Most people live anyway only to escape from themselves* (my italics). For them another weekday without work would only increase the emptiness and the disconsolateness caused by the idling away of spare time." What an extraordinary insight into the German soul!

With the failure of the campaign for the 40-hour week, the DGB devoted itself to preparing its affiliated unions for the first major post-war wage claims drive. Behind the drive was Dr. Viktor Agartz, the head of the DGB's Economic Research Institute in Cologne, and German labor's principal theoretician. Dr. Agartz was an insistent advocate of an "expansive wage policy" which he believed would lead to a higher level of productivity in Germany, and not, as the Federal Government feared, to the inflationary price spiral that has tormented Great Britain. In claiming that German industry could now afford to pay better wages, Dr. Agartz and the DGB had a better cause than when they had pressed for a 40-hour week. In 1954, 60 per cent of all male workers earned less than 300 DM ($72) per month. An ILO survey of November, 1953, concluded that it took a German worker 3.14 hours' labor to earn a given quantity of food that an

American worker could earn in 1 hour, or a British worker in 1.37 hours. Of the German worker's total earnings, at least half was spent on food. At the same time the disparity of wealth in Western Germany was growing apace in proportion to the numbers of Mercedes 300s owned by the new Ruhr barons.

The first wage strike began in Hamburg at the beginning of August, 1954, when 15,000 water, gas, electricity, and public transport workers paralyzed the great port for nine days. It was immediately followed by a strike of the Bavarian metal workers which lasted twenty-three days before the inexperienced (and almost non-existent) arbitrators could effect a compromise. By British standards, both strikes were disputes over an eggshell; in Bavaria the unions had been demanding less than 3 cents an hour increase. As it was the unions emerged badly battered from a war of attrition which management was better able to withstand. At the outset the Bavarian branch of the Metal Workers' Union (Germany's biggest) suffered an embarrassing reverse, when fewer than half of their estimated strength of 236,000 obeyed the union's call to strike on the appointed day. Commenting on the reluctance of the Bavarians to strike, *Die Zeit* of August 12th noted: "It is clear that the trade union functionaries did not act under pressure from the workers, but the workers under pressure from the functionaries." Finally, the Metal Workers' Union was forced to accept a compromise because after more than three weeks its limited resources were taxed to the point where it could barely afford to continue paying strike money to their unionists. The DGB's offensive was a failure, and although many of the wage claims remained unsatisfied, it was hesitant to follow up with strikes planned for other areas of the Federal Republic. German industrial peace was restored, but it was rather uneasier than before.

According to experts of the UK High Commission, the membership of the DGB in September, 1954, (after the Bavarian strikes had ended) had fallen to 4.5 million, from 6 million the previous September. If anything, the DGB's trial of strength had increased the disillusion of its members. Its power was further imperilled by the threat of a schism by Catholic unionists who want to form a separate Christian Federation of Trades Unions, such as Germany had prior to Hitler. The relative feebleness of German organized labor might seem highly enviable to British management faced with the scourge of over-powerful unions, but it holds certain grave political dangers for Germany, come a period of economic crisis. These dangers were underlined during the Bavarian strikes by prompt Communist action from Eastern Germany, in the form of sending hordes of functionaries over the interzonal frontier, armed with food parcels and "strike pay" for striking Bavarians which they distributed under the noses of the hard-pressed West German unions.

Almost exactly a year later, the Federal Republic received a still more cogent warning of the use that the Communists would make of industrial dissatisfaction over inadequate wage scales. At the beginning of August, 1955, *Die Zeit* published an article trying to put its finger on the cause of the "degeneration of the industrial climate" that had become perceptible. Recalling the times when worker and boss had put their best efforts into creating an existence out of "ruins, hunger and misery," *Die Zeit* pointed out that that period had come to an abrupt end. It was as if a *caesura* now separated the past where "one performed what was essential" and the future where "new desires will be constantly stimulated." As if in response to *Die Zeit's* speculations, a few weeks later the first major wave of unofficial strikes took the country completely by surprise. In Hamburg, shipyards dismissed 11,000 strikers, and at Kassel, the Henschel locomotive works was threatened with the loss of a $6 million Indian order by "wild cat" strikes of some 10,000 workers.

The Federal Government at once blamed the strikes on the Communists, and there is no doubt that Communist agitation was to a large degree responsible. That such agitation should have borne fruit was in itself an entirely new and sinister development in Western Germany. Moreover, the workers acting independently of their unions represented complete reversal of the situation in the industrial disputes of 1954. In contrast to the reluctance of members of the Metal Workers' Union in Bavaria to go on strike the previous year, union officials in Hamburg were forced to flee before crowds of angry workers enraged at the union's sloth in pushing wage demands. Even the increases they were demanding were nearly twice as high as those pressed the previous year. There is little doubt that German labor is developing a new and possibly ugly mood. In Great Britain since the war, we have come to appreciate the deadening effect that full employment can have upon the incentive to work; perhaps even the fabulous vigor of the German worker may succumb to this opiate in the years ahead. In any case, with the demands on the diminishing labor supply — particularly the supply of technicians — that German rearmament will soon be making, it seems that the Federal Republic can hardly escape a period of labor difficulties.

It is ominous that neither the warning of Communism in practice in the Eastern Zone nor full employment nor a high wage scale buttressed by great social efforts of management in the fields of housing and hospitalization can prevent successful communist activities in the labor field. This was clearly illustrated by a communist success in the Westfalenhütte, a major industrial complex at Dortmund where the workers recently elected a Works Council with an absolute communist majority. This is not surprising in view of fairly widespread infiltration. The Ministry for All German Questions reported late in 1955 that more than 1700 communist groups are believed to be active in German industrial establishments. More than 600 communist newspapers, bulletins and weeklies are circulated, some of them openly proclaiming their communist faith, others with their true nature cleverly disguised. Communist-front organizations are now said to number 250. It must be assumed that the powerful German trade unions will take intelligent action to combat this danger which threatens their existence and their control of the labor movement. Perhaps the real successes so far attained by the Communists are based less on dissatisfaction of the workers with their unions and more on the tactical skill of the Communists in making excellent use of the procedure for the election of Works Councils.

Labor problems are only one of the dark clouds overshadowing West Germany's future economic expansion. A really black cloud that has overcast the brilliant recovery right from the start is the coal supply. Coal production still lags behind pre-war figures. Between 1950 and 1954 production only increased from 123 million tons to 143 million tons, in spite of prodigious efforts by the Federal Government. Since the war, the problems facing the German coal mines have been very similar to those that have confronted Great Britain, declining coal reserves, and the difficulty of getting labor to go into the mines. Added to these, the Germans had their own peculiar problem of the acute shortage of capital to invest in badly needed new equipment.

In 1953 I went down one of the most modern German coal mines, Rheinpreussen's Pattberg shaft in the Northwest Ruhr. We ended up at a coal face named "Matilda," where an enormous coal plane shaped like an anchor was tearing down great chunks of coal along a 250 yard face, and automatically feeding the coal on to an endless conveyor belt. As fast as the plane cut through the seam, torrents of rubble and slag were being blown in by compressed air behind our backs; filling up the mine so as to make the workings doubly safe, and, incidentally avoiding the unsightly slag heaps and subsidences that are the curse of England's "black country." One hardly saw a miner at all, except for those fitting pit props as the mine moved itself automatically through the ground. The old wooden pit props had themselves been replaced by all-metal props that emitted frightening telltale noises as the roof of the working gradually subsided.

After leaving "Matilda" we were taken into the really impressive "Pestalozzi village" (named after the Swiss social reformer) built to house the miners. This was one of many government-subsidized schemes to attract permanent labor to the mines. The "Pestalozzi village" consisted of 14 well-built, light and airy houses, comfortably furnished. Each was allotted to a married "old time" miner, who had in his charge six young apprentices, aged 16 to 18. Many were refugees. One 17-year-old Pomeranian told me that he worked a 7½-hour shift on light jobs five days a week. The sixth day (which is a full working day for adult miners) he spent on sports and education. For this he received about $34 net a month, after his keep was deducted, but all of this except for $1.50 a week pocket money was put away for him. This was extremely high pay by German standards, but the coal miner has always had the reputation of being the "blue-eyed boy" of German wage structure.

In spite of all efforts to make coal-mining an attractive profession, fluctuation of the work force has proved a headache to the German coal industry. Between 1946 and 1953, 537,871 new miners enrolled in the industry — but 406,831 left. The industry has calculated that it costs approximately 1000 DM (about $250) and takes 3 months to train a new miner; on this basis they reckon that "fluctuation" has cost the industry something like $100 million. In addition, inexperience caused by fluctuation has greatly increased the accident rate — itself a deterrent to going down the mines. Productivity, in terms of man-tons mined per shift, is still only two-thirds of pre-war figures. Worst still, exhaustion of reserves has forced the industry to drive shafts down to previously unworked depths. The average depth of Ruhr workings is now 2,250 feet compared with 1,800 feet 20 years ago. (In Great Britain average working depth is little more than 1,000 feet; in France about 1,500). In the older mines of the South Ruhr, some shafts have now gone down to the staggering depths of well over 3,500 feet, and the additional operating costs threaten to make a considerable number totally uneconomical. Furthermore, at such extreme depths the temperature becomes uncomfortably high and has in some cases already exceeded the level of 83° F which German law prescribes as the highest in which miners can be asked to work.

A bright spot on the horizon, which promises to ease the pressure on coal is the discovery of oil. In 1947, a natural gas explosion in the bleak Ems valley near the Dutch frontier led to the discovery of substantial shale oil deposits in the area. Since then prospectors have discovered oil in several other parts of Germany; proved reserves are now put at some 60 million tons. On the basis of the oil discoveries, a thriving new industry has been set up. Annual output of crude oil is in the neighborhood of 3 million tons — or about 35 per cent of the Federal Republic's own needs. Refinery capacity has been increased from 1.3 million tons to over 10 million tons. But it is unlikely that German oil production will for long be able to fill the gap left by diminishing coal reserves, in view of the ever mounting consumption of electrical energy in Western Germany. Between 1948 and 1953, consumption of electricity has doubled; between 1953 and 1954 alone it rose by 14 per cent — but in the same period the increase in coal production was only 2.7 per cent. The gap was not filled by oil production, and substantial quantities of foreign coal had to be imported. Thus with electricity consumption and the needs of industry expanding out of all proportion to coal production, German industrialists are increasingly thinking in terms of new sources of power.

The coal shortage has inevitably had repercussions on the industry's biggest single customer, the Federal Railways. Apart from the fact that war destruction and reparations left the railways with practically nothing in the way of rolling stock, the high prices they have had to pay for coal have not helped them to make both ends meet. In 1953 the Federal Railways racked up a deficit of some 600 million DM ($150 million), and they are still one of the biggest black marks on the German economic scene — in spite of one or two expresses that have gained international repute for speed, efficiency and cleanliness.

The insolvency of the Federal Railways is also in part due to post-war policy of encouraging heavy road transport as the cheapest and quickest means of putting the German economy on wheels again. The result has been an extremely vicious circle; the railways are bankrupt and the roads among the worst and most dangerous in Europe. In spite of the fact that there are still only 2.1 vehicles per 100 Germans, compared with 4.7 in Great Britain and 29 in the US, the German accident rate is far ahead of both. Over twelve thousand people are killed every year on the German roads — or the equivalent of one of the new West German divisions! Perhaps the greatest accident-causer was the vast numbers of 30-ton trucks, usually towing two ten-ton trailers, which sway about at dangerously high speeds all over the autobahns, or else block the very poor secondary roads. Less than one per cent of German roads consist of autobahns, and the remainder are roads that, in the words of Dr. Nordhoff, "date from the Middle Ages." With new concrete autobahns now costing $840,000 a mile, it is unlikely that the strained Federal Treasury will find funds to expand adequately the present network for at least a decade. Meanwhile, unless Federal legislation is provided to shift heavy transport to the railways, German communications threaten to collapse in a *Göttedämmerung* of upturned monster lorries, and crumpled Volkswagens.

One worry (and it may turn out to be an even bigger worry for the western world) that German economists have about the future is what will happen when the ever expanding German economy comes up against a receding world market. Almost invariably the suggested answer is — turn to East-West trade. There are good precedents for trade with the Communist bloc; in 1938 it provided 16.9 per cent of Germany's export market, but in 1953 the trade was down to one-fifth of the 1938 level. In 1936 German exports to Russia totalled $73.5 *million*, in 1952 they totalled only $151 *thousand*; to Czechoslovakia $56 million in 1936, and $8 million in 1952. A favorite theme of West German businessmen was that NATO embargoes rigidly enforced by the Allied Occupation in Germany have prevented her from participating in East-West trade, while Western businessmen were constantly going behind the Iron Curtain to corner the lion's share. It is however a view hardly supported by the facts; indeed, in spite of "Allied restrictions" between 1952 and 1953 West Germany managed to increase trade with China ninefold. The initial German enthusiasm for trade with the East wore off noticeably (as indeed it has elsewhere in the West) with the realization that the Communist bloc often had little to offer in exchange but Chinese soya beans and Russian timber and grain. Nevertheless, the urge to exploit all channels of trade with the East remains, and the Chancellor was under heavy pressure from big business to include Professor Erhard and a strong trade delegation in his entourage at the Moscow talks in September 1955. One should never forget the possible power that Russian offers of large scale trade could exert over the West Germans come a time of trade recession in the West.

As a factor determining the Federal Republic's economic relationships with East and West, the European Coal and Steel Community (formed by the Schuman Plan) is of the utmost importance. A cloud on the German economic horizon, which may one day turn out to have been the first warning of a storm of European dimensions, was the Ruhr's dispute with the High Authority of the Schuman Plan, which reached a peak in April, 1954. The occasion was the High Authority's announcement of new coal prices, which unhappily coincided with the first big recession in the Ruhr coal mines since currency reform, and the Plan was blamed for it. The new regulations instructed the German coal mines to cease granting rebates to the insolvent Federal Railways, and at the same time increased the price of household coal by $3.50 a ton. With the money thus earned, German coal for industrial consumption was to be reduced by 47¢ a ton — although the price of French coal remained constant. The Ruhr howled — with a certain amount of justification — that the price cut would strike severely at the financial needs of reconstruction. Ever quick to cry "discrimination" against the High Authority and its French President, M. Monnet, it saw a sinister plot to provide France with cheap coal for her expanding steel industries — at the cost of the Ruhr. As an added insult in German eyes, the High Authority ordered the Germans to abolish their coal sales organization, Georg, whose price-fixing function, it was claimed, made possible the subsidizing of the old and unprofitable mines of the South Ruhr district.

Meanwhile coal and coke were piling up at the Ruhr pitheads, because the Schuman Plan appeared to be unable to sell enough steel to use up coke supplies. The Germans were forced to place some 25,000 miners on holiday shifts, an unprecedented step. The ill-feeling about the Schuman Plan was increased by the knowledge that outside the Plan's European markets, Great Britain and the US were able to sell all their expanded steel production. As the biggest coal and steel producers of the six Schuman Plan countries, West German industrialists noted resentfully that they were also paying the largest portion of the bill to subsidize the Plan — although it was impeding their own expansion. German press criticism of the High Authority reached such a pitch that Herr Franz Etzel, its German Vice-President, hastened to Bonn. In a brilliantly handled press conference, he most staunchly defended the Schuman Plan — identifying himself in this instance as a European first and a German second. In April, 1954, it was a most encouraging symptom. Herr Etzel's arguments were reinforced subsequently by the gradual disappearance of the coke piles, and the resumption of the German steel industry's upward trend. Concessions were allowed on Georg, and — most pleasing to the Ruhr — the High Authority agreed to allow reconcentration of some of the combines split up by the Allies. For the time being complaints against the Schuman Plan were muted.

But with France's rejection of the EDC in August, 1954, the future of the Schuman Plan at once became doubtful. At the time of the April dispute, a director of the big Klöckner steel combine had commented to me: "We joined the Schuman Plan because we wanted European integration, and we believed the Schuman Plan to be the economic forerunner to political integration. Now it seems to us that integration will not come, but we still have to foot the bill for the Schuman Plan." To many Germans, hopes of European integration did indeed seem to die with EDC; after the French vote, Dr. Dehler, leader of the Free Democrats and formerly a staunch supporter of the Schuman Plan, declared it to have become but a "torso."

Once Germany has received her sovereignty, and with it cast off the already relaxed grip of the Allied High Commission on her economic structure, the Schuman Plan will remain the principal guarantee that Germany does not once again misuse her industrial power. It will rest with the High Authority to see that the Ruhr does not rebuild the vast industrial empires and the monstrous system of cartels which cracked a whip over European trade in pre-war days. Since the Schuman Plan depends more on co-operation than control, it is up to the West to see that the Plan continues to function fairly enough not to give a future German Government a valid excuse for breaking away from it.

16

Atoms and Aircraft

OF ALL THE "INVISIBLE ASSETS" THAT MADE THE FEDERAL RE-
public's economic recovery possible, I have deliberately excluded
one of the most important because I consider that — with an eye
on the future — it merits a chapter on its own. This is the innate ingenuity of the Germans and the technical brilliance of
German scientists and engineers — or attributes that might be
summed up in the word *inventiveness*. The German contributions to science are well known; creative discoveries in chemistry
which opened up a whole new world of dyestuffs, chemicals and
drugs derived from coal, on the one hand, and on the other such
fiendish inventions as the V-1 and V-2 guided missiles that bombarded England indiscriminately in the last stages of World War
II. Unfortunately the abuse of science has generally gone hand
in hand with German inventiveness; the development of synthetic
nitrates for explosives enabled Germany to embark upon World
War I regardless of the certainty of being cut off from her sources
of natural nitrates abroad. Similarly German development of the
hydrogenation process for producing crude oil from coal and the
invention of synthetic rubber gave Hitler the essential raw materials without which he could not have entered a large scale
mechanized war in 1939.

Mindful of the misuse to which the Germans had put their
inventiveness in the past, the Allied occupiers placed the severest

curbs on German scientific research. As was so often the case, the Russian approach to the problem was the most effective and certainly (to them) the most advantageous: they simply carted off all the scientific equipment and any scientists on whom they could lay hands. The Western Allies for their part established far-reaching restrictions on the fields in which the Germans could carry on research and it was not until nearly five years after the war that any of the research organizations could get going again. Allied bans on research in the field of atomic science or aircraft production remained in force for yet another five years.

Of all the measures taken by the Allies, undoubtedly the most resented was the confiscation of German patents and trade marks. These were seized as reparations after the war and then auctioned off to private industries by the Allied governments; among them were such famous household names as "Bayer aspirin" and *4711 Eau-de-Cologne*. Most countries have by now concluded agreements with the Federal Republic to return these patents, the seizure of which — Professor Erhard claims — was, at one time, causing the Federal economy losses of not less than $200 million a year. The long abstention from research and the loss of the patents was undoubtedly a very serious handicap to Germany's recovery, insofar as her industrial goods on the export markets so often seemed out-dated in comparison with foreign equivalents. At the same time the all-pervading shortage of capital acutely limited any general expansion of industrial research. But the West Germans realized that they simply *had* to get back their old reputation for technical excellence in all fields in order to get sure footing in the export markets. As Professor Leo Brandt, the Minister for Economics and Transport of North-Rhine Westphalia and one of the key men in the German research program, commented in 1951: "Without *Technik* West Germany could only support one quarter of its population." The motto for West German industry became "research or die."

The principal body charged with the revival of German *Technik* is the "German Society for Research" (DFG) formed in 1951. The DFG is a private body financed almost entirely by public funds. It comprises some thirty to forty subsidiary and affiliated organs in various parts of the Federal Republic; in contrast to the research organization under the Third Reich, it has no centralized powers of coordination. (It is probably one of the more serious faults in the present set-up that inadequate coordination and excessive rivalry among the *Länder* apparently leads to an unnecessary amount of duplication.) One of the DFG's affiliated member organizations is the "Max Planck Institute for the Advancement of Science," a body chiefly concerned with pure science, renowned since before World War I. Another important body associated with the DFG and in close connection with both the "Federation of German Industries" (BDI) and the "European Productivity Agency" (EPA) is the *Rationalization Kuratorium* (RKW), to which I shall refer in detail later.

The research fields covered by the DFG now range all the way from nuclear physics to theology, but in spite of the immensity of its territory, the funds available for promoting research seem (on paper) to be more than modest. According to the DFG report they total only 20 million DM (about $5 million) a year. But this figure by no means represents the total West German annual expenditure on research, for the Max Planck Institute alone receives 40 million DM per year of its own, and an immense amount of research is financed by the *Länder* governments, and by private industry. Because there is no overall coordinating authority, and because of a somewhat evasive attitude of German officialdom where research is concerned, it is difficult to get an accurate figure for the amount spent annually on all forms of research. In the past five years, however, the Federal Government has multiplied its expenditure on research some tenfold. In 1954 it admitted that for the previous year 500 million DM ($125 million) had been spent from public sources alone. On this basis, Allied experts put current German research expenditure from all sources as high as 1,500 million DM ($375 million) a year — which, considering the population and financial structure, is a vast sum. It is perhaps worth relating to British and American figures, in so far as they are comparable. For 1954, Great Britain spent a total

(left) Between four rivers the Ruhr, Rhine, Emscher and Lippe, lie 23 per cent of the proven and 32 per cent of the estimated European coal reserves, some 40 billion tons. Annual production is well over 100 million tons.

(right) The Saar—Historically the region and its population of almost one million are German. So are the language, schools and social customs. Its coal fields are among the richest in Europe and produce roughly 15 million tons annually.

(left) A bridge across the Rhine nears its completion in Northrhine-West-phalia.

(right) A hydroelectric power plant under construction on the Danube near Passau at the Austrian frontier.

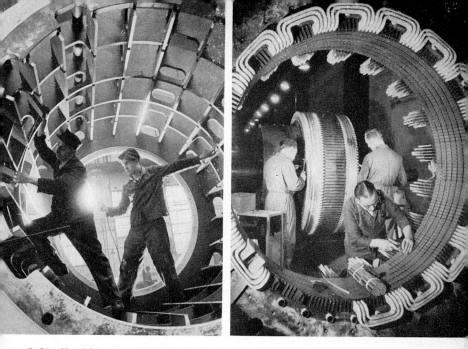

(left) Checking the measurements of the shell of an enormous turbo-generator.

(right) A large dynamo halfway through production.

Precision is the by-word of all German manufacturing.

West German steel production for 1955 was estimated at 23,300,000 tons, an increase of 6,000,000 tons over the 1954 figure. This increase put West Germany ahead of Great Britain in steel production for the first time since the end of World War II. Among the Western nations, only the United States produces more steel.

(far left) Not cannon, but multipurposed steel conduits are now being manufactured at this reconstructed plant in the Ruhr Valley.

(left) Steel plate is transported by huge electromagnets.

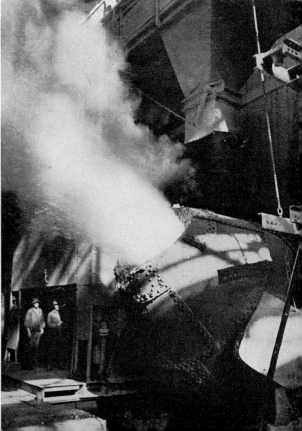

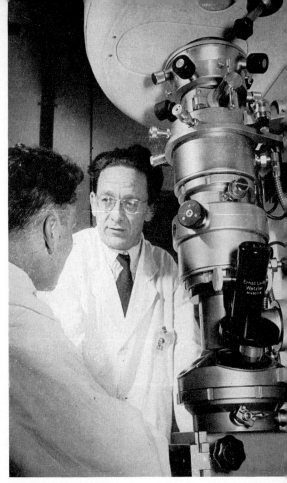

The most serious problem facing West German industrial expansion in the future is that of labor. Were it not for the influx of hundreds of thousands of skilled and semi-skilled workers from East Germany, West German production would have never attained the success it experienced in 1955. In that year West German economic progress was unequalled by any West European nation including England.

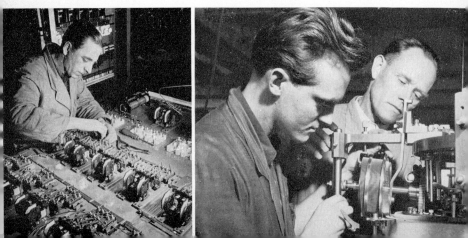

(top) The Pfaff Sewing Machine Company at the end of World War II.

The Pfaff Plant today—Women working on the assembly line, testing machines. Expanding production in Germany has increased the demand for women workers. German women today comprise 56 per cent of all gainfully employed persons in Germany. 2 million women are in key industries working in many categories requiring mechanical skills heretofore regarded beyond their capabilities or aptitudes.

The mile-long Volkswagen plant at Wolfsburg. Allied bombing demolished 65 per cent of this factory.

Professor Heinz Nordhoff, General Director of Volkswagen, received his training at General Motors. Volkswagen today produces approximately 1500 cars per day and employs over 30,-000 workers at the highest wages in Germany. High-power salesmanship has played a leading role in the company's success. Scores of bright young "customer consultants" are subject to intensive psychological training and are sent around the world without let-up.

Volkswagen assembly plants have been set up in South Africa, Brazil and Northern Ireland. More than 40 per cent of all Volkswagen production in 1955 was devoted to the export market.

West Germany's ship-building industry by the end of 1953 reached second place in world construction. By superhuman efforts, well over half the pre-war merchant fleet tonnage had been replaced by 1954—in addition to substantial foreign orders, which included the world's largest oil-tanker, the *Tina Onassis*.

Super-highway construction keeps pace with the production of trucks and passenger cars. Both of these strips are in the American zone of Southern Germany.

38 officers and enlisted men of the new German army which was activated on November 12, 1955, arrive at New York International Airport on January 2, 1956. These soldiers will be sent to various American Army installations to study and observe American military techniques.

With the creation of the new *Lufthansa* on April 1, 1955, Germany has once more taken up its position among the world's air-services. Within a few weeks regular service was established between Germany and London, Paris and Madrid. Trans-Atlantic service to New York began on June 8, 1955 and within six months eleven flights a week were scheduled between the continents. In April, 1956, service will be extended to Chicago via Montreal.

(allowing for some duplication of research funds) of between $600 and $750 million. Expenditures broke down into the following categories (in millions, approximately):

Civil atomic research and development	$ 75
Government, civil expenditure	56
Government, defense expenditure	442
Industry	140
Universities	17
Total (without allowing for duplications)	$730

In the year 1953–4, US expenditures totaled about $4 billion, representing about twice as much spent on research per capita of the population as in Great Britain, breaking down as follows (in millions, approximately):

Government expenditures	$2,500
Industry	1,500
Total	$4,000

Since however West Germany has as yet had no research expenditures in either the defense or atomic fields, these two items should be removed from the British list to make a fair comparison with German expenditure on purely civil research. This would leave a figure of some $210 million to compare with a German total of $360 million, which, if correct, would put German civil research expenditure proportionally closer the American than the British.

The great bulk of German research financing is carried out within the confines of private industry, which tends to conceal its extent from the public eye. For diverting profits into research channels, the same highly preferential and attractive taxation concessions prevail as in ploughing back profits to expand plant. Some idea of the scale on which German private industry has been investing in research can be gleaned from the fact that a firm like Siemens, Germany's No. 1 electrical industry, employs no less than 3,000 people in its research laboratories — a European record. Research workers receive extremely high wages in

Siemens — a so-called "scientific collaborator" ranks about on a par with a director of the company. In the chemical industry, the Bayer works of Leverkuesen alone spent 60 million DM (about $15 million) on research in 1954. The plant is just completing, at a cost of 15 million DM, its fourth new laboratory since 1953. All the successor companies to IG Farben are now devoting between 4 per cent and 5 per cent of their total turnover to research. It is interesting to compare this with Britain's mammoth Imperial Chemicals complex, which, although roughly four times the size of Bayer, both in personnel and turnover, spent a little over 2¼ per cent of turnover on research in 1954. That the vast sums invested by the German chemical industry in research are beginning to pay off is indicated by results produced by the highly technical plastics division of the industry, which at one time led the world. In 1947, West German production was under 3 per cent of world output; the Federal Republic is now second biggest producer in the world. One of the most remarkable research achievements in this field has been the development in 1954 of the "Ziegler process" for producing Polythene without pressure, an advance that promises to cut production costs to a fraction by doing away with the elaborate machinery previously required to produce Polythene under a pressure of over 1,000 atmospheres.

In the field of engineering, German ingenuity has also made valuable contributions. At Bochumer Verein, one of the big steel plants I used to visit in the Ruhr, a new technique has been perfected of casting vast steel shapes in a vacuum, a process which has reduced expensive faults due to cracks in 300-ton forgings to an almost negligible figure. Another steel works, Hüttenwerk Haspe, has pioneered an oxygen-blowing process which can produce from Germany's Bessemer steel furnaces steel of a quality and quantity comparable to America's "Open Hearth" steel. Other recent German developments include a type of bearing for heavy machinery that can be lubricated by compressed air instead of oil, and a gas turbine locomotive soon to come into service on the Federal Railways.

Of all the money spent publicly and privately on research a

very high proportion however goes into the quest for higher productivity in industry — or what the Germans like to call "rationalization," a favorite word in the German vocabulary. Rationalization and standardization have always been themes particularly dear to German hearts, but they realize all too clearly now how much ground they have lost over the past 20 years to their competitors. The following percentage increases in productivity between 1937 and 1955 are revealing: US, 36 per cent; Great Britain, 26 per cent; France, 24 per cent; West Germany, 14 per cent. Thus, in spite of the vast industrial expansion since 1948 and all the new American capital equipment that has replaced dismantled plant, German productivity still lags behind.

With lower wage scales, German steel plate yet costs about $22.40 a ton more than British steel. Agricultural productivity is only one half that of Great Britain, and German industrialists note aggrievedly that, in spite of all the German worker's diligence, Great Britain still achieves a gross national product 27 per cent higher than that of West Germany although the populations are almost exactly equal, and although the average British working week is only 44 hours compared to Germany's 49. Under the guidance of the *Rationalization Kuratorium* and its associated "German Committee for Standardization" (DNA) great efforts have been made to instill into German manufacturers new ideas of productivity, and to make them "time and motion" conscious. In the summer of 1953 an impressive productivity exhibition, entitled "A Better Life for All" was held in Düsseldorf under the auspices of the RKW. One of its main features was a complete mass production assembly line actually turning out motor crankshafts — from moldings to the finished article. At each of the 34 operations carried out by ultra-modern machinery, a chart was displayed explaining the number of worker-hours saved by employing "rational" methods. On another stand, a German commercial diesel manufacturer received excellent publicity for having produced a series of six engines, ranging from a single cylinder unit to a 200 horsepower V-8, all with fully interchangeable parts — including cylinders and pistons. In the corner of the exhibition stood an artificial "tree" sprouting some 2,000 bottles from its branches, representing the different varieties so "irrationally" produced by the German bottle industry.

Again, research funds invested in rationalization seem to be paying dividends. In 1950 the German radio industry produced some 450 different models: a year later it had been persuaded to concentrate on only 280 models. During 1954 overall productivity increased by 4 per cent over the previous year. But perhaps the most visible signs of the German rationalization drive are to be found in the curiously futuristic three-legged cranes which now form so integral a part of the scenery on Hamburg's reconstructed waterfront, and the new Rhine bridge south of Cologne. The Hamburg cranes, built by Demag, on an ingenious all-welded design, stripped of all but essentials, contain 25 per cent less steel than those they replace, and consequently cost about a third less. Similarly, the new bridge at Cologne (opened at the end of 1954), a graceful single span half a mile long slung between four immense pylons, represents half the weight in steel of the bridge demolished during the war. By 1956, it is reckoned that the number of apprentices available for specialized training in German industry will have diminished by a third due to the low birth rate of the war years; added to this problem the growing labor shortage in Germany will soon be aggravated by the demands of defense, so it can be expected that the German urge for more and more rationalization will continue, and in all probability automation will soon begin to make its appearance in the Ruhr.

In May 1955, with the restoration of sovereignty, two brilliant and vitally important scientific fields opened themselves to the West Germans, in which all experimentation and development had previously been banned. One was atomic energy and the other aircraft production.[1] Over both hovered a crucial question

[1] German activity in these two fields still however bears some restrictions: atomic development is limited to purely peaceful purposes, and under Western European Union there are limitations on the type and size of military air craft that may be constructed by West Germany. The guided missiles she may produce are limited to small anti-aircraft projectiles.

mark: could Germany ever catch up after ten years enforced inactivity — or would German "inventiveness" in a few years soon astound the world in these two fields also. In both fields the Germans have lost an immense amount of ground; in both initial progress is hamstrung not so much by shortages of equipment or finance, but by the catastrophic loss of technical experience and the almost total absence of trained men. This is especially the case in nuclear physics. In aircraft design, particularly in jet and rocket research, German scientists had much to offer the Allies in 1945; as a result many received excellent jobs after the war on projects in France, US, and Great Britain (to say nothing of the hundreds of German scientists who disappeared behind the Iron Curtain). Thus in this field Germany has a reserve of highly up-to-date knowledge on which she can call. In nuclear physics, however, by taking a wrong turn in their pursuit of the A-bomb during the war, German scientists ended in a cul-de-sac. Consequently, few German nuclear scientists were offered the opportunity to keep their hands in by working abroad. Of Germany's two leading nuclear physicists — both Nobel Prize winners — Professor Otto Hahn, the President of the Max Planck Institute, is 76 and no longer very active, and Professor Werner Heisenberg, 54, has relinquished the task of initiating West German atomic research after a dispute with the Federal Government. Even the theoretical training of nuclear physicists is still far behind the 1938 level in Western Germany.

To the responsible German, however, the development of atomic energy is considerably more urgent than the re-creation of the aircraft industry. For the reasons that I have cited in the previous chapter — declining coal reserves and rapidly increasing electricity consumption — the harnessing of atomic power on a large scale will be of paramount importance if Germany is to maintain its industrial position in Europe over the next twenty-five years. West German industrialists have watched developments in Great Britain, faced with an identical "energy gap," with some envy and alarm. Britain already has one atomic power station under construction and by the end of her first atomic "ten year plan" in 1965 expects to have twelve power plants in operation, capable of generating up to 2,000,000 kilowatts — or the equivalent of electricity produced by 5 or 6 million tons of coal. Some $140,000,000 are being spent annually on British atomic development, and it is estimated that the "ten year program" alone will cost over $850 million. By comparison with the British figures, official German investment in atomic energy is negligible, especially for a country starting off from scratch. So far the Federal Government has only granted 1.9 million DM (about $500,-000). The Government's parsimony, added to its dilatoriness in deciding on both an atomic program and a site for the first reactor, has brought the wrath of Professor Heisenberg on its head. In Heisenberg's calculations the first reactor itself would cost 17 million DM, and complete with the necessary ancillaries and administrative buildings the project would require some 28 million DM ($7 million) as an initial investment. Its high cost was explained by the fact that smaller, and cheaper, reactors can only operate on enriched uranium 235, or "heavy water" which the German industry will not be in a position to process for some considerable time.

Heisenberg's plans envisaged Munich, with its advanced technical institutes and concentrated industries, as the future site of the first experimental reactor. The Max Planck Institute, at present housed within the limited confines of Göttingen University, would move to Munich University, where it could draw upon some 17,000 students to provide a corps for nuclear training. As an additional attraction, the Bavarian Government promised Heisenberg 15 million DM —many times the amount of the Federal Government grant — to help finance the venture. A further consideration that may have affected Heisenberg's choice was that, in the event of reunification, Munich would be highly accessible to the uranium fields of Saxony, at present under Soviet control. Heisenberg had already got as far as choosing a building site in Munich when, in August, 1955, the Federal Government suddenly announced that the reactor would be erected at Karlsruhe. The Government explained that, for "strategic reasons," Karlsruhe on the middle Rhine was a sounder choice than Munich, but ugly remarks were passed around that parochial interests had persuaded Adenauer to place the seat of the atomic industry in his native Rhineland. In any case, it was the last straw for Heisenberg, and in a fit of pique he resigned from the project and withdrew, to the considerable embarrassment of the Government, from representing Germany at the United Nations conference on atomic energy that started the following week in Geneva.

Meanwhile the powerful *Land* of North-Rhine Westphalia, which has the bulk of heavy German industry, has also entered the lists with the object of ensuring that the first atomic plant producing power on a commercial scale should be set up in or near the Ruhr. Private industry appeared to be prepared to give such a venture a heavy financial backing. According to reports, a consortium of some 18 "atom interested" firms has been set up, including some of the most imposing names in German industry and headed by one of the big successor firms to IG Farben. Some idea of the seriousness with which this consortium views German atomic development is given by reports that each firm has subscribed 100,000 DM towards a general fund intended only to cover preliminary groundwork and travelling expenses to and from the US. The total of these contributions alone adds up to nearly as much as the Federal Government's whole grant for atomic research.

According to most recent reports from Germany, it now seems that small research reactors will be set up in rivalry at both Karlsruhe and Munich, and from the preliminary reconnaissance carried out in the Ruhr a project now seems to be emerging to build an industrial reactor at Oberhausen. Engaged in this project is the German subsidiary of Babcock and Wilcox — one of the British firms that pioneered the world's first atomic power station, now reaching completion at Calder Hall in the north of England.

This excessive rivalry between the *Länder* to acquire the future atom centers is typical of the situation that prevails in West German research as a whole—and is most detrimental to any long term planning. As will be seen shortly, inter-*Länder* rivalry is even more pronounced in efforts to grab the center of gravity of the new aircraft industry. It was not until late in 1955 that the Federal Government appointed a Minister, in the shape of energetic, forty-year-old Franz-Josef Strauss, to coordinate the country's atomic plans. As it is, at the time of writing, these plans still remain without a definite program or a site. The prospects facing it are bleak, and, unless much help from the US is forthcoming, commercial production of atomic energy will remain a distant dream for many a year to come.

What, then, of East Germany? Here one must interject a discussion of the enormous political significance of Germany's known uranium resources. Europe's biggest uranium deposits, and they are also among the most important in the world, lie in the *Erzgebirge* (which, in German, literally mean the "Ore Mountains"), partly in East Germany and partly in Czechoslovakia. There is good reason to believe that the Czechoslovak uranium fields provided one of the principal inducements to the Soviets to seize power there in 1948 — and the uranium veins in Saxony are reputedly far richer even than those lying in Czechoslovakia. This, in my opinion, is one reason why Russia will be extremely reluctant of *ever* giving up her hold on East Germany. In this atomic age, it may be a reason even more impelling to the Russians than political or ideological considerations for remaining in East Germany. Conversely, the Saxon uranium would make a united Germany immensely powerful. There are no substantial deposits of uranium yet located in Western Germany (a factor, which incidentally, threatens also to impede the development of its atomic energy projects), although extensive prospecting is going on in the Black Forest. Thus the uranium of East Germany should be looked upon by the West as a potentially dangerous enticement for any future West German government with neutralist tendencies to "make a deal" with the Russians.

In addition to mercilessly exploiting the East German uranium reserves for their own ends, the Russians have not neglected to cultivate the rich field of German "inventiveness." According to

West German physicists, in 1953 Jena and Halle universities alone turned out respectively 175 and 165 nuclear physicists, and East Germany is reported to be promised delivery of several small reactors. Like the Federal Republic, East Germany now has its own Minister for Atomic Affairs, Herr Willi Stoph. But she has already put herself a leap ahead by setting up a "scientific council" for atomic research. Its 21 members include the eminent German physicist Professor von Ardenne, who only returned from a prolonged "appointment" in the Soviet Union in 1945. If all the reports of East German activity were accurate, the comparison was a depressing one for the West Germans.

Although economic stimuli for re-entering the flying world are nowhere near so impelling as for the development of atomic energy in Western Germany (in fact industry as a whole is so far taking a distinctly reluctant attitude), the emotional impact is enormous. As the German representative of three big British aircraft firms told me, since May, 1955, the Germans have "gone flying mad." In countless open fields near big towns, gliding clubs have been set up, and the environs of airfields in the British zone are usually lined with young Germans watching RAF jet planes take off. The technical fascination even gives the RAF a distinctly greater popularity than other units of the occupation among Germans; a fact which I have heard remarked upon by several British servicemen. Since the wraps came off flying in May, 1955, numerous flying clubs have been set up — often built around one or two antiques purchased from abroad. With no organized body checking airworthiness, the accident rate is already high, and — as a British pilot remarked to me — "The German skies threaten to become as dangerous as the roads."

Behind the scenes an immense amount of activity, planning and counter-planning, is going on. In the foreground is the intense rivalry among the *Länder* to establish supremacy in the new aircraft industry. The principal contenders are Baden-Württemberg and North-Rhine Westphalia; the former because it was traditionally the seat of most of the great German aircraft factories, and feels it ought to be so again, and the latter because it claims it has better facilities for the creation of a new industry than any other area.

The efforts of North-Rhine Westphalia are coordinated by Professor Brandt, the Minister of Economics and Transport. The most important research organization, the "German Experimental Institute for Air Travel" (DVL) which up to 1945 was based at Adlershof near Berlin, now has its center of gravity in North-Rhine Westphalia. The headquarters of the DVL, although still in embryonic form, are at a disused airfield at Essen-Mülheim, but most of the active research is in fact at present being carried out at the Technical High School at Aachen. Also in North-Rhine Westphalia, what may turn out to be a highly important branch of the DVL has been set up at Bonn University. This is the "Institute of Flying Medicine," which will evidently concentrate on investigating the effects of high speed and high altitude on the human body. The Institute has already received first rate equipment and it seems that the Germans attach great significance to its work. Outside the *Land* the DVL also has two small branches at Munich and Garmisch in Bavaria. In addition to the DVL there are a number of private and semi-private air research bodies in North-Rhine Westphalia which receive financial support from Brandt. One of these is run by the former chief engineer of Arado's, Professor Walter Blume, at Duisburg. So as not to attract unwelcome publicity in the days before sovereignty, Professor Blume's organization rejoiced in the non-committal name of "Bureau for Light Metal Construction Technique," but was fundamentally concerned with the study of aircraft wing and fuselage construction.

Professor Brandt's chief rival in Baden-Württemberg is a body called the "Graf Zeppelin Union" formed by firms with such household names in the air world as Dornier, Heinkel, Messerschmitt, Bosch and Daimler-Benz. These companies are less interested in pure research than in the early re-establishment of some form of aircraft industry in which they would hope to be in on the ground floor. The "Graf Zeppelin" is however also partly financing advanced jet and rocket research at the "Institute for the Physics of Jet Propulsion." The latter was set up in 1954 at Stuttgart by Dr. Eugen Sänger, who helped design the V-2 with Professor Werner von Braun (now working in the US). Also in Stuttgart, attached to the Technical High School there, is the German "Helicopter Study Group," working under the famous designer Professor Focke.

Apart from the two main rival groups in North-Rhine Westphalia and Baden-Württemberg, there are smaller parallel research organizations at Brunswick and Göttingen in Lower Saxony. At the former is the "German Research Organization for Air Travel" (DFL) which did much experimental work on German jets during the war at Wölkenrode, just outside Brunswick, and at Göttingen is situated the "Aerodynamic Research Organization" (AVA).

With all this inter-*Länder* rivalry there is bound to be some considerable degree of duplication of research effort. At present the German scientists concerned tend to minimize the wastage by claiming that their main task in the first years will not be to develop revolutionary designs but to train technicians, during which phase duplication of research would not matter. The German air research program they envisage as divided into four basic stages:

1. The re-assembly of scientists from abroad.

2. The re-construction of equipment, most of which was dismantled.

3. The training of technicians.

4. The launching of large-scale development research.

The Germans have already gone far towards the completion of stage 1 — insofar as they are able. A prominent scientist told me that the call of the home country had met with varying responses; *all* the scientists employed in France had returned, one had even managed to get out of Russia, some had returned from England, but practically none of the hundreds working with Professor Werner von Braun has returned from America because "the research conditions and the pay there are too good; but they will probably come back as we progress here." Of those who returned, Professor Focke, now working on helicopters at Stuttgart, came back from Brazil where he had been constructing a monster passenger-carrying helicopter for the Brazilian Government. From France came Professor Quick, and Dr. Sänger, who up till recently had been working for the *Arsenal de l'Aeronautique,* the French Government establishment for military jet research. Professor Quick, one of Germany's greatest experts on aerodynamics, is now head of the DVL at Essen-Mülheim. Of the leading scientists who remained in Germany, Professor Seewald of Aachen's Technical High School is probably the most important. Seewald is one of the world's leading exponents of the ram jet, and played an important part in the development of the V-1. Since 1942, he has worked and taught at Aachen Technical High School — which was established as Germany's first aerodynamic experimental school as long ago as 1910. In 1947 Professor Seewald saw the wind tunnels and other equipment in Aachen dismantled by Allies, and since 1951 he has gradually been rebuilding and replacing. The initial reconstruction of the DVL has been almost entirely his work.

The two most prominent scientists working under Professor Quick at Essen-Mülheim are Professors Ebner and Esau. Professor Ebner is recognized as Germany's greatest expert on metal structure; while awaiting the go-ahead to work in the DVL, he kept his hand in by designing the new bridge at Cologne with its revolutionary steel-saving construction. Professor Esau is an expert in radar and high frequency work, for which a special research institute is already operating under the DVL at Essen-Mülheim. At Bonn the DVL's Institute of Flying Medicine is in the charge of Professor Ruff. Another name worth mentioning is that of Professor Blenk, who is the head of the DFL at Brunswick and who played a prominent part in German air research at Völkenrode during the war.

What are the Germans actually achieving in air research and

how far have they got? The answers at the moment are probably not much, and not very far. For years past, journalists in Germany have been speculating that a great deal of illicit work in this field was going on under cover, as after World War I. This is almost certainly not so. For one thing, the ubiquity of the Occupation and the activities of the Military Security Board have made large scale *practical* research almost impossible; for another, during the delicate political negotiations with the Western Allies over the past years, the Federal Government has itself been most anxious to avoid all stigma of "illicit" activities. Even the Blank Office maintained a very standoffish attitude to "bright" projects put up by German scientists prior to May, 1955. What the Germans have achieved before 1955 has mostly been on paper or on the scale of small laboratory experiments. The only case that has come to my ears of the Occupation authorities being bamboozled, I heard about through a chance conversation with one of the engineers concerned in the project, long after I had actually left my newspaper post in Germany. This "project" purported to be a testing ground for experimental ram jets on which Professor Seewald has been working. Ram jets make an immense amount of noise and, in testing, require fantastic quantities of electricity to produce compressed air for their operation. Thus experimentation is difficult to conceal. The DVL apparently solved the problem by setting up a proving station high in the Alps near Garmisch. The electricity required was supplied by a powerful plant which provided current for the mountain railway up the Zugspitze. The railway only operated during the daytime, thus leaving plenty of power for night-time research. The DVL testing ground may well have had a blind eye turned on it by the local occupation authorities; I don't know — such things did happen in the later days while ratification of the Treaties was in abeyance.

What funds were being channeled into air research is extremely difficult to discover, but I believe the DVL and others have at their disposal as much money as they can use at the moment. In Professor Brandt's Düsseldorf office, I was told that the money granted by the *Land* to the DVL in 1954 totalled only 3.5 million DM; but then almost immediately afterwards it was admitted that apart from this sum a further *10 million* DM was being devoted to the re-equipment of the Aachen Technical High School. Nor was any mention made of the millions of DM being invested in the development of Essen-Mülheim.

When I visited Essen-Mülheim from England in the summer of 1955, I was surprised by the modesty of what I saw. Unfortunately both Professors Quick and Ebner were away at the time, and I was met with a reluctance to talk about research. With some difficulty I persuaded them to show me around, and then I realized that what I had identified as fear of showing me too much was in fact largely embarrassment at having so little to show! There, in a remarkably dilapidated ancient pre-fab of Wehrmacht origin, in the middle of nowhere, were perhaps a score of scientists and assistants working with slide rules. The only place where any "laboratory" research seemed to be going on was in the small control tower of the airfield itself. Here scientists were studying the operation of their prize piece of equipment — an outdated jet combustion chamber given them by Rolls Royce. In the rest of the building, in two or three tiny rooms more work was in process on what looked like wartime radar equipment, and across the hall other research workers were listening to a technical lecture. That seemed to be the extent of the work — but outside large new halls and hangars were in the early stages of construction which suggested that in a few years Essen-Mülheim will be worth taking seriously. Perhaps of particular interest, in view of Germany's past achievements, is an institute to be housed at Essen-Mülheim about which very little is said. That is the institute for *Kybernetik* — or the study of remote controlled projectiles.

A few days after my visit to Essen-Mülheim, I made a trip to Aachen where Professor Seewald was working with some twenty technicians and forty students. Two wind tunnels have already been installed there (one drowned out most of my conversation with the Professor!) and two more are to be installed soon. One of these is to provide wind velocities of up to 3 mach (three times the speed of sound) in a tunnel of only one foot diameter with special application to Professor Seewald's ram jet experiments. The new tunnel was to cost 500,000 DM; but in both the US and Great Britain it would seem but a toy. Explaining the DVL research program to me Professor Seewald said that the Germans, in spite of all the ground they had lost, were wisely not going to chase after developments that other countries had already left behind them. There were fields in which Germany had once shone and in which he thought the West had not made as much progress as was possible. One particular field was his own beloved ram jet. This, he felt, held a great future for Germany — it was attractive to industry because its construction was so simple, having no moving parts. It also offered great possibilities for flight at speeds twice to three times the speed of sound. Professor Seewald smiled evasively when I asked how far he had got in his experiments. I learned however from a highly reliable source that some months earlier the Professor had privately claimed to have solved on paper the previously insuperable hitch with the ram jet engine: how to get it going from zero speed. (The ram-jet propelled V-1 projectiles had to be catapulted at high speed off their ramps before air pressure could start the engine.) Rocket assisted take-off to solve the urgent problem of longer and longer runways was also a field which the Germans felt worth exploring in the early stages of their research development; so was the problem of decreasing the noise factor in modern jet and turbine engines. Yet another field where Germans had once excelled (see Chapter 5) was in the development of heat resistant metal alloys. This is a field to which supersonic flight has now given even greater significance in the construction of both engines and fuselages, and in which the Germans hope they may be able to excel once more without elaborate transformation of existing industry.

Professor Seewald also felt that German "inventiveness" could play a major role in *rationalizing* production of aircraft components so as to cut ever mounting costs. In terms of time, he held optimistic views on the re-establishment of the German aircraft industry — contrary to the more sober — perhaps too sober — estimates of British aircraft manufacturers. He refused to believe that the techniques of construction had altered so much since 1945 as some people claimed. Granted licenses from abroad, and with technical assistance from the foreign "mother" company, he felt that German companies could be building complete airframes within one and a half years. Within five years Professor Seewald thought Germany should have a "solidly based" aircraft industry building competitive designs of its own. The magic figure of five years was one that I heard mentioned several times by scientists, officials and industrialists in Germany — most British experts with whom I have talked consider it will take more than twice as long.

Professor Seewald emphasized to me that any German re-entry into the air had to be based on new ideas. There is certainly no dearth of ideas in Germany; some exotic, of the order of wild dreams of interplanetary travel by rocket,[2] some not so exotic. It is perhaps worth mentioning briefly some of the specific projects of which I have either received information personally, or on which the German scientists have themselves reported. I have already described Professor Seewald's quest for a workable ram jet for supersonic flight. In this context, it is worth mentioning a project that was intended to make use of a Seewald ram jet unit. This was the designing of an anti-aircraft guided missile for the protection of German cities. A number of industrial firms showed interest in the project as did some members of the Blank Office, as long ago as 1954, and support was canvassed abroad to help experiment on the projectile outside the range of the prevailing Occupation bans. But as far as I know it has still not got beyond the drawing-board stage, but it can be expected to receive special priority once the Essen-Mülheim Institute for *Kybernetik* is in

[2] The Germans today take space travel extremely seriously — as indeed did the developers of the V-2 before the war. At all European "space" congresses, the Germans are generally better represented than most other people, and on one occasion were the only delegation to bring with them a civil servant — a representative of the Ministry of Transport.

operation. Also of some military significance is the preparatory work being done at Essen-Mülheim by Professor Esau's radar institute. Well before May, 1955, Professor Esau was reported at work on construction of a large diameter radar "mirror" up in the Eifel mountains. The "mirror" was nominally for astronomical observation, but little secret was made of its real use: research in aircraft detection radar.

But perhaps the most interesting glimpse of German thinking was provided in revelations — some of them sounding utterly fantastic — made by Dr. Sänger at the congress of the International Astronautical Federation held in Copenhagen in August, 1955. Dr. Sänger first told of German research into ram jet development, backing up what Professor Seewald had told me, and adding that the Federal Government (presumably through the DVL) was already investigating the practical possibilities of developing a large helicopter driven by ram jets on the rotor tips. He then went on to refer to work nearer his own heart that was already in progress: research on a device called "the hot water rocket" for assisted takeoffs. This was an old German project, and designed principally around the notion of heating a water-filled container to super-high temperatures and directing the steam formed through jet nozzles behind the aircraft. Dr. Sänger added that he was actively studying the idea of a 200 ton passenger plane, rocket-propelled and capable of speeds in the region of 2,000 mph, at 65,000 feet. But for Dr. Sänger's reputation, his revelations would have sounded fantastic. As it is, he is — I understand — regarded as one of the top world experts on rocket propulsion outside the United States; his work for the French is reported to have given French aviation an immeasurable boost, and he has already contributed to the newly founded German aeronautical periodical *Luftfahrttechnik* a highly advanced article analyzing the potentialities of rocket propulsion. However humble the present beginnings of German air research, the innate "inventiveness" of scientists like Seewald and Sänger will command attention in the Western world.

It would not do to end this brief survey of German strivings to get back a footing in aircraft development without making some reference to the practical end of the picture — the aircraft construction industry. The Germans themselves realize there are only two ways to get a prosperous aircraft industry going again on a large scale at this late date: one is through making parts, or even whole air frames, under license from foreign firms — to which I have referred already — and the other is by making military aircraft, both for West Germany's own air contingent and for NATO. If Germany is to have her own aircraft industry, construction of military aircraft must come; in this year of grace it is axiomatic that no country can keep a big aircraft industry going on civil production alone. It is just this prospect of going back into military production, that, recalling the grim fate of the industry in World War II, is making many big German industrialists hang back from rushing into it, quite apart from the enormous costs and risks that attend modern aircraft production. It is this reluctance — added to the muddle that rivalry is making of German research — that has made a poor impression on many of the British and American aircraft constructors who have visited Germany in recent years in hopes of doing business under license. So far nothing seems to have come of these attempts to get the German industry going by placing contracts to build under license.

When the industry does rise again, as it undoubtedly will sooner or later, there will be many old familiar names to the fore — such as those who have grouped themselves in the "Graf Zeppelin Union." Even before the Allied ban was lifted in Germany, Professor Messerschmitt and Herr Claudius Dornier were building planes in Spain. By September, 1955, Dornier announced its intention to start production of a light five seater civil aircraft, the Dornier 27, at a factory near Munich. Dornier's had a head start with this simple plane in that the firm had already developed it in Spain during the years when aircraft construction was banned in Germany. Similarly, Messerschmitt developed in Spain the ME 200 — a jet trainer powered by two small foreign-made jet engines. In Germany, both Heinkel and Messerschmitt have factories producing miniature three-wheel cars that closely resemble wingless planes, and to turn to producing light sports planes as an initial venture would not demand too radical a transformation. At Professor Blume's workshop in Duisburg, blueprints have already been completed for two small multi-purpose aircraft, the BI 501 and BI 502. It is reported that they will at first be produced at the Focke-Wulf factory in Bremen, with the first models appearing on the market sometime in 1956. But these are for the most part small, gap filling projects—perhaps more significant was the news at the end of 1955 that Henschels (once aircraft manufacturers, now locomotive builders) were negotiating with Sikorsky to construct American helicopters under license.

Since finance is one very significant obstacle to re-entry into aircraft construction on a big scale, eyes are naturally turning to three sources where there is known to be a lot of cash: Volkswagens, Flick and Krupp. Dr. Nordhoff has repeatedly denied any intention of entering the field, but the possibility cannot be excluded that, in the event Volkswagens is floated as a public company, some of its enormous resources might be channeled into the new aircraft industry. There is certainly no other German firm which had such a wealth of both trained technicians and capital.

Seventy-two-year-old Friedrich Flick, forced like Krupp to sell his coal and steel holdings, has already flirted with the idea of making airplanes. With the proceeds of his coal mines, Flick has already bought a large interest in Daimler-Benz (one of the firms in the "Graf Zeppelin Union"; financed the late Friedrich Siebel to build sports planes abroad prior to 1955; and financed Professor Blume's works in Duisburg. But Flick is now reported to have come to the conclusion that the prospect of early returns in German aviation are slim, to have dropped the above projects, and transferred his interest to ship-building.

Krupp's participation in the aircraft industry is much more likely. I have already pointed out Krupp's old interest in the metallurgy of aircraft design, and the news of the firm's entry into titanium production is extremely significant. Alfried Krupp himself has, with every sign of sincerity, stressed his desire to keep out of any production associated with armaments. But Krupp is under heavy pressure from his associates; moreover, more than any other German industrialist, he has the money available, and, in addition, he possesses a vast empty factory at Bremen, the machinery of which was removed by the Allies. The old Weser AG factory would be ideal for building aircraft. And one cannot help feeling that it was not just to watch the flying that brought both Alfried Krupp and his Managing Director, Herr Berthold Beitz, to the British aircraft display at Farnborough in 1955 as guests of Rolls Royce.[3]

Whoever may be its new leading men, the omens are that Germany will have a flourishing new aircraft industry in the near future — whether in two, five or ten years. And as long as the Federal Republic remains a loyal confederate within the Western Alliance the contribution that German "inventiveness" can make in this sphere should be of the greatest benefit to the common cause.

[3] Since writing the above, Krupps have announced their intention of going into the aircraft industry in partnership with other companies in North Germany. Exactly what and how great their role will be is not yet quite clear.

17

The Phoney Peace Conference

THE 4TH OF DECEMBER 1953 SAW THE OPENING OF THE momentous meeting of the three Western heads of state that had been postponed from early summer, owing to the simultaneous indisposition of both Sir Winston Churchill and the French Government. Amid the splendid Bermuda sunshine, the two old friends of the majestic days of the Grand Alliance, Churchill and Eisenhower, were once more reunited at the conference table. With them was M. Laniel, France's current premier.

At the top of their agenda was the subject of Germany, and the prospects of satisfying Western public pressure for early talks with Russia on Germany's future. Such a Four Power conference at the Foreign Ministers' level had come close to realization when the Russians showed a sudden change of heart in a note dispatched to the Western Powers barely ten days before the meeting in Bermuda.

It may be as well to recapitulate here the correspondence exchanged between the Russians and the West after the East German uprisings in June. The Allied proposal for talks "about the end of September," which had emanated from the Washington Foreign Ministers' conference on July 15th, was met by two Russian notes on August 4th and 15th. These counter-proposed the holding of a Five Power Conference, to include Red China,

with the vast and vague brief of discussing measures to relax
international tension — as well as German reunification. It was
a foregone conclusion that the West would not accept Chinese
participation in talks on Germany, and the West dismissed the
proposal for what it was — merely an attempt to influence the
forthcoming West German elections. It was abundantly clear
then that the Russians, still dealing with the chaos in Eastern
Germany, were not yet ready for talks. During September and
October the Allies endeavored to pin down the Russians to
specific talks on Germany at Lugano — first on 15th October,
then, as Russian evasive tactics continued, on November 9th.
The Russians replied with endless filibustering and repeated
efforts to bring in both Red China and representatives of East
and West Germany. By the middle of November, the Allies
had about concluded that the Russians did not want talks after all.
Then on November 26th, Moscow, apparently realizing that the
patience of the West was fraying, sent a note dropping China
temporarily and agreeing to join in a Four Power Conference
"in the near future" — and in Berlin.

The Soviets' delaying tactics had not only given them time to re-
organize East Germany, but also ensured a further postponement
of the ratification of the EDC. The French Assembly would do
nothing while there were prospects that talks with the Russians
might provide a solution of France's dilemma on German rearmament. With the passage of time, enthusiasm for the idea of
EDC had been waning — in France, in West Germany, and in
Britain and America. During the course of the Bermuda Conference, the Federal Government made little attempt to disguise the
return of old fears that the Western Allies might be preparing
to sacrifice EDC — and with it German sovereignty — to the
Russians in return for concessions on other vital issues, notably
the Far East. In spite of the promises Dr. Adenauer had obtained
earlier in the year that no decisions would be taken on Germany
without prior consultation with his Government, he uneasily
dispatched a series of memoranda to Bermuda, pressing his
views on the conduct of East–West talks. On no account, he

urged, should such talks be permitted to delay the process of West European integration. To the Federal cabinet, Dr. Adenauer expressed concern at the opportunities for splitting the West that might be offered by negotiation with the Russians at this stage. The big and accusing question-mark in Bonn was "What would happen to Germany if Molotov got Bidault into a corner in Berlin?" In the English version of the official *Bulletin* of January 21st, the Federal Government gave voice to its fears in a somewhat pointed parallel between Berlin 1954 and the Berlin Congress of 1878, which, it was noted, had led eventually to the Franco-Russian Entente.

The final communiqué from Bermuda on December 8th, with its reaffirmation of EDC, provoked an almost audible sigh of relief in Bonn. At the same time, the three Western Allies sent brief notes to Russia, accepting her proposal for talks in Berlin, and suggesting they begin on January 4th — at the former Allied Control Authority building, out of which Marshal Sokolovsky had marched in 1948. The Soviets had planned for yet a little more time, however, and on Boxing Day they replied that January 25th would be early enough, in view of the "appropriate preparation" that had to be made. Choice of the building, the note added, should be left to the four High Commissions in Berlin.

The "preparations" for the Berlin Conference, as understood by East and West, differed as radically as the viewpoints that were to be heard at the conference itself. Apart from the diplomats' wives who were buying themselves new wardrobes for the delicious social marathon that would accompany the conference, the West concentrated its efforts on sweeping out the cobwebs from the ACA building in West Berlin, where they hoped the conference would take place. Immediately after Bermuda, an army of painters, charwomen, electricians and carpenters were set to work in this vast deserted edifice of 500 rooms, which had long been dubbed "The Sleeping Beauty Castle" by the Berliners.

Soviet preparations were much more ambitious; hence, partly no doubt, the extra time required. Special canvassing squads

were set up throughout Eastern Germany to organize "spontaneous" mass appeals from the population, supporting Russian
proposals for German reunification. Up and down the country,
workers in factories and houswives at home were forced to
sign the monster lavatory rolls of signatures which form so vital
a part of the Communist fraud. By the end of the second week
of the conference, the Communists claimed to have collected
ten and a half million signatures. This farce was, however,
stripped of its striking power by the fact that at the same time
the Western Ministers were being inundated with hundreds of
letters smuggled out of the Soviet zone, beseeching them to pay
no attention to the rolls as their signatures were not given freely.

Along the Autobahn and at all vantage-points in Berlin where
they might attract the attention of Western diplomats and correspondents, vast hoardings were erected demanding participation at the conference of delegates from East and West Germany.
To stage in West Berlin the "mass popular demonstrations"
that the Communist Press were incessantly demanding, trainloads
of young Communists from the Ruhr set off for Berlin, completely equipped with interzonal passes, free tickets, money
and free accommodation in East Berlin. For the first time in
many a year, shops in East Berlin were filled wth enticing goods
— but not for the East Berliners. Fabulous silks from China,
cameras and binoculars from the Zeiss works were among the
goods on sale at about a quarter the prices in the West. Many a
diplomat's wife rose to the bait, and a photograph of her, buying
over a Communist counter, duly appeared in the East German
press as proof of the consumer hardships prevailing in the
capitalist West.

But the climax of the Russian overture to the Berlin Conference was the repatriation of some thousands of German
prisoners of war. It was a transparent and clumsy attempt to
win German sympathy while the negotiations were in train.
Among the POWs were many whose repatriation had been
halted the previous June by the East German uprising and postponed to a diplomatically more useful moment.

They came over the interzonal frontier in bedraggled batches of about a thousand at a time. Between September, 1953, and the opening of the conference, some 10,000 prisoners were repatriated in this manner, but at least another 15,000 were known to have remained behind — no doubt being kept as pawns for future moves in the inhuman Russian chess game.[1] Many of the Germans, survivors of Stalingrad, had been in Russian captivity for over eleven years. There were some pathetic sights as they reached the reception centers in Western Germany. One man, enfeebled by long years of forced labor, died of heart attack on the bus; another went mad as he heard the first cheers of German villagers along the wayside. At the camps, thousands of distraught German women sought frantically among the repatriates for men who were still somewhere in Russia; and many were the prisoners who returned home only to learn that their wives had long since remarried. With them the repatriates brought appalling tales of suffering in the Arctic labor camps; of the injustices of the Soviet system which had imposed sentences of up to twenty-five years' forced labor for such petty offenses as stealing a kilo of potatoes; and of the misery and squalor in which the Russian population themselves lived under the blessings of Communism. These stories received much prominence in the West German press, with the result that popular indignation against the Russians was, if anything, increased — quite the opposite of the effect desired by the Kremlin. It was yet another blatant example of how the Russians, with their essentially oriental outlook, completely fail to understand the psychology of the Germans — or, for that matter, of the West as a whole.

By the beginning of January, every room in Berlin had been booked by diplomats and their wives and the thousand journalists converging on the city from every part of the globe. On the 7th, the three Western Commandants met with their Russian opposite number to arrange administrative details. The meeting lasted

[1] Excluding some 103,000 POWs who, the German Red Cross claims, were known to have been alive in Russian captivity at the end of the war, but whose fate is now uncertain.

seven hours. A second meeting was held three days later, and lasted eight hours. The High Commissions were forced to admit that all was not going well. The choice of the site for the conference had turned into a vital battle of prestige. The Allies had hoped that all meetings could be held in the ACA building in the American sector, now being de-cobwebbed at great expense. With the onset of Russian resistance, they were prepared to accept one meeting in East Berlin to three in the West; arguing that this was just, since the four occupying powers had equal status. The Russians, however, insisted that all meetings take place in their Embassy in the East. After another lengthy session on the 12th, there was still a complete deadlock, and the whole thing was beginning to look to outsiders all too much like a scene from *The Love of Four Colonels*. The odds against the success of the conference as a whole rose sharply.

At last on the 17th — a week before the conference was due to begin — the West gave way after sixty hours of meetings, the last one lasting from 5 p.m. to 5 a.m. the following morning. During the first week of the conference the Foreign Ministers would meet in West Berlin; the second week, in the Soviet Embassy, and so on. To save the West the embarrassment of giving any recognition to the "Democratic Republic" of Eastern Germany, the Soviet Embassy would be known as "The Residence of the Russian High Commissioner in Germany," and the former Allied Control Authority building was to be disguised under the title of the "Four Power Building" to gratify Soviet susceptibilities. Murmurs promptly went up in Bonn that acceptance of the 1:1 ratio was an advance for the Russians towards their goal of putting East and West Germany on an equal footing. Not liking the spirit that was abroad, *Punch* of January 20th published a cartoon showing the three Western Foreign Ministers greeted at the Brandenburger Tor by the ghost of Neville Chamberlain, with the warning, "Beware the shades of Munich."

When January 25th at last came, the West Berliners — although they stood to gain more from a successful conference than any other West Germans — showed a remarkable degree of apathy, born of long-standing scepticism. Barely 2,000 spectators stood on the street corners to watch the Foreign Ministers arrive. The Berliners had few illusions that the conference was designed to be anything but a glorious propaganda spectacle, a sort of burnt-offering to the various electorates of the West. Whatever the outcome, they doubted very much that it would affect their lot.

That night each of the four Powers held rival Press conferences to give full accounts on the course of the first day's talks. (With a singular appropriateness, the Russians held theirs in what used to be Goebbels' old Propaganda Ministry, now the East German Press Office.) Mr. Molotov, it was revealed, had opened proceedings by tabling an agenda for the conference which would entail discussion on: (1) measures for reducing world tension in international relations, and the convening of a Five Power conference including China; (2) Germany; and (3) the Austrian State Treaty.

The second day brought the first surprise of the conference, when Mr. Dulles accepted the Molotov agenda "for the sake of getting on with our work." Mr. Molotov then followed up by proposing that a Five Power conference be convened in May or June of 1954. That night the round of diplomatic dinners began with M. Bidault accepting Mr. Molotov's hospitality at the Soviet Embassy. That he should have been first among the Western Foreign Ministers to be Mr. Molotov's guest was seized upon in Bonn's diplomatic circles as added grounds for their misgivings that a new Franco-Russian entente at Germany's expense might emerge from the Berlin Conference.

The third day was spent by the Western delegates shooting holes in Mr. Molotov's Five Power conference proposal, with Mr. Dulles commenting acidly that it seemed odd the conference should already be seeking to enlarge its tasks when it had not yet even tackled the particular task for which it had been convened. That night it was Mr. Molotov's turn to be entertained by Mr. Eden; this was later described by a member of the home team as "a very cordial social occasion."

On the fourth day, the West agreed to consider the Five Power conference proposal in a restricted session the next week. Mr. Dulles, with an eye on the clock, then suggested that as item 1 was exhausted, the conference could move on to item 2 of the agenda — Germany. This was forestalled by Mr. Molotov, who produced a surprise rabbit from his hat in the form of a new proposal to convene a World Disarmament Conference.

The fifth day opened with Mr. Molotov making strenuous efforts to get the meeting to discuss his disarmament resolution. When this failed, he reverted to the old theme of seats at the conference for East and West Germans during the discussions on Germany. There were, he claimed, already more than nine million Germans backing his proposal. Mr. Dulles taunted that it would be difficult to find an East German delegation that would be representative of the East Germans. At this point, Mr. Eden was able to interject with his five-point program for German reunification. There was really nothing very new about this program; it was, in fact, largely an amplification of the Western timetable for German reunification developed during the interchange of notes in 1952. In essence it provided for: (1) free elections throughout Germany; (2) the formation of an All-German Government as a result of these elections; (3) the negotiation, freely, of a Peace Treaty with this All-German Government. It offered one important concession to the Russians, however, dropping the original Western rider that the elections be supervised by a commission of neutrals. In 1952, the Russians had pounced on this as an excuse to veto the Allied reunification proposals, and refused entry to East Germany of a UN electoral investigating committee.

Although the Eden program was not even mentioned at the Soviet Press conference that night, Western hopes were raised on the following (sixth) day when Mr. Molotov not only dropped his demands for German representation at the conference, but also made some surprisingly mild preliminary remarks on the Eden proposals. This hint of moderation, added to the mere fact that the West had pinned down the elusive Mr. Molotov to talk on Germany at all after only five days of conference, brought the first week of the Berlin Conference to an end on a note of restrained optimism.

It was an optimism that was soon dampened. The following day the East German Government circulated an uncompromising memorandum which repeated all the former Russian demands put forward in their proposal of March 10th, 1952, for a German Peace Treaty. What little optimism remained after the weekend was shattered by Mr. Molotov's performance on the "Black Monday" of the conference.

As arranged, the second week opened in the massive building of the Soviet Embassy, built in 1951 at an estimated cost of $28,000 on Berlin's once fashionable Unter den Linden. To enter the conference room, the delegates passed through a great domed vestibule with a 60-foot-high stained glass window on which the Kremlin was portrayed. Everything was on a mammoth scale. The entrance to the conference rooms was flanked with two huge marble busts of Lenin and Stalin. Inside, the delegates sat underneath magnificent chandeliers hung from lofty ceilings supported by twenty columns of pink marble. As if infused with a sense of Soviet power generated by his imposing surroundings, Mr. Molotov abandoned his restraint of the previous days. In a speech that lasted nearly three hours, the Russian Foreign Minister revealed his cards for the first time.

Like the East German memorandum, his speech represented a complete reversion to the Soviet proposals of March 10th, 1952. EDC must be discarded, all occupation forces withdrawn from Germany, and a reunited Germany must form no alliances that might be taken as directed against any of her former enemies. Mr. Molotov went even further than the 1952 proposals, and demanded that the national forces of Germany should be restricted to those needed only for internal security, local frontier defense and anti-aircraft defense. He barely mentioned the vital issue of free All-German elections, and made no reference at all to the Eden program. One outstanding feature of his diatribe was apparently his all-out wooing of France, implying that between them France and Russia were the only two countries capable of settling the future of Europe. A British spokesman that evening described the Molotov speech as "very disappointing."

On the eighth day, the three Western Ministers rejected the Molotov proposals. With a remarkable display of spirit, M. Bidault countered the Molotov advances of the previous day, pointing out that if the Russian proposals were accepted, Germany would be left isolated in the heart of Europe. She would then require forces to defend herself and would once again play the game of see-saw they had seen after World War I.

Mr. Eden remarked: "I think it was Alice in Wonderland who said: 'The more we move, the more we stay in the same place.' That is horribly like our position today."

In Bonn, Professor Hallstein, Dr. Adenauer's right hand in the Foreign Ministry, summoned a small group of foreign correspondents to express the Federal Government's distress at the turn of events. The Molotov proposals meant nothing but the neutralization of Germany, "and eventually neutralization must equal *satellization*," he warned. Herr Ollenhauer seized the occasion to hurl a small dart at the Government with the rather stale accusation that it was its policy of Western integration that was making reunification impossible.

This day really marked the turning-point of the Berlin Conference. At least as far as Topic A, Germany, was concerned, the Western Ministers might just as well have packed their bags on the eighth night. The remainder of the conference was well summed up by Illingworth in *Punch*, in a cartoon depicting four phonographs all playing away at each other on top of a circular table. Time and again the delegates churned out the old familiar themes. With almost untiring repetition Mr. Molotov insisted that Germany would be tied for fifty years to the EDC if the Western proposals for free elections and a German Peace Treaty were adopted. Just as often the three Allies tried fruitlessly to convince him that a reunited Germany would not be pledged in advance to EDC. Mr. Molotov would not be drawn out on free All-German elections; he categorically rejected the Eden program for reunification, and the Allies rejected his plan. It was a stalemate on previous positions, with neither side willing to budge an inch.

During the third week of the conference, Mr. Molotov did contrive to produce one more surprise, which was as important as it was preposterous in that it gave the world a good look at the ultimate goal of Soviet policy in Europe. This was his draft for a fifty-year security treaty to include all European countries — but only European countries. The United States, it generously conceded, could attend meetings as an "observer" — a role which was also open to China. It would be a Sovietized NATO with the US and Canada replaced by the USSR — amounting to a Russian "Monroe Doctrine" for a neutralized Europe.

The Four Power talks on Germany were now suspended for a brief and tragic interlude which brought Dr. Figl, the Austrian Foreign Minister, to the Berlin Conference table. Despite failure to reach agreement on Germany, at least it was hoped that something might be achieved for Austria. A draft of the Austrian State Treaty had already been approved by all four Powers as long ago as 1949, with the exception of five relatively unimportant articles out of a total of forty-seven. Since then progress had been held up by the Russians on a variety of pretexts. But even on Austria Mr. Molotov would not yield. Until the conclusion of a Peace Treaty with Germany, he insisted, occupation troops of the Four Powers should remain in Austria, regardless of any Peace Treaty with her. Thus was poor little Austria doomed to be a Russian hostage in the battle for Germany.

There seemed now to be complete disagreement on every item of the Berlin Conference agenda; only in the restricted sessions had the Four concurred to hold a Five Power Conference on April 26th at Geneva to discuss Korea and Indo-China. On Thursday, February 18th, the conference limped to its end in weather that was symbolic of its final meetings. The thermometer had sunk to a nearly all-time low of thirty below zero, and Berlin seemed paralyzed in the grip of the Russian cold. In the terse final communiqué issued from the conference there was nothing from which the Berliners — or any other Germans — could derive an iota of consolation.

That afternoon rival demonstrations took place in East and West Berlin. More than 100,000 East Berliners shuffled past the Russian Embassy in the biting cold as a "manifestation of thanks to Comrade Molotov." Some carried crude slogans blaming the Western Ministers for the failure of the conference. In the Western sectors, the Berliners, uncoerced, felt they had little enough to thank anybody for; only some 10,000 turned out to protest against the Russians' refusal to permit free elections.

Later in the night of February 18th, a dramatic meeting took place between Dr. Adenauer and Mr. Dulles. On his flight back to America, Mr. Dulles touched down at Wahn airport, twenty miles from the Federal capital. Dr. Adenauer drove up from Bonn to meet him. Standing on the tarmac in a thin coat unmoved by the icy wind, the 78-year-old Chancellor looked unusually grim and depressed. Blithely undeterred by external events, the RAF were holding a dance in the airport restaurant. As Mr. Dulles stepped out of his plane and walked towards the waiting Chancellor, the sticky strains of "Charmaine" mingled incongruously with the whirl of the newsreel cameras. In contrast to Dr. Adenauer, Mr. Dulles seemed in a cheerful mood. Together, followed by the retinue of advisers, they were taken to a small room belonging to the airport manager, where they talked for over an hour. For the first time, Dr. Adenauer received the direct report of how the West's attempts to regain German unity had broken down. Now, he was told, the United States would devote herself with redoubled energy to achieving the rearmament of Western Germany. The intention to rearm Western Germany would not stop at a failure of the French Government to ratify the EDC, Dr. Adenauer was assured. After this momentous meeting, the American Secretary of State continued on his journey to Washington.

What was the net result of Berlin? There was precious little to show on the credit side for the West. The support of some political factions (notably the official British Labour Party) had been won for German participation in EDC, now that the attempt to negotiate with the Russians over Germany had been made and failed, but the attempt had not won over sufficient support in France to precipitate any action on EDC. The decision to hold a conference on the Far East was something of a mixed blessing to all but the French, desperately anxious as they were for any means of liquidating the "dirty war" in Indo-China. The French Government had vehemently denied that the prospect of negotiations on Indo-China would be allowed to interfere with the ratification of the EDC. But when the Viet-Minh launched their all-out offensive in March, followed by the heroic but shattering French defeat at Dien Bien Phu, the French Parliament determined to let no obstacle, such as a decision on EDC, stand in the way of getting the Communists to agree to end the fighting in Indo-China. If for no other reason, the Berlin Conference provided the Russians with a victory by causing one more crippling postponement of the EDC.

At least the Berlin Conference taught one lesson; it proved that there was a great deal of sense in Dr. Adenauer's steadfast view that one could only argue with the Russians from strength. The Allies had gone to Berlin, not in strength, but in weakness. After two years of Herculean efforts to integrate Western Europe and rearm Western Germany, no visible progress had been made. The realization of EDC was as distant as ever, and the stalemated EDC was hardly a stick or a carrot which the West could wield to induce the Russians to make any of the concessions they demanded. If indeed any idea had existed in French minds before Berlin that the EDC might have been used as a bargaining counter, they would have done well to recall the words of La Fontaine: "You should not sell the skin of a bear before you have killed it."

Throughout the whole conference the Russians never once gave any indication that they would yield on German reunification in return for abandonment of the EDC, in spite of the propaganda victory this might have won for them in the West. On the contrary, the Molotov Security Pact proposal showed all too clearly that the Russian plans for Europe lay far beyond just the thwarting of German rearmament. Mr. Molotov had left no doubts that the price for getting out of Eastern Germany was complete American withdrawal from Europe, thus opening to the Russians the rosy prospect of taking over the whole Continent in their own time. The Russian performance at Berlin was a slap in the face for the German Social Democrats, whose pet thesis had been that EDC was the chief stumbling-block to reunification; it was also a great disappointment to those in the West who believed that some marked moderation in Soviet policy over Germany — or Austria — should be perceptible a year after Stalin's death.

Perhaps one of the biggest single items on the debit account of the West after the collapse of the Berlin Conference was the effect that this had on German public opinion and morale. In this respect the oft-repeated warning of Dr. Adenauer, that an unsuccessful conference would be "disastrous" for the West, took on a new significant meaning. On February 25th Dr. Adenauer's statement to the Bundestag on the Berlin Conference drew loud and sustained applause from coalition deputies when he thanked the Allies for their "excellent" efforts in the cause of German reunification. But the enthusiasm of the deputies, living in the rarefied political climate of Bonn, was by no means echoed by their constituents in the country at large. Many Germans — and not just supporters of the Social Democrats — had the ugly feeling that the Western Ministers had simply not tried at Berlin. Old suspicions were revived in Germany that the West — especially Britain and France — would much rather have a truncated, controllable Western Germany than a reunited, giant Germany of uncertain sympathies. Their inarticulate thoughts were voiced to me by a German journalist during the Berlin Conference: "If they [the Western Ministers] have really come here for anything more than just propaganda, why do they not hold all the meetings of this phony conference at restricted sessions?" At Bonn, on the day after the conference ended, 3,000 sullen-faced students and professors of the University held a one-hour silent march through the capital in protest against the Berlin fiasco. Some time afterwards, a student who had taken part in the march told me: "We pretended that the Russians were responsible, but in our hearts we felt that all the Allies were equally to blame that German reunification got nowhere."

An even more disheartening symptom was the effect that the Allied failure to produce results at Berlin had in the Soviet zone of Germany. On my way to Hamburg in October of 1953, I gave a lift to the middle-aged wife of a schoolteacher from Chemnitz (now re-named "Karl-Marx Stadt"), who was on a visit to relatives in West Germany. She had been in Chemnitz at the time of the 17th of June uprisings. After the uprisings had been crushed by the Soviet tanks, she told me, East German morale had sunk to its lowest ebb since 1945.

"Now," she said, "everybody has pinned his final hope on the talks that are to come; if by January or February nothing has happened — or if the Allies show they are too weak to help us — I fear a mass surrender will begin in Eastern Germany. Opposition is nearly at an end; remember, young men who are now in their twenties have never known any other system than Hitlerism or Stalinism."

With the collapse of the Berlin Conference, this woman's prediction seemed to come close to reality; Allied observers reported a severe drop in morale among the East Germans, linked with a growing sense of hopelessness that they would ever be freed from the Communist yoke. No doubt many must have wondered seriously whether the courageous revolt of June 17th had been worthwhile. Their moral grounds for continued resistance, too, were being further sapped by the gradual, but substantial, improvement in living conditions which took place in East Germany throughout 1954, in step with the Malenkov "consumer program" in Russia.

Some of the feeling of despair and dangerous resentment against the West that was growing in the Soviet zone during 1954 was voiced in a moving letter from a young East German published in *Deutsche Kommentare,* a West German newspaper, from which I give some extracts:

"Many people in Western Germany, too many, passionately fight against hearing of our misery . . . The day is not very far off when you will lose us, when we shall become even more alien to you than, for instance, the French or the English . . . Yes, once we were active, and indeed delighted in our resistance to Communism; but now we have become weary and malleable — our backbone has been broken, down to the last man . . . We have nothing to which we can cling to save ourselves against the flood of Communist ideology; the tide is up to our necks . . . We stand at the end of our strength; we have no longer any belief, any hope. Apart from flight to the West, there now remains open to us two choices: to rise up once more against the regime, and then to fall forever — but for this the majority of us are already much too weary. There is only one other alternative: to become a follower of this new religion . . . "

Out of the wreckage of the Berlin Conference the Allies tried to pull something to bolster the sagging spirits of East and West Germans. After the conference the three Western High Commissioners appealed to Mr. Semeonov, their Soviet opposite number, to permit again the free movement of people, goods and literature over the interzonal frontier — which would have involved removing the barbed wire "death strip" laid down by the Russians after the signature of the EDC in May, 1952. But the implications of even this Western initiative were greeted with considerable reserve by large sections of the West German press. It was dubbed "the small solution," which Germans feared the West would accept on their behalf in lieu of reunification. *Die Zeit* of February 25th voiced typical German apprehensions in wondering whether it meant that the Allies might be preparing to acknowledge the *status quo* of the division of Germany, alleviated by such minor relaxations, as a way of bringing about a decrease in tension in Europe. As the word co-existence began to appear with increasing regularity in the mouths of Western statesmen during 1954, it was linked with the words *status quo* and provoked an ugly fear in German minds.

The Allied appeals, however, met with little success. As if to rub into the Germans the hopelessness of their position after Berlin, the Russians, on March 26th, elevated their zone to full satellite status by granting her the very nominal privilege of an "independent sovereign state." To agonized West German eyes, it seemed as if another few yards had been added to the chasm now separating the two Germanys. At the same time, even though the sovereignty bestowed on Eastern Germany was no more than a meaningless title, West Germans could not help remarking that they had still not got even that from their Western allies.

One of the very first moves by the Russians after conferment of sovereignty on Eastern Germany was to notify the Allied High Commissioners that their proposals should be dealt with by negotiations between the West German authorities and the "sovereign" East German Government. What was behind all these Russian attempts to get East and West Germans "around one table" was fairly obvious. It was all part of the campaign to isolate Germany. One day, they hoped, when the West Germans would be thoroughly disillusioned at the failure of their Western "Trustees" to procure reunification, they would utilize the links established by the Russians to take up direct talks with East Germans. With the West short-circuited, it might well be easier to induce the West Germans to accept terms of reunification rather more favorable to Russia.

While the post-Berlin disillusion was fresh there occurred in Bonn an unedifying episode which caused the very greatest harm to Western prestige in West German eyes. Now that the attempt to negotiate with the Russians had failed, Dr. Adenauer, bolstered up by the encouragement Mr. Dulles had given him at Wahn airport, set about with vigor to eliminate the remaining obstacles to the Treaties. The principal of these was the constitutional dispute over the EDC. In the spring of 1953, Dr. Adenauer had succeeded in pushing ratification through both Bundestag and

Bundesrat — leaving only the signature of President Heuss needed to complete the process. Here the matter stuck, after the President had given a personal promise to Herr Ollenhauer that he would not sign until the constitutional issues had been clarified. With the new enlarged parliamentary support he had gained at the Federal elections in September 1953, Dr. Adenauer decided to take the shortest and easiest cut to settling the dispute — by amending the Basic Law of the Federal Republic. So as not to give the Russians an additional excuse for intransigence at Berlin, Dr. Adenauer's advisers prevailed upon him not to take this step until after the conference.

On February 25th the important debate on the Conscription Amendment began in the Bundestag. To get it passed, the Government had to gain a two-thirds majority in both Houses. It was a close thing in the Bundestag; at full voting strength the four parties of the coalition (Christian Democrats, Free Democrats, German Party and Refugee Party) had a margin of only eleven votes over the Social Democrats. To make sure of the result, Government whips went to remarkable lengths; one deputy was flown back from New York, another was brought back from an expedition to Abyssinia, while an unfortunate deputy recently involved in a car accident was carried into the Bundestag on a stretcher. At the division the Government came through with a vote of 334 to 144; a few weeks later it also gained the required two-thirds majority in the Bundesrat. In the 100 per cent loyalty of his coalition supporters, the Chancellor had reaped the reward of his long-suffering diplomacy at the formation of his cabinet the previous October. (In the light of the wholesale rebellion over the Saar agreement a year later, it is perhaps doubtful whether he will ever again be able to command such undivided support from his coalition.)

But, to the astonishment of the Germans, their effort to ease the last hundred yards of the EDC's way by their legislation was greeted with a violently unfavorable reaction in France. On March 3rd the National Assembly's Foreign Affairs Committee called upon the French Government to announce its opposition to the amendment in strong terms to the Federal Government. The French argument was that, until France herself had pronounced on EDC, the Germans should not be allowed to take such a definite step towards rearmament. To an observer outside of France, it seemed a curiously confused piece of logic when for the past two years it had been the declared aim of French Government policy to get the EDC ratified by Germany; and it was not as if there was the remotest possibility of the Germans setting up their armed forces under the noses of the three occupying powers before the EDC had come into force.

Under the Occupation Statute, any amendment to the Federal Basic Law had to receive approval of the Allied High Commission; thus M. François-Poncet, acting on the Quai d'Orsay's instructions, was in a position to veto. It placed the British and American Governments, who had favored passage of the amendment, in a most embarrassing position. As a result of the French attitude, the Allied High Commission was forced to reserve its approval, and for weeks a deplorable uncertainty hung over Bonn, breeding much rancor in the hearts of the German supporters of EDC. The authoritative *Frankfurter Allgemeine* commented coldly on March 20th: "The Bundestag and Bundesrat did not vote for the rearmament amendment out of wild enthusiasm for German divisions, but first and foremost to bring into effect a political plan whose originator is France."

At last, on March 25th, the Allied High Commission informed Herr Blücher, the vice-Chancellor (Dr. Adenauer was away on a tour of Turkey and Greece), that it would give its approval to the amendment once the EDC Treaty came into force after ratification by all its members — but not before. It did little to take the edge off German bitterness. *Die Welt* of March 27th carried a cartoon depicting a French tailor shouting "Militarist!" accusingly at a German clad in an ill-fitting EDC uniform — labelled "made in France." The German's retort was: "But, after all, it's your model . . ."

With the passage of the Conscription Amendment, and the Allies' promise of approval, grudging as it was, President Heuss

now felt that his undertaking to Herr Ollenhauer had been fulfilled. On March 30th he signed both the Amendment and the
EDC Treaty and Bonn Conventions. Thus ended, though somewhat ignominiously, post-war Germany's most important piece
of legislation. It was a comment on the times, however, and a
sign of growing West German disillusion, that such a momentous
event as the President's signature of the Treaties after all the
months of struggle, was accorded only a minimum of prominence
in the great majority of German newspapers.

Hard on the heels of his drive to get the Conscription Amendment through Parliament, Dr. Adenauer pushed ahead with attempts to accelerate a Franco-German settlement on the Saar —
one of the pre-conditions to ratification of the EDC imposed by
the Mayer Government in 1953. At the beginning of March Dr.
Adenauer went to Paris to open a series of talks on the Saar with
M. Bidault. The first meetings aroused some optimism in Bonn,
when on March 9th it was announced that the two sides had
agreed to adopt as a basis for negotiations the van Naters Plan to
"Europeanize" the Saar (see Chapter 7).

In spite of the auspicious start, the Franco-German talks
reached a standstill by the end of March, a deadlock apparently
caused by M. Bidault's proposed amendments to the van Naters
Plan which would have had the effect of materially slowing down
the creation of the Saar's common market with Germany. In
Bonn, where feelings toward France were already — to say the
least — not at their friendliest following the Conscription
Amendment debacle, agreement on the Saar was hardly helped
by the Bundestag, which reaffirmed on April 30th its resolution
of the previous year, declaring the Saar to be an integral part of
German territory. Although the resolution had been forced by
the Socialist Opposition, some uncompromising speeches were
made by members of the Free Democrats against any sacrifice of
the Saar, and an unpleasant rift threatened within the coalition.
The wisdom of Dr. Adenauer's timing in getting his two-thirds
majority for the Conscription Amendment before negotiating on
the Saar became fully evident. Nevertheless, the Bundestag reso-

lution greatly embarrassed Dr. Adenauer, prepared as he was to concede the tentative detachment of the Saar from Germany in return for French acceptance of the EDC and the Bonn Conventions. At that time it seemed that the French might well have thrown in a few small concessions on the economic clauses of the van Naters Plan, to provide Dr. Adenauer with a face-saver. The fact that the French would do nothing to help Adenauer in his very genuine desire to compromise lent strength to ugly suspicions in Bonn that M. Bidault's advisers in the Quai d'Orsay, where an anti-EDC lobby was known to hold great power, were and had been utilizing the Saar to bring down the Treaties. On this occasion, the suspicions were not limited to German circles.

On May 20th, after a long discussion at Strasbourg, Dr. Adenauer and M. Teitgen, deputizing for M. Bidault, announced that they had concluded a Saar agreement in principle, based on the van Naters Plan, and that they had agreed to issue a joint declaration. The announcement was greeted with some jubilation in Bonn; but it was followed with a prompt disavowal from the Quai d'Orsay that anything definite had been settled. This was the high-water mark of the Bidault-Adenauer negotiations on the Saar, and within a few days the whole subject was thrust back into obscurity by over-shadowing events. In mid-June the Laniel Government collapsed under the strain of the Geneva talks on ending the war in Indo-China. An entirely new figure now entered the scene: M. Pierre Mendès-France, a man of action determined to bring a cease-fire to Indo-China but an entirely unknown quantity as far as the EDC and German rearmament were concerned. While he was crystallizing his policy, there was bound to be yet another unsettling delay for Western Germany.

18

Otto John Goes East

IF THE ELECTIONS OF SEPTEMBER, 1953, HAD MARKED THE high tide of Dr. Adenauer's five years as Federal Chancellor, events in the summer of 1954 certainly brought his fortunes to their lowest ebb. The disillusion born of the Berlin Conference, the endless delays in granting Western Germany the place of equality in the European community which the Treaties had promised her two years before, and mounting resentment at France's apparently implacable mistrust were all beginning to have a cumulative and disturbing effect on German political thinking. Although the Christian Democrats, at their party congress of May, 1954, gave Dr. Adenauer an overwhelming endorsement for his policy of West European integration, the other parties of the coalition were becoming increasingly restive.

The first serious manifestation of this restiveness came from within the right-wing Free Democrat Party, which had already joined battle with the Chancellor over the Saar. In April and May of 1954 this party's leading expert on foreign affairs, Dr. Karl-Georg Pfleiderer, launched a bombshell on Bonn with a bold proposal that the Federal Republic should establish direct relations with the Soviet Union. Dr. Pfleiderer suggested that as a first step a delegation of Bundestag deputies should go to Moscow to meet Soviet Church and the Red Cross authorities. Their aim would be to discuss the return of German prisoners still held in Russia, but Dr. Pfleiderer did not conceal that his ultimate goal was to establish relations looking toward talks on reunification, without the intermediation of the Western Allies. Nothing would have pleased the Russians more.

In view of the forthcoming series of *Land* elections, and the FDP's fight for survival as an independent party after its trouncing of the previous year, the Pfleiderer proposition might well have been dismissed as intended chiefly for internal consumption — but for the background of its originator. Now aged fifty-five, Pfleiderer had been a career diplomat before 1945. He had spent five years *en poste* in Russia, and ended up as Consul-General in Stockholm, where he was the last German diplomat to leave in 1945. While in Stockholm, Pfleiderer established close relations with the Russian diplomats there — among them Mr. Semeonov, who subsequently became first political adviser, and then Soviet High Commissioner, in Eastern Germany. On the creation of the Federal Republic, Pfleiderer resumed his association with Semeonov and thus became one of the few non-Communist West German politicians to be in regular touch with the Russians. In 1952 he achieved some renown as the author of the "Pfleiderer Plan," an alternative to the EDC which he believed would also be acceptable to the Russians. His proposal then was that the West should withdraw its occupation forces to the western bank of the Rhine and the Russians to the other side of the Oder–Neisse, leaving in between the greater part of Germany neutral and demilitarized, but reunited. The new "Pfleiderer Plan" was no doubt inspired at a meeting that took place between Semeonov and Pfleiderer at the Soviet HQ in Karlshorst immediately after the Berlin Conference.

His personality and independent line won Pfleiderer considerable popularity; in the 1953 elections, he was unique among the Bundestag contestants in that he got 8,000 more votes on the direct ticket than his own party gained on the indirect vote in the same constituency. The 1954 Pfleiderer Plan at once drew a respectable following from the ranks of all parties of the Bundes-tag, including most of the Free Democrats.

At one moment, it even looked as if Pfleiderer's mission to Moscow would receive the endorsement of the Chancellor him-self. Perhaps indeed Dr. Adenauer did at first toy with the idea of flying a kite in the face of the West as a warning of what might happen if the Treaties continued to stagnate — then changed his mind when he realized how dangerous the results might be. In any case, the full weight of a Chancellery veto was applied and the Pfleiderer project was dropped, amid much grumbling from the Free Democrats.

The grumbling had barely died down when a formidable figure from the past entered the lists. This was Dr. Heinrich Brüning, Chancellor of the Weimar Republic from 1930 to 1932 and one of the most able German leaders of that tragic period; a staunch anti-Nazi and a colleague of Dr. Adenauer's from the days of the old Catholic Center Party. Speaking at a private meeting of Düsseldorf's influential Rhein-Ruhr Club on June 2nd, Dr. Brüning accused Dr. Adenauer's foreign policy of being "too dogmatic." After reviewing the mediatory role Germany had played in central Europe in the period of Rapallo and Locarno, Dr. Brüning claimed that she had also had the same opportunity presented to her after World War II. Instead, the Federal Repub-lic had been drawn into a one-sided alliance with the West which had in no way helped to secure peace in Europe. Dr. Brüning concurred with the theme of the Social Democrats, when he added that he did not believe that Germany could be reunited if the condition was imposed that a united Germany should be tied to the West. Expressing fears of a new American slump, he warned against Germany becoming too dependent economically on the United States.

The Brüning speech provoked an instant and sharp retort from Dr. Adenauer. In a speech at Baden-Baden, he declared that Brüning was damaging Germany's good name and arousing sus-picions abroad that the Federal Republic might try to play off the East against the West. Dr. Adenauer deprecated the references to the Treaty of Rapallo between the Weimar Republic and the Soviet Union, and noted that its German exponent had been ex-Chancellor Dr. Joseph Wirth — now leader of the neutralist, fellow-travelling League of Germans.

Coming at this time, however, from such a respected personality as Dr. Brüning, the criticism of Dr. Adenauer's policy made a strong impression in Western Germany. The *Westdeutsche Allgemeine,* a paper which had generally supported the Chancellor, agreed with Dr. Brüning, noting that there were also complaints from within Dr. Adenauer's Government against his "dogmatic foreign policy."

How Dr. Brüning's thoughts echoed was revealed to me by a highly intelligent young student at Bonn University later in June.

"A few days ago," he said, "our *Stammtisch* discussed Adenauer's foreign policy. Everybody was critical of the old man, and we concluded that it was wrong that we, vigorous Germany, should be bound unilaterally to the modern 'sick man of Europe' — France. And there were those among us who thought Russia would be no worse a partner than France. Two years ago we were all heart and soul in favor of European union, but now — I'm afraid that things are beginning to change."

Realizing the critical state West German sentiment was reaching, the West stepped up its pressure on the French to ratify the Treaties. The prospects seemed increasingly slim. In April, Mr. Eden announced that Great Britain would place one of the British divisions in Germany under EDC command, and President Eisenhower pledged that American forces would continue to remain in Europe as long as the threat of aggression existed.

Both gestures met with a lukewarm reception in Paris; the first was regarded as "too little too late," and the second as no advance on earlier undertakings. On June 23rd Mr. Eden issued a stiff warning to France from the floor of the Commons: "You cannot ask Germany to put her name now again to precisely those things that Germany put her name to two years ago. Maybe she will. It is asking much even of a strong German Government. They have given up for the sake of this particular European conception rights and privileges they might well have thought they could in future enjoy . . . I say to our French friends again: with your clear and logical minds, do look at the alternatives before finally saying that you cannot vote for EDC."

At the same time, an Anglo-American study group began work on examining the Treaties to see whether the Bonn Conventions restoring German sovereignty could be implemented separately, should the French reject EDC. It seems that this could never have been intended as anything more than a move to frighten France; it would have been as impossible to grant Germany her sovereignty without French approval as it would have been un-thinkable to rearm her against the veto of France — moreover, no German Government could have accepted the truncated sov-ereignty which the Conventions alone gave her, with the con-tinuance of the occupation, devoid of any of the aspects of alli-ance in equality provided by the EDC.

While Her Majesty's Government was doing everything in its power to help the French decide for EDC, their endeavors were being largely cancelled out by the efforts of an important section of the British Press. Led by what *The Economist* aptly labelled the "Bevanbrook Press," a most violent attack had been launched against Germany in general and Dr. Adenauer in particular. There were mornings when it was difficult to tell whether one was reading the *Daily Express* or the *Daily Worker*.

In June, by twenty-four votes to eighteen, the Foreign Affairs Committee of the Assembly took the vital step of rejecting the EDC. On June 28th the results were announced of the *Land* elections in North-Rhine Westphalia, West Germany's biggest and most important state. The Christian Democrats' vote had dropped 6 per cent compared with the 1953 general elections, and the Social Democrats had gained 2 per cent. The CDU losses were not overwhelming, but they were sufficient for Dr. Adenauer to draw the conclusion that they would have been a great deal larger had it not been for the economic prosperity. When the British High Commissioner, Sir Frederick Hoyer-Millar, called on Dr. Adenauer that day, he found him more depressed than ever before. He said he saw his whole policy of European integration threatened with collapse. He had no confidence that M. Mendès-France would now ratify the EDC, and expressed fears that he might be induced to sacrifice it for better terms in Indo-China. The German people were growing very disillusioned by the delays over the Treaties, he said, and he feared that if they were not ratified there would be a revival of nationalist feeling in Germany, which would certainly be fanned and financed by the Russians.

Finally Dr. Adenauer for the first time abandoned some of his restraint in public. In a radio interview on July 2nd (which presumably had Anglo-American endorsement), he warned France that the only alternative to EDC would be a German national army. There could be no renegotiation of the present treaty by the five nations who had already ratified it. The Germans did not want a national army, he added. "We realize that it would only conjure up fresh mistrust and fears, especially in France . . . it would be an historical and political paradox if France herself should force us to create a German national army." Dr. Adenauer's words reflected, too, the mounting resentment in Germany that her sovereignty was still withheld after two years. "The Occupation Statute is not in keeping with the political maturity of which the Federal Republic has given proof. We have earned the sovereignty which alone can make us free partners of the democratic Western States."

Dr. Adenauer's broadcast was not the first warning France had received that a German national army would be the obvious alternative to EDC. Similar utterances had been made previously in Washington, in London, and by M. Spaak of Belgium. But it was "insupportable" that a *German* should address France in this manner.

A storm of indignation arose in Paris, and the Quai d'Orsay in a fit of pique at once cancelled the visit which the Secretary of State, M. Guérin de Beaumont, was to have made to Dr. Adenauer the following Wednesday. (Setting, as it were, a cap upon outraged French national dignity, a young German tourist unfor-

tunately chose that same week to make a daring night climb of
the Eiffel Tower!) The Chancellor was manifestly dismayed by
the uproar his broadcast had caused, and promptly set out to
remedy what he had done. Meanwhile, once again the harassed
Chancellor came under fire from his own press. The *Süddeutsche
Zeitung* questioned the wisdom of Dr. Adenauer's intervention at
this moment, and concluded that his declaration was a "shot
across the Rhine" which might well ricochet.

But all these slings and arrows of the early summer of 1954
were but pinpricks to Adenauer compared to the event which
took place on July 20th — the tenth anniversary of the anti-Hitler
bomb plot. In Berlin somber commemoration ceremonies were
held that day at the Bendlerstrasse and Ploetzensee [1] for those
who had died in the abortive revolt. Among those present was
Dr. Otto John, the chief of the Federal Republic's "Office for the
Protection of the Constitution" (Western Germany's FBI), one
of the most prominent survivors of the resistance movement. On
the night of July 20th, 1954, Otto John left the hotel in West
Berlin where he and his wife were staying, to call upon a mysterious physician, Dr. Wolfgang Wohlgemuth. He never returned.

Two days later the West German Government announced to
an incredulous public that Dr. Otto John had disappeared. A
letter had been left behind by Dr. Wohlgemuth, stating that John
had gone over to East Berlin of his own free will and "does not
want to return." He, Wohlgemuth, had accompanied him over
and would be remaining too, lest he be suspected of having "influenced" John. From this, and the fact that Wohlgemuth was
known to be both a Communist sympathizer and a narcotics
expert, the West German authorities deduced that John had been
drugged and then forcibly abducted to East Berlin. The police
in West Berlin, however, claimed to have collated evidence from
a taxi-driver and a check post on the sector boundary that led
them to believe that John had gone over voluntarily "in a fit of

[1] Respectively the headquarters of the conspirators in Berlin, and the Gestapo prison where eight of the leading plotters were garrotted on meat-
hooks.

depression" — a suggestion which was promptly refuted from Bonn.

At first the kidnapping theory seemed to be extremely water-tight. Kidnappings were as established a feature of Berlin life as homosexual night clubs; over the past four years 132 inhabitants of West Berlin were known to have been abducted to the East. Only three months previously, a Russian émigré leader, Dr. Truschnovitch, had been spirited spectacularly to East Berlin, apparently by the treachery of a friend. The MVD would have known well in advance that John was certain to be in Berlin for the 20th of July ceremonies; the Truschnovitch abduction might well have been a "dummy run" in preparation for securing the man whose knowledge of both West German and Allied intelli-gence secrets could provide the Russians with their greatest cloak-and-dagger victory of the cold war. To those who had known Otto John, it seemed unthinkable that he had gone over voluntarily to the Communists — he never left any doubt that he hated Com-munism only a little less than he hated Nazism. And nobody knew better than he what defectors to the East faced once they had served their purpose.

The bulk of the West German press, however, took a far less charitable view of John's disappearance right from the start. Foremost was *Die Welt,* until recently owned by the British High Commission, but now edited by the rabidly nationalist Hans Zehrer, who had long been gunning for John. In a deplorable piece of pre-judgment the very morning after the first Govern-ment announcement, *Die Welt* stated categorically that John had "defected" to East Berlin.

During the course of that day, the various Allied authorities came out with the statements in support of the Government's abduction thesis, the usually ultra-cautious British High Com-mission commenting that it was "still considered unlikely in view of his past record that he went over voluntarily."

So far not one single word about John had come from the East. Then, late that evening — I had just replaced the receiver after telephoning the Allied comments through to London — the report came in that John had broadcast from East Berlin. The following morning I listened to the tape recording of his speech in the NWDR broadcasting studios. A strained and hesitant voice, but unmistakably that of Otto John, started:

"To my German fellow-citizens: Germany is in danger of being torn asunder for ever through the dispute between East and West. Striking action is necessary in order to appeal to all Germans for an initiative for the reunion of Germany. For this reason I have taken a resolute step on the anniversary of the 20th of July, and established contact with the Germans in the East. In the German Federal Republic I have been deprived of the basis for political activity . . . I have been slandered continuously in my office by Nazis who are reappearing everywhere in political and public life . . . Prudent and politically experienced men have confirmed to me in recent conversations their conviction that German policy has got into a blind alley."

It is an eerie and unpleasant sensation to hear the voice of a person one has only recently spoken to in the flesh from across a chasm as dividing as the River Styx. Otto John was the only man I have known personally who took the awful leap, and he was a man for whom I had great respect. His defection left me feeling morally winded. One could not help wondering whether there was something deeply rotten in the West that could cause a man of John's integrity to take so desperate a step.

Even after the broadcast, the Federal Government still held tenaciously to its original position, although it was becoming increasingly untenable. On July 26th, Dr. Schröder, the Minister of the Interior and John's former chief, stated categorically that John had been "enticed and outwitted," and that there had been no treasonable intent. In support of this, Dr. Schröder produced the somewhat bizarre story that John had gone over to the Charité Hospital in East Berlin, where Wohlgemuth worked, in order to help a widowed friend of his with her pension. The explanation, however, fell on highly sceptical ears, and brought the Government a thoroughly bad press the following morning. In a leader entitled "This is not good enough," the usually pro-

Government *Frankfurter Allgemeine* termed Dr. Schröder's evidence "unbelievably inadequate." To add to the Federal Government's discomfort, within forty-eight hours of Dr. Schröder's press conference the East Germans gleefully broadcast another John statement.

The tension and confusion in Bonn was mounting to something approaching hysteria. Although John's Security Office carried on no activities in the Soviet zone, stories inspired from the East were in constant circulation of large-scale round-ups in the East of both German and Allied agents. Dr. Schröder's assurances that John had taken no office files with him did little to allay German misgivings.

The Federal Government came under increasingly heavy attack — both for appointing John in the first place and for its mishandling of the case. Dr. Adenauer, who was then on holiday in the Black Forest, was himself sharply criticized for not coming back to Bonn to direct operations personally; although the fact that he did not deem the situation so serious as to warrant interrupting his holiday probably did more to avoid panic in the long run than anything else. Capitalizing on the confusion John's disappearance had caused in the West, the Soviets rushed in on the 25th with yet another new proposal for "All-European" security talks.

On August 6th the Federal Government put its neck yet further into the noose that it must have realized would one day be pulled tight. While Dr. Adenauer was broadcasting to reassure public opinion at home and abroad, Dr. Schröder's ministry came out with the fantastic offer of 500,000 DM ($115,000) to anyone solving the mystery of Dr. John. It was asking for the cord to be yanked, and a few days later John solved his own mystery by holding a press conference in East Berlin.

Although he showed every sign of fatigue and excessive nervousness, John gave an impressive performance in the face of hot questioning from some 300 German and foreign correspondents, and left no doubt about the sincerity of his motives in going East. As expected, he devoted the main weight of his statements to the comeback in West Germany of former Nazis — naming among others Prof. Oberländer, the Minister of Refugees. It was on account of this trend that he had gone over to East Germany, as the only possible platform from which he could denounce Nazi influences in Western Germany and work for German reunification. Dr. John added that another reason for his defection had been his desire to inform the German people of the true significance of the Bonn and Paris Treaties. "While I was in America (in May) it became clear to me," he said, "that Germany was being forced to provide soldiers for an American crusade against Communism." He made constant, but vague, allusions to certain sinister "secret protocols" attached to the EDC. John's sponsors had certainly planned the timing of his revelation of the "aggressive" designs of EDC very well indeed; that same day in Paris the Mendès-France cabinet was holding its first vital meeting to discuss EDC.

In answer to numerous questions about his actual "disappearance" from West Berlin, John explained that "everything crystallized in my brain while I was in Berlin." Wohlgemuth, he claimed, had only helped by putting him into contact with the right people in the East. When asked why, although not a Communist, he had chosen voluntary exile in Eastern Germany rather than in a Western country, John answered that his wartime experience had taught him it was impossible to do political work from a foreign land, adding significantly — "one must work in *one's own country*." As the conference ended, Otto John strolled nonchalantly down from the platform to greet a British correspondent with whom he had worked during the war, with the words: "Hello, Karl — come and have some lunch."

Embarrassed by its own stupidity as much as by anything that John had done, the Federal Government — now forced to eat its hat — issued an angry statement with the dramatic title "The Traitor John."

Compared with the enormous damage that he had done to both his own Government and the whole Western cause, the personal tragedy of John was of small consequence. But he emerged as more than just someone who had lost his nerve in the cold war: his case was symbolic of the schizophrenia of modern, divided Germany. His personality, his past and his present motives, however misguided, all demanded more sympathy than such "secret" traitors as Fuchs, Nunn-May and Pontecorvo — or Burgess and Maclean. The background to Otto John's defection dated from 1938, when, as a young lawyer with leanings towards the Social Democrats, he first associated himself with the secret anti-Nazi forces. In 1944, he was enlisted by the Julyists to fly to Spain to make contact with the Allies and inform them of what was afoot. This he was able to do because of his position as legal adviser to Lufthansa — which also secured his escape to Portugal when the plot collapsed. There, Otto John once told me, a terrifying tug-of-war was fought over him between Gestapo agents and the British Secret Service. The Gestapo managed to persuade the Portuguese to transfer him to another place of internment — in the process of which they intended to kidnap him back to Germany. The Secret Service, however, got there first and John was spirited to England. For the remainder of hostilities, he worked with the Foreign Office in London, afterwards resuming practice as a lawyer in England, and not returning to Germany until 1949. During the first post-war period his intense idealism and hatred of the Nazis, who had murdered his brother Hans in the last days of the war, led him to an action for which, far more than on account of his wartime activity, few Germans have ever forgiven him. He gave evidence for the Allied prosecution of Field Marshal von Manstein — of all the war crimes trials, probably the most resented in Germany.

In 1949, John returned to Western Germany to take up the post of security chief, an appointment which the British High Commission had strongly favored on account of his pronounced pro-British sympathies. From the start the dice were loaded against him; on almost every occasion I saw him, he made the same complaint — that it was almost impossible to recruit the right people for his work. All the good men with intelligence and experience had either been killed by the Nazis, or had been implicated with them. He was made forcibly aware of his unpopularity when windows of his house in Cologne were broken by stones, and unpleasant slogans chalked up at night by an unknown hand. John was far too sensitive a man for his work and this sort of thing had an unduly depressing effect upon him. Most of his friends had died in 1944, and, he felt peculiarly isolated in post-war Germany. His small circle of friends there seemed to consist principally of German émigré artists and intellectuals — and British correspondents, with whom John felt almost more at home than among his own people after his five years in England.

After the 1953 general election, John's depression at the state of affairs in the Federal Republic grew more and more desperate. His own Minister of the Interior, Dr. Lehr, retired and was replaced by Dr. Schröder — a former Nazi Party member (though apparently a passive one). Dr. Adenauer himself, with whom John had had only two brief audiences in four years, made no bones about not liking his security chief; John's only access to the Chancellor's ear was via a man he hated — Dr. Globke, the State Secretary in the Chancellery, who had once been prominent as a lawyer to the Nazi Government. As John watched mounting numbers of ex-Nazis being brought into the Ministry of Refugees by its new Minister, Professor Oberländer, his obsession with the Nazis became almost a mania. He began to drink increasingly and would call on British correspondents late at night to unburden his mind — unusual behavior for the chief of an intelligence organization.

After the Naumann arrests, John felt that he had been let down by even the British authorities, who — although he had supplied them with so much of the information on the Naumann group — had not informed him of the action they were to take. At the same time, the Allies were beginning to share the Federal Government's opinion, because of several failures of the Security Office, that John was the wrong man for the job. By 1953 John himself would have gladly relinquished the post for a position on the resuscitated Lufthansa; but there too was a strong hostile clique. Unduly sensitive to criticism, John's personal frustration reached a peak only a few weeks before his defection; in the Bundestag he came under open attack for the shortcomings of his organization and rumors began to reach him that the Chancellor was preparing to transfer backing from his office to a rival intelligence organization run by a nebulous ex-General Gehlen. The last straw came in the week of John's departure for Berlin, when he heard that Dr. Schröder had indicated to a group of German journalists "in confidence" that John would be removed as soon as West German sovereignty was restored.

A person in a normal balance of mind, under similar circumstances, would have taken the obvious step and resigned. But Otto John was quite obviously not in a normal balance of mind; if he had been, he would not have closed his mind to the fact that there were just as many — if not more — ex-Nazis in the East German Government and that the "German Democratic Republic" bore an infinitely closer relation to the style of the Third Reich than the Federal Republic, whatever its deficiencies. In addition to this, John seems to have been suffering from a deluded sense of vanity — almost akin to that which drove Hess to Scotland — believing that he had a mystic mission to fulfil as a prophet of German unity.

The early notions that John had been drugged, abducted or enticed to East Berlin have been exploded, but one cannot ignore the possibility that John's defection on the anniversary of July 20th was in part the result of a brilliant psychological operation by the Soviets. Certainly the timing could not have been more devastating to the West. Much of the John case still remains a mystery, such as the inexplicable suicide of Wolfgang Höfer — an ex-German working for the American Intelligence in Berlin who had been a life-long friend of John's — and the precise role of the vanished Dr. Wohlgemuth. What is fact, however, is that the Russians were aware of John's "difficulties," and as early as March, 1954, sent from Eastern Germany another mysterious figure, Baron zu Putlitz, to sound him out. Putlitz, who had worked with John in London during the war, painted a rosy picture of life in Eastern Germany, and — on John's own admission — suggested that he come over, promising that he would be well looked after.

All three — John, Putlitz and Wohlgemuth — shared a common interest in modern art, and John was in the habit of visiting Wohlgemuth each time he went to Berlin, in spite of his known links with the Communists. Wohlgemuth, who features in all his photographs in the company of exceptionally attractive women, appears to have been a strange mixture of hedonist, brilliant but frustrated doctor, and a dilettante toying with dangerous political ideas. During the war he once saved Hans John from the Gestapo, a deed which seems to have given him a lasting hold over Otto John. He was recognized to be an extremely able psychologist, and in John's disturbed condition it is by no means unlikely that he had established himself in the relationship of father confessor to the West German security chief. Wohlgemuth had for years been angling for a post in the East Berlin Charité Hospital, and there is evidence that this was the reward offered him for bringing John over. Exactly what occurred in the mind of Otto John and what transpired on the night of July 20th can only be surmised. At the memorial ceremonies, several people remarked that John had been weeping and showing excessive emotion. According to one Julyist present at the Bendlerstrasse, John had grabbed him by the arm with the words, "Look, there are even Nazis here!" But there were none. After the grim memories which the ceremony recalled of the resistance against the Nazis — who, John believed, were now regaining power in Germany — it seems likely that he decided on the spur of the moment to accept the solution his "father confessor" had been repeatedly suggesting to him, and Wohlgemuth's chance came.

Perfidy for the cause of Communism evidently still does not pay. According to an informant of mine who was in East Berlin at the end of 1954, Wohlgemuth did not get his post in the Charité. His whereabouts are now unknown, and the waters of Communism also appear to have closed over the head of Otto John once his purpose had been fulfilled. Nearly a year later, a former colleague of mine met him in East Berlin, looking extremely dejected. He asked John pointblank: "Are you happy here?" John's answer was revealing: "I am no unhappier here than I was in Western Germany." [2]

In West Germany, John's defection caused havoc on four separate fronts. It did great harm to the cause of EDC both inside Germany and abroad. To the German man in the street, who was not aware of the intense personal drama of John — and especially to those who were now beginning to hold reservations about Adenauer's policy — the John episode appeared first and foremost as a new and grave warning that there was something wrong with Bonn's reunification program. Internally, it shook the Adenauer coalition probably more than any single event since the creation of the Federal Republic — a weaker Government handling it as ineptly might well have been brought down. It also struck heavily at the prestige of the Allies — particularly Great Britain, which was held entirely responsible for John's appointment. In a press whose more right-wing elements had gone so wild as to accuse John as having been simultaneously a Gestapo agent, a member of the Communist "Red Orchestra" network and a Julyist during the war, some wild accusations were made against Britain. The paper run by Naumann's old friends, *Deutsche Zukunft,* published a caricature of John Bull pointing to a drunken John with the caption: "Give him a good job! He's a good German — he betrayed his country!"

The most irreparable damage created by John's defection was suffered, tragically enough, by the very cause which meant most of all to him — the 20th of July. There were ugly mutterings both in the press and among the public — the theme of which was

[2] A few months after this conversation, the incredible occurred; Otto John escaped *back* to West Germany and put himself in the hands of the Federal Government. He thereby set up a record as the first "Cold War" defector to defect back; no mean feat even for a Houdini like John. Eighteen months in the "People's Paradise" of East Germany had been enough to make John realize that, whatever the shortcomings of Dr. Adenauer's Germany, he had truly leaped out of the proverbial frying pan into the fire. His return went far to balance out the great damage that had been done by his irresponsible departure.

"once a traitor, always a traitor." A prominent survivor of the Julyists now working in the Federal Government confided to me shortly after the John episode: "Already people are looking at me in a nasty way in my office. I fear many rats will begin to come out of their holes now."

His fears were soon confirmed; at an ex-Nazi rally in Lower Saxony that same week a Protestant pastor made the sinister remark: "It is a healthy sign of returning health to the German soul that the majority of the German people have turned against the oath-breakers of the 20th of July." One could only hope that the extremist pastor exaggerated; but at any rate there was no doubt that much of the repute of the 20th of July so laboriously built up by Professor Heuss and others had been demolished overnight by John's action. More than anything else, this was the saddest feature of his story.

On August 6th Dr. Adenauer made an impressive broadcast in an attempt to counter the damage caused by John's defection. Referring to the 20th of July, he said with great emphasis: "He who, out of love for the German people, undertook to smash tyranny — as did the martyrs of the 20th of July — is worthy of the esteem and veneration of everyone. He who at that time went into exile abroad deserves no censure." To reassure opinion abroad after the utterances of John, Dr. Adenauer continued: "I declare most emphatically that there is no reawakened National Socialism in Germany, and I pledge my word that it will *not* reawake."

Even before the dust had settled on the John affair, the Chancellor was faced with a new crisis from a totally different direction: West Germany's first major wave of strikes since the end of the war started in Hamburg and then moved on to paralyze virtually the entire metalworking industry in Bavaria for over three weeks. Much as the Communists might have liked to claim that the workers were striking against EDC it was, in fact, purely and simply a strike for higher wages. But the strikes left workers in many parts of the Federal Republic with a new and more bitter feeling towards the Government, which they believed had given its wholehearted support to management during the strikes. As the cost to the economy of the Bavarian strikes mounted ever higher, the Government was blamed from all directions for the ineptitude of its hitherto untried arbitration machinery.

While the strikes in Western Germany were still unresolved, out of the murk of EDC loomed the Brussels Conference. In hasty consultations with his cabinet, M. Mendès-France decided that the Treaty as it stood would never be approved by any French Parliament. In spite of the warnings of Dr. Adenauer and other EDC signatories that no alterations to the Treaty would be accepted if they involved ratification anew by the various parliaments, M. Mendès-France went ahead with drafting a series of modifications which were to be discussed among the EDC powers at Brussels on August 19th. In all, they included no less than sixty points, most of which were discreetly leaked to the press in Paris several days before the Brussels Conference began.

The amendments aimed firstly at postponing for eight years the supra-national aspects of the Treaty; secondly at allowing France to get out at such a time as either Germany became reunited or British and American troops withdrew from Europe. Thirdly (the worst discrimination against Germany) the EDC should only embrace "covering" troops, thus ensuring among other things that no German troops would be stationed in France. The Mendès-France modifications demanded even more than the Additional Annexes of the previous year. In Bonn they were greeted with hollow laughter; the *Düsseldorfer Nachrichten* commented bitterly: "The only provision missing is that German soldiers should hand in their rifles every evening."

As if to throw one more monkey-wrench into the nearly paralyzed works of EDC, the late Mr. Vyshinsky suddenly descended on Paris for talks at an hour's notice on the eve of the Brussels Conference. The intervention was hardly needed. In spite of the conciliatory attempts of that great European, M. Spaak, by August 22nd the Brussels Conference had broken down. For perhaps the first time in modern history, France found that her four neighbors had sided with Germany against her. Italy and the Benelux countries had stood firmly with Dr. Adenauer in rejecting the majority of the French demands on the grounds that they were contrary to the European idea of the Treaty, or imposed unacceptable additional discrimination against Germany. The conference adjourned, heavy with the realization that its failure spelt the final doom of EDC.

At Brussels, Dr. Adenauer, who was meeting M. Mendès-France for the first time, was unable to conceal his distrust and distaste for the French statesman. Apart from the firm conviction he still held that Mendès-France had sold EDC down the Red River at the Geneva Conference, all the world separated the two men in their personal background: Adenauer, the unbending Catholic Conservative of the old school, Mendès-France the mobile anti-clerical, Jewish radical. The alert *Spiegel* did not miss the opportunity to publish a photograph of Adenauer at the Brussels Conference with his back to, and apparently cutting, Mendès-France.

In the gloom that hung over the final stages of the Brussels talks, Dr. Adenauer's cup was still not yet full. On the last day of the conference, he received a telephone call from Germany to inform him that a Bundestag deputy of his own Christian Democrat party, Herr Schmidt-Wittmack, had followed in the footsteps of Otto John and gone to Eastern Germany to fight against his leader's foreign policy.

19

Adenauer's Defeat

and Triumph

A<small>T THE END OF</small> A<small>UGUST</small>, 1954, <small>FRANCE'S PARLIAMENT AT LAST</small>
came to grips with the EDC — twenty-seven months after her
statesmen had signed the Treaty and nearly four years since a
French Prime Minister had first launched the plan for a European
Army. In the intervening months of delays and exasperations the
plan, which had had as its lofty goal a lasting Franco-German conciliation, had in fact achieved the opposite: at no time since 1945
had relations between France and Germany been as strained.

After the resolute stand of the other five EDC Foreign Ministers against M. Mendès-France's demands at Brussels, the fate
of EDC was sealed. Even the French Prime Minister would not
make it an issue of confidence in the Assembly. On the evening
of August 30th, a few days before the 15th anniversary of the
outbreak of World War II, the EDC was simply dismissed from
the Assembly's agenda by a procedural vote of 319 to 264. The
vote was taken even before most of the supporters of the Treaty
had had a chance to state their cases. In was an ignominious end
for a scheme that once had inspired high hopes for all Europe
and on which so much toil, sweat and tears had been lavished.

On the day of the vital French debate, Dr. Adenauer was still
on holiday at the Black Forest health resort of Bühlerhöhe, which
had once also been the favorite retreat of the noted Chancellor

of the Weimar period, Dr. Gustav Stresemann. The news of the defeat of EDC was telephoned to Bühlerhöhe by the German Embassy in Paris. On being given the message, Dr. Adenauer returned without comment to the privacy of his own room. His thoughts must have been particularly bitter at that moment. Along with the EDC, which was to have been the preliminary to political federation, crumbled the keystone of his policy for a United Europe based on common institutions. The prospects for West German sovereignty and equality in the free world must have seemed to him little less remote than when he first came to office five years earlier. His whole policy of integration with the West and conciliation with France appeared to be set at naught. Even up to the eve of the Assembly debate, he had been reiterating again and again his simple faith — "I am convinced France will ratify." Particularly wounding to him must have been the almost casual way in which the French Assembly had flung aside all his efforts and hopes. One can well believe that at this moment his thoughts cast up the image of his predecessor, Stresemann, who too had based his policy on reconciliation with France; Stresemann, who said shortly before he died, a frustrated man, twenty-five years before: "I pledged myself to achieving a Franco-British-German concord. I gained the backing of 80 per cent of the German people for my policy . . . I gave and gave and gave until my own followers turned against me . . . If they could have granted me just one concession, I would have won my people. But they gave nothing. . . . That is my tragedy and their crime." The compassion of even Dr. Adenauer's personal adversaries went out to the lonely and disillusioned old man that night; Dr. Dehler said, "I am thinking at this hour of the Federal Chancellor, who has dedicated himself with such prophetic energy to this goal, and I hope that this will not affect him too sorely."

For the first forty-eight hours, uncertainty prevailed in Bonn as to how the Chancellor would react. On the 31st he set in train a flurry of action from his retreat at Bühlerhöhe. Both Herr von Eckardt and Herr Blankenhorn, his press chief and his political adviser from the Foreign Office, were called down from Bonn for consultations. Herr von Eckardt made the gruelling five-hour trip twice in the same day to hold a press conference in Bonn on his return. Under the chairmanship of Herr Blücher, the Vice-Chancellor, the Federal Cabinet held a crisis meeting in Bonn; the entire Cabinet then moved to the Black Forest to hold a second session the next day with the Chancellor himself presiding.

Afterwards a significant communiqué was issued, setting out the Federal Government's future policy. Western Germany would now aim for the prompt restoration of her sovereignty; Herr Strauss, a Minister without portfolio, amplified that this meant *full* sovereignty, and not the truncated version offered by the Bonn Conventions once EDC had been severed from them — a view which was resoundingly echoed in the German press the following day. In its policy of political integration, the Government would pursue its past line "with those people *in accordance* with it," and in military integration "with those countries *who have ratified the EDC, or are about to.*" Finally, the Federal Government would aim for negotiations without delay with the United States and Great Britain.

From each of the five points of the communiqué France seemed deliberately excluded. Was there some mistake? No, a spokesman of the Federal Press Office answered, "there is no mistake, and we have no comment to add. The communiqué must stand by itself." In a tense, rumor-laden atmosphere, the thought ran among the Bonn newspapermen that this was the first portent of some new Anglo-American-German *entente* — to the exclusion of France. It sounded impossible, and it sounded like the end of the Western Alliance; but one thing seemed to stand out of the dark confusion which followed the collapse of EDC — prospects of getting both Germany and France within the same defense organization were slim.

The Socialist Opposition at once pounced joyously on the Government for their exasperated communiqué. Its five points, they noted, contained no mention of reunification, and of course no policy could succeed which deliberately excluded France. The

Socialists were by now almost beside themselves with glee; at the news of EDC's collapse, Herr Ollenhauer, puffing himself up like Aesop's frog, had hastened to pronounce the Chancellor's policy "completely wrecked." Once again the SPD trotted out their nebulous scheme of a security system embracing everybody against nobody — coupled with a fresh proposal for Four Power talks with the Russians. Had their suggestion been taken seriously at that time, no more complete surrender of a defeated West could have been imagined. The triumphant gloating of the German Socialists at the collapse of a great conception and the failure of a great German's policy struck one as particularly squalid, coming as it did from a party that in five years of parliamentary opposition had contributed so little other than petty negativism.

On September 2nd Herr von Eckardt held another press conference, this time obviously to moderate the drastic impression the Cabinet's communiqué had caused. Although there was talk of a rump EDC without France, any effective defense of Europe, said Herr von Eckardt, must certainly include France. Furthermore, although what Germany now wanted was *full* sovereignty, she would be prepared later to renounce parts of that sovereignty should a new supra-national defense system materialize in Western Europe. But in spite of this apparent willingness of the Germans to make concessions on their sovereignty *afterwards,* the fact that they were now asking for it to be fully restored *before* entering into any new defense scheme clearly presented the Allies with a new and worrying situation. It threatened to reverse completely the reassuring arrangements of May, 1952, whereby Western Germany could only gain her sovereignty by first pledging to join in arms with the West. Once given sovereignty with no strings attached, anything might happen in Western Germany; between the granting of sovereignty and the opening of new defense negotiations a change of government could occur and an independent Western Germany might be forever lost to the West. But after the West's demonstration of its inability to put into effect the Treaties which it had signed with the Federal Republic two and a half years earlier, it seemed indeed difficult to delay any longer the process of restoring its unrestricted sovereignty. It was obvious that the West would have to act quickly if anything was to be rescued from the ruins of its German policy.

While new ideas were evolving in Western capitals, an interview took place between Dr. Adenauer and the former Bonn correspondent of *The Times,* John Freeman, who during his long stay in Germany had come closer to forming a personal friendship with the remote Chancellor than any other journalist or foreigner. Travelling all the way from Zagreb for the interview, Freeman received a warm welcome at Bühlerhöhe. He found the Chancellor very depressed and feeling his years, and — as he told me later — "not angry, but longing to let off steam." Dr. Adenauer's resentment against Mendès-France was very great; Mendès-France, he was convinced, had wanted to destroy EDC — but in doing so he had not had a majority behind him. According to *The Times* report of the interview, Dr. Adenauer went on:

> The good will which Germany has shown since the end of the war and the desire that we and the French should go forward in fellowship and friendship have been disappointed. What are the Germans now saying? They are saying something like this: "Stresemann negotiated with Briand, Brüning negotiated with Daladier, and Adenauer negotiated with Schuman — all to no purpose. Must we assume that the French do not wish for this understanding between our two countries? . . ."
>
> Think now of the younger generation of Germans. I think I can fairly claim that we had displaced the old conception of narrow nationalism with the European idea. If the European idea is wrecked by the action of France, will not that mean a return in Germany to an exaggerated nationalism? I do not mean a return to the Nazism of Hitler, but a return certainly to some form of nationalism. If Germany is rebuffed by the West and wooed by the East, do you not think that the new nationalism will look to the Soviet Union? This is a great danger.

Returning to France, Dr. Adenauer warned:

> If some French circles think that, with the help of Russia, they can play a decisive role in Germany, then they are making the same

mistake as Beneš and other peoples of the satellite States of to-day . . .

There is no question of isolating France. She had isolated her-self from Europe and from the United States.

But Dr. Adenauer added:

I am still of the opinion that without an understanding between France and Germany there will be no Europe, and that the fate of France and the fate of Germany are indivisible. Either both of us will fall into the hands of Russia or we shall both remain free. ·

During the conversation, Dr. Adenauer expressed some hope in the solidarity between the five other EDC partners, as witnessed at the Brussels Conference:

I am persuaded the European idea stands, and will stand. We require patience and discretion.

At a moment when vital new thinking had to be done on some alternative form of German rearmament which might be accept-able to France, publication of the Chancellor's private disillu-sionment seemed a questionable act. The French press at once reacted according to form; an "incredible interview" and an "in-tolerable interference," complained *Le Monde*. *The Times* inter-view met with hardly less displeasure in the German press; the *Frankfurter Allgemeine* printed a long leader by Paul Sethe, en-titled "Not Well Advised," commenting on the "disturbing im-pression that events had unbalanced the Federal Republic's lead-ership."

Suddenly hope began to spread through the bleak German scene. What many German newspapers and politicians had been pressing during the past months seemed about to take place: Britain moved to pick up the fragments of EDC and give Europe the new lead she so badly needed. On September 11th Mr. Eden embarked on a lightning fact-finding tour of the EDC capitals — which in a flippant mood he later described as "a bit of a scamper round the capitals of Europe." In Bonn the British Foreign Secre-tary's visit was greeted with unusually warm enthusiasm; even

Hans Zehrer, the editor of *Die Welt,* not previously renowned as an Anglophile, wrote of a "breathtaking display of intelligence" and exulted that "Britain is showing now that she is the only country which for centuries has had a world-wide position and an understanding of world problems." An excellently drawn cartoon in the *Stuttgarter Zeitung* portrayed a muscular Churchill in the garb of a Roman charioteer, flicking a whip over the jades of Europe — flanked by a wornout hack as West Germany and a rebellious, mettlesome beast as France.

But in spite of a glowing Chancellery communiqué announcing "complete agreement" during the talks, less optimistic Germans held sober reservations about the reception the Eden proposals would receive in Paris. As these were believed to involve some form of direct entry of a rearmed Western Germany into NATO, it was difficult to believe that they would be accepted by a French Parliament which had already rejected EDC with all its guarantees and safeguards. At any rate the boost which the Eden visit gave to Dr. Adenauer was a badly needed one; *Land* elections held in Schleswig-Holstein that same day showed that the Christian Democrats' support had fallen from the peak of 47 per cent in the 1953 Federal Elections to only 32.2 per cent. The Social Democrats could now claim an equal number of seats in the Diet of that *Land*. It was an alarming trend.

At the end of the following week, the seal was placed on the death of EDC by the return to Bonn of 200 disillusioned experts of the Blank Office, the German delegation to the EDC Interim Committee in Paris. They returned in a bitter mood; after nearly three years of work side by side with their French opposite numbers there had been no official farewell parties.

On September 28th the London Conference began under the Chairmanship of Mr. Eden. The nations which had negotiated the Bonn Conventions and the EDC Treaty were now increased to nine: the six EDC powers, US, Great Britain and Canada. The results of the first day's talks were apparently not such as to generate great confidence for the future. Late that night a solemn conversation in German took place in a corner of the foyer at

Claridge's between Adenauer, Spaak of Belgium, and Bech of Luxembourg. For the second time that month, the German Chancellor exposed to a foreign audience his fears of future developments inside Germany. This time Adenauer obviously did not expect his words to go beyond the trio — nor would they have done so but for one of those chances which occur perhaps once in the life of a journalist. Seated behind a pillar in the foyer some dozen feet away from the three ministers was a correspondent of the *Spiegel* who had come to London to cover the conference and who now pricked up his ears as he suddenly recognized Adenauer's Rhenish dialect. A full report of the conversation appeared in the *Spiegel,* together with some biting criticism of the Chancellor's lack of confidence in his countrymen. According to the *Spiegel,* Adenauer expressed his grave misgivings of where a new German national army, freed from the restrictions of EDC, would lead: "I am one hundred per cent convinced that the German national army, to which Mendès-France is driving us, will be a great danger for both Germany and Europe. *When I am no longer there,* I do not know what will happen to Germany if we have not yet succeeded in creating United Europe."

In France, just as in Germany, he feared the nationalists were ready to fall back into their evil ways, in spite of the experiences of the past. "They would rather," he said, "a Germany with a national army than United Europe — so long as they can pursue their own policy with the Russians. And the German nationalists think exactly the same way; they are ready to go with the Russians."

Here M. Spaak protested that such a development could not take place while the Christian Democrats and the Social Democrats were still the two strongest parties in Western Germany. But Adenauer expressed grave doubts about the Social Democrats: "Ollenhauer is a weak man and would not be able to keep his party from drifting. He lacks Schumacher's clear-sightedness and personality, and Schumacher's uncompromising attitude against Communism and the Soviets: he cherishes illusions of the possibility of a German policy in unison with Moscow, and other members of the SPD executive share this illusion."

Again and again, according to the *Spiegel,* Adenauer repeated his despondent theme of *après moi, le déluge,* with the words "when I am no longer there." He begged his listeners to "make use of the time while I am still alive, because when I am no more it will be too late. My God, I do not know what my successors will do; if they give way; if they are not obliged to follow along firmly pre-ordained lines, if they are not bound to United Europe . . ." As the one hope of the London Conference, Dr. Adenauer said: "We must regard the Brussels Pact as the starting-point for a new European Defense Community and exploit every possibility to achieve our goal — the integration of Europe . . . *and we have not got much time left.*"

The following day the conference took a spectacular turn for the better. Mr. Eden told the representatives of the nine nations that Great Britain would keep on the Continent her present forces of four divisions and one tactical air force for the duration of the new defense pact — fifty years. To commit the main weight of the regular army to the Continent of Europe for the next half-century in defiance of age-old tradition was a tremendous step for any British Government to take. That such a step had to be taken reflected the full seriousness of the situation in the West after the collapse of EDC; Mr. Eden must have seen that another failure to bring Germany into a Western defense set-up would almost certainly bring to pass the threatened "agonizing reappraisal" in the United States, followed by an American withdrawal from Europe. The British offer now fulfilled one of the most urgent French conditions for German rearmament: full British participation to hold the balance between the French and the German contingents in the defense system. It was tragic that the offer could not have been made two years before, when it was just as obvious that British divisions would be involved in the defense of the Continent for a great many years to come.

On October 3rd, after a rough passage created by M. Mendès-France's introduction of proposals for a European arms control organization, the London Conference ended in an unhoped-for atmosphere of success. The delegates appended their signatures to a series of preliminary agreements ending the Occupation in Germany, restoring sovereignty to Western Germany, rearming her within the framework of NATO and at the same time tying both her and Italy into the mutual security arrangements of the Brussels Treaty of 1948. That same afternoon, on the 25th anniversary of Stresemann's death, Dr. Adenauer left London in a far more buoyant frame of mind than when he had arrived. As he climbed out of the British Viscount turbojet at Wahn airport, he remarked: "I believe that the German people on both sides of the Iron Curtain will be satisfied by what we have achieved in London . . . I believe that France will now ratify the agreements."

Two days later Dr. Adenauer's report on the London talks was heard by an enthusiastic Bundestag, only so recently plunged in deepest gloom by the collapse of EDC. There was loud applause from the Government benches when the Chancellor said that the success of the talks redounded "to the lasting credit of the British Foreign Secretary." There was even louder applause when Adenauer termed the British offer of four divisions "a revolutionary act in British history" and "one of the most remarkable examples of British statesmanship." As he sat down at the end of his long statement, the Chancellor received one of the warmest and most prolonged ovations he had ever had from the Bundestag. Only the Socialists remained silent, although their leaders had in the past frequently stated that they would consider joining in a Western defense force, provided it embraced a wider framework than EDC — which was just what the London Agreements did.

Three weeks later, in Paris, the Fourteen Power North Atlantic Council convened to endorse Germany's entry into NATO. At the same time there were meetings of the Brussels Treaty signatories, and the three Western Powers plus Western Germany, to sign the detailed agreement, which ran to 30,000 words. On the eve of the talks, the British Foreign Secretary's triumph at the London Conference had been capped with the conferment of the Order of the Garter, and it was as Sir Anthony Eden that he came to Paris.

At the last moment, as so often in the past, the Saar question loomed up again to threaten the whole complex of the agreements with Germany. Once again France had stipulated that there could be no settlement with Germany until a satisfactory agreement had been reached on the Saar. On the eve of the signature of the Paris Agreements, Dr. Adenauer met M. Mendès-France to find an eleventh-hour answer to the problem he had been unable to solve in the past months and years of negotiations with M. Schuman and M. Bidault. Aware of the urgency with which the other Western delegates assembled in Paris were pressing for a solution on the Saar, M. Mendès-France resorted to the time-limit tactics which had been so successful at Geneva. This eleventh-hour diplomacy recalled, too, the French performance on the eve of the signature of EDC. It never seemed to fail.

Dr. Adenauer now found himself in the invidious position that if he rejected the Mendès-France Saar terms the whole Western world would then have cause to lay full responsibility on Germany for the collapse of the Paris Agreements. With the death of EDC, the prospects of a future United Europe of which the Saar would become the first "European Territory," as envisaged under the van Naters Plan, had become very slight. What Adenauer was now being asked to sign in fact entailed the risk of considerably greater sacrifice for Germany — and with it the prospect of still sharper resistance to it at home. He was, as *The Times* put it, giving "a bigger hostage to fortune over his Saar policy than by anything else he has done." With this in mind, Dr. Adenauer took the wise precaution of inviting to Paris first the leaders of his coalition parties, and then Her Ollenhauer, before committing himself to signing the Saar Agreement.

The Saar Agreement finally signed was a much shorter and less explicit document than the van Naters Plan, and almost immediately it was published dangerous ambiguities were picked out by both sides. Pending a German peace settlement, the Saar was to be given a Statute within the Western European Union to be formed under the Brussels Treaty. The Saarlanders themselves would be allowed to hold a referendum to express their views on the new Saar Statute. The previously banned pro-German political parties would now be licensed but they would be severed from any connection with their big brothers in Western Germany, who would be bound not to interfere in Saar politics. Economic relations between the Saar and Germany were to become *similar* but apparently not *identical* to those existing between France and the Saar. At the same time the agreement laid down that the Franco-Saar economic union should not be prejudiced by too precipitate increases in German-Saar trade. Thus, it seemed, France could object to any expansion of trade between the Saar and Germany.

One salubrious feature that emerged from the Saar talks at the time was the view expressed by M. Mendès-France that the Saar should henceforth be regarded as only a relatively unimportant corner of Franco-German economic problems, which should be tackled as a whole. Launching into this problem, M. Mendès-France raised a series of proposals for increasing Franco-German economic co-operation — including the widening of trade, joint participation in the industrial exploitation of North Africa, and a canalization of the Mosel River to connect the coal of the Ruhr more directly with the iron ore of Lorraine. At first sight, the Mendès-France approach seemed to offer a new basis for a Franco-German *rapprochement* that might be even sounder than the old ideas of co-operation by political integration that died with EDC. The talks on closer economic collaboration were later continued between M. Mendès-France and Professor Erhard, and indeed the principle behind them seems to have been adopted also by M. Mendès-France's successors, Messrs. Faure and Pinay.

A second gratifying feature of the Franco-German talks in Paris was a distinct improvement in the personal relations between Dr. Adenauer and the French premier. According to a German diplomat present at the Paris talks, Dr. Adenauer had revised his former distrust of M. Mendès-France and begun to appreciate him as the outstanding statesman that he undoubtedly is. Unfortunately, it was a friendship which had little time to mature before the Assembly guillotine did its work.

With the Saar Settlement disposed of, nothing stood in the way of the signature of the other agreements. This took place on October 24th, less than two months after the demoralizing fall of EDC. On examination of the lengthy documents, the achievement seemed all the more astonishing because of the remarkably good terms on which the West was getting German rearmament considering all that had transpired over the past two and a half years since the signature of EDC. Not only did the results reflect the wise guidance of Sir Anthony Eden, but also the stature of Dr. Adenauer and the flexibility of his Government. In spite of the sovereignty demands the Federal Government had made immediately after the collapse of EDC it was now dispensing with several of the privileges that *full* sovereignty would allow. The Paris Agreements did not offer Germany any great new advantages over the EDC-Bonn Conventions; on the other hand they provided the West with controls as under EDC — and, militarily, the scheme was probably a great deal more workable. Although the Federal Republic received full authority over both its internal and external affairs, the Western Allies still retained reserve rights where Berlin and German reunification were concerned. One important feature, though, was different: the Allies would no longer have the automatic right to keep their forces in Germany. Once the Paris Agreements entered into force, the consent of the Federal Republic would be required.

Unlike the EDC, national forces would no longer be submerged within a supra-national army; it will be recalled that this had always been a bugbear to the French (although they thought up the idea). France had never been able to shake off her fear that on reunification of Germany, the Federal Republic would withdraw from EDC — leaving the French army inextricably integrated within EDC for the remainder of the century. The German land forces — much as Dr. Adenauer and others had deprecated re-creating a national German Army — would now form an entity, integrated inside NATO at army-group level instead of divisional level as under EDC. Many Frenchmen had fought EDC because they feared it would revive the German General Staff; now, cynically enough, because of the collapse of EDC, Germany, granted its own army, would have to be allowed its own General Staff. But, under the extended powers of both NATO's Supreme Allied Commander (SACEUR) and the Brussels Treaty, the wings of the new German General Staff would be clipped pretty short. The Paris Agreements gave SACEUR control over the location of all forces under his command, over all "higher" training and over all logistics, as well as the right to inspect any forces at any time.

Although the tight control of the German contingent offered by the EDC system of integrated defense budgets, production and allocation of arms now fell away with Germany's entry to NATO, many of the safeguards of the EDC were taken over into the Brussels Treaty. The Treaty, which was negotiated in 1948 between Great Britain, France and the Benelux countries for the prime purpose of providing mutual security against a renewed threat of German aggression, was now converted into the Western European Union and extended to incorporate both Western Germany and Italy. It had none of the ambitious federal aims of the political community that was to have followed EDC; its object was simply "to promote the unity and to encourage the progressive integration of Europe." Within its framework, the German forces would be limited to their old maximum under EDC of twelve divisions. As also under EDC, the Federal Republic pledged itself not to manufacture any of the "ABC" weapons (atomic, bacteriological and chemical). In addition — together with all other Continental nations — she would be subjected to the checks of the arms control agency proposed by M. Mendès-France, which would be responsible to the Western European Union council. In theory the agency would control the production and purchase of every implement of war down to light firearms and "soft" vehicles; its officers would have the right to inspect any factory in the WEU. How it would work in practice was somewhat open to doubt. Post-Versailles experience indicated that arms controls and inspections provided no obstacle to any nation which might be bent on flouting them.

Declarations similar to those made at the signature of the EDC were also attached to the Paris Agreements. Western Germany pledged herself not to resort to force to achieve reunification, and the three Western Allies declared that they would regard any such recourse to arms as a threat to their own security.

After the signature of the Paris Agreements, the West breathed a deep sigh. The process of ratification had still to come; but in Germany Dr. Adenauer had a secure majority, and in France the Agreements now had the full backing of M. Mendès-France — a Frenchman who seemed to be able to get things done. Jubilation at the Paris achievement was immense; before leaving Paris, Mr. Dulles declared that Western Europe had "provided a new demonstration of its resources and of its capacity to act constructively."

For Dr. Adenauer the day the Agreements were signed was one of Franco-German reconciliation to find a parallel for which "it would be necessary to go back a thousand years in history." His talks with M. Mendès-France had reassured him that the prospects of United Europe remained as strong as before the collapse of EDC.

Comment in all but the extreme right- and left-wing German press echoed the Chancellor's enthusiasm. The *Frankfurter Allgemeine* spoke glowingly of "an era of trust, peace and close co-operation" which was succeeding the European enmities of the past centuries. The Catholic *Kölnische Rundschau* declared: "We have witnessed the birth of a new Europe."

20

The Dangerous Way Ahead

FOR ALL HIS JUBILATION AT THE SIGNATURE OF THE PARIS AGREE-
ments there was a strong element of defeat in Dr. Adenauer's
triumph. At last, by infinite patience, he had brought Western
Germany within sight of sovereignty. But had he brought her any
nearer reunification with the East? In October, 1954, Germans
asking themselves this question could only see darkly into the future. And what of Dr. Adenauer's own dreams of an integrated
Europe that he had dreamed in the golden days of the Schuman-
de Gasperi-Adenauer *entente*? Few observers shared Dr. Adenauer's optimism that a United Europe based on a gradual with-
ering away of national functions would yet arise from the West
European Union. The death of the European Defense Community seemed all too clearly to have sounded the death knell to
these dreams. Two and a half years further removed from the
lessons of World War II and Korea, a new European era seemed
to have opened where national collaboration would have to act
as a substitute for the earlier ideals of international federation.

Out of all the plans to make a European *whole,* there now remained but one tiny fragment destined under the Paris Agreements to have a "European Constitution" — the Saar. But barely
was the ink on the documents dry, than voices in Germany were
being raised against the Chancellor's "surrender" of the Saar.

Dr. Dehler, on the day of signature, said he thought that the Saar settlement would be final, for when was one to reckon with a German peace treaty? That other old rebel of the Free Democrat Party, Dr. Reinhold Maier, expressed fears that had long lurked at the back of German minds: would not separation of the Saar from Germany jeopardize her moral rights to the Oder-Neisse territory? After a nine-hour session on October 28th the Bundestag caucus of the Free Democrats decided to reject the Saar Agreement. It was soon clear that this "rebellion" within the coalition was highly dangerous. Matters worsened as subsequent statements from Bonn and Paris showed that both sides placed entirely different interpretations upon the ill-defined agreement; yet the French refused to meet Dr. Adenaur's requests for talks to "elucidate and amplify" the Saar Agreement. The Christian Democrat *Land* of the Palatinate began to ask ugly questions about the future of their territory which the French had arbitrarily annexed into the Saarland in 1947. Would this too be detached from Germany? Even Herr Kaiser, the Minister for All-German Questions, a member of Dr. Adenauer's own party, declared his opposition to the Saar Agreement.

When the vote on the Saar Agreement was held during the Bundestag's second reading of the Paris Treaties at the end of February, 1955, Dr. Adenauer's majority fell to sixty-one compared with the 190 that he had been able to muster for the Conscription Amendment when he was at the peak of his power a year earlier. Most of both the Free Democrat and Refugee Parties had voted against the Government. Even within Dr. Adenauer's Cabinet, one Free Democrat minister joined the Opposition; two more — and Herr Kaiser — abstained. Of the Free Democrat ministers, only the loyal Herr Blücher, the Vice-Chancellor, sacrificed his political future to support the Government. The vote, far more than just a protest against Dr. Adenauer's Saar policy in particular, was symptomatic of the restlessness that the years of uncertainty had brought about on the German political scene. Subsequent events, particularly the petty last-minute squabble over ownership of the Volklingen steel works, have shown that the Saar Agreement has still not provided the magic salve required to heal the ever-open wound of Franco-German discord.

Indeed, it is a wound that now threatens more than ever before to poison the peace of Europe. As on earlier occasions, when the Saar Agreement was drafted between the big neighbors too little attention was paid to what the Saarlanders themselves might want. As the time for the referendum on the Saar Agreement approached in the autumn of 1955, the licensing of the previously banned pro-German parties brought forth a wave of opposition to the Agreement far in excess of anything anticipated by the signatories. A surge of anti-French feeling, pent up by the repression of political freedom for so many years, went hand in hand with such an ardor of pro-German nationalism that observers were reminded all too vividly of the Nazi plebiscite of 1935. Some elements of the pro-German parties certainly did their best to revive this atmosphere. In an attempt to whip up feelings against the French and the Hoffmann Government, the newspaper of the Saar Democratic Party (the little brother of the German Free Democrats) resuscitated the "unatoned Geiger crime." Even the Saar Christian Democrats, affiliated to Dr. Adenauer's own party, came out against the Saar Statute on the ground that it would perpetuate separation from Germany. Paradoxically enough, the stipulation in the Saar Agreement banning German interference in Saar politics also worked against Dr. Adenauer in his efforts to persuade the Saar CDU to vote for the Statute.

On October 23, the day of the referendum, the inevitable occurred. The Saar's "European" Statute was rejected — but by an unexpectedly overwhelming majority of 423,434 against 201,-973 on a 96.7 per cent poll. By their votes, the Saarlanders made it quite clear that they still considered themselves Germans and wanted to return to the Fatherland. Their vote meant that, once again, the French and the Germans would have to get together to prepare a new Saar agreement — but this time it seemed impossible that any German government could agree to a settlement that envisaged any long term separation of the Saar from Germany. The Saar referendum was a terrible defeat for French foreign policy. As will be recalled, the French Government of M. Rene Mayer had in early 1953 stipulated that a Saar settlement favorable to France must be a pre-condition to French support for West German rearmament. Two years later, during the French debates on the London-Paris Agreements, the same M. Mayer commented, "The separation of the Saar from Germany is the only one of the goals of our foreign policy laid down in 1945 that we have achieved." After October, 1955, it must have looked to the average Frenchman as if West Germany had got rearmament and would now get the Saar too, with its vital balance of power in European coal and steel.

But the intelligent Frenchman, with his great capacity for self-criticism, must have found it difficult to absolve his own country from blame for the 1955 defeat. At the Saar elections of November 1952, only some 30 per cent of the Saar population showed their disapproval of the Hoffmann regime by spoiling their votes or abstaining; even though the pro-German parties were still banned, the chances then were that a settlement based on the van Naters' Plan would have gained the support of a majority of the Saarlanders. But the French dithered, and the status quo was maintained for another three years, during which French national prestige declined, and the attractions of Germany's ever-growing prosperity mounted hand-in-hand with resentment at the continued banning of the pro-German parties. Worst of all, though, was the French rejection of EDC, which, with its supra-national provisions, formed an integral part of the United Europe of which the Saar was to become the first genuine "European Territory." It may be being wise after the event, but there is no doubt that with the death of the EDC, a "European solution" for the Saar was doomed too. And this was the bitterest part of the tragedy that France has brought upon herself.

Will historians in future years look back on the Saar referendum as marking the end of that post-war period dominated by the European idea? Certainly at the time, in the minds of the soberest European observers the ultra-nationalist slogans chanted during the anti-Statute campaign awoke fears that they might be heralding in a return to the old narrow nationalism that has plagued Europe in the past. In Germany, there were few politicians who would express anything but varying degrees of relief when they heard of the rejection of the Saar Statute. But to the German architect of the Statute and the great exponent of the European Idea, then gravely ill with pneumonia, the rejection of his work by so overwhelming a majority must have come as a particularly savage blow. The Saar referendum, with its accompanying defeat for the European Idea, has given a great boost to the enemies of Adenauer in Germany — particularly to the neutralists and "unity firsters" already lured by the "Geneva spirit" to sail closer to Russia and further away from the West.

Depressing and dangerous though the Saar dispute had been both to the Adenauer Government and the solidarity of the Western world, in 1955 the most dangerous threat of all still came from the East. As soon as the London talks in 1954 had shown some prospect of replacing what had been lost with EDC, the Russians had pulled out every stop of the anti-rearmament organ. At the beginning of October, 1954, M. Molotov made a sudden tour of Eastern Germany. The East German press carried detailed reports of Molotov being embraced by "Stakhanovite" coal-miners, and ostentatiously making every show of amity for the East Germans. This display, clearly intended to emphasize to the West Germans the Soviet zone's integration with the Eastern bloc, was capped by Molotov in a long speech on the 6th, when he declared that the London Agreements would make reunification impossible, and once again proposed the withdrawal of all occupation forces from Germany. On October 18th, as another demonstration of how complete its sovietization was becoming, East Germany held national "elections" on the Communist pattern. Electors were marched in parties to the polls, where they were handed ballot slips each with the name of one single candidate taken from a single National Front Party list. Polling took place publicly — with no pencils or envelopes provided — and the elector was instructed simply to drop his ballot unmarked into a box. If he did, however, wish to vote privately there was a separate booth — with a secret police agent in close attendance to take down his name as he came out. As a result, the Government Socialist Unity Party registered a 99.3 per cent victory — it was only difficult to see how 0.7 per cent had discovered a way of casting a negative vote!

On October 25th, synchronized with the signature of the London-Paris Agreements, a new Soviet Note arrived in the West, calling for a Four Power Conference to convene in November to discuss German unity, the ending of the Occupation, and collective security in Europe. As there was still no mention of free elections, the invitation was declined by the West. Although it was so transparently a propaganda move, the bait got a nibble from Dr. Dehler, as well as the usual incautious bite from the Socialists. On November 13th another Soviet note followed up with a more precise proposal for a European Security Conference to take place in either Moscow or Paris. Of the twenty-three European nations invited, one-third — the Communist third — accepted, and an Eight Power conference duly took place in Moscow. On December 2nd the conference issued a communiqué announcing the Communist bloc's intention to form a military front in the East, including Eastern Germany, if Western Germany was rearmed. All that this, in fact, signified was the renaming of something that already existed, but it was another goad to the fears of the "unity firsters" of Western Germany.

On December 9th, shortly before the first reading of the London-Paris Agreements in the Bundestag, the Russians stepped up the imperative tone of their notes with a categorical refusal to discuss German unity once the decision to rearm Western Germany had been taken. It was a testing moment for German nerves. On December 16th, just before the debate in the French Assembly, the Russians switched fire momentarily to threaten France with denunciation of the Franco-Soviet Treaty of 1944. On the 20th — apparently on the sudden recollection that a similar treaty with Britain was moldering in the Kremlin archives — Moscow shipped off a minatory note to Great Britain. With the opening of the New Year, the Russians made their blandishments even more enticing to the West Germans. On January 15th, they proposed for the first time the holding of free All-German elections for German reunification under international supervision — provided the London-Paris Agreements were dropped. This was the very point which the Russians had previously refused to discuss, which refusal had indeed been the prime reason for the breakdown of the Berlin Conference. The climax of the Soviet campaign also coincided with the irresponsible "mass action" organized by the West German Social Democrats, in collusion with an assortment of left-wing trade-unionists, pacifist pastors and the "neutralist" party of Dr. Heinemann (which had made such a sorry showing as a puppet of the Russians in the 1953 elections). The aim of the "mass action" was to bring the Paris Agreements out of the confines of the Bundestag and place them before the German electorate, denouncing them as the monkey-wrench that would wreck the works of reunification once and for all.

On the representatives at Bonn, the Russian and the SPD actions had little influence. On February 27th, 1955, the Bundestag gave the Paris Agreements, except the one on the Saar, an overwhelming majority. But, almost immediately afterwards, the Russians followed up with their offer to grant Austria her freedom in return for guarantees of neutrality between East and West. The attractiveness of a treaty on the lines of that offered to Austria — plus the possibility of free elections — undoubtedly made a dangerously strong appeal to many West Germans.

In the summer of 1955, with the Geneva "Summit" Conference and Dr. Adenauer's subsequent visit to Moscow, the game for Germany entered a new and more dangerous stage. At Geneva — meeting within a day of the 10th anniversary of the Potsdam Conference — the Western heads of state encountered, instead of the stonewalling of Molotov, the benignity of Bulganin and the rough joviality of Kruschev. A wave of sickly optimism spread over the Western world, and even so responsible a statesman as the British Foreign Secretary was tempted into making his rather surprising remark: "There ain't gonna be no war." But, in spite of the smiles, there wasn't to be any agreement on Germany either; within the first 12 hours the Russian team made it quite clear that their terms had not altered since the Berlin Conference, a year and a half earlier. Just as after Berlin, Molotov had toured Eastern Germany to reaffirm Russia's determination not to relinquish it, so after Geneva did Kruschev and Bulganin stop off to assure the East German leaders that the Soviets would not "give up the achievements of Socialism" in the "German Democratic Republic." With a new buoyancy, Herr Grotewohl showed up the hollowness of the earlier Russian offer of free All-German elections. Since the ratification of the Paris Agreements, he claimed on August 12th, "a new situation has arisen which no longer allows of discussing All-German elections in the old form." As expected, the post-Geneva cockiness of the East German leaders brought with it a new slump in East German morale; for the month of July, the refugee figures of over 12,000 were higher than for any month since 1953.

In June, 1955, the Kremlin issued to the man it had for years been calumniating as a "Nazi warmonger" an invitation to talks in Moscow. After the Germans had got over their initial astonishment, there was almost universal jubilation in the Federal Republic. It seemed that perhaps Russia was planning to give way on Germany, in the same way that she had summoned Herr Raab to Moscow to concede Austria her independence. To the Christian Democrats, this was the leader's hour — the justification of his policy of "arguing from strength" with the Russians. Then, after Geneva, exuberance gave place to sobriety; fortunately for Adenauer, by the time he left for Moscow, the West German press was no longer expecting miracles. Within a few hours of his arrival in Moscow, talks on reunification had reached a stalemate. The key words of the conference were spoken by Kruschev — "We repeatedly and honestly warned you that the entry of the Federal Republic into the NATO would block the solution of this problem (reunification) in the nearest future." The statement was patently designed for West German consumption, as a direct refutation of Dr. Adenauer's repeated assertions that the Soviets would *not* refuse to talk reunification even after entry into force of the Paris Agreements. The conversations then turned to the subject of German prisoners of war, of which the West German delegation claimed the Russians still had some 100,000. The Russians replied that they only knew of 9,626 — and these were all "war criminals." Incensed by Dr. Adenauer's suggestions that the Russians had also committed "certain acts" on German soil, Kruschev shouted brutally: "The Italians too claimed we had some of their prisoners. Do you know where they are now? They're dead, dead, dead!"

Browbeating and cajolery, enticement and threats, *camaraderie* and brutality, that is the Communist negotiating procedure. The Chancellor seems to have been worn down and pushed into a corner. After five days of hard negotiating, in which the Russians had made it absolutely clear that they were quite prepared to let the surviving German prisoners continue to rot in Siberia if the Germans did not give them what they wanted, Dr. Adenauer gave in. What the Russians wanted was the establishment of full diplomatic relations — with the appointment of Ambassadors by Bonn and Moscow — a concession Adenauer before leaving Bonn had said he would only grant if the Russians made some substantial moves towards reunification. In return for a written agreement establishing diplomatic relations, all Dr. Adenauer got was a verbal undertaking to release the nine thousand odd prisoners of war whom the Russians claimed were the sole survivors. German correspondents gaped in amazement when the jubilant Russians announced the agreements at the end of the talks, and asked themselves what had happened to the "old man." This inhuman form of blackmail, using live beings as diplomatic counters, is an established part of Communist technique — the Japanese prisoners of war, the United Nations prisoners in Korea, the American airmen in China, and the Germans released before the Berlin Conference were all used in this fashion. Aware of the pressure of the German electorate upon him, Adenauer could not but bow to this blackmail.

Because of the promise he had gained that the prisoners would be released, on his return, at Wahn airport, Dr. Adenauer received one of his warmest ovations. There was a pitiful scene as a mother of one of the missing prisoners broke through the cordons to kiss the Chancellor's hand as he stepped out of his aircraft. But the Russians even contrived to deprive Adenauer of the credit for the prisoners' agreement. Twelve hours after Adenauer returned from Moscow, Herr Grotewohl was being received in the Kremlin, and the Russians announced that in fact the release of the prisoners had been arranged with Grotewohl some two months earlier.

There was no doubt that the Moscow talks had ended in a victory for the Russians; the *Daily Telegraph* of September 14th even went so far as to describe it as the "greatest Soviet diplomatic victory since the war." The Russians got a diplomatic foothold in Bonn which many West Germans feared would be used as a center for spying and for supporting the neutralists in their opposition to the Federal Republic's alignment with the West. In Moscow, the new West German Embassy would undoubtedly be subject to constant pressure to bring it into direct relations with the East German Embassy there. The Russians could feel confident that they had gone a long way towards realizing their old aim of putting West Germany on a basis of parity with the East German puppet state — which had been the meaning of the slogan "Germans at one table" at the Berlin Conference. The fact that the Adenauer visit had resulted in prospects of at least some of the German prisoners returning home did, however, give him a breathing spell before the reunification battle started up again in Western Germany. With a remarkable unanimity, the Bundestag gave Adenauer a hundred per cent endorsement for his transactions at Moscow. But it did not hide its dissatisfaction that no further progress had been made on reunification. It did not require Kruschev's coarse remark to Adenauer, "You are not immortal," to make Germans realize that at Moscow the Russians had been playing a game aimed more at Adenauer's successor than at the old Chancellor himself. Behind Kruschev's remarks about reunification only coming about through "a gradual growing together of two Germanies" could be seen the long-range Soviet policy on Germany: the two parts of Germany to discuss reunification through the agency of Russia — the one country to recognize both German governments — to the exclusion of the three Western Allies. It is a game that the Russians expect to be playing years after Dr. Adenauer has left the scene — preferably with a neutralist regime in power in Western Germany.

The success of the Russian maneuvers of 1955 have provided both the West Germans and their Allies with a grim reminder that the final card lies in Russian hands. Russia's combination of threats and bait have placed the Adenauer Government in a perilous position. A less strong German Government might well have quailed before the decision to ratify the Paris Agreements and risk being branded as "the Government that made reunification impossible." The two big questions for the years that lie ahead are whether the German people will eventually fall for the Soviet blandishments — and whether the Western Allies will allow them to fall, by plan or default.

Two years earlier, Dr. Adenauer could have relied unhesitatingly upon his people to repel Soviet advances out of mistrust for Soviet motives, and out of acceptance of his thesis that alliance with the West was the only sure way eventually to achieve reunification — on any other terms than slavery for all Germans. But things have changed radically in Western Germany since 1952. The international *détente* created by Malenkov's post-Stalin policy and the apparent *bonne volonté* of Kruschev-Bulganin have had their desired effect of stupefaction. Few Germans now look to the West out of fear of imminent onslaught from the East. The Semeonov "New Course" in the Soviet zone has also borne fruit. By their more benevolent treatment of the East Germans, and relaxations of interzonal travel, the Russians no longer appear to West Germans as an inflexible foe with whom it is impossible to negotiate.

At the same time, all the delays and disillusions of the past two years have left a deep mark on the West German's estimation of the West. Contrary to expectation, enthusiasm for rearmament at the side of the West has decreased, not increased — especially among German youth. In October, 1954, the Congress of the DGB — the trade union organization — with its 4–6 million members, voted overwhelmingly against rearmament — and among those who so voted were at least twenty-five to thirty delegates representing Catholic workers who previously would have supported Dr. Adenauer. In 1952, many young Germans unreservedly endorsed rearmament under the EDC because of the enthusiasm that the ideal of a reconciled United Europe then generated. With the death of EDC, that feeling largely died. The mistrust of Germany shown by France over the years has sown something like its counterpart in Germany; in spite of the nondiscrimination offered under the London-Paris Agreements, many young West Germans now ask themselves how they would fare if called to defend their homeland side by side with French troops. For many to whom "Western Integration" was once a rallying cry, "Unity" has taken its place. The young German who welcomed EDC out of idealism has to a large degree been replaced by a young German who views the Paris Agreements with the query, "What can we get out of it?"

Of all West German doubts about the Western Allies, perhaps the most dangerous have been those that were left by the Berlin Conference — and have not been dispelled by the Geneva Conference. The disappointment then felt somewhat inarticulately in West Germany has now been crystallized into an accusation and ugly fear summed up in the one word "co-existence" — meaning Allied acceptance of a perpetuation of the *status quo* along the Elbe — or the philosophy that Salvador de Madariaga has condemned as "live and let die."

After the Moscow declaration of January 15th the *Frankfurter Allgemeine,* which formerly had wholeheartedly supported the Chancellor's policy, set forth its belief that reunification could not now be achieved unless the Federal Republic was ready to jettison the London–Paris Agreements. The editorial went on to condemn Dr. Adenauer's policy in that, carried to its conclusion,

it would result in the Russians consolidating behind the interzonal frontier and refusing to give up an inch of Eastern Germany. British MP's at the annual Anglo-German conference at
Königswinter in April, 1955, were shocked to discover how many
German politicians, including coalition supporters, were already
talking in terms of trading membership in NATO for reunification on some basis of neutralization after the Austrian model.

There are still many thinking Germans who are not fooled by
Russian tactics into mistaking her strategy, who realize that the
Russians will never give up their key position in Eastern Germany unless assured that the surrender of all Germany coupled
with an American withdrawal from Europe could be achieved
that way. But how much support Dr. Adenauer could claim if he
went to the polls now is uncertain — in every *Land* election since
1953 the Christian Democrats suffered substantial losses to the
Social Democrats.

Moreover, at the end of 1954, a new and frightening factor
made its first appearance in the fortunes of the Christian Democrat party — the exhaustion of the leader. The cumulative effects
of the exertion and setbacks of the past months had begun to tell
on the Chancellor. During the tiring debates on the Paris Agreements, on December 16th — a few weeks before his 79th birth-
day — Dr. Adenauer suffered a mental blackout. According to
The Times correspondent in Bonn, "Twice on the second day he
was seen to be helpless under the pressure of Social Democrat
questioning. His mastery of the House was gone." Bewildered, his
supporters sat paralyzed and unable to help him. With the tragic
death of Dr. Ehlers in November, 1954, the early removal of Dr.
Adenauer's hand from the helm could spell disaster to Christian
Democrats. It would be an injustice to credit the stability and
success of the West German Government during the last five and
a half years entirely to the personality of Dr. Adenauer. Much of
the credit must go to the Allied High Commission for its wise
guidance in the early days, and later to the German people for
the ability they have shown to choose a responsible government.
That they are capable of governing themselves soberly and de-

cently is obviously the most encouraging omen for the future of Germany. But there can be no doubt that, in view of the critical days which still lie ahead before Western Germany is firmly ensconced within the Western Community, the departure of Dr. Adenauer would be a very great disaster for the West.

Events of recent years do not lead one to believe that Western Germany is in any imminent danger of being engulfed by a resurgent Nazism. But it would be wishful thinking to believe that all tendencies towards nationalism have been eradicated once and for all from the German mind. Whether it be among the football fans who allow themselves to be transported by *"über alles"* sentiments after a German victory, or among the disciples of Schumacher or Middelhauve, or among the neutralists who take upon themselves the mantle of Bismarck, the seeds of nationalism are still there. The West should give serious thought to Dr. Adenauer's various warnings that a Germany frustrated in its dealings with the West might give birth to a new form of nationalism with its head turned eastwards. One does not have to go back to Tauroggen for precedents of an alliance between German nationalists and Russia — one only has to recall the behavior of the West German neutralists in the period that this book covers — and it is now Russia alone which can offer the one prize a German nationalist regime would value above all others: reunification. There are those within the ranks of the Social Democrats, as well as of the right-wing parties of the present coalition, whose utterances in the past have shown them to be quite capable of leading Germany into a disastrous policy that would isolate her from the West in return for doubtful concessions from the East.

If the pro-West, pro-French Dr. Adenauer and his middle-of-the-road Government should eventually be replaced by a less co-operative, nationalist regime, it would be a terrible tragedy — but it would also be to a large degree the fault of the West. In the four years that have now followed signature of the EDC, the Western Allies have committed themselves to relaxing their victor's hold on Western Germany, but they have not so far managed to replace it by the fruition of their plans to integrate West Germany within the Western world. Largely because of the impetus passed on by the energetic M. Mendès-France, the Treaties restoring German sovereignty have been ratified by France, but ratification was only the end of the first stage. Many a fearful slip may yet occur before fulfilment of the Paris Agreements binds West Germany firmly to the West. With reunification now the No. 1 German interest, a dangerous period of Four Power talks, offers and counter-offers is bound to ensue — a period in which Western Germany might so easily become lost to the West. The indications are that the West Germans will be disappointed in reunification for perhaps many years to come. Sensible ones realize this in their heart of hearts, but the West will be constantly called upon to mitigate their disappointment. The most useful policy they can pursue is to see that German disappointment over reunification is balanced out by continuance of economic prosperity at home. Again, sensible Germans realize how closely this prosperity is linked with association with the West, and would surely hesitate when actually confronted with the uncertainty of neutralization in reunion with an impoverished Eastern Germany.

Germany, once more returned to power as a first-class force in world affairs, elevated from her cataclysmic defeat by the irony of history to a key position between East and West, holds the balance of power in the cold war. With her burning grievance in the East, she may well prove an uncomfortable ally, but if with all her resources and dynamic energy she is allowed to slip into the Russian maw, it will be the West's greatest defeat — probably a decisive one. The responsibility lies with the West — and particularly with France — not to fall back on a policy which once, through creating a hopeless sense of isolation in Germany, helped pave the way for Hitler, and that if repeated now would almost certainly throw the country into the arms of the Kremlin.

While writing this book, I submitted to Dr. Adenauer a number of written questions in the form of an interview, to which he replied in detail in February, 1955. However history may judge the achievements of Dr. Adenauer's policies, he will certainly stand out as the great architect of post-war Germany, and I can think of no more appropriate way of concluding this book than by recording his replies to my questions.

I asked Dr. Adenauer if he would reiterate his previous assurances that the spirit of aggression would not be allowed to reappear in the new German Army.

"Yes, most categorically," he replied, "and the German forces will in the future adopt a fundamentally different position in national life, compared with former days. A new constitution for the armed forces and a new training system will guarantee the education of the troops in a democratic spirit. The armed forces will moreover be subordinate to permanent parliamentary control. Our goal is the 'citizen in uniform.' The dominating principle will be the subjection of the military to civil authority. Recognition of this principle will be demanded from all officers, regardless of rank. From the external point of view, the German forces will also be in a radically different position from that of former days. The German forces will be part of a defense system and capable of military action only within the framework of this alliance. In addition to this comes the Federal Republic's voluntary renouncement of the production of ABC weapons and missiles of the former 'V-weapon' type. Seen from this point of view, German troops, in the event that they should ever stand alone on their own resources, would form only a weak military force. The revolutionary changes on the political and strategic scene, which have come about as a result of the last war, have opened up a completely new chapter in the relations between Germany and her neighbors, especially between Germany and Great Britain."

"How dangerous do you consider the threat of a revival of extreme nationalism in Western Germany?" I asked.

"Reviving nationalist tendencies in many countries have in the recent past created a definite threat to understanding between nations. In the Federal Republic, however, I see no acute danger that extreme nationalism will be able to play a role again. The most recent *Landtag* elections in Hesse, Bavaria, and Berlin have in every case reaffirmed what was already expressed by the Federal elections in September, 1953: extreme parties, no matter whether of the Right or of the Left, are finding no following among the German electorate. The proportion of the votes gained by radical parties fell far under 5 per cent at the last *Land* elections. Previous declarations of the Federal Government that it would take resolute measures against all radical tendencies of Right or Left coming to light, remain valid. On May 21st, 1953, in my speech to the Inter-Parliamentary Union in London, I gave the following assurance: 'The Federal Government is determined to permit the emergence of no radical phenomena that might aim to eliminate the democratic order; the Federal Government is determined not to allow any repetition of 1933.' "

With some hesitation, I questioned the Chancellor about his ultimate successor. He replied:

"It is not the business of a Federal Chancellor or of the Chairman of a Party to appoint a successor. Consequently it is also not his business to make a decision in this matter. I am, however, certain that my policy — particularly that of European co-operation — will be continued by my successors. In its basic features, this policy is so clearly prescribed by the developments of the times that no future Government will be able to forsake it — whatever the parties that may compose this Government. The Treaties of the West European Union, once they have entered into force, will lay down the course of German policy. As far as public opinion in the Federal Republic is concerned, all elections to date have reaffirmed that the great majority of the people stand behind the European policy which the Federal Republic has consistently followed since its entry into office in the autumn of 1949."

I reminded Dr. Adenauer of the hopes he had persistently expressed, even after the collapse of EDC, that a political integration of Europe would still take place. On what did he now base his hopes? He replied at some length, describing the prospects of finding a substitute for the political content of the EDC.

European integration, he felt, could still be effected through (1) strengthening the supra-national role of the "Schuman Plan" and (2) developing the provisions for "promoting European unity" contained within the West European Union Treaty. When asked about the spiritual paths that had led to the formulation of his "European policy," he replied:

"I first expressed my ideas on European integration and a conciliation between France and Germany in 1925, and I pleaded the same ideas before the Reich Cabinet of Marx, which was in office at that time. I was motivated by the conviction that it was essential for Germany and France — and for Europe — to make an end to the senseless strife. I have championed this cause since that time in my various offices and as a private person, and I have also dedicated my policy as Federal Chancellor to its service. In a Franco-German understanding I see the essential prerequisite for the unification of Europe. I repeat, the unification of Europe appears to me indispensable if our Continent will assert its position in the world, and if the Free World in its entirety wishes to survive in the proximity of the forces of totalitarianism which threaten it."

Finally, I asked Dr. Adenauer what course his Government might adopt to effect German reunification once a stronger position for bargaining with the Russians had been obtained on the entry into force of the Paris Agreements. His reply was:

"The way ahead is clearly signposted. We are partners of the Free World which has declared the reunification of Germany in peace and freedom to be also one of the objectives of its policy. Thus we shall be supported by the Free World, in particularly close understanding with Great Britain, America and France. We shall take advantage of every opportunity presenting itself to open up negotiations with Soviet Russia for reunification.

"The fact of the stronger bargaining position which will be attained on entry into force of the Treaties does not only concern the Federal Republic; it also concerns the whole of the Western world. Soviet Russia's consent to reunification in peace and freedom can only be achieved in common with the free nations."

Index

Abetz, Otto, 166
Achenbach, Dr. Ernest, 166, 167, 174, 177, 178, 181
Acheson, ——, 9, 17
Adenauer, Dr. Konrad, 2, 4, 9, 11, 22, 30, 31, 32, 33, 34, 35, 36, 38, 39, 40, 41, 45, 46, 47, 48, 52, 63, 64, 65, 73, 98, 99, 113, 122, 133, 134, 137, 138, 140, 141, 144, 145, 146, 147, 148, 150, 151, 152, 153, 154, 156, 157, 158, 159, 161, 164, 169, 171, 175, 179, 180, 182, 189, 205, 206, 212, 215, 217, 218, 219, 220, 221, 222, 223, 224, 225, 228, 229, 231, 232, 233, 234, 235, 236, 237, 238, 240, 241, 245, 247, 248, 249, 250, 251, 252, 254, 255, 256, 257, 258, 259, 260, 261, 262, 263, 269, 287, 290, 295, 297, 319, 334–35, 342, 344, 345, 346, 349, 350, 351, 352, 353, 354, 355, 356, 358–59, 363, 366, 369, 370, 371, 372, 373, 376, 378, 379, 380, 381, 382, 383, 384, 385, 387, 388, 389, 390, 392, 394, 396, 397, 398, 399, 400, 401
"Aerodynamic Research Organization," 323
Agartz, Dr. Viktor, 299
"Air Travel, German Experimental Institute for," 322, 324, 325, 327, 329
"Air Travel, German Research Organization for," 323, 324
AJDC. See American Joint Distribution Committee
Allensbach Institute, 218
All-German Peace Treaty, 139
All-German Party, 240
All-German People's Party, 224, 245, 246
Allied High Commissions, 3, 11, 55, 103, 106, 114, 132, 237, 259, 308, 338, 349, 351, 400
Allied Planners, 115
Altmaier, Jakob, 66
American Joint Distribution Committee, 67, 69, 70
Amnesty Act, 44
Ardenne, Professor —— von, 321
"Arrow Cross," the Hungarian, 71
"Association of German Soldiers," 171
Astronautical Federation, International, 329
Atlantic Pact, 12
Auerbach, Philipp, 62, 63
Austrian Treaty, 33
Auswärtiges Amt, 134

AVA. See Aerodynamic Research Organization
Axmann, Artur, 166, 167

"Balance Sheet of the Second World War, The," 58
Bank deutscher Länder, 285
BAOR, 129, 131
Bardeche, Professor Maurice, 169
Bathurst, Maurice, 177–78
Baudissin, Count, 81, 82, 83, 84, 100
Bavarian Party, 233
BdD. See League of Germans
BDI. See "Federation of German Industries"
Beaumont, Guérin de, 359
Beck-Broichsitter, ——, 167
Becker, ——, 141
Beitz, Berthold, 118, 332
Beneš, ——, 378
Benjamin, "Red Hilde," 207
Beria, ——, 207
Berlin Conference, 206, 335 ff., 354, 355, 395, 396, 397, 399
Bermuda Conference, 206, 264, 333 ff.
Berthawerk, 109, 118
Bevanites, 13
Bevin, Ernest, 5
Bidault, ——, 142, 335, 339, 342, 352, 353, 383
"Big Bertha," 103, 110
Bilanz des Zweiten Weltkrieges, 58, 87
Birley, Dr. Robert, 227
Bismarck, ——, 31, 104, 137, 222, 223, 295
Blankenhorn, ——, 159, 374
Blank Office, 325, 328, 379
Blank, Theodor, 73, 74, 75, 76, 77, 78, 79, 84, 85, 90, 93, 94, 100, 249
Blenk, Professor ——, 324
Blohm & Voss, 267
Blücher, ——, 141, 236, 351, 375, 389
Blumenfeld, Erik, 258
Blume, Professor Walter, 322, 331
Bochumer Verein, the, 272, 290, 314
Bohlen, Gustav von, 112
    See Krupp.
Boldt, Lieutenant, 58
Bonhoeffer, Pastor, 87
Bonin, Bogislav von, 82, 83, 85, 94, 95, 96, 97, 98
Bonn Coalition, 30
"Bonn Conventions, The," 1, 2, 3, 4, 5, 6, 14, 53, 122, 177, 221, 352, 353, 358, 375, 385
Bonn Treaties, 238, 364

Borbeck steelworks, 107, 111
Bor-Komorowski, General, 207
Bormann, Martin, 165–66
Bornemann, Dr. Karl Friedrich, 161, 169, 179, 180, 226
Brandt, Norbert, 67, 68
Brandt, Professor Leo, 311, 322
Brandt, Willi, 148, 239
Brauer, ——, 122
Braun, Professor Werner von, 323, 324
Breker, Arno, 166
Brentano, von, Heinrich, 149, 248, 256, 257
Briand, ——, 377
British Communist Party, 196
British Council, 262
British High Commission, 113, 125, 161, 162, 163, 193, 208, 222, 262, 360, 365
British Labor Party, 344
British Land Commissioners, 126
British Secret Service, 365
Brüderschaft, 45, 167
Brüning, Dr. Heinrich, 356, 357, 377
Brussels Conference, 371, 372
Brussels Treaty, 382, 384
Buchholz, Albert, 56
Bulganin, Marshal, 97, 394, 398
Bundesrat, 38, 92, 99, 100, 154, 155, 156, 157, 158, 218, 235, 350, 351
Bundestag, 12, 32, 35, 38, 39, 40, 44, 64, 65, 66, 99, 122, 137, 141, 146, 147, 148, 149, 150, 154, 155, 170, 205, 214, 215, 216, 217, 218, 219, 220, 223, 224, 226, 233, 239, 240, 247, 249, 255, 258, 349, 350, 351, 352, 355–56, 367, 382, 397
Bundestag Press Committee, 263
"Bureau for Light Metal Construction Technique," 322
Burgess, ——, 365
Bussche, Freiherr von dem, 83, 84, 85
Butler, R. A., 266, 283, 288

Caine Mutiny, The, 91
Capito and Klein, 108
Carroll, Earl J., 114
Catholic Center Party, 356
Catholicism in Germany, 253–55
CDV. *See* Christian Democrat Party
Central Intelligence Agency, 122
Center Party, 233–34
Chemische Werke Hüls, 273
Christian Democrats, 30, 32, 34, 36, 74, 99, 149, 156, 157, 163, 173, 187, 215, 221, 222, 223, 229, 232, 233, 234, 235, 238, 244, 248, 252,

254, 255, 256, 259, 260, 350, 354, 358, 372, 379, 380, 395, 400
Christian Factory and Transport Workers' Union, 73–74
Christian Socialists, 252
Churchill, Sir Winston, 31, 32, 33, 34, 49, 90, 158, 206, 222, 333, 379
Chuikov, General, 194
Clair, Colonel von, 84
Clark, General Mark, 27
"Co-Determination in Industry" Law, 296
Cohn, ——, 124, 125
Coleman, Major-General ——, 18
Communists, 3, 10, 12, 15, 16, 17, 19, 20, 21, 24, 27, 36, 39, 42, 45, 46, 50, 78, 121, 123, 124, 139, 146, 147, 148, 187, 188, 189, 191, 192, 193, 196, 199, 200, 204, 208, 209, 214, 215, 233, 239, 240, 241, 242, 243, 244, 294, 301, 302, 303, 336, 348, 360, 361, 364, 369, 370, 392, 396
Conant, Dr., ——, 159
Conrad, Dr. ——, 68
Conscription Amendment, 350, 351–52
"Constitution, Office for the Protection of the," 360
Consultative Assembly of the Council of Europe, 139
"Contractual Agreements, The," 1
Co-ordinating Committee, 260–61, 262, 263
Council of Europe, Consultative Assembly of the, 139
Credit Insurance Association, Ltd. of London, 283
CSU, 233, 248, 249, 252, 254

Daimler-Benz, 322, 331
Daladier, ——, 377
Daniel, Jens, 236, 237
Davies, John Paton, 124
DDR. *See* German Democratic Republic
Degrelle, Leon, 166, 169
Dehler, Dr., Thomas, 179, 180, 249, 250, 261, 308, 374, 389, 393
Demag, 297, 298, 316
Democratic Culture League, 244
Democratic Women's League, 244
Dertinger, Georg, 187
Deutsche Edelstahlwerke, 296
Deutsche Korrespondenz, 262
Deutsche Reichspartei, 175
"Devil's Colonel." *See* Bonin, Bogislav von
Devil's General, The, 91

Dewhurst, Claude, 20
DFG. *See* German Society for Research
DFL. *See* "German Research Organization for Air Travel"
DGB. *See* German Federation of Trade Unions
Dibelius, Bishop, 193, 196
Dibrova, Major-General, 201, 204
Diewerge, Wolfgang, 173, 174, 181
Discipline Is All, 24
Dithmar, Lieutenant, 58
DNA. *See* "German Committee for Standardization"
Dönitz, Frau, 167
Dönitz, Grand Admiral, 167, 175
Dork, Dr., ——, 44, 45, 173
Dormier, Claudius, 322, 330
DP, the, 168, 176
DP. *See* German Party
Draper, William, 153
Drewitz, Dr., ——, 169, 173
DRP. *See* German Reich Party
DUD, 163
Dulles, ——, 339, 340, 344, 349, 387
Dunlop, Dr., 126, 131
DVL. *See* "German Experimental Institute for Air Travel"

Ebner, Professor, ——, 324, 326
Eckhardt, —— von, 259, 262, 374, 375, 376
Economic Reconstruction Party, 233
EDC Assembly, 7
EDC *Council,* 7
EDC. *See* Treaty, European Defense Community
Eden, Anthony, 2, 5, 9, 17, 28, 62, 114, 161, 163, 176, 179, 206, 339, 340, 341, 342, 357, 378, 379, 381, 383
Edgley, Sir Norman, 177, 178
Ehlers, Dr. Herman, 40, 216, 218, 220, 232, 255, 400
Eilenstein, Irmgard, 108
Einstein, ——, 66
Eisenhower, President, 159, 333, 357
Elfes, Wilhelm, 243, 244
EMNID, 79, 127, 132, 209
EPA. *See* "European Productivity Agency"
EPU. *See* European Payments Union
Erhard, Professor ——, 384
ERP, 117
ERP-MSA, 286
Erhard, Professor Ludwig, 256, 257, 265, 266, 282, 283, 285, 286 ff.,

297, 307, 311
Esau, Professor ——, 324, 329
Essen-Mülheim Institute, the, 324, 326, 328
Etzel, Franz, 308
Euler, Martin, 252
European Coal and Steel Community, the, 307
European Defense Community Treaty, 1, 2, 3, 5, 6, 7, 8, 9, 10, 13, 14, 15, 23, 25, 28, 30, 38, 61, 75, 115, 122, 126, 131, 142, 143, 144, 145, 148, 149, 152, 153, 154, 157, 177, 194, 203, 205, 209, 212, 213, 219, 220, 221, 222, 234, 235, 244, 251, 264, 290, 308, 334, 335, 341, 342, 344, 345, 348, 349, 350, 351, 352, 353, 355, 357, 358, 359, 364, 369, 370–72, 373–76, 378, 379, 380, 381, 382, 383, 384, 385, 386, 387, 388, 391, 392, 399
European High Commission, 139
European Payments Union, 266
"European Productivity Agency," 312
"European" Statute, the Saar's, 390
Export Credit Company, West German, 283

Falkenhorst, Colonel-General von, 53
Farben, IG, 4, 119, 268, 272, 297, 314, 319
Farbwerke Hoechst, 268
Fascist, neo-, 164, 170
"Fascists," 72
Faure, ——, 384
FDJ agitators, 240, 241
FDP, 166, 168, 169, 171, 172, 173, 174, 175, 180, 181, 182, 223, 234, 247, 248, 250, 355
Fechner, Max, 207
Federal Constitution, 149, 152
Federalist Union, 233
Federal Press Office, 237
Federal Railways, 305, 307, 314
Federal Republic, 3, 4, 12, 15, 22, 33, 42, 72, 79, 95, 100, 133, 139, 158, 164, 171, 173, 179, 188, 195, 208, 211, 212, 266, 268, 271, 274, 282, 286, 289, 294, 301, 302, 305, 307, 310, 311, 312, 314, 321, 350, 354, 356, 359, 366, 369, 370, 376, 378, 385, 386, 395, 397, 399
    Constitution of the, 11
"Federation of German Industries," 312
Firma Lucht, 160, 163, 165
Five Power Conference, 333, 339, 343
Fleischmann, Charlotte, 244, 245

Flick, Friedrich, 105, 113, 331
Focke, Professor ——, 323, 324
Focke-Wulf factory, 331
Ford, 292
Foreign Affairs Committee, 358
Foreign Legion, 132, 133
Foreign Ministers' Conference, 206
Foreign Press Association, 40, 131, 172, 238, 287
Foreign Trade Information, 281
Four Power Foreign Ministers' Conference, 264, 333, 334
Fourteen Power North Atlantic Council, 382
Fragebogen, 60, 79
Franco-Soviet Treaty, 393
François-Poncet, M., 138, 350
Franke-Griecksch, Alfred, 45, 167
Frauenfeld, Alfred, 175
Free Democrats, 51, 68, 141, 155, 157, 158, 166, 179, 215, 222, 227, 233, 249, 250, 251, 252, 261, 350, 352, 354, 355, 389
"Free Jurists, League of," 39, 189
Freeman, John, 377
Free German Youth, 21, 25, 92, 240, 241
Freikorps, 167, 176
Freikorps Deutschland, 175
French Debt Agreement, 216
French High Commission, 113, 144, 259
Fritzsche, Hans, 169
From the Danube to the Yalu, 27

Gablonz glass, 211, 291
Gale, General Sir Richard, 131
Gambetta, ——, 103
Gasperi, de, ——, 388
"Gauleiter Group," 166, 167, 168, 170, 171, 174, 175, 176, 180, 181, 226
    See also Naumann
Gedanken zum Zweiten Weltkrieg, 88, 90
Gehlen, General ——, 367
Geiger, Georg, 141
General Motors, 275
"General Treaty, The," 1
"General War Pact," 1
Geneva "Summit" Conference, 97, 372, 383, 394, 399
German Central Bank, 285
"German Committee for Standardization," 315
"German Community, The," 175
"German Competition" (pamphlet), 283

"German Democratic Republic," 11, 395
"German Experimental Institute for Air Travel," 322, 324, 325, 327, 329
German Ex-Prisoners of War Association, 84
German Federation of Trade Unions, 74, 296, 298, 299, 300, 399
German Free Democrats, 390
Germaniawerft, 109
"German Miracle," 264 ff.
German Party, 223, 227, 233, 247, 249, 250, 252, 350
German Press Association, 259
"German Rally," 243
German Reich Party, 222, 224, 226, 227, 231, 233, 236
"German Research Organization for Air Travel," 323, 324
"German Society for Research," 311, 312, 313
"German Youth, League of," 121
Germany—Key to Peace, 136
Germany's Comeback in the World Market, 265
Gestapo, 365, 368, 369
Gerstenmaier, Dr. Eugen, 255, 258
Gille, General ——, 47
Globke, Dr. ——, 46, 366
GNP, 289
Goebbels, Dr. ——, 42, 160, 161, 168, 169, 174, 225, 228
Goerdeler, Mayor ——, 87
Goering, Hermann, 273, 274
Goettling, Willi, 202, 205
"Gomez, General." *See* Zaisser, Wilhelm
Göttingen University, 318
Government and Relief in Occupied Areas, 286
Government Socialist Unity Party, 393
"Graf Zeppelin Union," 322, 330, 331
"Grand Alliance," 2
Grandval, Gilbert, 136
Gretchko, Lieutenant-General Andrei, 194
Griffiths, Captain ——, 49
Grotewohl, Otto, 11, 12, 13, 21, 22, 24, 36, 184, 197, 198, 199, 203, 207, 395, 397
Grundherr, Dr. Werner von, 46
Guderian, Colonel-General, 58, 87, 171
Gussstahlfabrik, 108, 111, 118
GVP. *See* All-German People's Party

Hahn, Professor Otto, 317
Haile Selassie, Emperor, 116

Halbach, Arnold von Bohlen und, 108
Halbritter, Kurt, 24
Hallstein, Professor, 159, 342
Hamann, ——, 185, 187
Handke, ——, 185
Hanover-Hannibal coal mine, 108
Hanover Industries Fair, 284
Hardach, Dr., ——, 110
Harding, Field Marshall Sir John, 93
Haselmeyer, Dr. Heinrich, 160, 179
Hassel, —— von, 258
Hausser, General Paul, 171
Heimkehrer, Der, 49
Heine, Fritz, 233
Heinemann, Dr. Gustav, 245, 394
Heinkel, ——, 330
Heisenberg, Professor Werner, 317, 318
Hellwege, ——, 250
Henderson, Scott, 177
Henderson, Sir Nevile, 181
Henkels, 271
Hennigsdorf rolling mills, 199
Henschel locomotive works, 301, 331
Herchenröder, K. H., 116
Hermann Goeringwerke. *See* Reichswerke steel complex
Herrmann, Dr. ——, 112
Heusinger, General Adolf, 74, 84, 96
Heuss, Professor ——, 12, 86, 154, 156
Heuss, President, 55, 60, 65, 85, 87, 150, 151, 152, 154, 157, 219, 252, 350, 351, 370
High Authority, 307, 308, 309
Himmler, ——, 110
Hindenberg, ——, 57
Hitler, 29, 31, 32, 34, 35, 43, 44, 46, 55, 56, 62, 64, 68, 69, 74, 83, 84, 86, 87, 88, 89, 90, 95, 100, 102, 103, 105, 106, 125, 127, 131, 137, 138, 160, 167, 170, 211, 225, 226, 234, 243, 263, 266, 273, 296, 301, 310, 377
"Last Days of, The," 165
Hitler Youth, 166, 169
HO, the, 186, 280
Höfer, Wolfgang, 367
Hoffmann government, 390, 391
Hoffmann, Heinz, 24
Hoffmann, Johannes, 136, 138, 140
Home Service, Bureau for, 65, 85, 219–20, 259, 262
Hoyer-Millar, Sir Frederick, 358
"Hunting, Shooting and Fishing" exhibition, 284
Hütte, Friedrich Alfred, 107
Illingworth, ——, 342
ILO, 299

"Industries, Federation of German," 312
"Institute for the Physics of Jet Propulsion," 323
"Institute of Flying Medicine," 322
International Astronautical Federation, 329
Iron and Steel Industry Association (Ruhr), 160
"Iron Guard," the Rumanian, 71
Israel Reparation Scheme, 64

Jackson, Sir Edward, 178
Jesus, 123
"Jet Propulsion, Institute for the Physics of," the, 323
Jewish Restitution Office, 68
John, Hans, 365, 368
John, Dr. Otto, 161, 181, 360 ff.
Jost, Georg, 242, 243, 244, 246
Judas Iscariot, 123
Julyists, 43, 74, 85, 86, 87, 91, 94, 255, 360, 362, 365, 367, 368, 369, 370

Kaghan, Theodore, 124–25
Kaisen, Jakob, 122, 209, 210, 389
Kaiser Ministry, 142
Kaiser, the, 49, 103, 104, 105, 112
Kappe, Wilhelm, 53, 54, 58
Karst, Heinz, 100
Kaufman, Karl, 45
Kaufmann, Dr. Karl, 161, 167, 175, 179
Keitel, ——, 91
Kerneck, Heinz, 225
Kesselring, Field Marshal, 50, 52, 88, 89
Kielmannsegg, Colonel Count, 84
Kiesinger, Dr. Kurt-Georg, 258
Kirkpatrick, Sir Ivone, 28, 48, 52, 54, 162, 163, 164, 165, 176, 178, 181, 224
Klass, Gert von, 112
Kleist, Dr. Peter, 170
Klibansky, ——, 63
Klöckner steel combine, 308
Kohane, ——, 71
Kraft-Oberländer Refugee Party, 211
See Refugee Party, the
Kraft, Waldemar, 156, 176, 223, 251
Kressmann, Willi, 208
Krosigk, Count Schwerin von, 58
Krupp, Alfred, 105, 112, 113
Krupp, Alfried, 102, 104, 106, 107, 108, 110, 112, 113, 114, 115, 116, 118, 331-32

Krupp, Bertha, 103, 104, 112
Krupp, Berthold, 112
Krupp empire, 102 ff., 280, 291
Krupp Grusonwerk, 118, 201
Krupp, Gustav, 102, 104
Kruschev, ——, 394, 395, 396, 398
Kuhn, Hans, 53, 54, 58
KVP. *See* "People's Police," Barracked
Kuffhäuser Bund, 53

Labor Party, 47
Laniel, ——, 333, 353
"Late Homecomers" law, 54
Lawrence, D. H., 130
LOP. *See* Liberal Party
Leadership Ring of German Soldiers, 244
League of Free Jurists, 189
League of Germans, 224, 240, 244, 245, 246
"League of Germans True to the Homeland," 175
"League of German Youth," 121
BHE. *See* League of the Expellees; Refugee Party
League of the Expellees and Disenfranchised, 223
    See also Refugee Party
Leber, ——, 87
Lehr, Dr. ——, 44, 54, 366
Leipzig Trial, 57
Leitz Leica Works, 211
Lenin, 12, 195
Lenz, Dr. Otto, 232, 258, 259, 260, 261, 262, 263
Leuna synthetic oil works, 201
Leuschner, ——, 87
Leverkühn, Dr. Paul, 88
Lewis, John L., 296
Liberal Party, 187
Lindner, ——, 173
Linse, Dr. ——, 39, 40, 189
List, Field Marshal, 50
Lloyd, Selwyn, 207
Lloyd's Register, 267
Locarno Treaty, 158, 356
London Conference, 379, 380, 382
London Debt Agreement, 215, 266, 290
London-Paris Agreements, 392–93, 394, 399
    See also Paris Agreements, the
"Long Max," 103
Loritz's Economic Reconstruction Party, Dr., 226
Löwenberg, Dr. ——, 68
Loewenthal, Rix, 173
Lucht, Herbert, 166

Lüdde-Neurath, Walter, 88
Ludendorff, ——, 57

Mackensen, General, 50
Maclean, ——, 365
Macmillan, Harold, 271
Madariaga, Salvador de, 399
Madgeburg Grusonwerke, 115
Mahlberg, Dr. Josef, 169
Maier, Dr. Reinhold, 155, 156, 157, 158
Malenkov, ——, 192, 194, 195, 347, 398
Mann, Anthony, 93
Mannesmann, 119
Manstein, Field Marshal von, 50, 52, 88, 89, 93, 95, 365
Marshall, ——, 265
Marshall Aid, 276, 286
Marx, 292
"Max Planck Institute for the Advancement of Science," 312, 313, 317, 318
Mayer, Rene, 142, 143, 144, 146, 391
McCarthy, Senator, 124, 125
McCloy, ——, 102
"Medicine, Institute of Flying," 322, 324
Mellies, ——, 99
Mende, Dr. Erich, 51, 54
Mendès-France, Pierre, 353, 359, 371, 372, 373, 377, 380, 381, 383, 384, 386, 387
Menuhin, Yehudi, 297
Menzel, Dr., ——, 122
Merkatz, —— von, 250
Messerschmidt, Professor ——, 322, 330
"Metal Construction Technique, Bureau for Light," 322
Metal Workers' Union, 205, 300, 302
Middelhauve, Dr. Friedrich, 171, 172, 173, 174, 182, 234, 401
Military Penal Code, 91
Military Security Board, 325
Ministry for All German Questions, 302
Mitford, Nancy, 130
Molotov, ——, 339 ff., 392, 394, 395
Molotov-Ribbentrop pact, 44
Montgomery, F. M., 90
Morgenthau, ——, 265
Moscow Conference, 266, 393
Mosley, Sir Oswald, 169, 177
Muenzel, Major General, 167
Müller, Philip, 15
Munich University, 318
Mussolini, ——, 171

MVD, 361
Machfolger der Ruhrkonzerne, Die, 116

Napoleon, 237
Naters, van der Goes van, 139, 352, 353, 383
National Democrat Party, 187
National Front Party, 392
"National Opposition," 168, 170, 171, 175
National Socialist Party, 44, 107, 164, 166, 169, 173, 175
NATO, 5, 6, 7, 8, 10, 26, 27, 77, 84, 94, 95, 96, 101, 306, 330, 343, 379, 382, 385, 386, 395, 400
Naumann, Dr. Werner, 45, 97, 160 ff., 220, 223, 224, 225, 226, 227, 228, 233, 234, 236, 249, 263, 366, 369
Nazi Propaganda Ministry, 259
Nazis, 3, 13, 40, 41, 43, 45, 46, 47, 50, 59, 61, 64, 65, 66, 67, 68, 74, 85, 90, 100, 125, 134, 137, 160, 161, 163, 165, 168, 170, 172, 174, 175–76, 177, 178, 180, 181, 214, 218, 223, 224, 226, 227, 228, 234, 239, 256, 262, 273, 275, 281, 362, 364, 365, 366, 367, 368, 390
Nazi Students' League, 160
NOP. *See* National Democrat Party
Neguib, General ——, 44, 167
Nemesis of Power, The, 117
NEP, 195
Nerreter, Dr. Paul, 252
Neugablonz. See Gablonz glass
Neumayer, Fritz, 252
Neurath, —— von, 60, 61
Niemoeller, Pastor, 97
Noell, Friedrich, 56
Nord-Deutsche Steelworks, 109
Nordhoff, Heinz, 275 ff., 295, 299
North Atlantic Council, 143
Nunn-May, ——, 365
Nuremberg Race Laws, 46
Nuremberg Trials, 59, 169
Nuschke, ——, 200
NWDR broadcasting studios, 362

Oberländer, Professor Theodor, 209, 223, 251, 364, 366
Occupation Statute, 351
Occupied Areas, Government and Relief in, 286
Occupation Statute, 3, 359
Ollenhauer, Erich, 36, 37, 38, 121, 148, 154, 221, 222, 232, 238, 342, 350, 352, 376, 380, 383

Opel works, 275
Operation Friendly Hand, 128
Operation Lorelei, 240–41
Oradour Trial, 143
Oxborrow, Brigadier, 115

Paris Agreements, 385, 387, 388, 394, 395, 396, 398, 400
See also London-Paris Agreements
Paris Conference, 5
Paris Treaty, 364, 389
Paulus, Field Marshal, 89, 98
PAYE system, 298
"People's Chamber," 40
"People's Council," 10, 11
People's Police, 12, 15, 16, 21, 23, 187
Barracked, 24, 25, 97, 100
See also Vopos
"People's Republic," 72
"People's Scooter," 280
"Pestalozzi Village," 303
Peters, Anneliese and Arno, 123
Pfeffer, Professor, 59
Pfleiderer, Karl-Georg, 354 ff.
Picht, Werner, 85, 87
Pieck, Wilhelm, 12, 21, 280
Pinay, ——, 384
Pinay-Schuman Government, 142
"Pleven Plan," 5
Polythene, 314
Potsdam Conference, 2
Preusker, Dr. ——, 270
Principal Committee against Remilitarization, 244
"Productivity Agency, European," 312
Protestantism in Germany, 253–55, 257
Punktal steelworks, 161
Putlitz, Baron —— von, 366, 367

Quick, Professor ——, 324, 326

Raab, ——, 395
Radio House, blockade of the, 17 ff.
Ramcke, General ——, 47, 48, 142, 167, 171
Ramcke, ——, 60
Rapallo, Treaty of, the, 356, 357
Rathenau, ——, 175
Rationalization Kuratorium, 312, 315
Rau, ——, 193, 197
Refugee Party, 156, 168, 176, 222, 227, 233, 234, 235, 247, 251, 252, 350, 389
Reichswerke steel complex, 273–74
Reimann, Max, 39, 239, 242, 243
Reinhardt, Colonel-General, 52

Remer, Major-General Otto Ernst, 42, 43, 44, 86, 167, 168, 171, 173, 175, 224, 226
Renner, ——, 45, 239
Restitution Laws, 67, 68
"Research, German Society for," 311, 312, 313
Rendulic, General, 50
Reuter, Professor Ernst, 189, 193, 237
"Rexist" movement, 166
Rhee, Syngman, 22
Rheinberg Mine, 107
Rheinhausen Steel Co., 107, 108, 118
    See also Stahlbau Rheinhausen
Rheinpreussen's Pattberg shaft, 303
Rhein-Ruhr Club, 356
Ribbentrop, ——, 46
Ribbentrop-Molotov Non-Aggression Pact, 196
Ridgeway, General ——, 27
Riecke, Hans Joachim, 58
Rische, ——, 215, 239
RKW. *See Rationalization Kuratorium*
Robespierre, 123
Robinson, Joseph S., 114
Rogers, ——, 178
Rolls Royce, 326, 332
Rommel, Field Marshal, 74
Ronzhin, Major, 193
Rosenberg, Ludwig, 296
Roske, Karl, 280
Rossenray mine, 107
Rubarth. *See* Stern—Rubarth, **Edgar**
Rudel, Colonel, ——, 175
Rudel, Hans, 171, 224, 226
Ruff, Professor ——, 324
Russell, Lord ——, 61

Saar agreement, the, 350, 383, 384, 385, 389, 390
Saar Christian Democrats, 390
Saar Democratic Party, 390
Saar Statute, 392
SACEUR, 386
Salisbury, Marquess of, 206
Salomon, Ernst von, 60, 87
Sänger, Dr. Eugen, 323, 324, 329
Schaefer, Hermann, 97
Schäfer, Emmanuel, 55
Schäfer, Joh., 116
Schäffer, Fritz, 76, 248, 252, 257, 268, 269, 271, 289, 290, 298
Scharnhorst, ——, 237
Scharpeng, Dr. Karl, 161, 179
Scheel, Dr. Gustav, 160, 163, 167, 175, 179
Schine, ——, 124, 125
Schlueter, Leonhard, 227

Schmid, Professor Carlo, 220
Schmidt-Wittmack, ——, 35, 372
Schneider, Dr. Ernst, 295
Schneider, Lieutenant-General, 88
Schnitzler, —— von, 19
Schnurpfeil, Paul, 56
Schoerner, Field Marshall Ferdinand, 80
Schramm, Ruth, 189
Schröder, Dr. ——, 362–63, 366, 367
Schröder, Lieutenant-General Oskar, 51
Schubert, Dr. Hans, 251
Schumacher, Kurt, 33, 35, 36, 37, 38, 218, 222, 233, 237, 239, 380, 401
Schuman Plan, 11, 119, 137, 138, 139, 140, 221, 307, 308, 309
Schuman Plan Assembly, 7
Schuman, Robert, 2, 9, 134, 137, 138, 140, 145, 377, 383, 388
"Schuyler Plan," 94
Schwabenstein, 267
"Science, Max Planck Institute for the Advancement of," 312
Scourge of the Swastika, The, 61
SED. *See* Socialist Unity Party
Seebohm, Dr. Hans-Christoph, 211, 249, 250
Seeckt, Colonel-General von, 97
Seewald, Professor ——, 324, 325, 326, 327, 328, 329
Selbmann, ——, 198
Semeonov, Vladimir, 194, 195, 203, 207, 355, 398
Sethe, Paul, 165, 378
Shaw, 292
Siebel, Friedrich, 331
Siepen, Heinz, 161, 177, 179
Sikorsky, ——, 331
"Six Year Plan," 269
Skorzeny, Otto, 171, 174
Slansky Trial, 189
Social Democrats, 4, 13, 34, 35, 36, 37, 38, 39, 46, 52, 99, 106, 121, 133, 143, 148, 149, 150, 152, 153, 154, 155, 156, 165, 173, 205, 221, 222, 223, 232, 233, 237, 238, 239, 254, 258, 346, 350, 356, 358, 365, 376, 379, 380, 381, 394, 400, 401
Socialist Reich Party, 42, 43, 44, 45, 168, 175, 224, 226
Socialists, 10, 38, 39, 78, 99, 107, 121–22, 149, 150, 155, 156, 164, 216, 219, 222, 232, 352, 375, 376
Socialist Unity Party, 14, 45, 183, 187, 195, 196, 198, 199, 241
Sokolovsky, Marshal ——, 10, 335
Soviet High Commission, 355